Intergroup Conflicts and Their Resolution

FRONTIERS OF SOCIAL PSYCHOLOGY

Series Editors:
Arie W. Kruglanski, *University of Maryland at College Park*
Joseph P. Forgas, *University of New South Wales*

Frontiers of Social Psychology is a series of domain-specific handbooks. Each volume provides readers with an overview of the most recent theoretical, methodological, and practical developments in a substantive area of social psychology, in greater depth than is possible in general social psychology handbooks. The editors and contributors are all internationally renowned scholars whose work is at the cutting edge of research.

Scholarly, yet accessible, the volumes in the *Frontiers* series are an essential resource for senior undergraduates, postgraduates, researchers, and practitioners and are suitable as texts in advanced courses in specific subareas of social psychology.

Published Titles

Negotiation Theory and Research, Thompson
Close Relationships, Noller & Feeney
Evolution and Social Psychology, Schaller, Simpson & Kenrick
Social Psychology and the Unconscious, Bargh
Affect in Social Thinking and Behavior, Forgas
The Science of Social Influence, Pratkanis
Social Communication, Fiedler
The Self, Sedikides & Spencer
Personality and Social Behavior, Rhodewalt
Attitudes and Attitude Change, Crano & Prislin
Social Cognition, Strack & Förster
Social Psychology of Consumer Behavior, Wänke
Social Motivation, Dunning
Intergroup Conflicts and Their Resolution, Bar-Tal

Forthcoming Titles

Explorations in Political Psychology, Krosnick & Chiang
Goal-Directed Behavior, Aarts & Elliot
Group Processes, Levine
Social Metacognition, Briñol & DeMarree
Social Judgment and Decision Making, Krueger
Behavioral Economics, Stapel & Zeelenberg

For continually updated information about published and forthcoming titles in the *Frontiers of Social Psychology* series, please visit: **www.psypress.com/frontiers**

Intergroup Conflicts and Their Resolution

A Social Psychological Perspective

Edited by
Daniel Bar-Tal

Psychology Press
Taylor & Francis Group

New York   London

Psychology Press
Taylor & Francis Group
270 Madison Avenue
New York, NY 10016

Psychology Press
Taylor & Francis Group
27 Church Road
Hove, East Sussex BN3 2FA

© 2011 by Taylor and Francis Group, LLC
Psychology Press is an imprint of Taylor & Francis Group, an Informa business

Printed in the United States of America on acid-free paper
10 9 8 7 6 5 4 3 2 1

International Standard Book Number: 978-1-84169-783-3 (Hardback)

Library of Congress Cataloging-in-Publication Data

Intergroup conflicts and their resolution : a social psychological perspective /
   [edited by] Daniel Bar-Tal.
     p. cm. -- (Frontiers of social psychology)
   Includes index.
   ISBN 978-1-84169-783-3 (hardcover : alk. paper)
   1. Conflict management. 2. Intergroup relations. I. Bar-Tal, Daniel.

HM1126.I55 2011
303.6--dc22
                                                       2010036972

Visit the Taylor & Francis Web site at
http://www.taylorandfrancis.com

and the Psychology Press Web site at
http://www.psypress.com

Contents

Editor

Daniel Bar-Tal is Branco Weiss Professor of Research in Child Development and Education at the School of Education, Tel Aviv University, Israel. His research interest is in political and social psychology studying socio-psychological foundations of intractable conflicts and peace making, as well as development of political understanding among children and peace education. He has published more than 15 books and more than 200 articles and chapters in major social and political psychological journals and books. He served as a president of the International Society of Political Psychology and received various awards for his work. In 1991 and 2009, he was awarded the Otto Klineberg Intercultural and International Relations Prize of SPSSI, and in 2000–2001, he was awarded the Golestan Fellowship at the Netherlands Institute for Advanced Study in the Humanities and Social Science. In 2006, his book, coauthored with Yona Teichman, *Stereotypes and Prejudice in Conflict* (Cambridge University Press, 2005), received the Alexander George Award of the International Society of Political Psychology for the best book in Political Psychology. He also received in 2006 the Peace Scholar Award of the Peace and Justice Studies Association for great scholarship and hard work in studying conflicts and peace making.

Contributors

Daniel Bar-Tal
School of Education
Tel Aviv University
Tel Aviv, Israel

Klaus Boehnke
Bremen International Graduate
    School of Social Sciences (BIGSSS)
Jacobs University Bremen
Bremen, Germany

Marilynn B. Brewer
School of Psychology
University of New South Wales
Sydney, Australia

and

Ohio State University
Columbus, Ohio

Aleksandra Cisłak
Warsaw School of Social Sciences and
    Humanities
Polish Academy of Sciences
Warsaw, Poland

Dawna K. Coutant
Department of Psychology
University of Hawaii at Hilo
Hilo, Hawaii

Guy Elcheroth
Institute of Social Sciences
University of Lausanne and Free
    University of Brussels
Lausanne, Switzerland

Ronald James Fisher
School of International Service
American University
Washington, DC

Shira Fishman
National Consortium for the Study of
    Terrorism and Responses to
    Terrorism (START)
University of Maryland
College Park, Maryland

James J. Gross
Department of Psychology
Stanford University
Stanford, California

Eran Halperin
Lauder School of Government
Interdisciplinary Center (IDC)
    Herzliya
Herzliya, Israel

Marcelo Hanza
Department of Psychology
University of Hawaii at Hilo
Keàau, Hawaii

John T. Jost
Department of Psychology
New York University
New York, New York

Herbert C. Kelman
Department of Psychology
Harvard University
Cambridge, Massachusetts

Margarita Krochik
Department of Psychology
New York University
New York, New York

Arie W. Kruglanski
Department of Psychology
University of Maryland
College Park, Maryland

James Hou-fu Liu
Centre for Applied Cross Cultural
    Research
Victoria University of Wellington
Wellington, New Zealand

Dario R. Paez
Departamento de Psicologia Social
University of the Basque Country
San Sebastian, Spain

Dean G. Pruitt
Institute for Conflict Analysis and
    Resolution
George Mason University
Bethesda, Maryland

Janusz Reykowski
Warsaw School of Social Sciences and
    Humanities
Polish Academy of Sciences
Warsaw, Poland

Nadim N. Rouhana
Fletcher School of Law and
    Diplomacy
Tufts University
Medford, Massachusetts

Henning Schmidtke
Bremen International Graduate
    School of Social Sciences (BIGSSS)
Jacobs University Bremen
Bremen, Germany

Maor Shani
Bremen International Graduate
    School of Social Sciences (BIGSSS)
Jacobs University Bremen
Bremen, Germany

Keren Sharvit
Department of Psychology
University of Maryland
College Park, Maryland

Dario Spini
Institute of Social Sciences
University of Lausanne
Lausanne, Switzerland

Stephen Worchel
Department of Psychology
University of Hawaii at Hilo
Hilo, Hawaii

Preface

My interest in conflicts began almost 30 years ago when I realized that living in a conflict-ridden region, where violence and wars are part of life, does not allow being an academic bystander. I felt that it is my duty as a human being, an Israeli co-patriot and as a social psychologist to engage in the venture of trying to understand the socio-psychological foundations that lead to societal involvement in intractable conflicts and then to elucidate the socio-psychological dynamics that can facilitate peace making—all in the context of the natural laboratory of the Middle East. This book reflects my long journey in the field of social-political psychology of conflicts and peace building. It was a privilege and honor to be invited to edit the book and I would like to thank the editors of the series Frontiers of Social Psychology, Arie W. Kruglanksi and Joseph P. Forgas, who provided me with this great opportunity.

The title of the book includes the words *social psychological perspective*. They are there in order to emphasize the particular approach of the book. I hoped to produce a book that sheds light on various socio-psychological processes, states and structures that are inherent part of conflicts such as their eruption, mobilization, escalation, maintenance, peace building, negotiation and media-tion, peaceful resolution or reconciliation. Chapters of the book use accumulated socio-psychological knowledge and apply it to the analysis of various issues that stand at the core of research of conflicts, though contributions of other disciplines of social sciences are recognized and acknowledged. Special efforts were made to edit a book that has also a holistic nature where the chapters complement each other and eventually provide a coherent and systematic understanding about a conflict and peace making.

An attempt was made to go beyond the research in social psychology to refer to and describe real life cases of conflicts. This attempt reflects a desire to be close to the problems that preoccupy citizens of this world. In fact the issue of conflict is not only an issue of basic scientific problems, it is also a theme that concerns lay people in the world. Moreover, efforts were made to prepare a volume that is not only relevant to the real life issues, but also to provide knowledge that can be used by practitioners who try hard to resolve conflicts peacefully and/or prevent them from occurring. In addition, this book intends to extend its scope of distribution also to lay individuals who are interested in one of the most prevailing phenome-non of our lives—intergroup conflicts that serious have implications on the well being of the individuals and the collectives on our globe.

All the contributors tried to provide the readers with comprehensive and original knowledge that helps an understanding of intergroup conflicts. Such illumination hopefully will widen the horizon and perspective and contribute to the practice of making peace. This is an opportunity to thank all the contributors who worked hard to provide very enlightening chapters that fit well into the holistic picture that the book tries to illuminate.

Introduction
Conflicts and Social Psychology[*]

DANIEL BAR-TAL

*C*onflicts are defined as situations in which two or more parties *perceive* that their goals and/or interests are in direct contradiction with one another and *decide* to act on the basis of this perception. This definition suggests two conditions for eruption of the conflict: identification of the contradiction and the decision to act on this basis. Accordingly, it is not enough that each of the parties will identify the contradiction in goals and/or interests: In order for a conflict to erupt, it is necessary that at least one party will decide to act upon this contradiction and bring it into the light, at least in a verbal expression. This means that conflicts may erupt also when in the first stage only one side perceives that its goals and/or interests are in direct contradiction with the goals or interests of another party and decides to act on the basis of this perception. Such a move causes the other side to note the contradiction and act as well, leading to the surge of the conflict.

Conflicts are inseparable and significant part of human life on every level of interaction; there are interpersonal conflicts, intragroup, intergroup, interorganizational, intrasocietal, and interethnic as well as international conflicts and even intercivilization conflicts—to note the most salient ones as we move from the micro to mega conflicts (Galtung, 2004). They take place constantly and continuously because it is unavoidable that human beings will not have disagreements over goals, interests, values, and/or beliefs. It is just simply natural that people, as individuals and groups, who differ in aspects such as belief systems that include aspirations, values, goals, needs, as well as in ways of socialization, cultural environments, or political and economic systems will have conflicts over almost every tangible or nontangible element of desire.

In this vein it is necessary to say that not all the conflicts have negative meaning and are negative in their nature. Conflicts are also necessary for enabling progress and innovation as human beings come with new ideas or inventions that contradict old stagnated dogmas, values, habits, or practices. Conflicts also erupt to abolish various types of immorality that human beings practice such as discrimination, injustice, inequality, exploitation, occupation, and even ethnic cleansing and genocide. Often only through conflicts groups can achieve what they deserve according to international laws or moral codes of the international community. This is so because very rarely groups willingly provide to other groups with what these groups

[*] I would like to express gratitude to Shai Fuxman, Nimrod Goren, Dana Guy, Dennis Kahn, Shiri Landman, Rafi Nets-Zehngut, Amiram Raviv, Nimord Rosler, Ofer Shinar, and Doron Tsur, who reviewed the earlier draft of the chapter and provided valuable comments.

ought to have according to these laws and codes. Many of the attempts to correct injustice are then met with strong resistance and rejection which lead to serious conflicts. Moreover, there is need to note that conflicts differ in their symmetrical–asymmetrical dimension on various parameters. The two distinguished parameters refer to the military–economic–political might that the sides in conflict have and to the level and extent of violation of moral codes that the sides in conflict practice. On both parameters there might be differences between the rival sides. In general, it can be said that those are not the conflicts themselves which necessarily reflect the ugly side of the humane species, but some of their causes and some of the ways they are managed.

MACRO LEVEL CONFLICTS

The present volume focuses on particular types of conflicts—macro level conflicts that involve societies and with this focus the volume will analyze mostly serious and harsh conflicts in which society members participate. A society denotes a large, unique and stable social system with established boundaries that differentiates it from other societies. It consists of collective of people, who have at least some feeling of belonging, share societal beliefs, experience solidarity, coordinate to at least some extent of activities and have a sense of common identity. Using Giddens's (1984) terminology, societies are "social systems which 'stand out' in bas-relief from a background of a range of other systemic relationships in which they are embedded. They stand out because definite structural principles serve to produce a specifiable overall 'clustering of institutions' across time and space" (p. 164). These social collectives endure, evolving a tradition, culture, collective memory, belief systems, social structures, and institutions (Griswold, 1994). Those are binding and integrating elements that unite differing groups into one society (Hoebel, 1960).

Many of the macro societal conflicts involve ethnic societies. Ethnic societies or groups refer to collectives, whose membership is determined on the basis of perceived common past, common culture, common language and common destiny. It means that ethnicity is based also on perception and awareness of shared characteristics, as well as cognized differences from other groups (Anderson, 1991; Barth, 1969; Brubaker, 2004; Connor, 1994; Geertz, 1973).

The reference to the macro level conflicts indicates that they involve society members as being part of collectives, as a result of their identification with the collective and an emergence of the collective identity (David & Bar-Tal, 2009). This implies that in times of a conflict, members of a society in many cases, sharing with each other feelings, beliefs, values and norms, act in coordinated ways. That is, macro level conflicts concern collective goals and interests such as rights, territories, self-determinations, resources, prestige, values, ideologies, and so on—both tangible and nontangible societal commodities that individuals as members of a society value, desire, aspire, or need for their collective entity. As a result, society members mind, care, are emotionally involved, and participate in conflicts as members of their collective. These conflicts also involve individual interests and goals, but central preoccupation concerns the well-being of the society. Moreover, society members are aware that this preoccupation is shared by other members who also identify with the collective (Ashmore, Deaux, & McLaughlin-Volpe, 2004). With this awareness, society members do not have to experience the conflict directly in order to feel that they are part of it. As members of a society they are exposed to the events of the conflict via various channels of communication and societal institutions and thus become vicarious participants of all aspects of the conflict through the process of identification with their society.

The care and concern for the well being of the society or even direct participation does not mean that all society members must agree with the way the conflict is managed. Some of them may not even support the goals of the conflict. They may disagree on various issues related to conflict and carry out debates and activities that reflect these disagreements. These disagreements may even lead to deep schism reflecting intrasocietal conflicts that may evolve at any phase of the macro inter-societal conflict.

SOCIO-PSYCHOLOGICAL PERSPECTIVE

The analysis of the macro level intergroup conflicts involves many different perspectives such as, for example, historical, political, sociological, economic, or cultural ones. Each of these perspectives offers different concepts, theoretical frameworks, models or even ways of collecting data that provide unique outlooks and emphases. Thus, the historical perspective focuses on the historiography of the outbreak of the conflict and its continuation, attempting to describe the course of the events in most accurate way; or the political perspective tries to elucidate the role of political systems and dynamics in conflicts.

However, it seems to me that first of all there is a need to recognize that those are human beings who initiate conflicts, take part in them, manage them, sometimes peacefully resolve them and even may reconcile. Human beings perceive, evaluate, infer and act. These human psychological behaviors* are integral parts of conflicts' interactions as human beings are the only actors on the conflict stage. As noted, those are human beings who decide to disseminate the idea about the necessity of conflicts, to mobilize societies' members to participate in them, to socialize their children to continue them, to carry them violently, or to reject their peaceful resolution (see Chapter 1).

Mobilization is a necessary condition for carrying out a successful macro level intergroup conflict. Mobilization is an act of deliberate recruitment of society members to be involved in the causes of the conflict. It can be seen as a kind of persuasion process with the goal of convincing group members to support the conflict and participate in it actively. The necessary basic precondition for mobilization is that individuals who are society members will greatly identify with their group, in general, and specifically with the posed conflict's goals of their society (Simon & Klandermans, 2001; see also Chapter 5). Moreover, mobilization means not only that individuals identify with the group and accept the goals related to

---

* The term behavior is used in the most general psychological way to refer to perception, cognition, experiencing affect and emotions and acting.

conflicts, but also approve the direction of the actions that the group takes and are ready to carry some kind of action themselves on behalf of the group which often involves killing the rival and at the same time, readiness to be killed (Klandermans, 1988). This process is carried through messages that include beliefs which are relevant, concrete, appeal to the social identity, negate the present situation as unacceptable, note important cherished values are threatening and arouse strong emotions. It is clear that harsh and violent conflicts cannot evolve and gain strength without the participation of at least some of the group members in conflict, which is manifested by their total devotion and readiness to sacrifice their lives (Bar-Tal & Staub, 1997).

In view of the premises stated above, the study of conflicts cannot take place without the contribution of the field social psychology. More explicitly, social psychology provides the core knowledge that is necessary to form the foundations for the understanding of the conflicts' dynamics and their peace making. Socio-psychological perspective does not try to describe what the "real" course of the conflict was, but rather to analyze what people think and feel in this situation, as this is extremely important for the understanding of why they act in the particular way. Krech, Crutchfield, and Ballachey (1962) rightly noted years ago that "man acts upon his ideas, his irrational acts no less than his rational acts are guided by what he thinks, what he believes, what he anticipates. However bizarre the behavior of men, tribes, or nations may appear to an outsider, to the men, to the tribes, to the nations their behavior makes sense in terms of their own world views" (p. 17).

This means that people behave in a conflict according to their psychological repertoire which includes not only those beliefs, attitudes, emotions, and intentions of behaviors acquired in the course of the conflict, but also according to the ones that were acquired over a long period of time in different contexts, before the conflict erupted. Various past experiences and acquired knowledge also have determinative influence on the manner in which a collective acts in a conflict situation. Thus the socio-psychological approach tries to reveal these thoughts, feelings, and behaviors that are underlying the evolvement and maintenance of the conflict as well as later its eventual resolution and reconciliation. Thus, also a possibility of peace building must also be initiated in human minds first. This idea should then be propagated and adopted by the same human beings who were engaged in initiating and maintaining the conflict.

STUDY OF CONFLICTS IN SOCIAL PSYCHOLOGY

In view of the above presented premises about intergroup conflicts it is not surprising that the founding fathers of social psychology realized that their study should be one of its main endeavors (Deutsch, 1980). One research direction of the early seeds of studies of conflict is summarized by Murphy, Murphy, and Newcomb (1937) in their textbook of social psychology. On one hand, empirical studies focused on individual cooperation and competition in the framework of task performance. On the other hand, in the first half of the twentieth century, the study of conflict was an integral part of the study of prejudice, as prejudice was viewed as one of the salient indications of intergroup conflict and violence (Cantril, 1941; Harding, Kutner, Proshansky, & Chein, 1954; Newcomb, 1950). However, this state changed with time. Presently, the study of prejudice is omitting deeper analysis of conflicts and their resolution (Stephan, 1985).

In the mid-twentieth century, when the modern social psychology evolved, the study of conflicts was part of the main stream. Kurt Lewin believed that conflicts are inseparable part of human behavior and social psychologists can illuminate various aspects of this phenomenon. The edited volume *Resolving Social Conflicts* (Lewin, 1948) presented and analyzed different types of conflicts ranging from intrapersonal to intergroup using socio-psychological conceptual framework. Based on Lewin's theory, Deutsch, one of the pioneers of modern social psychology, began to develop a theory of cooperation and competition, which has served as a basic conception for the study of a conflict (Deutsch, 1949a, 1949b). During this period, the knowledge about conflicts began to crystallize and the classical text-book *Theory and Problems of Social Psychology* by Krech and Crutchfield (1948) already devoted two chapters to conflicts: one regarding industrial conflict and the other about international tension.

The classical studies by Sherif and his colleagues about conflict and coopera-tion are undoubtedly the most compelling examples of seminal contributions to the understanding of how conflicts evolve and how they can be resolved (Sherif, 1966; Sherif, Harvey, White, Hood, & Sherif, 1961). The so-called "Robber Cave experi-ments" provided experimental real life opportunity to observe first the formation of two groups, then the emergence of a conflict between them and its various implications and finally ways of resolving this conflict peacefully via setting a series of super-ordinate goals. Approximately at the same time the paradigm of simulat-ing conflicts as games was imported from game theory to social psychology allow-ing for the use of experimental method in the investigation of various hypotheses in intergroup conflicts and their resolution (Deutsch, 1958; Kelley et al., 1970; Rapoport, 1960). This paradigm enabled precise measures of outcomes, easy manipulation of various situations and strict control of variables (Pruitt & Kimmel, 1977). The most popular paradigm was the *prisoners dilemma*, but with time other paradigms were invented including trucking game by Deutsch and Krauss (1960) that allowed to study mixed motive conflicts.

The very early work by Klineberg (1950) was signaling the growing preoccupa-tion with international conflicts by social psychologists . In the 1960s, a clear trend in this direction emerged in social psychology. The edited book by Kelman (1965), as well as books written by Stagner (1967) and White (1970), offered a social psychological perspective to the analysis of large scale intersocietal conflicts, high-lighting issues such as intergroup perceptions, violence, leadership, or negotiation. The seminal contribution of Tajfel (1979, 1982) on social identity also has direct implication for intergroup conflicts, suggesting not only a crucial mechanism for group formation and functioning, but also a determinative element that leads to intergroup differentiation as well as to conflicts.

From the present perspective, it is possible to say that although the theme of studying conflict never achieved a longstanding primary place as did the studies of prejudice or conformity, it succeeded to establish itself as a legitimate part of the social psychology. A number of textbooks included this topic in their agenda (Myers, 1993; Raven & Rubin, 1976; Saks & Krupat, 1988) and a number of leading social psychologists such as Morton Deutsch, Herbert Kelman, late Jeffrey Rubin, late Ralph White, or Dean Pruitt to name only a few, devoted their entire career to studying this topic. For years social psychologists have played the major role in developing and establishing peace psychology and political psychology which have been preoccupied with the study of conflicts and peace making. In 1990 division 48 within the American Psychological Association (APA) namely the Society for the Study of Peace, Conflict and Violence was established. Few years later the society began to publish a journal *Peace and Conflict: Journal of Peace Psychology*.

Today there is a growing interest in the social psychology of a conflict and many of the younger generation of social psychologists concentrate on various aspects of this area. Throughout the recent years, books, chapters, and journal articles, have been published and many papers have been presented in social psychology conferences on various aspects of conflicts and peace making (Vollhardt & Bilali, 2008). Also several "small meetings" of the European Social Psychology Association were organized about the social psychology of conflicts and their resolution and several issues of *Journal of Social Issues* and *Group Processes & Intergroup Relations* were devoted to this theme as well. A few years ago a second edition of the handbook about conflict resolution (Deutsch, Coleman, & Marcus, 2006) was published by social psychologists and recently a few important collections have appeared providing impetus to the psychological study of conflict and peace building (de Rivera, 2009; Fitzduff & Stout, 2006).

The present book is taking a social psychological perspective to the analysis of conflicts. It mainly focuses on the socio-psychological foundations and dynamics of harsh and destructive intergroup conflicts (but not only), illuminating their eruption, management, resolution, and peace making.

DESTRUCTIVE CONFLICTS

There are different types of societal conflicts, which may be classified in various ways. One of the more meaningful classification focuses on their severity and longevity. In fact this dimension represents the level of destructiveness of the conflicts. Different terms were used to describe the two opposing poles of this dimension on which it is possible to locate the various intergroup conflicts—though they may dynamically move on this dimension with time. The concepts of tractable and intractable conflicts* will be used. Thus, on the one pole of this dimension are found tractable conflicts which are over goals of low importance and last for a short period of time, during which the parties in dispute view them as solvable and are interested to resolve them quickly through negotiation. In addition, the involved societies avoid violence, do not mobilize society members to support their cause, and recognize and take into account mutual interests, goals and needs, and view

---

* The term intractable became popular in recent years among social scientists (Coleman, 2000, 2003; Lewicki, Gray, & Elliot, 2003 and http://www.crinfo.org).

their conflict as being of mixed motive nature. Some of the conflicts between allied states such as France and Germany or Britain and United States are examples of this type of conflicts.

On the other pole are found intractable conflicts. These conflicts are over perceived important goals; they involve great animosity and vicious cycles of violence; are prolonged because neither side can win and therefore are perceived as unsolvable and self-perpetuating; at the same time both sides are not interested in compromising and resolving them in a peaceful way; in contrast, each side mobilizes society members to participate in them and is focusing only on own needs and goals (see also different characterizations of intractable conflicts, Azar, 1990; Burton, 1987; Deutsch, 1985; Huth & Russett, 1993; Kriesberg, Northrup, & Thorson, 1989; Mitchell, 1981; Mor & Maoz, 1999). The interethnic conflicts between Protestants and Catholics in Northern Ireland, between Chechens and Russians in Chechnya, between Tamils and Singhalese in Sri Lanka, between Turks and Kurds in Turkey, between Moslems and Hindus in India's Kashmir and in the Middle East, between Jews and Palestinians provide or provided in different periods prototypical examples of intractable conflicts. This type of long-lasting, severe and violent conflicts have serious implications for the societies involved, their individual members as well as for the whole world community. Therefore, understanding the foundations and dynamics of intractable conflicts is of special challenge for social scientists, including social psychologists. Many chapters of this book focus especially on this type of conflicts.

The present characterization of conflict's intractability is based on Kriesberg's characteristics (Kriesberg, 1993, 1998). He suggested the following four necessary characterizing features:

1. Intractable conflicts are violent involving physical violence in which society members are killed and wounded in either wars, small-scale military engagements or terrorist attacks.
2. They are perceived as unsolvable because society members involved in intractable conflict do not perceive the possibility of resolving the conflict peacefully.
3. They demand extensive investment as the engaged parties make vast material (i.e., military, technological, and economic) and psychological investments in order to cope successfully with the situation.
4. They are protracted as they persist for a long time, at least a generation. Their long duration implies that the parties in conflict have had many confrontational experiences and as a result they have accumulated animosity and hostility.

In addition to these features, Bar-Tal (1998a, 2007a) proposed to add three necessary characteristics that further elaborate the nature of intractable conflicts.

5. Intractable conflicts are total as they are perceived to be about essential and basic goals, needs and/or values that are regarded as indispensable for the group's existence and/or survival.

6. They are perceived as being of zero sum nature, without compromises and with adherence to all the original goals. In addition, parties engaged in intractable conflict perceive any loss suffered by the other side as their own gain, and conversely, any gains of the other side as their own loss.
7. They are central because they occupy a central place in the lives of the individual group members and the group as a whole. Members of the society are involved constantly and continuously with the conflict.

To conclude this characterization, some of the above described essential features of intractable conflict are purely psychological such as the manner the conflict is perceived as being existential, irresolvable, and of a zero sum nature. Other features are associated with different realms of personal and collective experiences. Even level of violence or extent of investment in the conflict is evaluated subjectively. Only the characteristic of longevity is absolutely an objective one. This does not mean that evaluation of intractability is imagined. People evaluate conflicts on the basis of their experiences and provided information and there is not doubt that conflicts differ in their severity and thus in the clearness of the situation. Wars or high level violence provide unequivocal basis for the evaluation of the severity of the conflict. But there are also situations and lasting conditions that are not as clear and then society members are dependent more on supplied information and acquired knowledge in their judgment.

All the six features (except longevity) may evolve with time and each of them has its own pace of development. Once all of them appear, the state of intractability begins and each characteristic adds to this chronic and harsh reality. It is possible to assume that violence plays a major role in characterizing the severity of the conflict and that it is difficult to evaluate the contribution of each of the other elements to its level of intractability. Nevertheless appearance of the six characteristics without longevity may lead to a very severe, intense and vicious conflict with very heavy losses as the bitter memory of War World II teaches us. The feature of longevity adds a particular element of accumulation of hostility over a long period of time and evolvement because of the continuing violence, which anchors the conflict in system beliefs. It also indicates the inability to bring the conflict to an end either by force through a military victory or by a peaceful resolution. Thus only when all the seven features emerge in their extreme form, typical nature of intractable conflicts emerges. In reality, intractable conflicts differ in terms of the intensity with which each of the seven features occurs. Moreover, intractable conflicts fluctuate, as they may deescalate and then escalate again. Thus, over time each of the seven features may vary in its intensity.

One of the most salient signs of conflict escalation takes place when a party or parties resort to violence (see Chapter 7). In many cases the use of violence is perceived as necessary part to achieve the goals either by one or both sides to the conflict (Brubaker & Laitin, 1998; Opotow, 2006). In conflicts that are over existential goals related to the social identity of the group and which are viewed as of zero sum nature, the use of violence is almost inevitable as the contentions are of such a large scale that very rarely they are satisfied with good will when they emerge. Violence also erupts often in conflicts in which one party is not recognized as a legitimate side to contentions, when there is a great disparity of power and when one side believes that it can ignore the demands of the other side and then the other side feels the need to demonstrate its determination; when there are no institutionalized ways to deal with the grievances, and/or when a party believes that using violence is the best way to achieve its goals.

In most of the cases the beginning of violence by one side immediately evokes violent response from the other side to the conflict. From this point onwards the acts of violence become a part of the conflict and the meaning of initiation and retribution for specific acts is lost. Once the violence erupts it immediately changes the nature of the conflict because it involves harm to society members. Physical violence includes all forms of harm inflicted on human beings beginning with destruction, injuring through torturing, raping, murdering, and can at times leads up to mass killing, ethnic cleansing and even genocide. Physical harm is usually accompanied by symbolic violence such as humiliation or discrimination. The harm is often not only inflicted on military forces but also on civilians (Chapter 8). The harm violates codes of moral behavior, involves group members, gives rise to a sense of collective victimhood, arouses strong emotional reactions, leads to dele-gitimization of the rival and eventually escalates the conflict (Bar-Tal, 2003). Also, particularly important in the context of interethnic conflict is the fact that although individuals perform violent acts, the violence is initiated and carried out within the social system. That is, the societal–political system provides the rationales and the justifications for the violence, mobilizes group members to carry it out, trains individuals to perform violent acts and then glorifies the violent acts and those who perform them.

As noted before, parties involved in intractable conflict cannot win and do not perceive a possibility of resolving it peacefully, instead they continue the confrontation for many decades until intractability is eventually overturned, that is, either one side wins eventually, or both sides finally decide to resolve it peacefully. In any event in interethnic conflicts it is very difficult to win it militarily and therefore they continue through decades and centuries until sometimes both sides turn to peaceful resolution (Sandole, Byrne, Sandole-Staroste, & Senehi, 2009; Worchel, 1999). Even when one side conquers the territory and even when establishes a cooperative regime to own wishes, the conflict may erupt again until the basic needs and goals of the conquered group are satisfied (see, e.g., the conflicts in Chechnya, Rwanda, Middle East, or Sri Lanka). In a few cases interethnic conflicts ended with ethnic cleansing or even a genocide (e.g., the case of Aborigines in Australia). Of crucial importance for the continuation of intractable conflict and lack of its peaceful resolution are the shared beliefs of the rival societies' members suggesting—that they have the human and material resources to continue the conflict, that their goals are sacred and therefore cannot be compromised, that the other side cannot be trusted and/or that time is on their side which means to them that they can improve their situation with time, and may even win the conflict. When even one of these beliefs is hegemonic it greatly inhibits an achievement of peaceful settlement of the conflict.

CONCEPTUAL FRAMEWORK

My own academic work over the last 25 years focuses entirely on the study of conflicts, their resolution, and also in general on peace building. Specifically, I focused on the development of conceptual framework that elaborates the process and the contents of the repertoire that maintains prototypic intractable conflicts. On the basis of this conceptual framework I later developed a conception for analyzing peace building and reconciliation. This line of thoughts served as a scheme for the planning and organization of the present edited book. It provided the rational for the holistic, coherent and systematic structure of the chapters and therefore will be described in details.

Challenges of Intractable Conflicts

On the basis of the previously described characteristics of intractable conflicts, it is assumed that this type of conflicts inflict severe negative experiences such as threat, stress, pain, exhaustion, grief, traumas, misery, hardship, and cost, both in human and material terms on the involved in them societies (Cairns, 1996; de Jong, 2002; Robben & Suarez, 2000). This situation is chronic, as it persists for a long time. Thus, members must adapt to the conditions in both, their individual and collective lives (Hobfoll & deVries, 1995; Shalev, Yehuda, & McFarlane, 2000). I would like to suggest that from a psychological perspective, in order to adapt to the harsh conditions of the intractable conflict, three basic challenges must be met (Bar-Tal, 2007a, 2007b, manuscript in preparation; Bar-Tal & Salomon, 2006).

First, it is necessary to develop ways to satisfy needs that are usually deprived during intractable conflicts, like, for example, psychological needs of knowing, mastery over the destiny, safety, positive identity, and so on (Burton, 1990; Staub, 2003; Tajfel, 1982). Second, it is necessary to learn to cope with the chronic stress, fears, and other negative psychological phenomena that accompany intractable conflict situations. Third, adaptation to the conflict requires development of psychological conditions that will be conducive to successfully withstanding the rival group, that is, to attempts to win the conflict or, at least, not to lose it.

Thus my primary proposition is that to meet the above described challenges, societies in intractable conflict develop a specific socio-psychological repertoire that includes shared beliefs, attitudes, motivations, and emotions[*] (Chapter 2). It eventually turns into a socio-psychological infrastructure, which means that the shared repertoire gradually crystallizes into a well organized system of societal beliefs,[†] attitudes and emotions and penetrates into institutions and communication channels' of the society. As this socio-psychological infrastructure plays a determinative role in intractable conflict, it will now be described and analyzed,

---

[*] This idea is based on conceptual and empirical literature which suggests that successful coping with threatening and stressful conditions requires construction of a meaningful world view (Antonovsky, 1987; Frankl, 1963; Janoff-Bulman, 1992; Taylor, 1983).

[†] Societal beliefs are cognitions shared by society members on topics and issues that are of special concern for their society and contribute to their sense of uniqueness (Bar-Tal, 2000).

especially referring to its adaptive roles in meeting the psychological challenges that have to be met in the context of intractable conflict.

Socio-psychological Infrastructure in Intractable Conflicts

My suggestion is that the socio-psychological infrastructure in intractable conflict consists of three elements: collective memories (Chapter 4), ethos of conflicts and collective emotional orientation (Chapter 3). These elements have mutual interrelations and maintain each other, as well as mutually effect the development of each of them, yet there is a merit in analyzing them separately.

Collective Memory of Conflict   Collective memory is defined as representations of the past remembered by society members as the history of the conflict (Kansteiner, 2002). It presents a coherent and meaningful socially constructed narrative that has some basis in actual events (Cairns & Roe, 2003; Halbwachs, 1992; Liu & Hilton, 2005), but is biased, selective and distorted in ways that meets the present needs of the society. During the conflict, collective memory focuses on at least four of the following themes:

It justifies the outbreak of the conflict and the course of its development.
It presents own society in a positive light (Baumeister & Gastings, 1997).
It describes the rival society in delegitimizing ways (Bar-Tal, 1990; Oren & Bar-Tal, 2007).
It portrays own society as the victim of the opponent (Bar-Tal, Chernyak-Hai, Schori, & Gundar, 2009; Mack, 1990; Volkan, 1997).

All these themes appear in the description of the history of the conflict.

It follows that opposing groups in a conflict will often entertain contradictory and selective historical collective memories of the same events. By selectively including, or excluding, certain historical events and processes from the collective memory and by characterizing positively the in-group and very negatively the out-group, a group views itself and its historical experiences in unique and exclusive ways (Baumeister & Gastings, 1997; Irwin-Zarecka, 1994). Collective memory provides a black and white picture, which enables parsimonious, fast, unequivocal, and simple understanding of the "history" of the conflict.

Ethos of Conflict   During prolonged intractable conflict, in addition to the narrative of collective memory, societies involved develop also a particular ethos— ethos of conflict (Bar-Tal, 1998, 2000a). Ethos is defined as the configuration of shared central societal beliefs that provide a particular dominant orientation to a society at present and for the future (Bar-Tal, 2000a). Ethos of conflict which evolves through the long years of confrontations supplies the epistemic basis for the hegemonic orientation of the society, provides a clear picture of the conflict, its goals, its conditions, requirements, images of the own group and of the rival. It indicates the direction and goals for individual and societal behavior, gives meaning to the societal life, imparts legitimacy to the social system, and explains and justifies leaders' decisions.

It is proposed that ethos of conflict consists of eight themes of societal beliefs (Bar-Tal, 1998, 2007a, 2007b; Rouhana & Bar-Tal, 1998).* It includes the following:

Societal beliefs about the justness of own goals, which outline the goals in conflict, indicate their crucial importance and provide their justifications and rationales.

Societal beliefs about security refer to the importance of personal safety and national survival, and outline the conditions for their achievement.

Societal beliefs of positive collective self-image concern the ethnocentric tendency to attribute positive traits, values and behavior to own society.

Societal beliefs of own victimization concern collective self-presentation as a victim.

Societal beliefs of delegitimizing the opponent concern beliefs which deny the adversary's humanity.

Societal beliefs of patriotism generate attachment to the country and society, by propagating loyalty, love, care, and sacrifice.

Societal beliefs of unity refer to the importance of ignoring internal conflicts and disagreements during intractable conflict in order to unite the forces in the face of the external threat.

Societal beliefs of peace refer to peace in general and amorphic terms as the ultimate desire of the society.

Ethos of conflict together with the collective memory constitutes the ideological epistemic basis of the conflict and complements each other with similar contents. But while the collective memory provides the narrative of the history of the conflict, ethos of conflict enlightens the present and future orientation of the society. In addition to the epistemic–cognitive basis which is constructed with societal beliefs, the socio-psychological infrastructure includes collective emotional orientation.

Collective Emotional Orientation   Societies may develop characteristic collective emotional orientations, with an emphasis on one, or a number of particular emotions (Bar-Tal, Halperin, & de Rivera, 2007; Barbalet, 1998; Kemper, 1990; Mackie & Smith, 2002).† Societies involved in intractable conflict, tend to be dominated by a number of collective emotional orientations. The most notable is the collective orientation of fear, but in addition, they may be dominated by hatred, humiliation and anger, as well as guilt, shame, or pride (Bar-Tal, 2001; Halperin, 2008; Petersen, 2002; Scheff, 1994).

---

* The proposed eight themes of the ethos were found in the public opinions of the Israeli Jewish society between 1967 and 2000 and served as their organizing scheme (Oren, 2005). They were also found to be central motifs in the Israeli school textbooks (Bar-Tal, 1998a, 1998b). Finally, recently they were extensively analyzed as providing foundations for the culture of conflict in the Israeli society (Bar-Tal, 2007b).

† Collective emotional orientation refers to the characterizing tendency of a society to express a particular emotion. That it, the emotion and the beliefs that evoke a particular emotion are widely shared by society members and appear frequently in the society's public discourse, cultural products, and educational materials (Bar-Tal, 2001).

Functions   As indicated, the above described infrastructure of collective memory, ethos of conflict and emotional collective emotional orientations fulfills important functions in meeting the delineated challenges that are facing societies engaged in intractable conflicts. This is especially observable when the conflict is in its climax and no signs of possible peace process appear (Burton, 1990; Staub & Bar-Tal, 2003). First, it provides a meaningful and coherent picture of the conflict to society members (Antonovsky, 1987; Frankl, 1963; Janoff-Bulman, 1992; Taylor, 1983). Second, it serves to justify the acts of the in-group toward the enemy, including violence and destruction (Apter, 1997; Jost & Major, 2001). Third, it prepares the society members to be ready for threatening and violent acts of the enemy, as well as for difficult life conditions (Antonovsky, 1987; Lazarus & Folkman, 1984). Fourth, it has the function of motivating for solidarity, mobilization, and action (Bar-Tal & Staub, 1997). Finally, it creates a sense of differentiation and superiority (Sandole, 1999; Sidanius & Pratto, 1999).

Consequences   The socio-psychological infrastructure, which evolves in the context of intractable conflict and is characterized with the above described features, has serious consequences. The societal beliefs of the infrastructure often are rigid and turn into a kind of ideological conflict supporting beliefs (Chapter 6). The socio-psychological infrastructure with these beliefs and the emotions affects the way information is handled through selective, biasing and distorting way, serving as a barrier to peaceful resolution of the conflict (Chapter 9). Specifically, on the psychological level, socio-psychological infrastructure affects the way incoming information is anticipated, selectively attended to, encoded, interpreted, recalled and acted upon (Bar-Tal & Geva, 1986). It becomes a prism through which society members construe their reality, collect new information, interpret their experiences and then make decisions about their course of action. That is to say, socio-psychological infrastructure tends to "close minds" and stimulate tunnel vision which excludes incongruent information and alternative approaches to the conflict (Jervis, 1976; Vertzberger, 1990; White, 1970). It is proposed that on the basis of the socio-psychological infrastructure the involved societies form a stable view of the violent intractable conflict, while the continuous stream of negative information and experiences validate and reinforce it. This negative repertoire is thus individually stored, frozen and continuously accessible. We can say that those are not the disagreements themselves over the goals that are crucial in any analysis of intergroup conflicts but the social psychological repertoire that includes hostility, hatred, fear, resentment, anger, delegitimization, mistrust, and more that leads to tragic consequences.

Obviously society members differ in the extensity and intensity of sharing the described infrastructure. It depends on various factors such as the level of the perceived threat to the society, unity of goals, strong leadership, availability of communication channels for mobilization, held collective memory about past dangers, and so on. In some societies a hegemonic consensual repertoire of conflict develops, while in the others there may be serious disagreements and schism about conflict goals and about other themes related to the conflict. Also, the extensity and intensity of sharing the infrastructure changes through the time of conflict.

Societies may begin the conflict with consensual agreement which later may dissipate and lead to schism in the society and also conflicts may begin with a disagreement but later with the appearance of a real threat society members may rally under the patriotic umbrella of unity.

Evolvement of Culture of Conflict

In view of the above described processes societies that live under prolonged experiences of intractable conflict with the dominant socio-psychological infrastructure evolve a culture of conflict (Bar-Tal, 2010). A culture of conflict develops when societies saliently integrate into their culture tangible and intangible symbols of conflict which are created to communicate a particular meaning about the prolonged and continuous experiences of living in the context of conflict (Geertz, 1973; Ross, 1998). These symbols of conflict become hegemonic elements in the culture of societies involved in intractable conflict. They provide a dominant meaning about the present reality, about the past, and about future goals, and serve as guides for practice-all as a reflection of the conflict. Moreover, with time, the beliefs of collective memory and ethos of conflict serve as content's basis for the formation of social identity of both societies (Ashmore, Jussim, & Wilder, 2001; Cash; 1996; Oren, Bar-Tal, & David, 2004; Ross, 2001; Worchel, 1999; see also Chapter 5).

Culture of conflict indicates that the socio-psychological infrastructure goes beyond the institutions and communication channels' of the society to become part of the stable political, societal, cultural, and educational context in which society members live and thus turns dominant repertoire (Ross, 1993). In essence, culture of conflict encompasses all the domains of individual and collective life (Kimmel, 2006). Specifically, the repertoire of culture of conflict is not only widely shared by society members but also appears to be dominant in public discourse via societal channels of mass communication. Moreover, it is often used for justification and explanation of decisions, policies and courses of actions taken by the leaders. In addition socio-psychological infrastructure is expressed in cultural products such as literary books, TV programs, films, theater plays, visual arts, monuments, and other products. It is also expressed in institutional ceremonies, commemorations, memorials, and so on. Finally, the socio-psychological infrastructure appears in the school textbooks, is used by teachers and appears prominently even in higher education. The latter building block is of special importance because the beliefs presented in the educational textbooks reach all of the younger generation (Bar-Tal, 2007b for an extensive analysis of the Israeli Jewish society as an example). On one hand the culture of conflict implies that the repertoire of conflict is widely disseminated, imparting its hegemonic views while on the other hand, it reflects the reality as viewed by the society.

Obstacles to Resolve Conflicts Peacefully

In effect, culture of conflict with the described particular repertoire that emerges in times of conflict serves as a major factor for the continuation of the conflict and a barrier for resolving it; in fact it is part of the vicious cycle of the intractable conflict. Considering that this process occurs simultaneously to the two parties in the conflict (what is called a mirror image), it is obvious how the vicious cycle of violence operates (Sandole, 1999). As the conflict evolves, each of the opponents develops the described culture of conflict with the repertoire, which initially fulfills important functional roles, on both the individual and collective levels. With time, however, this repertoire comes to serve as the major motivating, justifying, and rationalizing factor of the conflict. Any negative actions taken by each side toward the rival then serve as information validating the existing negative socio-psychological repertoire and in turn magnify the motivation and readiness to engage in conflict. With the tuning toward the evilness of the rival, the behaviors of each side confirm the held negative socio-psychological repertoire and justify harming the opponent. Both societies practice moral disengagement, moral entitlement, and self-focusing, blocking any empathy, accountability, and responsibility toward the suffering of the rival and the performed perpetration by own group. In this situation it is extremely difficult to change the minds of the involved society members to resolve the conflict peacefully.[*]

Observation of the serious, harsh, and violent conflicts indicates that it is much easier to mobilize society members to participate in them than to persuade them to embark on the road of peace making. Society members can be mobilized with much enthusiasm to support even violent conflicts, in which many human lives are lost, within days; but it takes years to persuade them to stop the bloodshed and suffering in order to settle the conflict via negotiation that requires compromises.

There are several reasons for this asymmetry. At least few of the reasons that are somewhat related are as follows:

1. Evolutionary psychology tells that human beings are more tuned to threats than to peaceful signs (Bigelow, 1969; Ross, 1991; van der Dennen & Falger, 1990). The instinct for survival in times of threat is strong and very basic (Duntley, 2005). People do not take risks and therefore cope with perceived threats with speed and determination in order to avert possible harm (Riek, Mania, & Gaertner, 2006; Stephan & Renfro, 2002). This tendency reflects adaptive behavior since negative information, especially related to threats, may require immediate functional reactions to the new situation (Fox, 1992; Gil-White, 2001), including aggression (Eibl-Eibesfeldt, 1979).

2. High fear, which dominates society members engaged in intractable conflict, usually overcomes hope because is processed unconsciously and

---

[*] It should be noted that intergroup conflicts of a macro scale are not necessarily symmetrical on various dimensions. Of special importance for the understanding asymmetrical conflicts is the level of military-economic power. Such an asymmetry has a great influence on the way the conflict is managed. These asymmetries have to be taken into consideration in the analysis of conflicts. Nevertheless the present conception and many of the chapters focus on the psychological forces that operate independently of the asymmetry, though it is well recognized that the asymmetry has an effect also on socio-psychological processes and dynamics (Aggestam, 2002; Rouhana, 2004; Rouhana & Fiske, 1995).

evokes simple feelings, while hope needed for peace is always based on conscious piecemeal cognitive activity (Lake & Rothchild, 1998; Petersen, 2002). In addition, whereas fear is activated automatically, without effort and cognitive control, hope always relies on thinking and requires various intellectual skills (Jarymowicz & Bar-Tal, 2006). On the behavioral level, fear may lead to defensive and/or aggressive behaviors, often already used in the past as it is based on memorized patterns of reactions (Eibl-Eibesfeldt & Sutterlin, 1990), while hope requires conceiving new behaviors to achieve the desired, positively valued goal and attempts to realize it (Snyder, 2000). In this human programming people are guided by high fear which inhibits a rise and development of hope that is one of the conditions for driving society members toward peace making.

3. Negative information about potential harm has more weight than positive information about peace opportunities. This proposition is based on considerable evidence in psychology to the effect that negative events and information tend to be more closely attended and are better remembered, and that they strongly impact evaluation, judgment, and action tendencies (see reviews by Cacioppo & Berntson, 1994; Christianson, 1992; Lau, 1982; Peeters & Czapinski, 1990; and studies by Ito, Larsen, Smith, & Cacioppo, 1998; Wagenaar & Groeneweg, 1990). This negativity bias is an inherent characteristic of the negative motivational system, which operates automatically at the evaluative-categorization stage. It is also structured to respond more intensely than the positive motivational system to comparable levels of motivational activation (Cacioppo & Gardner, 1999).

4. Finally, social psychological theory of terror management (Pyszczynski, Greenberg, & Solomon, 1997; Solomon, Greenberg, & Pyszczynski, 1991) proposes that innate anxiety of annihilation, combined with the human knowledge of inevitable death, creates an ever-present potential for terror. One of terror management theory's central propositions, strongly supported by research (Greenberg, Solomon, & Pyszczynski, 1997), is that conditions in which mortality is made salient, which characterize many negative threatening contexts, arouse the potential for terror and the immediate need to protect against it. In other words conditions of heightened mortality salience lead to a desire to bolster beliefs in the need to defend and select behaviors that uphold those beliefs, as well as a readiness to reject and even annihilate outsiders who are viewed as threatening the society.

Once collectives rally to engage in conflict and then continue it for a long period of time, additional reasons may explain the dogmatic adherence of the society members to repertoire that maintains conflict and is resistant to alternative information. Some of those several reasons explaining this tendency are as follows:

1. Intractable conflicts often concern protected values that needed to be compromised in order to reach a peace agreement. Protected (or sacred) values are perceived by members of societies involved in conflicts as

fundamental for defining their identities, world views and ideologies, and thus they become protected against any trade-offs or compromise (Baron & Spranca, 1997; Fiske & Tetlock, 1997). Giving up on these values implies for them moral bankruptcy, and even the thought about their compromise stimulates a strong psychological response in the form of moral outrage (Tetlock, 2003; Tetlock, Kristel, Elson, Green, & Lerner, 2000).

Protected (or sacred) values may be abstract (e.g., human rights, justice, etc.), or may be symbolized in a tangible asset, such as a holy site (Skitka, 2002). In other cases, they are associated with a specific policy that is perceived as reflecting the protected value (e.g., building Jewish settlements in the West Bank). Since protected values are nonnegotiable by definition, if the core issues of an intergroup dispute are perceived by the parties as protected values, the conflict will be stubborn and difficult to solve (Landman, in press).

2. Intractable conflicts lead to the evolvement of culture of conflict that penetrates to every societal institution and channel of communication (Bar-Tal, 2010; Ross, 1998). It appears, for example, in public discourse, cultural products, educational material and channels of mass communication. It is very difficult to change cultures in general and especially culture of conflict as it is well entrenched and supported by the conditions of conflict. Dominance of this culture serves as an inhibiting environment that discourages evolvement of alterative ideas that advance peace making.

3. Many of the intractable conflicts are viewed as being related to collective identity (Kelman, 1999a). According to Rothman (1997), these conflicts are "deeply rooted in the underlying human needs and values that together constitute people's social identities," (p. 6). In times of intractable conflict the generic features of collective identity become conducive to the management of the societal mission (David & Bar-Tal, 2009). Also, societal beliefs of ethos of conflict and collective memory offer contents par excellence that imbue social identity with meaning, which maintains the conflict (Barthel, 1996; Cairns, Lewis, Mumcu, & Waddell, 1998; Gillis, 1994; Oren, Bar-Tal, & David, 2004). The challenges of introducing new beliefs that support peace making provide threat to the well established foundations of the collective identity. Any change of these contents is slow and requires an establishment of secure new foundations for the new emerging identity.

4. The intractable conflicts are supported by ideological conflict supporting beliefs that are frozen because of structural and motivational factors and serve as socio-psychological barriers to peace making (Bar-Tal, Halperin, & Oren, in press; Cash, 1996). Rigidity structures imply that they are resistant to change, being organized in a coherent manner with little complexity and great differentiation from alternative beliefs (Tetlock, 1989; Rokeach, 1960). The motivational force that contributes to the freezing is a specific closure need (Kruglanski, 1989, 2004), which motivates society members to view the held conflict supporting beliefs as being truthful and valid because they fulfill for them various needs. It is thus extremely

difficult to overcome these barriers, as at least segments of society members are well entrenched in them.

5. Societies involved in intractable conflict exert great efforts to assure that society members would adhere to the dominant conflict supporting repertoire and ignore alternative information. In other words, the society constructs mechanisms to guarantee that the themes of collective memory and the ethos of conflict, as well as collective emotions, will be maintained and alternative knowledge about possibilities of peace making will not penetrate into the social sphere and even when penetrates would be rejected (Bar-Tal, 2008; Horowitz, 2000; Kelman, 2007). Examples of such mechanism are control of the mass media, censorship on information, delegitimization of alternative information and its sources, closure of archives, and so on.

6. Individuals as well as collectives learn through the years of the protracted conflict how to deal with the situations and conditions of violent confrontations and how to adapt to it. They live with the feeling that the conflict context is meaningful, unambiguous and predictable. Peace making requires changes of well established ways of coping and adaptation. Such changes arouse uncertainty, unpredictability, and ambiguity. Thus society members prefer to continue the known, certain and predictable instead of moving into unknown that causes stress and threat (Mitzen, 2006).

7. Parties engaged in an intractable conflict make vast material (i.e., military, technological, and economic) investments in order to cope successfully with the situation. These investments include mobilization of society members, training the military, development of military industries, acquisition of weapons, and development of supportive infrastructure in all spheres of collective life (Mintz, 1983). They eventually constitute obstacles to peace making because they provide a particular lines of developments, rationale, organizational frameworks, human staff, budgets, resources, and systems that by their nature know only to continue the course of conflict for which they were established. The investments then provide a rational to continue the situation of conflict (Koistinen, 1980).

8. There is no doubt that in every intractable conflict there are segments in the involved society that profit from the continuation of the conflict. Those are investors in the military–industrial complex, military personnel who gain status and prestige, sectors that profit in the conflict territories or gain other resources, and so on (Zertal & Eldar, 2007). These sectors become the agents of conflict during its management and spoilers of the peace process when this possibility appears.

9. Societies engaged in intractable conflict suffer heavy human losses. These losses eventually often constitute an obstacle to peace making. The ultimate sacrifice by society members may lead often to object to any peace move that results in compromise because the feeling is that the sacrifice was in vain as the collective gave up its goals. In a similar line, peace settlement that appears, as was possible in the past, also raises a feeling that it was possible to avoid the sacrifice. Both views lead the families who

lost their dearest to object to needed compromises in conflict settlement (Bar-Tal, 2007b).

10. Finally leaders who lead to intractable conflicts, using coherent and well elaborated justification, have later great difficulty to change their mind and persuade the same audience in the need of peace making. On the individual level the leaders face a cognitive dissonance between attitudes, beliefs and actions during the conflict and those needed to lead a peace process (Bar-Siman-Tov, 1996). On the social level, their previous political and ideological commitments, as well as the leaders' fears from potential political and electoral criticism furthers enhance their tendency to avoid major changes in policy (Auerbach, 1980; Janis & Mann, 1977). In societies engulfed by intractable conflict the prospective dissonance may lead to loss of public support and legitimacy, and even to perceiving the leader as a traitor (Bar-Siman-Tov, 1996; Kelman & Fisher, 2003). Therefore, many scholars consider leadership change as a precondition for shift in policy toward peacemaking (Bennett, 1997; King, 1997; Licklider, 1993).

In spite of the delineated list of obstacles, conflicts do not only outbreak and are managed, but also some are resolved (see Chapter 10). Groups sometimes find ways to resolve the contradiction between their goals and other group goals (Sandole, Byrne, Sandole-Staroste, & Senehi, 2009).

All this does not mean that all the conflicts are similar. On contrary, they are different, involving parties with different level of responsibility, of justified contentions, or of used violence. But almost all of them require peace making process in order to end them.[*] The next section elaborates this process.

EMBARKING ON THE ROAD OF PEACE BUILDING

Embarking on the road of peace building begins when at least a number of society members begin to think that the conflict should be resolved peacefully and also begin to act to realize this idea. Once such an idea emerges and is propagated by society members, a long process of moving the society to resolve the conflict peacefully begins. There are various terms to describe these processes (Galtung, 1975; Rouhana, 2004). Peace building process can be defined as continuous exerted efforts by society members, society's institutions, agents, channels of communications and the international community to realize full lasting peaceful relations with the past rival within the framework of culture of peace. Peace building thus includes all the acts that are done to facilitate the achievement of this goal that is reflected in reconciliation (de Rivera, 2009; Lederach, 1997). Peace making in contrast focuses only the acts toward reaching an official settlement of the conflict which is a formal agreement between the rival sides to end the confrontation

---

[*] There is the hidden assumption in this chapter and other chapters that it is desirable to solve intergroup conflicts peacefully. In general this assumption is well accepted but I do recognize that this assumption may not apply to very few conflicts that require a complete victory in accordance to moral standards. One such clear example is the violent conflict of the World War II because the evilness of the Nazi regime required a full victory to stop it.

(Zartman, 2007). Within the process of peace making, conflict resolution refers to the negotiation process that takes place between decision-makers to reach its formal settlement.

In order to pave the route to the settlement of the conflict and later to the lasting peace, a new repertoire must be formed and disseminated among society members. This repertoire should include ideas about the need to resolve the conflict peacefully, about personalization and legitimization of the rival, changing goals that fueled the conflict, cessation of violence, initiating compromises, optional solutions for conflict resolution that could be accepted by both sides, building trust and constructing beliefs that the agreement can be implemented, developing goals about new peaceful relation with the rival, and eventually recognition in the need to reconcile and construction of new climate which promotes the above presented new ideas about peace making and building (Bar-Tal, 2009). These ideas have to be adopted by society members who must be mobilized for the peace process, if it would be successful. Thus in principle there is need to move the society from what is known, well entrenched in the minds of society members and well practiced for many years to new ideas that portray unknown, uncertain and unpredictable future that is dependent on the delegitimized rival. The above described change therefore constitutes long, complex, and nonlinear process, which does not necessarily end with the new peace supporting repertoire or with peaceful conflict settlement (see Chapter 13).

Peace Making

According to the classic conception offered by Lewin (1947) every process of cognitive change, in individuals and groups, requires unfreezing. Hence a precondition for the acceptance and internalization of any alternative content about the conflict or peace building depends on the ability to destabilize the rigid structure of the socio-psychological repertoire about the conflict that dominates the involved societies.

This endeavor is especially challenging because in many of the conflict situations, this process begins with a minority who needs also to have courage in order to present the alternative ideas to society members. This minority is often viewed by the great majority of the society members at best as naive and detached from reality, but more often as traitors, who harm the patriotic cause and hinder the group cause. Nevertheless the emergence of this minority is not only important for the own society but also for the rival group as well. It may ignite a similar process in the other group or reinforce it. With time, this small minority may gain support and its persistence may serve as a basis for a movement and a change of the context that eventually will open the possibilities to launch an effective campaign for resolving the conflict peacefully.

Peace making requires support of formal leaders for its realization and indeed some of the leaders may join the process of peace making in its early phase trying to initiate conflict resolution. In most of the cases, peace making involves, on one hand, bottom-up processes in which groups, grass roots, and civil society members support the ideas of peace building and act to disseminate them also among leaders.

On the other hand, it also needs top-down processes in which emerging leaders join efforts and begin to persuade the society members in the necessity of peaceful settlement of the conflict and begin to carry it out.

Peace making process must get also a support from the elites and institutions of the society and eventually must be shared by at least a substantial portion of society (Bar-Siman-Tov, 2004; Knox & Quirk, 2000; Weiner, 1998). Of special importance is the role of mass media and other societal channels of communication and institutions that can first buttress the formation of peace orientation, and next transmit and disseminate the new system of beliefs among the society members. The presentation of new beliefs which provide the goals, plans, information, images, considerations, arguments, and justifications for peace building subscribes to the principles of persuasion. These new beliefs should form a new prism for understanding the reality and processing new information. In any event these new alternative ideas must be spread, be legitimized and eventually institutionalized in the society if peace making process is to succeed (Bar-Tal, Landman, Magal, & Rosler, 2009 conception).

Unfreezing process may be facilitated in many of the cases with changes in the context which signal to society members a need to reevaluate the held repertoire that fueled the continuation of the conflict. A few of the possible changes to be noted are: First, the context may change as a result of accumulation of conflict experience like fatigue, vast human and property losses, continuous stalemate and lack of effective governance. Second, it may change as a result of major events like the outbreak of a war, dramatic peace gesture or extreme violent events. Third, this may happen as a consequence of conciliatory and trust-building actions by the rival, which lead to perceived change regarding the opponents' character, intentions, and goals. Fourth, change may take place because of internal events or processes unrelated to conflict (recession, hunger, appearance of a new enemy) that indirectly create the motivation to reassess the centrality and importance of the conflict. Fifth, a third powerful party may change the context by an intervention. This intervention can take various forms such as mediation, providing incentives, persuasion, bombing, sending troops or even economic boycott. Sixth, coming to power of new leaders, who are less committed to the ideology of conflict and thus can develop new approaches to the conflict and create a new context. In addition, arriving of a new generation which has a different look at the conflict and its implications may create a new context. Finally, a need to reevaluate the situation may be the result of more global geopolitical processes and events that are not directly related to the conflict (collapse of a superpower and international climate), but may eventually affect the parties.

Obviously, embarking on the road of peace depends in fact mostly on the societies involved in the severe and harsh conflict. A number of contributions tried to elucidate the conditions of ripeness that may facilitate peacemaking process and reaching conflict settlement. For example, Zartman (2000)—proposed if the (two) parties to a conflict (a) perceive themselves to be in a hurting stalemate and (b) perceive the possibility of a negotiated solution (a way out), the conflict is ripe for resolution (i.e., for negotiations toward resolution to begin)" (pp. 228–229). On the basis of the prospect theory (Kahneman & Tversky, 1979), it was also proposed that societies may begin negotiations for peaceful settlement of the conflict when society members realize that the loses resulting form the continuation of the conflict exceed significantly the losses that a society may incur as a consequence of the compromises and outcomes of peaceful settlement of the conflict (Bar-Tal & Halperin, 2009). It seems that the great majority of society members are usually mobilized to support the peace process on the basis of self-utilitarian considerations. Only a very small minority approach and weigh the situation from moral perspective.

Eventually, conflicts may de-escalate and move toward their peaceful resolution when society members are demobilized from supporting the goals of the conflict and are mobilized for its peaceful resolution (Gidron, Katz, & Hasenfeld, 2002). But without determination and persistence of peace forces which actively act, peace cannot be achieved because it is not enough just to want peace. Almost everyone on this earth cherishes the value of peace and wants to live under its wings. But this is not so simple—peace making requires parting from far-fetching and ideal dreams, descending to concrete steps of pragmatism and transforming the psychological repertoire that served for many years as a compass for continuing the conflict. Even goals that are underlined by justice and moral values have to be eventually compromised with practical considerations if peace making process is to succeed.

This process is complex. The psychological roots of conflict are not easily eliminated. The collective memories of the conflict and ethos of conflict are well organized in the memory system are automatically activated when threats, real or symbolic, are perceived. Thus, the orientation for peace needs not only to inhibit the automatic activation of thoughts associated with conflict, but also to replace them with new beliefs and behaviors. These new beliefs must be attended, comprehended, accepted and practiced, before they can serve as an alternative to the automatically activated repertoire of conflict.

This challenge meets many obstacles because although during the peace making process the conflict may stop being intractable, it still continues to exist and still may have violent expressions such as terror attacks on civilians, military encounters, aggressive rhetoric, or agitation. Hostile and aggressive acts do not stop at once, but usually continue for years, even after achieving formal agreement to settle it. When signs of conflict still occur, this is a challenging task because not only the conflict repertoire becomes accessible, but also these signs are used by spoilers of the peace making process who wait for these types of events and know how to inflame the animosity, fear and hatred. In such a situation the reaction of leaders and the media to the threatening cues is crucial. When they frame the events in support of the conflict orientation, then peace process has very low chances to evolve. But, when in contrast, the leaders and media on both sides explicitly condemn the acts and their perpetrators, when they minimize their importance, reassure the public, and repeat their commitment to peace goals, then the chances are high that the peace making process will survive and gain momentum and reach the stage of conflict settlement.

Conflict Settlement

Ending the conflict resolution process with settlement is a turning point in the relation between the rival parties engaged in intractable conflict. This point in most of the cases is reached after a long process of persuading society members to support it and mostly when the leaders decide to take the determinative decision to settle the conflict peacefully. It refers to a political process through which the parties in conflict eliminate the perceived incompatibility between their goals and interests, and establish a new situation of perceived compatibility (Burton, 1990; Deutsch, 1973; Fisher, 1990; Kriesberg, 1992). It usually ends with an agreement, negotiated by the representatives of the two opposing groups, which outlines the details of the settlement that allows viewing the goals as not being contradictory (see Chapter 11). Conflict resolution can be seen also as a psychological process, since it requires that the negotiators will change their beliefs regarding own goals, and/or other group's goals and/or the extent of contradiction between these two sets of goals, and/or the conditions of the political environment, and/or the situation of the own group and/or the situation of the adversary group (Bar-Tal, Kruglanski, & Klar, 1989; Bercovitch, 1995; Burton, 1987, 1990; Fisher, 1990, 1997; Kelman, 1997; Kriesberg, 1992; Ross, 1993; Worchel, 1999).

An agreement of conflict settlement is a very important phase in the course of the confrontational relations between the rivals. It formally indicates an end of the conflict and specifies the terms of its settlement, which are based on uncertain and ambiguous future benefits. In most of the cases they require to put aside dreams and aspiration in order to accept the possible and practical present.

But it has to be clear that in order for the agreement to resolve the conflict will contribute determinately to the peace building process and change the conflictive relations there are a number of conditions:

It has to satisfactorily address the issues that stood at the core of the conflict.

It has to satisfy the basic needs and goals of both parties.

It has to address the justice within practical limitations.

It has to provide observed changes in the conditions that benefit the ex-rivals.

It has to create a basis for the emergence of the new psychological repertoire that supports the peace making.

It has to signal a strategic decision that changes the nature of the relations between the rival parties.

It has to provide foundations for new policies and new courses of actions which strengthen the peaceful settlement of the conflict, and move the involved societies on the road of peace building.

Nevertheless, peaceful settlement of the conflict does not have a unitary meaning, as peace can take many different forms, ones is achieved. It can range from cold peace that indicates lack of violent acts and minimal relations up to warm peace that is geared toward major transformation of building completely new peaceful relations (see the difference between negative and positive peace by Galtung, 1969). In any event reaching a peaceful and satisfactory settlement of an intractable conflict with the support of the rival societies is probably one of the most impressive and significant achievements that human beings attain.

Thus, it becomes apparent that reaching successfully conflict settlement is only the first formal step in the peace process. Peace building does not end with peace making (Cohr & Boehnke, 2008). Of special importance is the societal process of reconciliation that requires change of the socio-psychological repertoire of culture of conflict among society members that fed the conflict and served as a barrier to the peace process. Moreover, it has become evident that even when the formal peaceful settlement of the conflict is reached it may fall far short of establishing genuine peaceful relations between the former adversaries. The repertoire that fed the conflict does not change overnight even when the groups' leaders resolve the conflict peacefully and sign a peace agreement. What is needed is reconciliation which does not take place unintentionally, but requires also reciprocal planned and active efforts in order to overcome many obstacles and facilitate its solidification (see Chapter 12).

Reconciliation

Students of reconciliation in the present decade agree that it concerns the formation or restoration of genuine peaceful relationships between societies that have been involved in intractable conflict, after its formal resolution is achieved (Nadler, Malloy, & Fisher, 2008). Reconciliation goes beyond the agenda of formal conflict resolution to changing the motivations, goals, beliefs, attitudes, and emotions by the great majority of the society members regarding the conflict, the nature of the relationship between the parties, and the parties themselves (De Soto, 1999; Kelman, 1999b; Lederach, 1997; Nadler, 2002; Rouhana, 2004; Shonholtz, 1998; Wilmer, 1998).

There is not doubt that the first condition for reconciliation is legitimization, personalization, humanization, and equalization of the rival (Bar-Tal & Teichman, 2005). This recognition allows viewing the rival as a legitimate partner to peace and as human entity that deserves equal humane treatment. In addition reconciliation requires viewing the conflict as solvable and recognizing that both sides have legitimate contentions, goals, and needs and there is need to satisfy them in order to solve the conflict and then establish peaceful relations. These basic changes open the road for the process of reconciliation to progress.

On the general level, a number of definitional specifications have been proposed by different writers. Thus, for example, Marrow (1999) pointed out that reconciliation "is reestablishment of friendship that can inspire sufficient trust across the traditional split" (p. 132). In emphasizing trust, he asserts that the basic thrust of reconciliation is to be sensitive to other's needs, the principal question being not what they have to do, but what we have to do to promote the reconciliation process. Lederach (1997) focused mainly on intrasocietal reconciliation and posits four elements of it which can also be extended to intersocietal conflicts, namely:

Truth, which requires open revelation of the past, including admission, acknowledgment, and transparency.
Mercy, which requires acceptance, forgiveness, compassion, and healing for building new relations.

Justice, which requires rectification, restitution, compensation, and social restructuring.

Peace, which underscores common future, cooperation, coordination, well being, harmony, respect, institutionalized mechanisms for conflict resolution, and security for all the parties.

This view is similar to Long and Brecke (2003) model which suggests that reconciliation is based on truth telling about the harm done by both parties, forgiveness which requires new view of both parties, giving up retribution and full justice and building new positive relationship. Kriesberg (2004) added the following to the list:

Regard, which includes mutual recognition of humanity and identity of the societies.

Security which ensures that both society are safe from physical harm.

Kelman (1999b) presented elaborated components of reconciliation in what he calls a positive peace. In this view, reconciliation consists of the following components:

a. Solution of the conflict, which satisfies the fundamental needs of the parties and fulfils their national aspiration.
b. Mutual acceptance and respect of the other group's life and welfare.
c. Development of sense of security and dignity for each group.
d. Establishment of patterns of cooperative interactions in different spheres.
e. Institutionalization of conflict resolution mechanisms (Bar-Siman-Tov, 2004).

In a later paper, Kelman (2004) defined reconciliation as "the development of working trust, the transformation of the relationship toward a partnership based on reciprocity and mutual responsiveness, and an agreement that addresses both parties' basic needs" (p. 119). In his view reconciliation requires change of identity via process of internalization.

As the process of reconciliation proceeds, there is wide agreement that the successful outcome requires the formation of a new common outlook of the past. It is suggested that once there is a shared and acknowledged perception of the past, both parties take a significant step toward achieving reconciliation. As Hayner (1999) noted "where fundamentally different versions or continued denials about such important and painful events still exist, reconciliation may be only superficial" (p. 373). This is the place to note that a number of social psychologists in recent years directed their lines of research exactly to this important observation by studying such phenomena, guilt feelings, taking responsibility, or apologizing (Branscombe & Doosje, 2004; Cehajic & Brown, 2008).

There is no doubt that only reconciliation can address the symptoms of the asymmetrical conflicts in their different aspects: First it should deal with the situation existing before the eruption of the conflict and during its course when on party carried various types of injustices as for example discrimination, exploitation, or occupation. Then it should also deal with the way the conflict was managed and thus refer to various unacceptable types of violence, especially against the civilian population performed such as deportations, mass killing, collective punishments, terrorism, ethnic cleansing, and even genocide. This means that in many cases reconciliation requires major restructuring of the relations as well as the societies involved in order to carry this process. Those are necessary political–economic–societal–cultural processes without which reconciliation cannot succeed.

Socio-psychological Conditions for Reconciliation

On the socio-psychological level reconciliation has been suggested as an outcome that requires mutual recognition and acceptance, invested interests and goals in developing peaceful relations, mutual trust, positive attitudes as well as sensitivity and consideration of the other party's needs and interests (Bar-Tal, 2009). All these elements of reconciliation apply to postconflict situations in which the two groups build peaceful relations in two separate political entities—their states, as well as to situations in which the two rival groups continue to live in one political entity. But, this long process of peace building usually begins before the act of reaching agreement on the peaceful resolution of the conflict. After violent and prolonged conflict, reconciliation is probably the most complex and difficult challenge that collectives can face.

The outlined changes can be carried on through coordinated efforts of the parties that were engaged in intractable conflict and/or via process of self-collective healing through which each party heals itself independently of the other party (Nets-Zahngut, 2009). In view of the socio-psychological dynamics that dominated the years of intractable conflict, reconciliation usually requires a defined policy, planned initiatives, and wide variety of activities; all in order to convince the society members in the necessity, utility, value, and feasibility of the peace process. Eventually, reconciliation supports and solidifies the peace as a new form of intergroup relations and serves as stable foundations for cooperative and friendly acts that symbolize these relations.

With regard to knowledge, of special importance is changing the following major themes of ethos of conflict and collective memory of conflict (Bar-Tal & Bennink, 2004).

Societal beliefs about group's goals. An important challenge for reconciliation process is changing the societal beliefs regarding the justness of the goals that underlay the outbreak and maintenance of the conflict. The new beliefs must present new goals for the society that allow compromise and therefore lead to peaceful conflict resolution.

Societal beliefs about the rival group. Additional crucial objective of reconciliation is a change of the images of the adversary group. It is important to legitimize and personalize its members.

Societal beliefs about the relationship with the past opponent. Reconciliation needs to facilitate formation of new societal beliefs about the relations between the two rival groups that emphasize the importance of new just, equal, cooperative, and friendly relationships.

Societal beliefs about the history of the conflict. Reconciliation requires also a change of collective memories that were dominating the engaged societies during the conflict. There is need to revise these narratives that fueled the conflict into outlook on the past that is synchronized with that of the former rival. Within this theme, past injustices, immoral acts, or violent atrocities have to be addressed.

Societal beliefs about peace. Reconciliation requires forming new societal beliefs that describe the multidimensional nature of peace, specify the conditions and mechanisms for its achievement, realistically outline the benefits and costs of achieving it, connote the meaning of living in peace, and especially emphasize the conditions for its maintenance.

Reconciliation also requires construction of general positive affects and specific emotions about the peaceful relations with the past opponent. Positive affects should accompany the described beliefs and indicate good feelings that the parties have toward each other and toward the new relations. With regard to emotions, reconciliation requires a change in the collective emotional orientations of high level fear, anger, and hatred, which often dominate societies in intractable conflict. Instead, there is need to develop at least emotional orientation of hope to establish peaceful relations with the past rival, which reflects the desire for positive goals of maintaining peaceful and cooperative relations with the other party. This emotional orientation indicates positive outlook for the future, expectations of positive events, without violence and hostilities.

The described changes in groups engaged in intractable conflict, in the framework of reconciliation, is a very complicated, painful, threatening and full of resistance and obstacles process. In order for such a process to succeed, there must be a societal climate of openness and motivation to search and absorb new information, which provides alternative perspective to the conflict. It has to be noted that the process of reconciliation in which ethos of peace evolves is a political, social, cultural, and educational process which involves all the societal institutions and channels of communication (Gawerc, 2006). But, it is not a formal process that can be fully controlled. It depends on a number of major factors.

First of all, it depends on successful conflict resolution, which terminates the conflict formally and is expressed in signed agreement by both sides. This is a determinative factor; without it, reconciliation cannot advance. Second, it depends on the course of events and acts of the past rivals which reflect the desire to change the conflictive relations into peaceful relations. Third, should be noted external supportive conditions such as the peaceful international climate, pressure from influential allies, or rise of a new external common goal (e.g., threat), which may be determinative in the acceleration of the reconciliation process. Fourth, the progress of reconciliation depends on the strength of the opposition to the peace process within the involved societies. Strong opposition of political parties and/or nonparliamentary organizations, which have the support of the elite and/or the masses, may impede the reconciliation process. Fifth, of great importance are the acts and determination of those parts in the engaged societies who support the reconciliation process. Sixth, the success of reconciliation depends on the mobilization of the educational, societal, and cultural institutions for support of the reconciliation process. Finally, the success of the reconciliation process depends also on the activities of various organizations which promote the reconciliation among the in-group members and initiate joint acts with the former adversary group.

It is assumed that the coming years, in the new millennium, we will witness a major effort to study and practice reconciliation. This endeavor is necessary because conflict resolution, especially in the cases of intractable conflicts, is only a part of the reconciliation process. Without reconciliation, seeds of the conflict feed the society members and conflict may outbreak again, as it happened in the past (e.g., in Bosnia or Rwanda). Reconciliation assures in more fundamental way that the past rivals form peaceful relations and view themselves and each other in a way that is functional to the completely new relations (as it happened in the French–German case).

THE PRESENT BOOK

Although the present book deals with various types of conflict, it is skewed toward harsh and intense intergroup conflicts of which the intractable conflicts are of the extreme type. It also concentrates mostly on macro level conflicts and thus by and large concerns destructive conflicts that do harm to societal life. Chapters of the book trying to analyze various aspects of conflicts with the socio-psychological perspective are organized according to the presented scheme in this introduction. With this scheme the book describes a full cycle beginning with the outbreaks of conflicts and finishing with their resolution and peace building through the reconciliation process. It thus provides a holistic and comprehensive outlook on the socio-psychological dynamics that characterize each stage and aspect of intractable conflicts. Each chapter of the book systematically elucidates a particular part of the chain of the cycle describing the theoretical frameworks and concepts, as well as presenting empirical data that was accumulated through the years.

About two-third of the chapters are devoted to unveiling the outbreak of the conflict, its escalation, and the factors that contribute to its maintenance. Chapter 1 explains why intergroup conflicts outbreak by discussing various reasons and causes for their eruption. Chapter 2 discusses the perceptual-cognitive factors involved in conflicts, since the assumption is that perceptions pay an important role in the evolvement of intergroup conflicts and their maintenance. Chapter 3 elaborates on the nature and role of the emotions involved in intergroup conflicts and their resolution. Chapter 4 examines the processes by which collective remembering of conflict's past affects the course of current conflicts. Chapter 5 explains how the role identity and identification play a role in conflicts and describes identity-based conflicts. It focuses on the relationship between social identity and outbreak, and on the maintenance of intergroup conflicts. Chapter 6 adds an important element to the analysis of conflicts, which is an ideology that often inflames them. Chapter 7 illuminates the evil phenomenon of violence in conflicts. It analyses the reasons for the outbreak of violence, the factors that lead to the continuation of the violence and the influence of violence on the development of conflicts, their continuation and resolution. Chapter 8 has special relevancy to the present situation that is sometimes labeled as an age of terror. Many of the conflicts in the present times involve terrorism and the chapter attempts to unveil the reasons for its evolvement. Chapter 9 describes the socio-psychological barriers that hinder and inhibit peace making. Rest of the chapters concerns processes related to peace building. Chapter 10 presents the process of conflict resolution and focuses on various variables that facilitate or inhibit this process. Chapter 11 elaborates on the processes of intergroup negotiation and mediation, since they constitute an essential part of the peace making process. Chapter 12 questions the traditional approach to the study of reconciliation and points out that in cases of asymmetry a new perspective is needed. Finally, Chapter 13 specifies the various socio-psychological approaches and ways to building and maintaining peace including peace culture.

These chapters present an opportunity to get acquainted with the central issues that stand at the core of the discussion in the social psychology of conflict. They may not be exhaustive, but uncover, even if partially, the state of accumulated knowledge in this area. There is no doubt that they do not come to conclude, but to instigate interest in one of the major topics that has a direct relevance to the well being of the human species.

REFERENCES

Aggestam, K. (2002). Mediating asymmetrical conflict. *Mediterranean Politics, 7*(1), 69–91.

Allport, G. W. (1960). *Personality and social encounter*. Boston: Beacon Press.

Anderson, B. (1983). *Imagined communities: Reflections on the origins and spread of nationalism*. London: Verso.

Anderson, B. (1991). *Imagined communittles: Reflections on the origin and spread of nationalism* (rev. ed.). London: Verso.

Antonovsky, A. (1987). *Unraveling the mystery of health: How people manage stress and stay well*. San Francisco: Jossey-Bass.

Anzulovic, B. (1999). *Heavenly Serbia: From myth to genocide*. New York: New York University Press.

Apter, D. E. (Ed.). (1997). *Legitimization of violence*. New York: New York University Press.

Ashmore, R. D., Deaux, K., & McLaughlin-Volpe, T. (2004). An organizing framework for collective identity: Articulation and significance of multidimensionality. *Psychological Bulletin, 130*, 80–114.

Ashmore, R. D., Jussim, L., & Wilder, D. (Eds.). (2001). *Social identity, intergroup conflict, and conflict reduction*. Oxford: Oxford University Press.

Auerbach, Y. (1980). *Foreign policy decisions and attitude changes: Israel–Germany 1950–1965*. Unpublished dissertation, The Hebrew University of Jerusalem (in Hebrew).

Azar, E. E. (1990). *The management of protracted social conflict*. Hampshire, UK: Dartmouth Publishing.

Barbalet, J. M. (1998). *Emotion, social theory, and social structure: A macrosociological approach*. Cambridge: Cambridge University Press.

Bargh, J. A. (2007). *Social psychology and the unconsciousness: The automaticity of higher mental processes*. New York: Psychology Press.

Baron, J., & Spranca, M. (1997). Protected values. *Organizational Behavior and Human Decision Processes, 70*(1), 1–16.

Bar-Siman-Tov, Y. (1996). *The transition from war to peace: The complexity of decisionmaking—The Israeli case*. Tel-Aviv: Tel-Aviv University (in Hebrew).

Bar-Siman-Tov, Y. (Ed.). (2004). *From conflict resolution to reconciliation*. Oxford: Oxford University Press.

Bar-Tal, D. (1990). Israel-Palestinian conflict: A cognitive analysis. *International Journal of Intercultural Relations, 14*, 7–29.

Bar-Tal, D. (1998a). Societal beliefs in times of intractable conflict: The Israeli case. *International Journal of Conflict Management, 9*, 22–50.

Bar-Tal, D. (1998b). The rocky road toward peace: Societal beliefs functional to intractable conflict in Israeli school textbooks. *Journal of Peace Research, 35*, 723–742.

Bar-Tal, D. (2000). *Shared beliefs in a society: Social psychological analysis*. Thousand Oaks, CA: Sage.

Bar-Tal, D. (2001).Why does fear override hope in societies engulfed by intractable conflict, as it does in the Israeli society? *Political Psychology, 22*, 601–627.

Bar-Tal, D. (2003). Collective memory of physical violence: Its contribution to the culture of violence. In E. Cairns & M. D. Roe (Eds.), *The role of memory in ethnic conflict* (pp. 77–93). Houndmills, UK: Palgrave Macmillan.

Bar-Tal, D. (2007a). Sociopsychological foundations of intractable conflicts. *American Behavioral Scientist, 50*, 1430–1453.

Bar-Tal, D. (2007b). *Living with the conflict: Socio-psychological analysis of the Israeli–Jewish society*. Jerusalem: Carmel (in Hebrew).

Bar-Tal, D. (2009). Reconciliation as a foundation of culture of peace. In J. de Rivera (Ed.), *Handbook on building cultures for peace* (pp. 363–377). New York: Springer.

Bar-Tal, D. (2010). Culture of conflict: Evolvement, institutionalization, and consequences. In R. Schwarzer & P. A. Frensch (Eds.), *Personality, human development, and culture: International perspectives on psychological science* (Vol. 2, pp. 183-198) New York: Psychology Press.

Bar-Tal, D. (in press). Culture of conflict. In D. J. Christie (Ed.), *Encyclopedia of peace psychology*. New York: Wiley-Blackwell.

Bar-Tal, D. (in preparation). *Intractable conflicts: Psychological foundations and dynamics*. Cambridge: Cambridge University Press.

Bar-Tal, D., & Bennink, G. (2004). The nature of reconciliation as an outcome and as a process. In Y. Bar-Siman-Tov (Ed.), *From conflict resolution to reconciliation* (pp. 11–38). Oxford: Oxford University Press.

Bar-Tal, D., Chernyak-Hai, L., Schori, N., & Gundar, A. (2009). A sense of self-perceived collective victimhood in intractable conflicts. *International Red Cross Review, 91*, 229–277.

Bar-Tal, D., & Geva, N. (1986). A cognitive basis of international conflicts. In S. Worchel & W. B. Austin (Eds.), *Psychology of intergroup relations* (2nd ed., pp. 118–133). Chicago: Nelson-Hall.

Bar-Tal, D., & Halperin, E. (2009). Overcoming psychological barriers to peace process: The influence of beliefs about losses. In M. Mikulincer & P. R. Shaver (Eds.), *Prosocial motives, emotions and behaviors: The better angels of our nature* (pp. 431–448). Washington, DC: American Psychological Association Press.

Bar-Tal, D., Halperin, E., & Oren, N. (in press). Socio-psychological barriers to peace making: The case of the Israeli Jewish society. *Social Issues and Policy Review*.

Bar-Tal, D., Halperin, E., & de Rivera, J. (2007). Collective emotions in conflict situations: Societal implications. *Journal of Social Issues, 63*, 441–460.

Bar-Tal, D., Kruglanski, A. W., & Klar, Y. (1989). Conflict termination: An epistemological analysis of international cases. *Political Psychology, 10*, 233–255.

Bar-Tal, D., Landman, S., Magal, T., & Rosler, N. (2009). *Societal-psychological dynamics of peace-making process—A conceptual framework*. Paper presented at the small meeting of the European Association of Social Psychology about Resolving Societal

Conflicts and Building Peace: Socio-psychological Dynamics." Jerusalem, Israel, September 7–10, 2009.

Bar-Tal, D., & Salomon, G. (2006). Israeli–Jewish narratives of the Israeli–Palestinian conflict: Evolution, contents, functions and consequences. In R. Rotberg (Ed.), *Israeli and Palestinian narratives of conflict: History's double helix* (pp. 19–46). Bloomington: Indiana University Press.

Bar-Tal, D., & Staub, E. (Eds.). (1997). *Patriotism in the life of individuals and nations.* Chicago: Nelson-Hall.

Barth, F. (1969). *Ethnic groups and boundaries.* Boston: Little, Brown.

Barthel, D. (1996). *Historic preservation: Collective memory and historical identity.* New Brunswick, NJ: Rutgers University Press.

Baumeister, R. F., & Butz, J. (2005). Roots of hate, violence and evil. In R. J. Sternberg (Ed.), *The psychology of hate* (pp. 87–102). Washington, DC: American Psychological Association.

Baumeister, R. F., & Gastings, S. (1997). Distortions of collective memory: How groups flatter and deceive themselves. In J. W. Pennebaker, D. Paez, & B. Rimé (Eds.), *Collective memory of political events: Social psychological perspectives* (pp. 277–293). Mahwah, NJ: Lawrence Erlbaum.

Bennett, D. S. (1997). Democracy, regime change and rivalry termination. *International Interactions, 22*(4), 369–397.

Bercovitch, J. (Ed.). (1995). *Resolving international conflicts.* Boulder, CO: Lynne Rienner.

Bigelow, R. (1969). *The dawn warriors: Man's evolution towards peace.* Boston: Little Brown.

Branscombe, N. R., & Doosje, B. (Eds.). (2004). *Collective guilt: International perspectives.* New York: Cambridge University Press.

Brubaker, R. (2004). *Ethnicity without groups.* Cambridge, MA: Harvard University Press.

Brubaker, R., & Laitin, D. D. (1998). Ethnic and nationalist violence. *Annual Review Sociology, 24,* 423–442.

Burton, J. W. (1987). *Resolving deep-rooted conflict: A handbook.* Lanham, MD: University Press of America.

Burton, J. W. (Ed.). (1990). *Conflict: Human needs theory.* New York: St. Martin's Press.

Cacioppo, J. T., & Berntson, G. G. (1994). Relationship between attitudes and evaluative space. A critical review, with emphasis on the separability of positive and negative substrates. *Psychological Bulletin, 115,* 401–423.

Cacioppo, J. T., & Gardner, W. L. (1999). Emotion. *Annual Review of Psychology, 50,* 191–214.

Cairns, E. (1996). *Children in political violence.* Oxford, UK: Blackwell.

Cairns, E., & Roe, M. D. (Eds.). (2003). *The role of memory in ethnic conflict.* New York: Palgrave Macmillan.

Cairns, E., Lewis, C. A., Mumcu, O., & Waddell, N. (1998). Memories of recent ethnic conflict and their relationship to social identity. *Peace and Conflict: Journal of Peace Psychology, 4,* 13–22.

Cantril, H. (1941). *The psychology of social movements.* New York: Wiley.

Cash, J. D. (1996). *Identity, ideology and conflict: The structuration of politics in Northern Ireland.* Cambridge: Cambridge University Press.

Cehajic, S., & Brown, R. (2008). Not in my name: A social psychological study of antecedents and consequences of acknowledgment of ingroup atrocities. *Genocide Studies and Prevention, 3,* 195–211.

Christianson, S. A. (1992). Remembering emotional events: Potential mechanisms. In S. A. Christianson (Ed.), *The handbook of emotion and memory* (pp. 307–340). Hillsdale, NJ: Lawrence Erlbaum.

Cohr, J. C., & Boehnke, K. (2008). Social psychology and peace: Introductory overview. *Social Psychology*, *39*, 4–11.

Coleman, P. T. (2000). Intractable conflict. In M. Deutsch & P. T. Coleman (Eds.), *The handbook of conflict resolution: Theory and practice* (pp. 428–450). San Francisco: Jossey-Bass.

Coleman, P. T. (2003). Characteristics of protracted, intractable conflict: Towards the development of a metaframework—I. *Peace and Conflict: Journal of Peace Psychology*, *9*(1), 1–37.

Connor, W. (1994). *Ethnonationalism: The quest for understanding*. Princeton: University Press.

de Jong, J. (Ed.). (2002). *Trauma, war, and violence: Public mental health in socio-cultural context*. New York: Kluwer Academic/Plenum Publishers.

David, O., & Bar-Tal, D. (2009). A socio-psychological conception of collective identity: The case of national identity. *Personality and Social Psychology Review*, *13*, 354–379.

de Rivera, J. (Ed.). (2009). *Handbook on building cultures for peace*. New York: Springer.

De Soto, A. (1999). Reflections. In C.J. Arnson (Ed.), *Comparative peace processes in Latin America* (pp. 385–387). Stanford: Stanford University Press.

Deutsch, M. (1949a). A theory of cooperation and competition. *Human Relations*, *2*, 129–153.

Deutsch, M. (1949b). An experimental study of the effects of cooperation and competition upon group process. *Human Relations*, *2*, 199–232.

Deutsch, M. (1958). Trust and suspicion. *Journal of Conflict Resolution*, *21*, 265–279.

Deutsch, M. (1973). *The resolution of conflict*. New Haven, CT: Yale University Press.

Deutsch, M. (1980). Fifty years of conflict. In L. Festinger (Ed.), *Retrospections on social psychology* (pp. 46–77). New York: Oxford University Press.

Deutsch, M. (1985). *Distributive justice: A social psychological perspective*. New Haven, CT: Yale University Press.

Deutsch, M., Coleman, P. T., & Marcus, E. C. (Eds.). (2006). *The handbook of conflict resolution: Theory and practice* (2nd ed.). San Francisco: Jossey-Bass.

Deutsch, M., & Krauss, R. M. (1960). The effect of threat on interpersonal bargaining. *Journal of Abnormal and Social Psychology*, *61*, 181–189.

Driskell, J. E., & Salas, E. M. (Eds.). (1996). *Stress and human performance*. Hillsdale, NJ: Erlbaum.

Duntley, J. D. (2005). Adaptation to dangers from humans. In D. M. Buss (Ed.), *The handbook of evolutionary psychology* (pp. 224–249). Hoboken, NJ: John Wiley& Sons.

Eibl-Eibesfeldt, I. (1979). *The biology of peace and war*. New York: Viking.

Eibl-Eibesfeldt, I., & Sütterlin, C. (1990). Fear, defense and aggression in animals and man: Some ethological perspectives. In P. F. Brain, S. Parmigiani, R. J. Blanchard, & D. Mainardi (Eds.), *Fear and defense* (pp. 381–408). London: Harwood.

Fisher, R. J. (1990). *The social psychology of intergroup and international conflict resolution*. New York: Springer-Verlag.

Fisher, R. J. (Ed.). (1997). *Interactive conflict resolution*. Syracuse: Syracuse University Press.

Fiske, A. P., & Tetlock, P. E. (1997). Taboo trade-offs: Reactions to transactions that transgress the spheres of justice. *Political Psychology*, *18*(2), 255–297.

Fitzduff, M, C., & Stout, C. (Eds.). (2006). *The psychology of war, conflict resolution and peace* (3 Vols.). Westport, CT: Praeger.

Fox, R. (1992). Prejudice and the unfinished mind: A new look at an old failing. *Psychological Inquiry*, *2*, 137–152.

Frankl, V. E. (1963). *Man's search for meaning*. New York: Washington Square Press.

Galtung, J. (1969). Violence, peace and peace research. *Journal of Peace Research*, *6*, 167–101.

Galtung, J. (1975). Three approaches to peace: Peacekeeping, peacemaking and peace-building. In J. Galtung (Ed.), *Peace, war and defence—Essays in peace research* (pp. 282–304). Copenhagen: Christian Ejlers.

Galtung, J. (2004). *Transcend and transform: An introduction to conflict work*. London: Pluto Press.

Gawerc, M. I. (2006). Peace building: Theoretical and concrete perspectives. *Peace & Change, 31*, 435–478.

Geertz, C. (1973). *The interpretation of cultures: Selected essays*. New York: Basic Books.

Giddens, A. (1984). *The constitution of society*. Berkeley, CA: University of California Press.

Gidron, B., Katz, S. N., & Hasenfeld, Y. (Eds.). (2002). *Mobilizing for peace: Conflict resolution in Northern Ireland, Israel/Palestinian and South Africa*. New York: Oxford University Press.

Gillis, J. (1994). Memory and identity: The history of a relationship. In J. Gillis (Ed.), *Commemorations: The politics of national identity*. Princeton: Princeton University Press.

Gil-White, F. J. (2001). Are ethnic group biological "species" to the human brain? Essentialism in our cognition of some critical categories. *Current Anthropology, 42*, 515–554.

Greenberg, J., Solomon, S., & Pyszczynski, T. (1997). Terror management theory of self-esteem and cultural worldviews: Empirical assessment and conceptual refinements. In M. Zanna (Ed.), *Advances in experimental social psychology* (Vol. 30, pp. 61–139). San Diego: Academic Press.

Griswold, W. (1994). *Cultures and societies in a changing world*. Thousands Oaks, CA: Pine Forge Press.

Halbwachs, M. (1992). *On collective memory*. Chicago: University of Chicago Press.

Halperin, E. (2008). Group-based hatred in intractable conflict in Israel. *Journal of Conflict Resolution, 52*, 713–736.

Harding, J., Kutner, B., Proshansky, H., & Chein, I. (1954). Prejudice and ethnic relations. In G. Lindzey (Ed.), *Handbook of social psychology* (Vol. 2). Cambridge, MA: Addison-Wesley.

Hayner, P. B. (1999). In pursuit of justice and reconciliation: Contributions of truth telling. In C. J. Arnson (Ed.), *Comparative peace processes in Latin America* (pp. 363–383). Stanford: Stanford University Press.

Hobfoll, S. E., & deVries, M. W. (Eds.). (1995). *Extreme stress and communities: Impact and intervention*. New York: Kluwer Academic/Plenum Publishers.

Hoebel, E. A. (1960). The nature of culture. In H. L. Shapiro (Ed.), *Man, culture, and society* (pp. 168– 181). NY: Oxford University Press.

Horowitz, D. L. (2000). *Ethnic groups in conflict*. Berkeley: University of California Press.

Huth, P., & Russett, B. (1993). General deterrence between enduring rivals: Testing three competing models. *American Political Science Review, 87*, 61–72.

Irwin-Zarecka, I. (1994). *Frames of remembrance: The dynamics of collective memory*. New Brunswick, NJ: Transaction.

Ito, T. A., Larsen, J. T., Smith, N. K., & Cacioppo, J. T. (1998). Negative information weighs more heavily on the brain: The negativity bias in evaluative categorizations. *Journal of Personality and Social Psychology, 75*, 887–900.

Janis, I. L., & Mann, L. (1977). *Decision making: A psychological analysis of conflict, choice, and commitment*. New York: The Free Press.

Janoff-Bulman, R. (1992). *Shattered assumptions: Towards a new psychology of trauma*. New York: The Free Press.

Jarymowicz, M. (2008). *Psychologiczne podstawy podmiotowości (The Self as a subject: Psychological bases)*. Warszawa: Wydawnictwo Naukowe PWN (in Polish).

Jarymowicz, M., & Bar-Tal, D. (2006). The dominance of fear over hope in the life of individuals and collectives. *European Journal of Social Psychology, 36*, 367–392.

Jervis, R. (1976). *Perception and misperception in international politics*. Princeton: Princeton University Press.

Jost, J. T., & Major, B. (Eds.). (2001). *The psychology of legitimacy: Emerging perspectives on ideology, justice, and intergroup relations*. New York: Cambridge University Press.

Kahneman, D., & Tversky, A. (1979). Prospect theory: An analysis of decision under risk. *Econometrica, 47*, 263–291.

Kahneman, D., Slovic, P., & Tverski, A. (Eds.). (1982). *Judgment under uncertainty: Heuristics and biases*. New York: Cambridge University Press.

Kansteiner, W. (2002). Finding meaning in memory: Methodological critique of collective memory studies. *History and Theory, 41*, 179–197.

Kelley, H. H. et al. (1970). A comparative experimental study of negotiation behavior. *Journal of Personality and Social Psychology, 16*, 411–438.

Kelman, H. C. (Ed.). (1965). *International behavior: A social psychological analysis*. New York: Holt, Rinehart and Winston.

Kelman, H. C. (1997). Social-psychological dimensions of international conflict. In I. W. Zartman & J. L. Rasmussen (Eds.), *Peacemaking in international conflict: Methods and techniques* (pp. 191–237). Washington, DC: United States Institute of Peace Press.

Kelman, H. C. (1999a). The interdependence of Israeli and Palestinian identity: The role of the other in existential conflicts. *Journal of Social Issues, 55*(3), 581–600.

Kelman, H. C. (1999b). Transforming the relationship between former enemies: A social-psychological analysis. In R. L. Rothstein (Ed.), *After the peace: Resistance and reconciliation* (pp. 193–205). Boulder: Lynne Rienner Publishers.

Kelman, H. C. (2004). Reconciliation as identity change: A social psychological perspective. In Y. Bar-Siman-Tov (Ed.), *From conflict resolution to reconciliation* (pp. 111–124). Oxford: Oxford University Press.

Kelman, H. C. (2007). Social-psychological dimensions of international conflict. In I. W. Zartman (Ed.), *Peacemaking in international conflict: Methods and techniques* (rev. ed., pp. 61–107). Washington, DC: United States Institute of Peace Press.

Kelman, H. C., & Fisher, R. J. (2003). Conflict analysis and resolution. In D. O. Sears, L. Huddy, & R. Jervis (Eds.), *Oxford handbook of political psychology* (pp. 315–353). Oxford: Oxford University Press.

Kemper, T. D. (Ed.). (1990). *Research agendas in the sociology of emotions*. Albany, NY: State University of New York Press.

Kimmel, P. R. (2006). Culture and conflict In M. Deutsch, P. T. Coleman, & E. C. Marcus (Eds.), *The handbook of conflict resolution: Theory and practice* (2nd ed., pp. 625–648). San Francisco: Jossey-Bass.

King, C. (1997). *Ending civil wars*. Adelphi Paper 308. New York: Oxford University Press.

Klandermans, B. (1988). The formation and mobilization of consensus. In B. Klandermans, H. Kriesi, & S. Tarrow (Eds.), *From structure to action: Comparing social movement research across cultures* (Vol. 1, pp. 173–196). Greenwich, CT: JAI Press.

Klineberg, O. (1950). *Tensions affecting international understanding*. New York: Social Science Council Bulletin.

Knox, C., & Quirk, P. (2000). *Peace building in Northern Ireland, Israel and South Africa: Transition, transformation and reconciliation*. London: Macmillan.

Koistinen, P. A. C. (1980). *The military-industrial complex: A historical perspective*. Westport, CT: Praeger.

Krech, D., & Crutchfield, R. S. (1948). *Theory and problems of social psychology*. New York: McGraw-Hill.

Krech, D., Crutchfield, R. S., & Ballachey, E. L. (1962). *Individual in society.* New York: McGraw-Hill.

Kriesberg, L. (1992). *International conflict resolution.* New Haven, CT: Yale University Press.

Kriesberg, L. (1993). Intractable conflicts. *Peace Review, 5*(4), 417–421.

Kriesberg, L. (1998). Intractable conflicts. In E. Weiner (Ed.), *The handbook of interethnic coexistence* (pp. 332–342). New York: Continuum.

Krieberg, L. (2004). Comparing reconciliation actions within and between countries. In Bar-Siman-Tov, Y. (Ed.), *From conflict resolution to reconciliation* (pp. 81–110). Oxford: Oxford University Press.

Kriesberg, L., Northup, T. A., & Thorson, S. J. (Eds.). (1989). *Intractable conflicts and their transformation.* Syracuse: Syracuse University Press.

Kruglanski, A. W. (1989). *Lay epistemics and human knowledge: Cognitive and motivational bases.* New York: Plenum.

Kruglanski, A. W. (2004). *The psychology of closed mindedness.* New York: Psychology Press.

Kunda, Z. (1990). The case for motivated reasoning. *Psychological Bulletin, 108,* 480–498.

Lake, D. A., & Rothchild, D. (Eds.). (1998). *The international spread of ethnic conflict: Fear, diffusion, and escalation.* Princeton: Princeton University Press.

Landman, S. (in press). Protected values as barriers to solving the Israeli–Palestinian conflict: A new perspective on the core issues of the conflict. In Y. Bar-Siman-Tov (Ed.), *Barriers to the resolution of the Israeli–Palestinian conflict.* Jerusalem: Jerusalem Institute for Israel Studies (in Hebrew).

Lau, R. R. (1982). Negativity in political perception. *Political Behavior, 4,* 353–377.

Lazarus, R. S., & Folkman, S. (1984). *Stress, appraisal, and coping.* New York: Springer.

Lederach, J. P. (1997). *Building peace: Sustainable reconciliation in divided societies.* Washington, DC: United States Institute of Peace Press.

Lewicki, R., Gray, B., & Elliott, M. (Eds.). (2003). *Making sense of intractable environmental conflicts: Frames and cases.* Washington, DC: Island Press.

Lewin, K. (1947). Frontiers in group dynamics. *Human Relations, 1,* 5–41.

Lewin, K. (1948). *Resolving social conflicts.* New York: Harper & Row.

Licklider, R. (1993). What have we learned and where do we go from here? In R. Licklider (Ed.), *Stopping the killing: How civil wars end* (pp. 303–322). New York: New York University Press.

Liu, J. H., & Hilton, D. J. (2005). How the past weighs on the present: Social representations of history and their in identity politics. *British Journal of Social Psychology, 44,* 537–556.

Long, W. J., & Brecke, P. (2003). *War and reconciliation: Reason and emotion in conflict resolution.* Cambridge, MA: MIT Press.

Mack, J. E. (1990). The psychodynamics of victimization among national groups in conflict. In V. D. Volkan, D. A. Julius, & J. V. Montville (Eds.), *The psychodynamics of international relationships* (pp. 119–129). Lexington, MA: Lexington.

Mackie, D. M., & Smith, E. R. (Eds.). (2002). *From prejudice to intergroup emotions: Differentiated reactions to social groups.* Philadelphia, PA: Psychological Press.

Marrow, D. (1999). Seeking peace amid memories of war: Learning form the peace process in Northern Ireland. In R. L. Rothstein (Ed.), *After the peace: Resistance and reconciliation* (pp. 111–138). Boulder: Lynne Rienner Publishers.

Mintz, A. (1983). The military-industrial complex: The Israeli case. *Journal of Strategic Studies, 6*(3), 103–127.

Mitchell, C. R. (1981). *The structure of international conflict.* London: Macmillan.

Mitzen, J. (2006). Ontological security in world politics: State identity and the security dilemma. *European Journal of International Relations, 12,* 341–370.

Mor, B. D., & Maoz, Z. (1999). Learning and the evolution of enduring rivalries: A strategic approach. *Conflict Management and Peace Science, 17,* 1–48.

Murphy, G., Murphy, L. B., & Newcomb, T. M. (1937). *Experimental social psychology* (rev. ed.). New York: Harper and Brothers.

Myers, D. G. (1993). *Social psychology.* New York: McGraw-Hill.

Nadler, A. (2002). Post resolution processes; instrumental and socio-emotional routes to reconciliation. In G. Salomon & B. Nevo (Eds.), *Peace education: The concept, principles and practice in the world* (pp. 127–143). Mahwah, NJ: Lawrence Erlbaum.

Nadler, A., Malloy, T. E., & Fisher, J. D. (Eds.). (2008). *The social psychology of intergroup reconciliation.* New York: Oxford University Press.

Nets-Zahngut, R. (2009). The collective self healing process of the aftermath of intractable conflicts. (Submitted for publication.)

Newcomb, T. M. (1950). *Social psychology.* New York: Holt-Dryden Books.

Nisbett, R., & Ross, L. (1980). *Human inferences: Strategies and shortcomings of social judgment.* Englewood Cliffs, NJ: Prentice-Hall.

Opotow, S. (2006). Aggression and violence. In M. Deutsch, P. T. Coleman, & E. C. Marcus (Eds.), *The handbook of conflict resolution: Theory and practice* (2nd ed., pp. 509–532). San Francisco: Jossey-Bass.

Oren, N., & Bar-Tal, D. (2007). The detrimental dynamics of delegitimization in intractable conflicts: The Israeli–Palestinian case. *International Journal of Intercultural Relations, 31,* 111–126.

Oren, N., Bar-Tal, D., & David, O. (2004). Conflict, identity and ethos: The Israeli–Palestinian case. In Y-T. Lee, C. R. McCauley, F. M. Moghaddam, & S. Worchel (Eds.), *Psychology of ethnic and cultural conflict* (pp. 133–154). Westport, CT: Praeger.

Peeters, G., & Czapinski, J. (1990). Positive–negative asymmetry in evaluations: The distinction between affective and informational negativity effects. *European Review of Social Psychology, 1,* 33–60.

Petersen, R. D. (2002). *Understanding ethnic violence: Fear, hatred, and resentment in twentieth-century Eastern Europe.* Cambridge: Cambridge University Press.

Pruitt, D. G., & Kimmel, M. J. (1977). Twenty years of experimental gaming: Critique, synthesis, and suggestions for the future. *Annual Review of Psychology, 28,* 363–392.

Prunier, G. (1997). *The Rwanda crisis: History of a genocide.* New York: Columbia University Press.

Pyszczynski, T., Greenberg, J., & Solomon, S. (1997). Why do we need what we need? A terror management perspective on the roots of human motivation. *Psychological Inquiry, 8,* 1–20.

Rapoport, A. (1960). *Fights, games, and debates.* Ann Arbor: University of Michigan Press.

Raven, B. H., & Rubin, J. Z. (1976). *Social psychology: People in groups.* New York: John Wiley.

Riek, B. M., Mania, E. W. M., & Gaertner, S. L. (2006). Intergroup threat and outgroup attitudes: A meta-analytic review. *Personality and Social Psychology Review, 10,* 336–353.

Robben, A., & Suarez, O. M. M. (Eds.). (2000). *Cultures under siege: Collective violence and trauma.* New York: Cambridge University Press.

Rokeach, M. (1960). *The open and closed mind.* New York: Basic Books.

Ross, M. H. (1991). The role of evolution in ethnocentric conflict and its management. *Journal of Social Issues, 47*(3), 167–185.

Ross, M. H. (1993). *The culture of conflict: Interpretation and interests in comparative perspective.* New Haven, CT: Yale University Press.

Ross, M. H. (1998). The cultural dynamics of ethnic conflict. In D. Jacquin, A. Oros, & M. Verweij (Eds.), *Culture in world politics* (pp. 156–186). Houndmills: Macmillan.

Ross, M. H. (2001). Psychocultural interpretations and dramas: Identity dynamics in ethnic conflict. *Political Psychology, 22,* 157–198.

Rothman, J. (1997). *Resolving identity-based conflict in nations, organizations, and communities.* San Francisco: Josey-Bass.

Rouhana, N. N. (2004). Group identity and power asymmetry in reconciliation process: The Israeli–Palestinian case. *Peace and Conflict: Journal of Peace Psychology, 10,* 33–52.

Rouhana, N., & Bar-Tal, D. (1998). Psychological dynamics of intractable conflicts: The Israeli–Palestinian case. *American Psychologist, 53,* 761–770.

Rouhana, N., & Fiske, S. T. (1995). Perception of power, threat and conflict interest in asymmetric intergroup conflict. *Journal of Conflict Resolution, 39,* 49–81.

Saks, M. J., & Krupat, S. (1988). *Social psychology and its applications.* New York: Harper & Row.

Sandole, D. (1999). *Capturing the complexity of conflict: Dealing with violent ethnic conflicts of the Post-Cold War era.* London: Pinter/Continuum.

Sandole, D. J. D., Byrne, S., Sandole-Staroste, I., & Senehi, J. (Eds.). (2009). *Handbook of conflict analysis and resolution.* New York: Routledge.

Scheff, T. J. (1994). *Bloody revenge: Emotions, nationalism, and war.* Boulder: Westview.

Scheff, T. J., & Retzinger, S. (1991). *Emotion and violence: Shame/rage spirals in intermiable conflicts.* Lexington: Lexington Books.

Shalev, A. Y., Yehuda, R., & McFarlane, A. C. (Eds.). (2000). *International handbook of human response to trauma.* Dordrecht, Netherlands: Kluwer Academic Publishers.

Sherif, M. (1966). *The common predicament: Social psychology of intergroup conflict and cooperation.* Boston: Houghton Mifflin.

Sherif, M., Harvey, O. J., White, B. J., Hood, W. R., & Sherif, C. W,, (1961). *Intergroup cooperation and competition: The Robber Cave experiment.* Norman, OK: University Book Exchange.

Shonholtz, R. (1998). Conflict resolution moves East: How the emerging democracies of Central and Eastern Europe are facing interethnic conflict. In E. Weiner (Ed.), *The handbook of interethnic coexistence* (pp. 359–368). New York: The Continuum Publishing Company.

Sidanius, J., & Pratto, F. (1999). *Social dominance.* New York: Cambridge University Press.

Simon, B., & Klandermans, B. (2001). Politicized collective identity. *American Psychologist, 56,* 319–331.

Skitka, L. J. (2002). Do the means justify the ends, or do the ends justify the means? A test of the value protection model of justice. *Personality and Social Psychology Bulletin, 28,* 588–597.

Snyder, C. R. (Ed.). (2000b). *Handbook of hope: Theory, measures, & applications.* San Diego: Academic Press.

Solomon, S., Greenberg, J., & Pyszczynski, T. (1991). A terror management theory of social behavior: The psychological functions of self esteem and cultural worldviews. In M. P. Zanna (Ed.), *Advances of experimental social psychology* (Vol. 24, pp. 91–159). San Diego: Academic Press.

Staal, M. A. (2004). *Stress, cognition and human performance: A literature review and conceptual framework.* Hanover, MD: NASA, Center for Aerospace Information.

Stagner, R. (1967). *Psychological aspects of international conflict.* Belmont, CA: Brook/Cole.

Staub, E. (2003). *The psychology of good and evil: The roots of benefiting and harming other.* New York: Cambridge University Press.

Staub, E., & Bar-Tal, D. (2003). Genocide, mass killing and intractable conflict: Roots, evolution, prevention and reconciliation. In D. O. Sears, L. Huddy, & R. Jervis (Eds.), *Oxford handbook of political psychology* (pp. 710–751). New York: Oxford University Press.

Stephan, W. G. (1985). Intergroup relations. In G. Lindzey & E. Aronson (Eds.), *Handbook of social psychology* (Vol. III, pp. 599–658). New York: Addison-Wesley.

Stephan, W. G., & Renfro, C. L. (2002). The role of threat in intergroup relations. In D. Mackie & E. Smith (Eds.), *From prejudice to intergroup emotions* (pp. 191–207). Philadelphia, PA: Psychology Press.

Tajfel, H. (Ed.). (1978). *Differentiation between social groups: Studies in the social psychology of intergroup relations*. London: Academic Press.

Tajfel, H. (1982). *Social identity and intergroup relations*. Cambridge: Cambridge University Press.

Taylor, S. E. (1983). Adjustment to threatening events: A theory of cognitive adaptation. *American Psychologist*, *38*, 1161–1173.

Tetlock, P. (2003). Thinking the unthinkable: Sacred values and taboo cognitions. *Trends in Cognitive Science*, *7*, 320–324.

Tetlock, P. E. (1989). Structure and function in political belief system. In A. R. Pratkanis, S. J. Breckler, & A. G. Greenwald (Eds.), *Attitude structure and function* (pp. 126–151). Hillsdale, NJ: Erlbaum.

Tetlock, P. E., Kristel, O. V., Elson, S. B., Green, M. C., & Lerner, J. F. (2000). The psychology of the unthinkable: Taboo trade-offs, forbidden base-rates, and heretical counterfactuals. *Journal of Personality and Social Psychology*, *78*(5), 853–870.

Waganaar, W. A., & Goreneweg, J. (1990). The memory of concentration camp survivors. *Applied Cognitive Psychology*, *4*, 77–88.

van der Dennen, J., & Falger, V. (Eds.). (1990). *Sociobiology and conflict: Evolutionary perspective on competition, cooperation, violence and warfare*. London: Chapman & Hall.

Vertzberger, Y. (1990). *The world in their minds: Information processing, cognition and perception in foreign policy decision making*. Stanford: Stanford University Press.

Volkan, V. (1997). *Bloodlines: From ethnic pride to ethnic terrorism*. New York: Farrar, Straus and Giroux.

Vollhardt, J. K., & Bilali, R. (2008). Social psychology's contribution to the psychological study of peace: A review. *Social Psychology*, *39*, 12–25.

Weiner, E. (Ed.). (1998). *The handbook of interethnic coexistence*. New York: The Continuum Publishing Company.

White, R. K. (1970). *Nobody wanted war: Misperception in Vietnam and other wars*. Garden City, NY: Anchor Books.

Wilmer, F. (1998). The social construction of conflict and reconciliation in the former Yugoslavia. *Social Justice: A Journal of Crime, Conflict & World Order*, *25*(4), 90–113.

Worchel, S. (1999). *Written in blood: Ethnic identity and the struggle for human harmony*. New York: Worth.

Zartman, I. W. (2000). Ripeness: The hurting stalemate and beyond. In P. C. Stern & D. Druckman (Eds.), *International conflict resolution after the cold war* (pp. 225–250). Washington, DC: National Academy Press.

Zartman, I. W. (Ed.). (2007). *Peacemaking in international conflict: Methods and techniques* (rev. ed.). Washington, DC: United States Institute of Peace Press.

Zertal, I., & Eldar, A. (2007). *Lords of the land: The settlers and the State of Israel, 1967–2007*. New York: Nation Books.

1

Pigs, Slingshots, and Other Foundations of Intergroup Conflict

DAWNA K. COUTANT, STEPHEN WORCHEL, and MARCELO HANZA

*T*he roots of social psychology are deeply embedded in the study of groups. Psychologists have been both intrigued and perplexed by group behavior. Of all the questions that have been raised about groups, perhaps the most important ones concern intergroup conflict. Why is the existence of a group so often accompanied by conflict with other groups? Why does this conflict and hatred become so deeply engrained that it can persist for generations? No period of history and no corner of the world have been spared tragic consequences from intergroup conflict, and as human ingenuity develops more creative weapons of destruction, the understanding of intergroup conflict takes on increasing urgency.

It would be natural to believe that a behavior that has the potential to destroy humankind would have incredibly complex causes. But history and literature suggest that this is not necessarily the case. Take, for example, the remote valleys and hollows along the Big Sandy River in the United States that divides Kentucky and West Virginia. Like a people who time forgot, two extended families, Hatfields and McCoys, populated this isolated region. The families existed side by side, often intermarrying. One morning in 1873, Floyd Hatfield drove his pigs into his pigsty. A few days later, his brother-in-law, Randolph McCoy stopped by to chat. He noticed the pigs and on inspection determined that one of them looked like one of his, "Floyd, that ain't yo' hog … hit's mine" (Jones, 1948, p. 18). The two men squabbled over ownership of the pig, and eventually turned the matter over to a local court. The jury ruled that Floyd could keep the pig, but the ruling ignited a feud between the Hatfields and McCoys that lasted more than 50 years and resulted in nearly 100 deaths. The root of the conflict was disagreement over the ownership of a pig.

One might think that this story is an exception. But before embracing this conclusion, let's examine some children's literature. In *Gulliver's Travels* (Swift, 1735) Gulliver relates a longstanding conflict between people who opened their boiled egg on the big end and those who cracked their eggs on the narrow end. And a more recent "classic" tells a similar tale. Dr. Seuss (1984) writes about two groups, the Zooks and Yooks, who were separated by a stone wall and by their eating habits. "… every Zook eats his bread with the butter side down! But we Yooks, as you know, when we breakfast or sup, spread our bread, Grandpa said, with the butter side up" (Suess, 1984, pp. 5–6). This uneasy coexistence was broken one day when a "very rude Zook" shot a rock with his slingshot at a Yook. This event ignited an arms race that eventually led each side to the development of an ultimate weapon of mass destruction.

Moving from fiction to reality, the breadth and the simplicity of the foundation of intergroup conflict is evident in the responses of youth who attended "peace programs" aimed at bringing together people from groups engaged in protracted and violent conflict. Worchel and Coutant (2004, 2008) asked participants (aged 14–18) from war-torn areas in the Middle East and Balkans to give their views on the underlying causes of conflict in their regions. The large majority of responses identified the "other side" as being responsible for the conflict. In addition, many respondents targeted numerous "group" factors as contributing to the conflict, including the "history of the groups," religion, government, and teachers. There was a certain resignation that the conflict was caused by conditions outside the control of individuals, and, therefore, the conflict was destined to remain until "something" changed these contextual factors. One particularly intriguing response was that the conflict between the groups was "natural," and that the violence may be reduced, but the conflict would forever remain.

The conclusion that intergroup conflict is "natural" or expected is certainly food for contemplation. But whether one concludes that intergroup conflict is the norm or an aberration, few would disagree about the destructive consequences that can result from the conflict. For more than a half-century, social psychologists have theorized about and carefully examined the conditions that lead to intergroup conflict, and literature focusing on these causes is both extensive and varied. Therefore, the task of summarizing the approaches in a single chapter is formidable. After slicing and dicing the literature in several ways, we determined that the best method to present the theories was to classify them by their focus. Some theories emphasize the individual and the psychological processes that give rise to conflict. Others see the roots of intergroup conflict growing from the conditions within the groups. A third approach emphasizes specific factors that exist between the groups as the culprit of hostility and conflict between groups. And, finally, investigators have implicated the cultural context as a contributing factor in intergroup conflict.

Before beginning our examination, it is important to clarify two points. First, our classification of approaches is employed as an organizational framework that is based only on the emphasis of approaches. We do not wish to suggest that a specific theory focuses on only one domain or level of analysis. However, since the focus of this chapter is on groups and intergroup relations, we have chosen to present those approaches that may be applicable at several levels, at the group level. For example, research demonstrates the impact of relative deprivation on individuals and groups. In order to avoid being redundant, and for the sake of brevity, we address the work on relative deprivation in the section devoted to group-based factors. Second, the various theories are not mutually exclusive; no single approach is the explanation for intergroup conflict. Instead, the various levels of explanation should be viewed as comprising a system that recognizes that factors at all levels contribute to inter-group conflict. Specific conflicts may be more influenced by factors at certain levels, but in most cases, the conflict is nurtured by factors and processes at all levels of analysis. With these points in mind, let us begin the exploration of the foundations of intergroup conflict.

FOCUS ON THE INDIVIDUAL

Psychology is a science of the individual, and accordingly several theories of intergroup conflict focus on processes within the individual. These theories range from the instinctive approaches of aggression, through personality and attitudinal tendencies that lead to nationalistic views (Adorno et al., 1950; Stangor & Jost, 1997) to human dispositions to conform and be obedient. One of the more popular theories in this domain is social identity theory (SIT).

Perhaps the most influential of these is SIT, which argues that an individual's identity is based largely on two sources (Tajfel, 1970; Tajfel & Turner, 1986). One, personal identity, comes from his or her unique characteristics such as personality, accomplishments, and physical attributes. The other social identity is based on the groups to which one belongs. Individuals are motivated to create the most positive identity possible, and because "positive" is often a relative term, people engage in social comparison with others (Festinger, 1954). Do I have more money than others? Are the groups (in-groups) to which I belong better than the groups to which I am not a member (out-groups)? At first glance, this appears to be a relatively harmless process. Why should conflict, interpersonal or intergroup, be sparked by an individual's desire to learn about themselves or have a positive self-image?

Tajfel and Turner (1979), and Turner, Brown, and Tajfel (1979) supply the answer by emphasizing the egocentric motivation to have a positive self-image: Individuals want to be "better" than others. The desire to be better than others can lead to (mis)perceptions of oneself or one's group relative to others. Blake and Mouton (1962) found that when members of a human relations training program were asked to judge the quality of a solution of the in-group and the out-group on a task, individuals over estimated in-group performance and under-estimated the out-group performance. Likewise, Worchel, Axsom, Ferris, Samaha, and Schweitzer (1978) found that when two groups worked together on a common task, failure led participants to attribute the cause of the poor performance to the out-group. Finally, Hastorf and Cantril (1954) interviewed Princeton and Dartmouth students after a particularly violent football game. During the game, Dartmouth was flagged for more infractions than Princeton. But when asked to estimate the number of infractions by each team, Dartmouth students recalled that each team had an equal number of fouls while Princeton students overestimated the number of infractions by Dartmouth (their out-group). These types of misperceptions allow one to perceive his/her group as being better than the out-group. By allowing the individual to perceive the out-group in a negative light, these perceptions sow the seeds of conflict between individuals in different groups, but, on their own, they do not ignite hatred and discrimination.

Unfortunately the comparison process is not limited to memory and cognition, it also involves behavior. According to SIT, individuals engage in actions to benefit their own group and disadvantage the out-group, with an emphasis on enhancing the relative difference between the two groups (Hogg & Abram, 1988; Mullen, Brown, & Smith, 1992). There are some intriguing twists and turns within these discriminatory behaviors. For example, individuals may choose a path that harms their own group in an absolute sense, so long as this action increases the relative difference between the in-group and out-group. In one study, participants were supposedly divided into groups based on their preferences to slides of two Flemish painters, then asked (individually) to choose a matrix to divide points. The researchers cleverly designed these matrices to assess the strategies individuals would use to discriminate between another in-group member and an out-group member. Researchers found that equally (and nonsignificantly more) important than maximum profit for the in-group member was maximum differentiation between the out-group. The motive to separate the in-group by suppressing profit for the out-group was as strong as or stronger than simply maximizing profit (Turner, Brown, & Tajfel, 1979). Even when experimental controls have manipulated expectations of reciprocity by the in-group, similar findings are seen (Gagnon & Bourhis, 1996). The critical point is that individuals are willing to hurt their own group if this act increases the discrepancy between the groups. For example, an employer may reject hiring a member of the out-group, who could help his company, in favor of hiring a less qualified in-group member, who may be of marginal help to the company.

SIT has been the catalyst for a wonderfully diverse and prolific body of research. Some studies have dissected the issue of whether discrimination typically involves advancing the in-group, disadvantaging the out-group, or both. SIT raises the disturbing possibility that intergroup conflict results from the mere existence or formation of distinct groups or social categories. And since groups are a fact of life in our social landscape, the pointed message is that intergroup conflict is endemic to human existence. This disturbing thought aside, numerous questions can and have been raised about the social identity process. One important issue deals with group formation. Each of us belongs to numerous groups at any point of time: gender group, political party, nation, religion, ethnicity, age group, sexual orientation, etc. In fact, the constellation of in-groups that describe any individual may be unique. If we follow SIT, this would ultimately lead each individual to be in constant conflict with every other individual. In an effort to address this question, the theory of self-categorization (Turner, Hogg, Oakes, Reicher, & Wetherell, 1987) argued that individuals can and do cognitively divide their social world into groups and categories around in-groups and out-groups. The categories are formed by paying attention to specific characteristics that separate individuals. There is an egocentric flavor to the categorization because individuals use themselves as the frame of reference; people who share a characteristic with the individual are the in-group and all others are the out-group. Certain groups will be salient at any specific time, and those groups that happen to be salient will influence inter-group behavior. "Salience" is influenced by a host of factors including the other people present and the groups to which they are members, how positively they are viewed, and the mood of the individual, and whether there are any superor-dinate groups to which the individual and others present share (Brewer, Ho, Lee, & Miller, 1987; Crisp & Hewstone, 2000; Hewstone, Islam, & Judd, 1993; Schmitt, Branscombe, Silvia, Garcia, & Spears, 2006). Terror management theory (Arndt, Greenberg, Pyszczynski, & Solomon, 1997) offers another perspective by sug-gesting that when individuals are faced with recognizing their own mortality (e.g., threat of impending death), bonds with significant in-groups become more salient and intergroup discrimination is likely to result.

Although much of the work on SIT suggests that in-group favoritism is closely linked with out-group discrimination and intergroup conflict, other research in both real world settings (Struch & Schwartz, 1989) and in an intergroup prisoner dilemma game paradigm (Halevy, Bornstein, & Sagir, 2008) have found that in-group favoritism and intergroup aggression may be unrelated. It may be possible to obtain positive self-identity with an in-group without derogating an out-group. It is not clear what factors determine when social categorization and social compari-son will result in intergroup conflict and when they will not. The critical point of this research is that individual psychological processes can and do contribute to conflict at the intergroup level.

A FOCUS ON DYNAMICS OF GROUPS

Although social categorization and SITs offer important insights into why indi-viduals engage in conflict, discrimination, and violence directed toward out-groups, there are still many nagging questions. In keeping with social cognition, these theories view groups as cognitive categories developed by individuals. But one cannot escape the fact that groups are more than cognitive structures that reside within the minds of individuals. They involve interaction between, and action by, individuals. Intergroup conflict often includes confrontation and violence between groups of individuals acting in unison. How does the field of play move from cognitive representations to collective actions by individuals against common targets?

This is not a new question, and efforts to address it go back to Le Bon's (1908) explanations of crowd behavior. Crowd psychology argues that the behavior of groups cannot be completely understood by focusing on individuals; "It is impor-tant to realize that within crowd psychology the focus on the individual" does not necessarily imply the explanation of mass phenomena by individuals (Graumann, 1986, p. 221). Worchel (2003) argued that to understand group behavior, such as intergroup conflict, we must look to traditional group dynamics research that demonstrates how such factors as leadership, conformity and contagion, deindi-viduation, and norm formation bind individuals together and galvanize action toward a common goal. These dynamics not only goad individuals to see themselves as a group and act together, but they may also be the fountain from which conflict with out-groups springs.

One approach to understanding group behavior maintains the central role of identity, but moves from the domain of individual to that of group identity (Crocker & Luhtanen, 1990; Worchel & Coutant, 2004). This approach argues that groups, like individuals, develop social identities called group or collective identities. Collective identity involves the mutual awareness that members of the same group share the same social identity (David & Bar-Tal, 2008; Klandermans & de Weerd, 2000; Mellucci, 1989). This identity takes place on three planes: cognitive, emotional, and motivational. The cognitive plane involves the individual's categorization of the self with that of a larger group. Research suggests that as this happens, the individual identity is "depersonalized" in lieu of the collective identity (David & Bar-Tal, 2008; Hogg & McGarty, 1990; Turner, 1999). The emotional aspect of collective identity, on the other hand, involves the extent to which the individual experiences feelings such as pride, devotion, and concern toward the collective (Bar-Tal, 1993). And finally, the motivational plane concerns the individual's willingness to belong to the group. Researchers postulate that an individual's willingness to be part of a group stems from basic human needs which are met by membership in a collective. These include the need to create interpersonal relationships, to preserve a positive self value, and to feel secure and protected (Baumeister & Leary, 1995; Mack, 1983). Important for our purposes, collective identities often result in a sense of a "common fate" in which the fate of each individual depends on the outcome of the collective. A collective identity also results in the perception of "uniqueness," in which the collective views itself as different from other groups, focusing on group characteristics such as beliefs, values, norms, and language that set the group apart from others (David & Bar-Tal, 2008). Often, the resulting expression of difference between groups is intergroup conflict.

Groups also experience both shared beliefs and shared emotions. This position has its roots deep in early sociological examinations of crowd behavior that posited a "group mind" and the contagion of emotion (Le Bon, 1908). Several investigators have reacquainted group behavior with this tradition through such concepts as "societal beliefs" (Bar-Tal, 1990a, 2000) and "collective guilt" (Miron & Branscomben, 2008). This perspective suggests that beliefs and emotions can be carried at the level of the group. Societal beliefs not only unify in-group members, but justify and direct their actions toward out-groups (Bar Tal, 1990b, 2000).

Societal beliefs are shared beliefs that bind society together (Bar-Tal, 2000). Such beliefs often serve as the basis for group formation and influence the behavior of the group. Societal beliefs, such as history, myths, and religion allow members of a society to create and maintain psychological connections with each other. These connections are a major factor in group formation. Societal beliefs also serve to distinguish one group from the other—those who share the same beliefs, and those who do not. Eidelson and Eidelson (2003) describe five belief domains that precipitate a beginning of intergroup conflict: superiority, injustice, vulnerability, distrust, and helplessness. They argue that these beliefs occur at both the individual and collective level and while operating separately, are parallel to one another.

Societal beliefs are rooted in the histories and myths of the in-group. These stories not only describe the group and its attributes, but also define the relevant out-groups that are sources of comparison and pose potential threats to the group. Evidence of this process is seen in the school textbooks about the history of groups. These shape children's views of their own group and the out-groups (Luke, 1988). Bar-Tal (1998) content-analyzed 124 textbooks approved by the Israeli Ministry of Education, from a variety of disciplines, including: history, geography, and literature. Certain themes emerged regarding societal beliefs of security, positive identity, and the victimization of Jews. Embedded within these accounts of Israeli history were negative stereotypes of Arabs who were portrayed as posing consistent threats to the security of Israel.

Collective emotions, on the other hand, can be characterized as emotions that are shared by a large number of group members (Bar-Tal, Halperin, & de Rivera, 2007; Stephan & Stephan, 2000). Group emotions may include fear, hatred, guilt, hope, and security. While some collective emotions can be considered beneficial, binding society together in a shared experience, others may be detrimental. Fear is a collective emotion which tends to mobilize societies toward conflict by limiting the perspective of its members, linking past negative experience to the present. When met with conflict or threatening conditions, a society that experiences fear as a collective emotion is likely to act out in violence (Bar-Tal, Halperin, & de Rivera, 2007). Contrastingly, collective hope can serve as a mobilizing force toward collective goals such as equality, security, and peace.

Bar-Tal (2007) adds yet another dimension by introducing the concept of collective memories (see Chapter 4). These memories, which include a collective emotional orientation and shared societal beliefs are the socio-psychological infra-structure of intractable conflicts. Collective memories include historic incidents such as when a group was victimized by out-groups. These memories are passed down from one generation to another and are evident in the cultural products such as literature, myths, or songs. But like any memory, these memories undergo trans-formation and shaping, so ultimately they are subjective interpretations of events. It is these interpretations that become the shared beliefs, but are accepted as objective, "truthful" accounts. These accounts, in turn, not only justify and legiti-mize intergroup conflict but also spin a positive image of the in-group.

Whether the focus is on group beliefs, emotions, or memories, there is a unique twist that gives them added power to affect group behavior and intergroup con-flict. Like lovers whose hearts flutter when they hear a song that was playing during their first kiss, group memories often incite emotions that grip group members (see Chapter 3). These emotions not only color the evaluative component of the memory, but they also arouse the group and prepare it for action. Intergroup emo-tions theory (Mackie, Devos, & Smith, 2000) suggests that group emotions are experienced by a member of a group who strongly identifies with her or his group. Although they are experienced individually, the emotions are shared with other members of that group and influence both inter and intragroup relations. (Smith, Seger, & Mackie, 2007). Group emotions expand the study of intergroup relations to include a more complex description than simply positive or negative. And this very complexity can help explain why a single out-group can elicit both a positive stereotype attribute and a negative perception at the same time (Yzerbyt, Dumont, Wigboldus, & Gordijn, 2003). For example, Fiske and her colleagues have documented target out-groups that were rated high on competence (positive) but were not rated positively on issues related to likeability (Fiske, Cuddy, Glick, & Xu, 2002).

Although all children may be introduced to the group's history and its enemies through the same textbooks, the impact of these messages differs. Some children will embrace the message and it will guide their behavior toward the out-group. Others, however, will not accept the message and may actively challenge it. Clearly there are a variety of sources that compete for the minds and hearts of group members; friends, parents, religious leaders, and media to name a few. However, there is another interesting factor that appears to affect whether or not individuals adopt the messages from the in-group and become willing participants in intergroup conflict. That factor is the degree to which individuals identify with the group and incorporate group identity into their personal identity (see Chapter 5). Sahdra and Ross (2007) found that individuals who strongly identified with their group were more likely to remember positive rather than negative historical incidents of their own group's action. Furthermore, individuals with low group identification recalled more incidents of in-group violence and hatred than those with high group identification. At the same time they tend to remember better the harm done to their group by an out-group (see Chapter 4). Thus, group identity is a powerful force because it involves not only protecting the group from present threats, but it excites members to preserve loyalty to the group for future generations.

These approaches that focus on group identity, group beliefs, and group memories share the common bond of locating the foundation of intergroup conflict within the group. They represent broad strokes of the theoretical brush that identify general factors of intergroup conflict. They are, however, less suited to identifying specific factors that determine how and when a specific conflict will erupt. In order to refine the focus and craft more specific predictions, we must turn to a large, often unrelated, body of research that takes a more microscopic look than group factors. Because of the breadth of this research, we will examine several representative examples of this work.

Cyclical Patterns

Whether we examine the history of nations, ethnic groups, or other groups such as labor management, we find that periods of conflict and violence tend to occur in periodic waves punctuated by periods of relative peace, even if the peace is uneasy. For example, despite the tense, often violent, relationship between Israelis and Palestinians, there are numerous cease fires and times, often lasting several years, of relatively peaceful coexistence. Unfortunately, hopes for conflict resolution are dashed when violence and hatred once again grip the region. How do we explain the fact that intergroup conflict occurs at some times, but not others?

In order to address this question several investigators have focused on the developmental cycle of groups, arguing that there are specific points in this cycle where a group is susceptible or actually seeks out conflict with the other groups (Lacoursiere, 1980; Worchel, Coutant-Sassic, & Grossman, 1992). Worchel et al.

(1992) observed a variety of groups over time and found regular patterns in their development. They suggested that groups first engage in group identification efforts to define their group. They then focus on issues related to group productivity, individual identity, and decay in that order. In one study, they asked group members what type of relationship they desired with the out-group (and the in-group). Group members indicated that they desired competition with the out-group during the initial group identity stage. The investigators argued that intergroup conflict and competition play several functions for a group in the formative period. First, conflict helps define the boundaries of a group, clearly defining who is in the group and who is not. In fact, Sassenberg and colleagues (Sassenberg, Moskowitz, Jacoby, & Hansen, 2007) have even identified a "carry-over effect" for intergroup prejudice after competition. Groups that competed with one out-group, subsequently displayed prejudice and perceptions of out-group homogeneity toward a different out-group that had not been involved in the competition. Second, conflict with out-groups enhances group cohesiveness (Campbell, 1958; Gairtner & Schopler, 1998), giving group members a common purpose that binds them together. Finally, intergroup conflict often leads members to accept centralized leaders, thereby aiding the development of a clear group structure (Allport, 1979; Bekkers, 1976; Rabbie & Bekkers, 1978). And inversely, recategorizing of former conflictive out-groups as subgroups of a more inclusive in-group, may predispose that group to a new conflict with a new out-group (Kessler & Mummendey, 2001). For example, many Polynesian groups (Maoris, Tahitians, and Native-Hawaiians) from different islands have historically viewed themselves as separate groups. But periodically they recategorize themselves as Polynesians to become a more inclusive in-group which can then instill confidence and support for a confrontation with, or challenge to, an out-group such as the United States or Western Europeans.

Leaders

The Iraq War was a difficult event for Americans for a variety of reasons. One consequence of the war was that people in other countries "hated us." However, on closer examination, the position of people in other countries was that they did not hate the "American people" or hold them responsible for the war in Iraq; it was the leaders that they detested and blamed (Pew Research Center for the People & the Press, 2004). This response illustrates the recognition that group leaders play critical roles in instigating intergroup conflict and violence. Leaders clearly have a stake in intergroup conflict and often benefit from this conflict. Allport (1979) pointed out that leaders who view their power as eroding may attempt to consolidate support by inviting conflict with an out-group. Fear of the threat from an out-group leads to in-group cohesion and the acceptance of centralized leadership. Beckers and Rabbie (1978) confronted group leaders with either a threat or no-threat of losing their leadership position. They found that threatened leaders were more likely to choose intergroup competition rather than cooperation tactics when given a choice.

The tendency to blame the out-group for in-group ills is not confined to leader behavior. Scapegoat theory (Berkowitz & Green, 1962) posits that when individuals in a society are struggling with economic or other situational factors, they often blame an out-group, typically a low-power or minority out-group for their difficulties. Based on frustration–aggression theory (Dollard, Doob, Miller, Mowrer, & Sears, 1939), scapegoat theory suggests that violence and aggression against a low-power out-group are more likely to occur when resources become more scarce. Nazi Germany's persecution of Jews as a result of depression is one example (Berkowitz & Green, 1962). Hoveland and Sears (1940) found that during the Great Depression, falling cotton prices in the southern United States were accompanied by increased violence and lynchings of African–Americans. It was argued that dropping cotton prices raised the level of frustration in the region, and resulted in blaming Blacks for the condition. However, this general explanation has been called into question by findings that this relationship disappears when periods outside the Great Depression are examined (Berkowitz, 2005). Still other research failed to find a relationship when other indicators of economic assessment and other target groups are included (Green, Glaser, & Rich, 1998). Thus scapegoating does not occur in all financial hardship situations and other factors clearly play a role.

Lickel, Miller, Stenstrom, Denson, and Schmader (2006) took the concept of displaced aggression one step further and proposed the concept of vicarious retribution as the underlying cause of intergroup conflict. Vicarious retribution occurs when an individual who witnesses or learns of an aggressive act against an in-group member (but was not personally impacted by the action) is motivated by their group identification, to aggress against uninvolved members of the out-group. Thus, this phenomenon moves an interpersonal provocation onto the intergroup playing field.

Relative Deprivation

Clearly, broad social conditions such as hunger or poverty have been related to acts of evil, especially ones directed toward out-groups (Pinstrup-Anderson & Shimokawa, 2008; Staub, 1996, 1999; Thelsen, 2008). However, other investigations have moved the focus away from simple frustrations (e.g., impoverished conditions) all together. Rather, the focus has been on relative deprivation. Although it has been clearly demonstrated that feelings of deprivation are not directly related to actual deprivation, there are situational conditions for a group that appear to be related to the feelings of deprivation (Corning, 2000; Crosby, 1976). Although having several different forms (Crosby, 1976; Gurr, 1972; Runciman, 1966), relative deprivation is derived from the discrepancy between the expectation or desire to have something and the inability to actually have that something. An important delineation is made between an actual discrepancy and a perceived discrepancy. A sense of unfairness arises from the feelings of entitlement and the belief that the desired object should be obtainable, but through no perceived fault of one's own, it is not. Relative deprivation results in anger, resentment, and a negative identity that again, stems not from a difference in objective differences in outcomes, but in subjective evaluations of unfairness.

In a field study with East Germans after German unification, Mummendy, Kessler, Klink, and Mielke (1999) compared SIT and relative deprivation theory in predicting behavioral strategies that individuals use to manage a negative social identity in unsatisfying intergroup relations. They found that relative deprivation theory explained collective responses such as social competition whereas SIT explained individual strategies such as recategorization.

The thrust of these positions is that situations within a group can lead it to invite conflict with other groups. Indeed, the research shows that the relationship between intergroup conflict and group dynamics is reciprocal. That is, intergroup conflict can also have a marked impact on the dynamics within groups. This reciprocal relationship may be one of the reasons that intergroup conflict is so tenacious and resists attempts at reduction. Groups adapt their structure, focus, norms, and roles to deal with intergroup conflict, and these changes support the conflict.

INTERGROUP RELATIONS

In many ways, it would be comforting to conclude that conflicts between groups have their roots within each group. This would suggest that the solution to intergroup conflict would involve "fixing" what ails each group. But the seeds of intergroup conflict are also found in the situation that exists between groups. In one of the earliest examinations of intergroup conflict, Sherif, Harvey, Hood, White, and Sherif (1961) argued that intergroup conflict results when groups are in competition for scarce resources. This observation became the backbone of realistic conflict theory (Sherif & Sherif, 1953). Although similar to the concept of relative deprivation discussed earlier, realistic conflict theory is based on actual competition between groups for a scarce resource, whereas relative deprivation is based on group expectancies, which in fact may have little or no relationship to actual resource availability. Sherif et al. (1961) created a number of competitive contests that resulted in a winner and loser, in order to create hostility between groups of campers. For example, the groups engaged in athletic competitions (one winner and one loser) and contests to determine which group had the cleanest bunkhouse. As expected, the result was that the groups quickly became enemies, each trying to sabotage the efforts of the other. It is important to recognize that the competition may be real (e.g., only one winner) or perceived (e.g., situations where sharing of resources is possible, but not recognized or wanted). Indeed it seems almost trite to state that intergroup competition leads to intergroup conflict; the terms competition and conflict are often used interchangeably.

On closer examination, however, the distinction between competition and hostile conflict is important. Not all competition leads to hatred and violence. Why does some competition lead groups to focus on enhancing their skills and developing better coordination, while other competitions lead to conflict and hate? Stephan and his colleagues (Corenblum & Stephan, 2001; Stephan & Stephan, 2000; Stephan, Ybarra, & Bachman, 1999) argue that interactions between groups that lead to fear are most likely to foster conflict and violence. They focused on the role of perceived threat in intergroup relations, and proposed an integrated threat model of prejudice. The model proposes a category of ante-cedent factors, such as strong in-group identification, negative out-group contact and a history of intergroup conflict. It suggests that these antecedent variables predict threat variables, which are factors related to perceptions of both realistic and symbolic threats as well as intergroup anxiety. These threat variables in turn predict prejudice and negative attitudes toward the out-group. This model was tested in Canada with Whites and First Nation. For the First Nation participants, realistic threats, such as perceptions of economic and political power, symbolic threats, such as perceived violations of in-group culture, traditions, or language, and intergroup anxiety were significant predictors of negative out-group attitudes (Corenblum & Stephan, 2001). In addition, in-group (ethnic) identity as well as negative intergroup contact (both antecedent variables) predicted intergroup anxiety (a threat variable); thus linking a group level factor (in-group identification) and intergroup factors. The interesting aspect of the research on threat is that the nature of the threat can be internal to the group or external, related to the behav-ior (real or perceived actions) and the intentions of the out-group.

Worchel and Coutant (2008) expanded the fear model and demonstrated how fear of the out-group could result in protracted conflict that escalated over time. They suggested that specific fears regarding group security and existence ignite intractable conflict. Indeed, many competitions between groups can be concluded by an acceptable division of resources and compromise. However, in some cases, the competition leads the group to perceive the out-group as threatening its identity and security, not just its resources. In these cases, and often abetted by opportu-nistic leaders, the fear grows and engulfs the group. But irrational fear cannot exist for long on its own, and in an effort to justify and explain the fear, the group builds on the perception of the out-group as diabolical. Increasing the perception of the evil intentions not only justifies existing fears, but gives rise to increased fears and concern for security. This, in turn, leads to still more negative impressions of the enemy. This situation was clearly evident in the growth of hostility and hatred of Al-Qaeda after the attack on the World Trade Center on September 11, 2001. The initial incident and fear fed quickly growing perceptions of Al-Qaeda as a well-organized enemy who would launch imminent attacks aimed at destroying the United States. This new perception increased the level of fear and led to greater conflict and, in turn, led people to view Al-Qaeda as even more dangerous.

The point of realistic conflict theory and related approaches is that certain factors, especially competition igniting fear and concerns for group security, involving the relationship between groups can be the foundation for intergroup conflict. These factors often ignite conflict that is both violent and protracted. But competition is only one of the intergroup culprits that have been identified as giving rise to intergroup conflict. Power, the root of many evils in interpersonal relations, has also been implicated.

Power differences between groups is a situational factor that is as omnipresent in real world settings as disparities in social conditions. Moul (2003), comparing theories from the field of political science, conducted an archival study of the outbreak of war from the years 1816–1989 and whether hostilities between two countries with power-balanced situation as predicted by balance of power theory

(BOP) (Morgenthau, 1967) versus imbalanced situation as predicted by power transition theory (PT) (Organski, 1968) were more likely to lead to war. BOP theory suggests that armed conflict will be less likely to occur when the groups in conflict are equal, or "balanced" in power. Alternately, PT posits that a stable power disparity will be less likely to escalate into armed conflict than when a lower power group approaches parity (or equal) power. According to PT, as a low power group strives for a power balance, the high power group is likely to make a preemptive strike if the upcoming group is perceived as closing the gap, in order to maintain the power disparity. Moul found support for the PT, in that inter-nation armed conflict was more likely to occur when power situations approached and were approximately equal.

Rothgerber and Worchel (1997) examined the influence of power differences on intergroup conflict in a laboratory setting. They found that low power groups are more likely to disadvantage another low power group than the high power group. Again, conflict, in this case from low-power groups, was more tempting with another low-power group (approximately equal power) than with the advantaged group (unequal, high power group). Coutant (2006) further demonstrated that not only the amount of power in the intergroup relationship, but also the stability of a power difference, impacts on how low power group members process information about high power outgroup members. In an unstable situation lower power individuals are more likely to use individuated processing whereas in stable situations they tend toward stereotyped processing. Stereotyping is in turn more likely to lead to dehumanization of the out-group, which makes conflict more acceptable. For example, in South Africa under apartheid the power difference between blacks and whites was very stable for many years. This stable power differentiation likely lead to stereotyped processing of out-groups which lead to blacks being seen as "less-than" whites, and during revolts of blacks, horrific acts of violence being committed against whites. As the low power group, blacks, gained world-wide support for an end to apartheid, and the power situation began to appear more stable, processing of the out-group probably became more individuated so that black leaders could differentiate which white leaders would be better to work with and more open to change.

The role of intergroup conditions is interesting because it demonstrates that violent conflict can occur even when groups are relatively comfortable with their situations. It further shows that factors outside the control of either in-group or out-group can sow the seeds of conflict.

CULTURE: THE CRUCIBLE OF CONFLICT

We have explored a variety of conditions within the individual, group, and between groups, that affect the development of intergroup conflict. There is still another domain that should not be overlooked. This sphere helps explain why conflict is more likely to occur in one situation than in another even though similar conditions exist in both. The catalyst here is culture. One can think of a culture as the glasses through which we see the world, our ideas of right, wrong, acceptable behavior and what is taboo. Culture includes those implicit attitudes and expectations that are below our level of awareness. Cultural differences in acceptance of conflict and power disparities also impact intergroup relations.

Several theorists have identified cultural values related to an acceptance of power discrepancies, Hofstede's (Hofstede, 1984; Hofstede & McRae, 2004) high versus low power distance, Schwartz's (1992, 1994) hierarchy versus egalitarianism, and Project GLOBE's (House, Javidan, & Dorfman, 2001) power distance. These researchers have identified these components in which a culture varies on their tolerance, or acceptance of power differences. A culture high on power distance would have clear distinctions between superiors and subordinates, with unquestioning dependence and compliance by subordinates. Thus what in one culture may appear a grievous injustice, in need of rectification, in another culture might be received with stalwart, unswerving compliance.

Kluckholn and Strodbeck (1961) described a cultural value of human nature orientation, in which cultures vary in whether they perceive the nature of people as basically good or basically evil. Clearly, self-fulfilling prophecy would suggest that how one views out-group members can be expected to drastically effect behavior toward that out-group depending on this underlying assumption. The expectations of an out-group's willingness to change or be flexible in negotiations would be affected by an individual's belief of a basically "good" versus basically "evil" opponent.

Schwartz (1992, 1994) also identified a cultural value of mastery versus harmony; another likely candidate to impact intergroup conflict. This dimension suggests that some cultures tend to value individual control over society and natural resources, whereas a culture with more of a harmony value would appreciate the preservation of indigenous societies and natural resources. A group from a culture high on mastery would be expected to view conquering an out-group to obtain resources as a more positive step for the in-group than one from a culture high on harmony. For example, Native-American Indian tribes differed along this dimension. Some tribes such as Apache or Blackfoot were fierce hunters and followed their prey, wherever necessary, to get what they needed. The Blackfoot people in particular had flexible social units so that an individual could move from one group to another to be more successful. Hopi Indians, on the other hand, tend more toward harmony. Thus the Hopi were known as the peaceful people as their harmony culture encouraged preserving whereas the Blackfoot rewarded successful mastery.

At a more diffuse level, cultural differences in communication or negotiation styles can cause intergroup disagreements to escalate. Hall (1976) identified a cultural dimension of contextuality in communication. Cultures high on context convey most of the information of a message through the person who transmits the message, location of the communication, and the method (face-to-face, letter, telephone) of transmission rather than the explicit wording of the transmitted part of a message. More emphasis is placed on the relationship between the communicators in a high context, rather than low context culture. Low context cultures, alternatively, invest most of the information in the actual wording of a message, with less information conveyed through the context. Kimmel (2006) suggested that a lack of understanding of context played a role in unsuccessful negotiations between Iraq and the United States prior to Iraq's invasion of Kuwait and the resulting US attack on Iraq in the first Persian Gulf Crisis. "An explicit, written statement from one head of state to another was the wrong kind of message sent in the wrong way to the wrong person. As a result of their different cultural expectations and assumptions, Aziz and the Iraqis decided that the Americans were not serious about negotiating and were deliberately insulting them" (Kimmel, 2006, p. 626).

Research in the area of international business relations has also diagnosed intercultural communication differences that commonly lead to conflict. For example, the misinterpretation of silence was identified (Graham & Sano, 1984) as a frequent cause of problems between the United States and Asian firms. Silence is frequently used as way to politely signal an objection by Asians whereas in the United States it is interpreted as consent. Alternatively a direct, assertive, verbal critique of an opponent's argument, while a common and respected practice in the US culture, is considered a rude, lack of respect by an individual from an Asian culture.

CONCLUSION

We have traveled a long and winding road through the causes of intergroup conflict. Although the theories and research are diverse and raise complex issues, there are several important conclusions to reach. First, the foundation for intergroup conflict can occur at all levels of social relationships: The individual, the group, intergroup situation, and culture. These levels are not mutually exclusive, and in most conflicts, causes can be identified at all levels. Further, conditions that exist on one level are likely to create conditions at other levels. For example, the striving of individuals to create positive social identities may excite groups to become concerned about the group identity and the threat to this identity posed by an out-group. This, in turn, may lead the group to focus on its power relative to the out-group. Likewise, disharmony within a group may simultaneously lead individual members to become concerned about their social identities, and lead groups to emphasize competition with out-groups.

These points lead to a better understanding of why intergroup conflict is so resistant to resolution. Not only does the conflict have roots at many levels of social interaction, but many factors nurture the conflict once it develops. Leaders, for example, find that their power is often augmented by intergroup conflict. Hence, they have reason to feed and prolong the conflict. Individuals, who may be marginal to the group during periods of calm, find the group more willing to accept them in periods of conflict. And, we must recognize that conflict is arousing and energizing. It goads people to action and lends purpose to lives. But even more basic, as implied by SIT, intergroup conflict may be a natural by-product of everyday living and the inevitable formation of groups and social categories: "Intergroup conflict happens." These various theories and research give us some perspective about why it happens and the conditions under which it is most likely to occur.

In addition to illuminating the causes of intergroup conflict, the theories can serve as a road map toward the management of conflict. There is a seductive force to the idea that science will ultimately identify the method to reducing and/or managing intergroup conflict, so that an isolated pig-shooting will remain just that, isolated, rather than escalating into a decades-long violent feud. This magic bullet may come in the form of peace camps, arbitration by third parties, or the elimination of social ills such as hunger or disease. But the multitude of causes of intergroup conflict (from a single pig-shooting to sending the "wrong" person as a national representative) caution against embracing this position. For just as there are numerous causes of conflict and levels at which conflict is instigated, so, too, should there be many approaches to reducing intergroup conflict. And the most effective approach to reducing conflict may reside in the ability to match the approach to the cause of the conflict. For example, a conflict that is fed mainly by the dynamics that occur within a group may best be addressed by efforts that also focus on issues internal to the group.

Lastly, theories about the causes of intergroup conflict can play a role beyond guiding efforts to manage conflict. Indeed, the research demonstrates how resistant conflict is to efforts to reduce it. However, knowing the causes of conflict can help identify ways to prevent intergroup conflict or at least mute its occurrence. The research clearly points to the seeds that can grow to create conflict. This research can also galvanize responses to ensure that the seeds do not mature into violent confrontations between groups. For example, recognizing that poverty can be a group factor that predisposes it to seek conflict and confrontation, efforts can be directed toward reducing poverty within the group before it leads to intergroup violence.

Hence, the disturbing message is that the causes of intergroup conflict are many and varied. The encouraging note is that understanding these causes can offer an equally varied selection of approaches to reduce and/or prevent the conflict.

REFERENCES

Abrams, D., & Hogg, M. A. (1988). Comments on the motivational status of self-esteem in social identity and intergroup discrimination. *European Journal of Social Psychology*, 8, 317–334.

Adorno, T. W., Frenkel-Brunswik, E., Levinson, D. J., & Sanford, R. N. (1950). *The Authoritarian Personality*. Oxford, England: Harpers.

Allport, G. W. (1979). *The nature of prejudice*. Oxford, England: Addison-Wesley.

Arndt, J., Greenberg, J., Pyszczynshi, T., & Solomon, S. (1997). Subliminal exposure to death-related stimuli increases defense of the cultural worldview. *Psychological Science, 8*, 379–385.

Bar-Tal, D. (1990a). Group beliefs: A conception for analyzing group structure, processes, and behavior. *Springer series in social psychology* (p. 140). New York, NY: Springer-Verlag Publishing.

Bar-Tal, D. (1990b). Causes and consequences of delegitimization: Models of conflict and ethnocentrism. *Journal of Social Issues, 46*, 65–81.

Bar-Tal, D. (1993). Patriotism as fundamental beliefs of group members. *Politics and Individual, 3*, 45–62.

Bar-Tal, D. (1998). The rocky road toward peace: Beliefs on conflict in Israeli textbooks. *Journal of Peace Research, 35*, 723–742.

Bar-Tal, D. (2000). *Shared beliefs in a society: Social psychological analysis*. Thousand Oaks, CA: Sage.

Bar-Tal, D. (2007). Sociopsychological foundations of intractable conflicts. *American Behavioral Scientist, 50*, 1430–1453.

Bar-Tal, D., Halperin, E., & de Rivera, J. (2007). Collective emotions in conflict situations: Societal implications. *Journal of Social Issues, 63*, 441–460.

Baumeister, R. F., & Leary, M. R. (1995). The need to belong: Desire for interpersonal attachments as a fundamental human motivation. *Psychological Bulletin, 117*, 497–529.

Bekkers, F. (1976). A threatened leadership position and intergroup competition (a simulation experiment with three countries). *International Journal of Group Tensions, 6*, 67–94.

Berkowitz, L. (2005). On hate and its determinants: Some affective and cognitive influences. In R. J. Sternberg (Ed.), *The psychology of hate* (pp. 155–183). Washington, DC: American Psychological Association.

Berkowitz, L., & Green, J. A. (1962). The stimulus qualities of the scapegoat. *The Journal of Abnormal and Social Psychology, 64*, 293–301.

Blake, R. R., & Mouton, J. S. (1962). Overevaluation of own's group's own product in intergroup competition. *Journal of Abnormal Social Psychology, 64*, 237–238.

Brewer, M. B., Ho, H. K., Lee, J. Y., & Miller, N. (1987). Social identity and social distance among Hong Kong schoolchildren. *Personality & Social Psychology Bulletin, 13*, 156–165.

Campbell, D. T. (1958). Common fate, similarity, and other indices of the status of aggregates of persons as social entities. *Behavioral Science, 3*, 14–25.

Corenblum, B., & Stephan, W. G. (2001). White fears and native apprehensions: And integrated threat theory approach to intergroup attitudes. *Canadian Journal of Behavioural Science, 33*, 251–268.

Corning, A. F. (2000). Assessing perceived social inequity: A relative deprivation framework. *Journal of Personality and Social Psychology, 78*, 463–477.

Coutant, D. K. (2006). The effect of a power-imbalanced situation on the cognitive processing of low-power group members. *Group Dynamics: Theory, Research, and Practice, 10*, 71–83.

Crisp, R. J., & Hewstone, M. (2000). Crossed categorization and intergroup bias: The moderating roles of intergroup and affective context. *Journal of Experimental Social Psychology, 36*, 357–383.

Crocker, J., & Lutanen, R. (1990). Collective self-esteem and ingroup bias. *Journal of Personality and Social Psychology, 58*, 60–67.

Crosby, F. (1976). A model of egoistical relative deprivation. *Psychological Review, 83*, 85–113.

David, O., & Bar-Tal, D. (2008). Collective identity and nations: A socio-psychological conception.

Dollard, J., Miller, N. E., Doob, L. W., Mowrer, O.H., & Sears, R. R. (1939). *Frustration and aggression*. New Haven, CT: Yale University Press.

Dr. Seuss. (1984). *The butter battle book*. New York: Random House Publishing.

Eidelson, R. J., & Eidelson, J. (2003). Dangerous ideas: Five beliefs that propel groups toward conflict. *American Psychologist, 58*, 182–192.

Festinger, L. (1954). A theory of social comparison processes. *Human Relations, 7*, 117–140.

Fiske, S. T., Cuddy, A. J. C., Glick, P., & Xu, J. (2002). A model of (often mixed) stereotype content: Competence and warmth respectively follow from perceived status and competition. *Journal of Personality and Social Psychology*, 82, 878–902.

Gagnon, A., & Bourhis, R. Y. (1996). Discrimination in the minimal group paradigm: Social identity or self-interest? *Personality and Social Psychology Bulletin*, 22, 1289–1301.

Gairtner, L., & Schopler, J. (1998). Perceived ingroup entitativity and intergroup bias: An interconnection of self and others. *European Journal of Social Psychology*, 28, 963–980.

Graham, J., & Sano, Y. (1984). *Smart bargaining: Doing business with the Japanese.* Cambridge, MA: Ballinger.

Graumann, C. F. (1986). Crowd mind and behavior: Afterthoughts. In C. F. Graumann & S. Moscovici (Eds.), *Changing conceptions of crowd mind and behavior* (pp. 217–228).

Green, D. P., Glaser, J., & Rich, A. (1998). From lynching to gay bashing: The elusive connection between economic conditions and hate crime. *Journal of Personality and Social Psychology*, 75, 82–92.

Gurr, T. R. (1972). The calculus of civil conflict. *Journal of Social Issues*, 28, 27–47.

Halevy, N., Bornstein, G., & Sagiv, L. (2008). "In-group love" and "out-group hate" as motives for individual participation in intergroup conflict: A new game paradigm. *Psychological Science*, 19, 405–411.

Hall, E. (1976). *Beyond culture.* Garden City, NY: Doubleday Anchor Books.

Hastorf, A. H., & Cantril, H. (1954). They saw a game: A case study. *The Journal of Abnormal and Social Psychology*, 49, 129–134.

Hewstone, M., Islam, M. R., & Judd, C. M. (1993). Models of crossed categorization and intergroup relations. *Journal of Personality and Social Psychology*, 64, 779–793.

Hofstede, G. (1984). *Culture's consequences: International differences in work related values.* London: Sage.

Hofstede, G., & McCrae, R. R. (2004). Personality and culture revisited: Linking traits and dimensions of culture. *Cross-Cultural Research: The Journal of Comparative Social Science*, 38, 52–88.

Hogg, M. A., & McGarty, C. (1990). Self categorization and social identity. In D. Abrams & M. A. Hogg (Eds.), *Social identity theory: Constructive and critical advances* (pp. 10–27). New York: Harvester Wheatsheaf.

House, R., Javidan, M., & Dorfman, P. (2001). Project GLOBE: An introduction. *Applied Psychology: An International Review. Special Issue: Leadership and culture in the Middle East: Norms, practices, and effective leadership attributes in Iran, Kuwait, Turkey, and Qatar*, 50, 489–505.

Hoveland, C. I., & Sears, R. R. (1940). Minor studies of aggression: VI. Correlation of lynchings with economic indices. *Journal of Psychology: Interdisciplinary and Applied*, 9, 301–310.

Jones, V. C. (1948). *The Hatfields and the McCoys.* Chapel Hill, NC: University of North Carolina Press.

Kessler, T., & Mummendey, A. (2001). Is there any scapegoat around? Determinants of intergroup conflicts at different categorization levels. *Journal of Personality and Social Psychology*, 81, 1090–1102.

Kimmel, P. R. (2006). Culture and conflict. In M. Deutsch, P. T. Coleman, & E. C. Marcus (Eds.), *The handbook of conflict resolutions: Theory and practice* (2nd ed., pp. 625–648). Hoboken, NJ: Wiley.

Klandermans, B., & de Weerd, M. (2000). Group identification and political protest. In S. Stryker, T. J. Owens, & R. W. White (Eds.), *Self, identity, and social movement— Social movements, protest, and contention* (Vol. 13, pp. 68–90). Minneapolis: University of Minnesota Press.

Kluckholn, F. R., & Strodbeck, F. L. (1961). *Variations in value orientations*. Evanston, IL: Row, Pearson.

Lacoursiere, R. B. (1980). *The life cycle of groups: Group development stage theory*. New York, NY: Human Science Press.

Le Bon, G. (1908). *The crowd*. London: Unwin.

Lickel, B., Miller, N., Stenstrom, D. M., Denson, T. F., & Schmader, T. (2006). Vicarious retribution: The role of collective blame in intergroup aggression. *Personality and Social Psychology Review, 10*, 372–390.

Luke, A. (1988). *Literacy, textbooks, and ideology*. London: Falmer.

Mack, J. (1983). Nationalism and the self. *The Psychohistory Review, 11*, 47–69.

Mackie, D. M., Devos, T., & Smith, E. R. (2000). Intergroup emotions: Explaining offensive action tendencies in an intergroup context. *Journal of Personality and Social Psychology, 79*, 602–616.

Mellucci, A. (1989). *Nomads of the present: Social movements and individual needs in contemporary society*. London: Hutchinson Press.

Miron, A. M., & Branscomben, N. R. (2008). Social categorization, standards of justice, and collective guilt. In A. Nadler, T. E. Malloy, & J. D. Fisher (Eds.), *The social psychology of intergroup reconciliation* (pp. 77–96). New York, NY: Oxford University Press.

Morgenthau, H. J. (1967). *Politics among nations: The struggle for power and peace* (4th ed.). New York: Knopf.

Moul, W. (2003). Erratum: "Power parity, preponderance, and war between great powers, 1816–1989". *Journal of Conflict Resolution, 47*, 706.

Mullen, B., Brown, R., & Smith, C. (1992). Ingroup bias as a function of salience, relevance, and status: An integration. *European Journal of Social Psychology, 22*, 103–122.

Mummendey, A., Kessler, T., Klink, A., & Mielke, R. (1999). Strategies to cope with negative social identity: Prediction by social identity theory and relative deprivation theory. *Journal of Personality and Social Psychology, 76*, 229–245.

Organski, A. F. K. (1968). *World politics* (2nd ed.). New York: Alfred A. Knopf.

Pew Research Center for the People & the Press. (2004, March). *A year after Iraq war: Mistrust of America in Europe ever higher, Muslim anger persists*. Washington, DC: Pew Global Attitudes Project.

Pinstrup-Anderson, P., & Shimokawa, S. (2008). Do poverty and poor health and nutrition increase the risk of armed conflict onset. *Food Policy, 33*, 513–520.

Rabbie, J. M., & Bekkers, F. (1978). Threatened leadership and intergroup competition. *European Journal of Social Psychology, 8*, 9–20.

Rothgerber, H., & Worchel, S. (1997). The view from below: Intergroup relations from the perspective of the disadvantaged group. *Journal of Personality and Social Psychology, 73*, 1191–1205.

Runciman, W. G. (1966). *Relative deprivation and social justice: A study of attitudes to social inequality in twentieth-century England*. Berkeley, CA: University of California Press.

Sahdra, B., & Ross, M. (2007). Group identification and historical memory. *Personality and Social Psychology Bulletin, 33*, 384–395.

Sassenberg, K., Moskowitz, G. B., Jacoby, J., & Hansen, N. (2007). The carry-over effect of competition: The impact of competition on prejudice towards uninvolved outgroups. *Journal of Experimental Social Psychology, 43*, 529–538.

Schmitt, M. T., Branscombe, N. R., Silvia, P. J., Garcia, D. M., & Spears, R. (2006). Categorizing at the group-level in response to intragroup social comparisons: A self-categorization theory integration of self-evaluation and social identity motives. *European Journal of Social Psychology, 36*, 297–314.

Schwartz, S. H. (1992). Universals in the content and structure of values: Theoretical advances and empirical tests in 20 countries. In M. P. Zanna (Ed.), *Advances in experimental social psychology* (Vol. 25, pp. 1–65). San Diego, CA: Academic Press.

Schwartz, S. H. (1994). Beyond individualism/collectivism: New cultural dimensions of values. In U. Kim, H. C. Triandis, C. Kagitcibasi, S. Choi, & G. Yoon (Eds.), Individualism and collectivism: Theory, method, and applications. *Cross-cultural research and methodology series* (Vol. 18, pp. 85–119). Thousand Oaks, CA: Sage Publications.

Sherif, M., Harvey, O. J., White, J., Hood, W., & Sherif, C. W. (1961). *Intergroup conflict and cooperation: The robber's cave experiment.* Norman: University of Oklahoma, Institute of Intergroup Relations.

Sherif, M., & Sherif, C. (1953). *Groups in harmony and tension.* New York: Harper.

Smith, E. R., Seger, C. R., & Mackie, D. M. (2007). Can emotions be truly group level? Evidence regarding four conceptual criteria. *Journal of Personality and Social Psychology*, 93, 431–446.

Stangor, D., & Jost, J.T. (1997). Commentary: Individual, group and system levels of analysis and their relevance for stereotyping and intergroup relations. In R. Spears, P. Oakes, N. Ellemeres, A. Haslam (Eds.) *The social psychology of stereotyping and group life*, (pp. 336–358). Malden: Blackwell Publishing.

Staub, E. (1996). Cultural-societal roots of violence: The examples of genocidal violence and of contemporary youth violence in the United States. *American Psychologist*, 51, 117–132.

Staub, E. (1999). The roots of evil: Social conditions, culture, personality, and basic human needs. *Personality and Social Psychology Review. Special Issue: Perspectives on Evil and Violence*, 3, 179–192.

Stephan, W. G., & Stephan, C. W. (2000). An integrated threat theory of prejudice. In S. Oskamp (Ed.), *Reducing prejudice and discrimination* (pp. 23–46). Hillsdale, NJ: Erlbaum.

Stephan, W. G., Ybarra, O., & Bachman, G. (1999). Prejudice toward immigrants. *Journal of Applied Social Psychology*, 29, 2221–2237.

Struch, N., & Schwartz, S. H. (1989). Intergroup aggression: Its predictors and distinctness from in-group bias. *Journal of Personality and Social Psychology*, 56, 364–373.

Swift, J. (1735). *Gulliver's travels.* Benjamin Motte, London.

Tajfel, H. (1970). Experiments in intergroup discrimination. *Scientific American*, 223, 96–102.

Tajfel, H., & Turner, J. C. (1979). An integrative theory of intergroup conflict. In W. G. Austin & S. Worchel (Eds.), *The social psychology of intergroup relations* (pp. 33–47). Monterey, CA: Brooks-Cole.

Tajfel, H., & Turner, J. C. (1986). The social identity theory of intergroup behavior. In S. Worchel & W. Austin (Eds.), *Psychology of intergroup relations* (pp. 7–24). Chicago: Nelson Hall.

Thelsen, O. M. (2008). Blood and soil? Resource scarcity and internal armed conflict revisited. *Journal of Peace Research*, 45, 801–818.

Turner, J. C. (1999). Some current issues in research on social identity and self categorization theories. In N. Ellemers, R. Spears, & B. Doosje (Eds.), *Social identity: Context, commitment, content* (pp. 6–34). Boston: Blackwell.

Turner, J. C., Brown, R. J., & Tajfel, H. (1979). Social comparison and group interest in ingroup favouritism. *European Journal of Social Psychology*, 9, 187–204.

Turner, J. C., Hogg M. A., Oakes, P. J., Reicher, S. D., & Wetherell, M. S. (1987). *Rediscovering the social group: A self-categorization theory* (p. 230). Cambridge, MA: Basil Blackwell.

Worchel, S. (2003). Come one, come all: Toward understanding the process of collective behavior. In M. Hogg & J. Cooper (Eds.), *The Sage handbook of social psychology*. London: Sage Publications.

Worchel, S., & Coutant, D. (2004). It takes two to tango: Relating group identity to individual identity within the framework of group development. In M. B. Brewer & M. Hewstone (Eds.), *Self and social identity. Perspectives on social psychology* (pp. 182–202). Malden, MA: Blackwell Publishing.

Worchel, S., & Coutant, D. (2008). Between conflict and reconciliation: Toward a theory of peaceful co-existence. In A. Nadler, T. E. Malloy, & J. D. Fisher (Eds.), *The social psychology of intergroup reconciliation*. New York: Oxford University Press.

Worchel, S., Axsom, D., Ferris, F., Samaha, G., & Schweitzer, S. (1978). Determinants of the effects of intergroup cooperation on intergroup attraction. *Journal of Conflict Resolution, 22,* 429–439.

Worchel, S., Coutant-Sassic, D., & Grossman, M. (1992). A developmental approach to group dynamics: A model and illustrative research. In S. Worchel, W. Wood, & J. A. Simpson (Eds.), *Group processes and productivity* (pp. 181–202). Thousand Oaks, CA: Sage Publications, Inc.

Yzerbyt, V., Dumont, M., Wigboldus, D., & Gordijn, E. (2003). I feel for us: The impact of categorization and identification on emotions and action tendencies. *British Journal of Social Psychology, 42,* 533–549.

perceptions, attitudes, and values of individuals involved in a conflict relationship are important determinants of their behavior toward the other party and their response to the conflict. According to a recent explication of the social psychology of national and international group relations, "... individuals, their thought processes, and the manifestations of those processes in interpersonal interactions, are a fundamental aspect of intergroup and international dynamics" (Dovidio, Maruyama, & Alexander, 1998, p. 832). We view international conflict as a process driven by collective needs and fears—by nonfulfillment or threats to the fulfillment of basic human needs, including such psychological needs as security, identity, recognition, autonomy, self-esteem, and a sense of justice (Burton, 1990). Subjective forces linked to basic needs and existential fears contribute heavily to the escalation and perpetuation of international conflict. Thus, a wide range of perceptual and cognitive structures, processes, and biases at the level of individuals and groups need to be examined in order to fully understand the genesis and escalation of intergroup and international conflict.

Second, a social-psychological approach analyzes perceptual and cognitive processes in the context of group functioning and intergroup relations, which are the domains in which social conflict arises and is pursued. These processes operate differently in the group and intergroup environment than they do when an individual responds independently to stimuli without reference to their social implications. Muzafer Sherif and his colleagues were among the first to stress that behavior in an intergroup context is characterized by the fact that individuals interact with members of other groups in terms of their group identifications (Sherif, 1966). This idea was elaborated in social identity theory (SIT) (Tajfel, 1982; Tajfel & Turner, 1986), which posits that individuals' perceptions and interactions in intergroup contexts are governed by their respective memberships in social categories. SIT provides a series of propositions that link social categorization to individual self-esteem and positive identity by the mechanism of self-serving social comparison with other groups. According to this analysis, the intergroup and international context of social perception and cognition needs to be understood in terms of the formation and existence of social groups, particularly identity groups, which are defined by racial, religious, ethnic, cultural, and/or national markers and share a common history and a common fate. Individual members identify with such groups in cognitive, functional, and emotional terms, and their membership thus constitutes an important element of their social identity and self-concept.

It appears that the mere fact of social categorization, in differentiating among groups, gives rise to the perception of heightened similarities within groups alongside exaggerated differences between groups. As a consequence, the processes of group formation and social identity help to plant the seeds of ethnocentrism by producing positive attachments and attitudes toward the in-group. The full expression of ethnocentrism, involving prejudice toward out-groups as well, seems to require the existence of real conflicts of interest between the groups, which—according to realistic group conflict theory (RCT) (LeVine & Campbell, 1972)—are the necessary conditions for intergroup conflict and all that goes with it, including out-group prejudice. In other words, incompatible goals and competition for scarce resources result in the perception of threat, which increases ethnocentrism and drives invidious group comparisons. Once ethnocentrism is pushed to a moderate level through the sense of threat and related mistrust, perceptions of intragroup similarity and intergroup difference are enhanced by further cognitive distortions fostering the development of negative stereotypes, mirror images, selective perceptions, and self-serving biases (Fisher, 1990).

Third, a social-psychological approach views the interaction between the parties, in interplay with subjective elements, as fundamental in determining the course and outcomes of international conflict. Interactions between the parties are shaped by their initial and continuing orientations, especially on the dimension of cooperativeness versus competitiveness, and by the communication processes—their openness, accuracy, and complexity—that prevail at all levels of the societies. In line with this emphasis on interaction at all levels of the conflicting societies, a social-psychological approach views international conflict as an intersocietal process, rather than simply an intergovernmental phenomenon, which also reminds us that interactions within each society play an important role in the course of an international conflict. Furthermore, a social-psychological approach views international conflict as a multifaceted process of mutual influence, not only a contest in the exercise of coercive power; and as an interactive process with an escalatory, self-perpetuating dynamic, not merely a sequence of action and reaction by stable actors. Thus, the manner in which an intergroup or international conflict unfolds, particularly the escalatory dynamic of conflict interaction, is a prime focus for analysis from a social-psychological perspective.

Fourth, a social-psychological approach affirms that intergroup and international conflict can be understood only through a multilevel analysis, ranging from the individual to the social-system level, with special attention to the power of group and intergroup dynamics. According to Dovidio et al. (1998), social psychology has the power to bridge intrapsychic processes, individual behavior, and collective action at the policy level. It is essential, however, to begin any analysis at the level of the phenomenon in question, in this case the intergroup or international level, and to then blend in concepts and models from lower levels of analysis as they appear to be useful (Fisher, 1990). Thus, psychological factors must be understood in their context, and therefore the value of their contribution depends on the correct identification of the appropriate points of application. Furthermore, while a social-psychological perspective can add depth and richness to the analysis of intergroup and international conflict, it cannot by itself provide a comprehensive theory of conflicts at these levels.

The four features of a social-psychological approach to intergroup and international conflict that we have laid out provide the general framework for the more specific discussion of the role of perceptual processes in international conflict to which the remainder of this chapter is devoted. Perceptual processes—along with the normative processes that prevail in conflicting societies—are social-psychological processes that contribute importantly to the generation of conflict and particularly to its escalation and perpetuation once it has started (Kelman, 2007b). The images that the parties hold of each other and themselves, and of the conflict as such, are rooted in the collective needs and fears that drive the conflict, and therefore contribute to the escalatory, self-perpetuating dynamic of the interaction between them. We focus on two perceptual processes that can account for the impact of subjective factors on conflict escalation and perpetuation: the formation of enemy and self-images, and the resistance of these images to contradictory information.

THE FORMATION OF ENEMY AND SELF-IMAGES

The course of intergroup relations is significantly set by each group's perception of the other group, which typically has ramifications for the group's self-perception. A central feature of this phenomenon is the concept of stereotype, which is generally defined as a set of simplified and rigid beliefs about the attributes of another social group. The term was coined by journalist Walter Lippmann in 1922 to refer to *pictures in our heads* and was soon picked up by social psychologists (Katz & Braly, 1935) whose initial interest was in measuring the content of stereotypes toward various minority groups (Hamilton, Stroessner, & Driscoll, 1994). This early focus on assessing the content and continuity of stereotypes ultimately gave way to the cognitive revolution in social psychology, which emphasized the role of stereotypes as cognitive structures that function to influence perceptions and judgments about the other groups (Fiske, 1998; Hamilton, 1981; Rothbart & Lewis, 1994). Stereotypes build on the process of social categorization and the effect of perceived out-group homogeneity, in that members of another group tend to be seen as sharing similar characteristics, more so than members of one's in-group. In addition, stereotypes incorporate the out-group derogation side of ethnocentrism, in that the simplistic beliefs about another group often have negative connotations. Stereotypes abound in the world of intergroup relations at low levels of conflict escalation, and can be relatively innocuous misperceptions of group reality; they may also contain a *kernel of truth* (Triandis & Vassiliou, 1967) and exhibit many of the same characteristics as all cognitive generalizations (Schneider, 2004). However, at higher levels of escalation, stereotypes can drive more insidious processes, such as self-fulfilling prophecies, and can provide part of the justification for destructive behaviors, such as discrimination and dehumanization.

Once established, primarily through in-group socialization, stereotypes serve as one of the cognitive structures that drive selectivity in perception, a basic process of some necessity in a very complex and fast-moving world. Unfortunately, in the intergroup context, the effects of social categorization and ethnocentrism appear to increase as the distinguishing characteristics of groups are clearer and more marked, for example, in language, manner of dress, or skin color. Thus, stereotypes between such distinctive groups become filters through which information that is consonant is attended to and encoded while contrary or irrelevant information is ignored or discounted (Hamilton, 1979; Hamilton et al., 1994). Furthermore, the perceptual effects of stereotypes appear to be automatic, operating outside conscious awareness, in facilitating the rapid identification of congruent information. As a result, individuals appear more similar to their stereotype than they are in reality (Fiske, 1998). In addition, this automatic assimilation effect seems to operate more quickly with the encoding of positive in-group attributes than negative out-group characteristics, thus producing a self-serving in-group bias in perception. The pressures of conflict escalation, with its attendant perception of threat, distrust, and hostility, likely enhance these perceptual distortions.

A useful example of the nature of stereotypes in the context of intractable conflict is provided by the work of Bar-Tal and Teichman in their comprehensive conceptualization of the etiology, maintenance, and effects of stereotypes. They apply their conceptual scheme to the Israeli–Palestinian conflict, with particular reference to the stereotype of "Arabs" held by a range of Israeli Jews from children to adults (Bar-Tal & Teichman, 2005). Using a variety of measures, including interviews, questionnaires, and human figure drawings, Bar-Tal and Teichman (2005) document the existence of the Arab stereotype in a range of domains, including the public discourse, school textbooks, literature, and the entertainment media. Direct, empirical studies of the Jewish stereotype of "Arabs" yields an unflattering picture with themes of "low intelligence, primitivism, dishonesty, fanaticism, conservatism, violence, and lack of value for human life, but on the other hand, positive attributes such as hospitality, sociability, and diligence" (p. 228). The innovative element of this work is its use of human figure drawings and other methods to chart the acquisition of stereotypes of Arabs, Israelis, and Jews by children and youth, thus addressing the critical question of how such simplistic representations are maintained from generation to generation.

The in-group glorification side of ethnocentrism also posits perceptual selectivity and distortion, which now operate in the direction of elevating and exalting the in-group. According to SIT, the self-serving biases that operate here are due to the need for enhanced self-esteem, provided by heightened in-group distinctiveness and out-group derogation through invidious comparisons. Simply put, individuals tend to perceive positive behaviors more often on the part of in-group members and negative behaviors more often on the part of out-group members, and even evaluate the same behaviors differently when they are associated with in-group versus out-group members (Pruitt & Kim, 2004). These self-serving biases are important in their own right, but gain in significance as conflict escalates, because they contribute to more extreme perceptual distortions.

In the study of international and intercommunal conflict, the concept of image has been widely used to capture the mutual perception of enemy and self. Indeed, the study of images has been proposed as a valuable approach to a number of topics in international relations, foreign policy research, and political psychology (Herrmann, 2003; Herrmann & Fischerkeller, 1995). Images can be defined as the organized representations of a social object in a person's cognitive system (Kelman, 1965). Viewed in its full complexity, an image is more than a stereotype in that it is comprised not only of cognitive attributes of the social object, but also of an affective component that involves liking or disliking, and a behavioral aspect that consists of appropriate actions toward the social object (Scott, 1965). In this view, the concept of image shows considerable similarity to the common definition of attitude in social psychology, and thus much of the research on social attitudes at the intergroup level can be applied to the functioning of images at the international level. In fact, according to Herrmann and his colleagues (Alexander, Brewer, & Herrmann, 1999), social-psychological interest in stereotypes has its parallel in international relations, where the origins and consequences of images have been studied, particularly in the context of international conflict. Specifically, the concept of stereotype has found a parallel in the concept of the enemy image, wherein the cognitive attributes of the adversary are typically described as evil, immoral, conspiratorial, opportunistic, and yet fundamentally weak—a "paper tiger." Thus, the concepts of stereotype and enemy image refer to the same perceptual phenomenon, but at different levels, that is, the intergroup versus the international. The biasing effects on perception and cognition of enemy images are strikingly similar to those of stereotypes. Once a threatening enemy image is formed, biases tend to enter into all phases of information processing, from attention, encoding, and memory to attributions for behavior and expectations for future actions (Silverstein & Flamenbaum, 1989). Silverstein and Flamenbaum (1989) review studies and report research that demonstrates the biasing power in a number of domains of the American enemy image of the Soviets during the Cold War.

In a significant contribution to the study of perception in international conflict, social psychologists have identified in particular the phenomenon of mirror image formation as a characteristic of many conflictual relationships. Both parties tend to develop parallel images of self and other, except with the sign reversed; that is, the two parties have similarly negative enemy images and similarly positive self-images. The phenomenon was first described by American social psychologist, Urie Bronfenbrenner, in the context of American-Soviet relations during the early period of the Cold War (Bronfenbrenner, 1961). Being fluent in Russian, he engaged Soviet citizens in conversations about the two competing superpowers during an academic visit, and at first he was disturbed by what he saw as the distorted view of the United States held by the Russians. However, he soon came to a more sobering realization: The typical Russian image of America was very similar to the average American's image of Russia—a negative mirror image that saw the other's country and policies as aggressive, untrustworthy, and verging on madness, with a government that exploits and deludes its own people, most of whom are not really sympathetic to the regime. Bronfenbrenner's conceptualization was soon supported by the work of Ralph White and others who applied the concept to various intergroup and international conflicts (Haque, 1973; Haque & Lawson, 1980; White, 1965, 2004).

The core content of mirror images is captured by the good–bad dimension: each party sees itself as good and peaceful, arming only for defensive reasons, and willing to engage in open and flexible compromise. At the same time, each party sees its enemy as evil and hostile, arming for aggressive reasons, and understanding only the language of force. Influenced by these polar opposites, the parties engage in counterproductive if not destructive interaction in attempts to unilaterally achieve their objectives in the conflict situation.

A typical corollary of the good–bad image in protracted conflicts is the view that the other side's aggressiveness is inherent in its nature: in its ideology (e.g., Zionism or PLO nationalism), in its political/economic system (e.g., capitalist imperialism or communist expansionism), in its religion, or in its national character. On the other hand, if one's own side ever displays aggressiveness, it is entirely reactive and defensive. In the language of attribution theory, the tendency on both sides is to explain the enemy's aggressive behavior in dispositional terms and one's own in situational terms (Jones & Nisbett, 1971). To perceive the enemy's evil action as inherent in its nature is tantamount to demonization and dehumanization of the other, with all the dangerous consequences thereof. Once a group perceived as threatening one's own welfare is excluded from the human family, almost any action against it—including expulsion, dispossession, torture, rape, genocide, and ethnic cleansing in its various forms—comes to be seen as necessary and justified (Kelman, 1973). For example, recent research on the Israeli–Palestinian conflict has demonstrated that dehumanization of Palestinians, expressed as disgust and contempt toward them, in a national sample of Israeli Jews, was related to support for coercive policies toward Palestinians, such as administrative detention, the use of rubber bullets, demolishing homes, and torture (Maoz & McCauley, 2008).

Another common corollary of the good–bad image—one that derives from the virtuous self-image—is the assumption on each side that the enemy knows very well *we* are not threatening them. Our own basic decency and peacefulness, and the provocation to which we have been subjected, are so obvious to us that they must also be obvious to the other side (Ross & Ward, 1995). Thus, the assumption is that they see us as we see *ourselves*—when in fact they see us as we see *them*. This feature of the mirror image process contributes significantly to the escalatory dynamic of conflict interaction, to which we shall return below.

A third—though less common—corollary, first noted by Bronfenbrenner (1961) and extended by White (1965, 1970), involves the separation of the masses from the elites on the other side. The people, in this view, are basically decent but have been misled, brainwashed, or intimidated by their rulers. By contrast, there is complete harmony between rulers and citizens on "our" side. A related element often found in mirror images—as, for example, in the Israeli–Palestinian case—is the view that, in contrast to the genuine unity on one's own side, the enemy's unity is artificial and sustained only by its leaders' effort to keep the conflict alive.

Apart from such generic features of mirror images, which arise from the dynamics of intergroup conflict across the board, mirror images in any given case may reflect the dynamics of the specific conflict. Thus, a central feature of the Israeli–Palestinian conflict over the years has been mutual denial of the other's national identity, accompanied by efforts to delegitimize the other's national movement and claim to nationhood (Kelman, 1978, 1987). Other mirror images that have characterized the Israeli–Palestinian and other intense ethnic conflicts (such as those in Bosnia and Northern Ireland) include:

- Mutual fear of national and personal annihilation, anchored in the view that the project of destroying one's group is inherent in and central to the other's ideology.
- A mutual sense of victimization by the other side, accompanied by a tendency to assimilate the image of the current enemy to the image of the historical enemy and the current experience of victimization to the collective memories of past experiences.
- A mutual view of the enemy as a source of the negative components of one's own identity, such as the sense of humiliation and vulnerability.

While mirror images are an important and central feature of the dynamics of conflict, the concept requires several qualifications, particularly because it is often taken to imply that conflicts are necessarily symmetrical—an idea vehemently rejected by the parties engaged in conflict. The mirror image concept implies that *certain* symmetries in the parties' reactions arise from the very nature of conflict interaction, and that it is important to understand them because of their role in escalating the conflict. There is no assumption, however, that *all* images of self and enemy are mirror images. In the Israeli–Palestinian conflict, for example, both sides agree that Israel is the more powerful party (although Israelis point out that their conflict has been not only with the Palestinians but with the entire Arab world and much of the Muslim world). Furthermore, there is no assumption that the images on the two sides are equally inaccurate. Clearly, the mirror image concept implies that there is some distortion, because the two views of reality are diametrical opposites and thus cannot both be completely right. It is also presumed that there is probably some distortion on each side because both sides' perceptions are affected by the conflict dynamics. This does not mean, however, that both sides manifest equal degrees of distortion.

A third qualification is that the mirror image concept does not imply empirical symmetry between the two sides. There is no assumption that the historical experiences or the current situations of the two sides are comparable on all or even the most important dimensions. To take one dimension as an example, many conflicts are marked by asymmetries in power between the parties, which have significant effects on the parties' perceptions of the conflict (Rouhana & Fiske, 1995). Finally, the mirror image concept does not imply moral equivalence in the positions of the two parties. To note the symmetry in the two sides' perceptions of their own moral superiority is not to postulate moral symmetry in their claims or their actions. Thus, for example, one can point to mirror images with many similar elements in the relationship between Serbs and Muslims in Bosnia and still make the moral judgment that it was the Serbian side that committed genocide.

With these qualifications in mind, one can trace the common tendency among parties in conflict to form mirror images to the dynamics of the conflict relationship itself. Since each party is engaged in the conflict and subject to similar forces generated by that engagement, parallelism in some of their images is bound to develop. Parallel images arise out of the motivational and cognitive contexts in which parties in conflict generally operate. Motivationally, each side is concerned with "looking good" when blame for the conflict events is being apportioned; political leaders, therefore, feel a strong need to persuade themselves, their own people, the rest of the world, and future historians that the blame rests with the enemy—that their own cause is just and their own actions have been entirely defensive in nature. Cognitively, each side views the conflict from its own perspective and—painfully aware of its own needs, fears, historical traumas, grievances, suspicions, and political constraints—is convinced that it is acting defensively and with the best intentions. Furthermore, each side assumes that these circumstances are so self-evident, they must be equally clear to the enemy; signs of hostility from the enemy must therefore be due to its aggressive intent.

When both sides are motivated to deflect blame from themselves and are convinced that their own good intentions are as clear to the other as to themselves, mirror images are formed. Mirror images increase the danger of escalation, as illustrated in the classical pattern of arms races. They produce a spiraling effect because each side interprets any hostile action by the other as an indication of aggressive intent against which it must defend itself, but its own reactions—whose defensive nature, it assumes, should be obvious to the enemy—are taken by the other as signs of aggressive intent. The effect of mirror images is accentuated insofar as the enemy's ideology or national character is perceived to be inherently aggressive and expansionist, because this essentialist view provides a stable framework for explaining the other's behavior. In addition to their escalatory effect, mirror images tend to make conflicts more intractable because the sharp contrast between the innocent self and the aggressive other makes it difficult to break out of a zero-sum conception of the conflict.

Intergroup and international conflict that is not managed effectively in the early stages has a built-in tendency to escalate, that is, to increase in intensity and hostility with a growing gap in the difference between winning and losing. That is to say, the stakes in the conflict continue to increase in both number and value in terms of a cost–benefit analysis. As conflict escalates, a series of transformations occur in the orientations and behavior of each party and thereby in their interaction (Pruitt & Kim, 2004). One of these changes relates to the motivation of the parties, which shifts from doing well in achieving their goals, to winning in the contest with the other party, and finally to hurting the other party. At higher levels of escalation and intractability, mirror images develop beyond the initial good–bad distinction toward more exaggerated and variegated forms, identified in the work of Ralph White as major forms of misperception, including the diabolical enemy image, the virile self-image, and the moral self-image (White, 1970). The diabolical enemy image embodies a view of the opponent as an evil, monster-like entity that is simply outside of one's moral universe. The virile self-image portrays one's own party as powerful and uncompromising, views strength as a virtue and military superiority as the path to beneficial outcomes, and promotes the further bias of military overconfidence. The moral self-image exaggerates the good–bad element of the ethnocentric mirror image to the point where one's own party is seen as the defender and arbiter of all that is desirable in the human condition.

The diabolical enemy image finds its expression in the demonization of the enemy, which White found to be an almost universal misperception in his forty years of studying the most serious conflicts of the past century (White, 2004). A concomitant of demonization is the dehumanization of members of the enemy group, which helps to justify aggressive behavior toward them, as noted earlier. Dehumanization, in turn, is accompanied by deindividuation, a process whereby members of a group experience a loss of personal identity and become submerged in the group's cognitive reality (Festinger, Pepitone, & Newcomb, 1952). In intergroup conflict, as group members come to see themselves, as well as members of the out-group, less as individuals and more as members of a social category (Pruitt & Kim, 2004), the constraints against aggression toward the out-group are reduced both because of a decline in their sense of personal responsibility and because of the exclusion of the other from their moral community. The mutual victimization characteristic of highly escalated intergroup conflicts is in part due to the enabling effects of extreme images and their associated cognitive biases.

The accumulation of all of these enemy and self-images as conflict escalates results in a sense of victimization for the in-group and allows for more severe aggressive responses toward members of the enemy group, which further increases the intensity of the conflict. This sense of victimhood has been defined as "a mind-set shared by group members that results from a perceived intentional harm with severe consequences inflicted to a collective by another group that is viewed as undeserved, unjust, and immoral and one that the group could not prevent" (Bar-Tal, Chernyak-Hai, Schori, & Gundar, 2009, p. 238). The sense of victimhood in intractable conflicts serves multiple functions, which include attributing the responsibility for the conflict to the other side, serving as a basis for solidarity, and motivating and mobilizing group members for action against the other. It thus contributes to the continuation of the conflict and to the severity of the conflict through violent retributions. An estimate of the extent of victimhood in intractable conflicts is provided in a survey study completed in 2001 in Northern Ireland in the 26 Council Areas that had experienced the "Troubles" (Cairns, Mallet, Lewis, & Wilson, 2003). In the random sample of 1000 adults, 12% reported that they often or very often thought of themselves as victims of the Troubles, while 16% were classified as being direct victims (injured in a sectarian incident, home damaged by a bomb, or intimidated outside their home) and 30% as indirect victims (family member or close friend injured, intimidated, or home damaged by a bomb). Not surprisingly, those seeing themselves as victims or reporting direct or indirect victimization showed lower levels of psychological well-being as measured by a general health questionnaire.

At higher levels of escalation, enemy images become increasingly resistant to contradictory information and are confirmed as accurate representations of social reality. Concurrently, the conflict moves into a protracted phase, taking on characteristics of intractability that render it resistant to resolution (Coleman, 2003, 2006), including *polarized collective identities* constructed partly through self-serving biases and distortions of the other. We turn next to a consideration of the conditions that contribute to the resistance of enemy images to contradictory information and, as a consequence, to the intractability of the conflict.

RESISTANCE OF IMAGES TO CONTRADICTORY INFORMATION

Conflict images are highly resistant to new information that challenges their validity. The persistence of these images inhibits the perception of change and the expectation of future change that might create possibilities for conflict resolution, and thus helps to perpetuate the conflict.

A great deal of social-psychological theorizing and research has addressed the general phenomenon of the persistence of attitudes and beliefs in the face of new information that, from an observer's point of view, is clearly contradictory—information that should at least call the existing attitudes into question but is somehow neutralized or ignored. This is not to say that attitudes never change; indeed, there is considerable evidence that individuals' and societies' attitudes constantly change—sometimes gradually, sometimes drastically—in response to new events and experiences. But change always occurs in the face of some resistance.

Resistance is motivated in the sense that we tend to hold on to our attitudes because they perform certain important functions for us: They help us interpret social reality, express our values, support our self-esteem, and maximize our rewards in life (Katz, 1960). Beyond that, however, resistance is built into the very functioning of attitudes: Since attitudes help shape our experiences and the way new information is organized, they play a role in creating the conditions for their own confirmation and for avoiding disconfirmation. Research has focused on several types of mechanisms that account for resistance to contradictory information: selectivity, consistency, attribution, and the self-fulfilling prophecy.

The concepts of selective exposure, selective perception, and selective recall all point to the fact that our stereotypes and attitudes help determine the kind of information that is available to us. Our political attitudes, for example, determine the organizations we join, the meetings we attend, and the publications we receive. Consequently, we are more likely to be exposed to information that confirms our views than to information that contradicts them. We also tend to seek out confirmatory information because we enjoy it more, trust it more, and find it more useful—for example, to support our position in subsequent discussions. Furthermore, as noted earlier, we are more likely to perceive the information to which we are exposed in a way that is congruent with our initial stereotypes and attitudes, because these predispositions create expectations for what we will find and provide a framework for making sense of it (Fiske, 1998). Finally, we are more likely to remember confirmatory information because we have a preexisting framework into which it can be fit and because we are more likely to find it useful.

The processes of selectivity also operate in interpersonal and intergroup relations. We are less likely to communicate with people whom we dislike; as a result we have less opportunity to make new observations that might conceivably lead to a revision in our attitudes (Newcomb, 1947). Similarly, our initial attitudes and images—sometimes based on first impressions or group labels—create expectations that affect our subsequent observations and provide a framework for how we perceive a person's behavior and what we recall about it. A review (Rothbart, 1993) of the processes of intergroup perception indicates that initial group categorizations are "reinforced by selective memory for events that confirm the implicit expectations generated by the initial categorization" (p. 98). For example, in one study, subjects were presented with information about behaviors of individuals in a group that was previously described as either "friendly" or "intelligent." Subjects exhibited higher recall for behaviors congruent with the label they had been provided with (Rothbart, Evans, & Fulero, 1979). Rothbart (1993) also reviews studies indicating that memory effects are different for in-groups and out-groups in that individuals are more likely to remember favorable in-group behaviors and less favorable out-group behaviors. In short, the memory process involves "a self-confirmatory cognitive system that appears 'determined' to derogate the out-group" (Rothbart, 1993, p. 98).

Cognitive consistency has received a great deal of attention in experimental social psychology. Among the different models explored in numerous studies, the two most influential ones have been Fritz Heider's theory of cognitive balance and Leon Festinger's theory of cognitive dissonance (Festinger, 1957; Heider, 1958). The general assumption of the various consistency models is that inconsistency between different cognitive elements (e.g., between feelings and beliefs about an object, between our attitudes and our actions, or between our attitudes and the attitudes of important others) is an uncomfortable psychological state. It creates tension, which we seek to reduce by whatever means are most readily available to restore consistency. The study of cognitive dissonance has pursued a number of research paradigms, including the belief-disconfirmation paradigm, in which individuals are exposed to information that is inconsistent with their beliefs (Harmon-Jones & Mills, 1999). If individuals do not change their beliefs outright to reduce the dissonance, a number of other alternatives are available, including the misperception or misinterpretation of the information, which is of interest here. Alternatively, individuals may refute the information, or look to support from others who agree with them or try to persuade others who do not.

The role of consistency mechanisms in reaction to new information is thus rather complex. Inconsistent information is often an important instigator of change in attitudes and behavior, provided the information is compelling and challenging and situational forces motivate the person to seek out new information. At other times, however, consistency mechanisms serve to reinforce selective exposure, perception, and recall: People screen out information that is incongruent with their existing attitudes and beliefs and thus maintain cognitive consistency. This reaction is especially likely when the existing attitudes are strongly held and have wide ramifications—as is the case with enemy images. Perhaps the earliest application of these concepts to international conflict in a comprehensive manner was undertaken by Robert Jervis, whose case analyses demonstrated how policy makers assimilated new information into pre-existing beliefs and cognitive categories in ways that rendered the information cognitively consistent (Jervis, 1976). The power of these cognitive mechanisms in producing an *irrational consistency* has been well supported by further research (Jervis, 1988; Tetlock & McGuire, 1985). Particularly in foreign policy decisions, these cognitive biases can lead not only to selective attention to information, but also to premature cognitive closure in which decision makers stop searching for information once they have enough to support pre-existing beliefs (Levy, 2003). For example, Levy cites the Israeli failure in the 1973 Middle East war to incorporate and act on information signaling an Egyptian attack, because of the Israeli belief that Egypt would not go to war since it could not strike deep into Israeli territory. In general, there is a continuing assertion in the field of political psychology that the need for consistency in attitudes is a powerful force in information processing (Taber, 2003).

Attribution theory has been another central focus for research on social cognition. This theory addresses the ways in which people explain their own and others' behavior—how they assess the causes of behavior. Causal attributions are significant in human interaction because they affect emotional and behavioral responses to other people's actions. One of the key distinctions in the field, to which we referred in the preceding section, has been between dispositional and situational attributions: The perceived cause of a particular action may be placed in the actor's character and underlying nature, or in situational forces (Jones & Nisbett, 1971). When observing the behavior of others, people have a strong tendency to make dispositional attributions—to commit what has been called *the fundamental attribution error* (Ross, 1977). On the other hand, when explaining the causes of their own behavior, people are much more likely to make situational attributions, because they are aware of the many pressures and constraints that affect their behavior at any given time and place. Most of the initial work on attributional biases focused at the level of individuals and interpersonal relations, but it has since been extended to the intergroup and international levels (Betancourt, 1990; Hewstone, 1988, 1990). One conclusion relevant to the fundamental attribution error is that in a conflict relationship, dispositional attributions of the enemy's behavior tend to produce an image of the enemy as *inherently* aggressive, which is far more likely to be resistant to disconfirming information.

The resistance of enemy images to disconfirmation is further intensified by what Thomas Pettigrew called the ultimate attribution error—a cognitive bias that, according to him, is particularly strong in intergroup relations that are marked by highly negative stereotypes and intense conflict (Pettigrew, 1979). When people explain their own behavior or that of members of their in-group and its allies, they tend to make dispositional attributions for positive acts and situational attributions for negative acts; when they explain the behavior of out-group members or enemies, they are inclined to do the reverse, attributing undesirable acts to dispositional causes and desirable acts to situational causes. These tendencies were confirmed in several studies of international conflict (Heradstveit, 1981; Rosenberg & Wolfsfeld, 1977; Rouhana, 1997). A cogent example is provided in the context of the Northern Ireland conflict in which Catholic and Protestant university students were presented with newsreel clips showing scenes of violence by in-group versus out-group members (Hunter, Stringer, & Watson, 1991). After viewing the clips, respondents were asked to explain what they thought was happening and why those involved had behaved as they had. Statements dealing with causality were coded by two blind, independent coders as demonstrating either internal or external attributions. As predicted by Pettigrew's hypotheses, for both Protestants and Catholics, respondents made significantly more internal attributions for out-group members' violence and more external attributions for violence perpetrated by their own group's members. Thus, attribution mechanisms—like consistency mechanisms—promote confirmation of the original enemy image. Hostile actions by the enemy are attributed dispositionally and thus provide further evidence of the enemy's inherently aggressive, implacable character. Conciliatory actions are explained away as reactions to situational forces—as tactical maneuvers, responses to external pressure, or temporary adjustments to a position of weakness—and therefore require no revision of the original image.

The concept of the self-fulfilling prophecy refers to the effect of expectations about another person or group on the other's actual behavior. Our expectations are communicated, perhaps subtly and unconsciously, in the way we approach others in the course of interaction. In doing so, we often create conditions that cause others to behave in line with our expectations, thus confirming the original stereotype. Such effects were initially studied in educational settings, where it was found that teachers' expectations about the capabilities of their students were related to the students' subsequent performance, apparently through teachers' differential treatment of the students (Jussim, 1986; Rosenthal & Jacobson, 1968). The effect has also been documented in interpersonal relations, where stereotypes of another generate subtle cues that lead to confirmatory behavior in the other (Snyder, 1984; Snyder, Tanke, & Berscheid, 1977). In the context of intergroup conflict, a group's expectation of hostility from the other may cause it to act in a cold and defensive manner toward the other, which in turn might elicit a hostile response, thus confirming the initial image. In negotiation, for example, a party that enters the exchange with the expectation that the other party will be unyielding may engage in particularly hard bargaining and offer proposals that the other party is bound to reject, thus living up to the original expectation. Expectations thus create self-fulfilling prophecies, with the consequence that enemy images are not only confirmed, but strengthened for the next round of interactions. Self-fulfilling policies can also play out around specific policy decisions. For example, in the context of the intractable Cyprus conflict (Fisher, 2001), the Greek Cypriot administration in 1990 unilaterally applied for membership in the European Union, a move that outraged and alienated the Turkish Cypriots. When asked why a joint application was not attempted, one Greek Cypriot response was that the Turkish Cypriots would have refused, a prediction then confirmed by their opposition to the application.

The mechanisms that account for resistance to disconfirming information—selectivity, consistency, attribution, and self-fulfilling prophecy—are particularly powerful in a conflict relationship for several reasons. First, images of the enemy and conflict-related self-images are central aspects of the national consensus. In an intense conflict, there are strong social pressures toward maintaining uniformity of opinion, especially in a crisis atmosphere. Softening the image of the enemy breaks the consensus and invites accusations of disloyalty. The militant elements resist a revision of the enemy image because they see it as weakening the national resolve, lowering defenses, and signaling a readiness for hazardous compromise. Their objections may have a broad appeal because the assumption that the risks of underestimating the enemy's hostility are more dangerous than the risks of overestimating it (and thus underestimating the opportunities for peace) is widely shared—and only the former invokes the charge of disloyalty. In short, the mechanisms of resistance to disconfirming information are reinforced by normative pressures in a conflict situation.

Second, enemy images are especially resistant to disconfirmation because, in a conflict relationship, the opportunities for taking the perspective of the other are limited, and the capacity for doing so is impaired. In normal social interaction, participants' mutual attitudes often change in response to new information they acquire and/or evaluate by taking each other's perspective. However, interaction among parties in conflict—if it occurs at all—is governed by a set of conflict norms.

Under these circumstances, the empathy required for taking the other's perspective is difficult to achieve and is, in fact, frowned upon. As a result, each party's analysis of the enemy's society is dominated by its own perspective. In the Arab–Israeli case, for example, both parties tend to overestimate how much the other knows about their own intentions and concerns: parties' estimates of what the other knows are based on what they themselves know (an important source of the escalatory effect of mirror images, as noted earlier). Other consequences of looking at the other primarily from one's own perspective are:

- A lack of differentiation among various strata and segments of the other society and a tendency to categorize it in terms of one's own concerns (e.g., pro-PLO versus anti-PLO Palestinians, Zionist versus anti-Zionist Israelis) rather than the society's internal dynamics.
- A self-centered view of the other side's opposition groups, equating them with supporters of one's own cause (which is bound to lead to disappointment once one discovers that even the dovish opposition elements have not switched sides).
- A self-centered view of the other's ideology that perceives the destruction of one's own national existence as the entire meaning and sole purpose of the other side's national movement.

These and similar failures to take account of the other's perspective reduce the impact of potentially new information. Lacking the appropriate context, the parties may not notice or adequately appreciate the varieties, changes, and signs of flexibility in the other side's views.

Third, the resistance of enemy images to disconfirmation is magnified by strong beliefs concerning the unchangeability of the enemy. Such beliefs are typically part of the mirror image, which regards the enemy's hostility as inherent in its ideology and character (i.e., the mirror image attributes such hostility to dispositional causes). Thus, for many years, both Israelis and Palestinians insisted that there had been no real change in the enemy's position, only tactical maneuvers; that view changed over the years—especially after the Oslo agreement in 1993—but, with the failure of the Camp David talks in 2000 and the outbreak of the new intifada, it reemerged in full force. One reason for underestimating the amount of change on the other side is that the two parties use different anchors in assessing movement. The side taking a given action measures the amount of change it represents in terms of how far it has moved from its original position; the other side measures it in terms of how close it has come to its own position. Thus, in the Palestinian view, the 1974 decision of the Palestine National Council to accept a "national authority" on any part of Palestine that is liberated represented a major change—one that was bitterly contested and divided the movement, because it was seen as a step toward a two-state solution. Israelis, however, saw no significance in this move because it was still a long way from recognizing Israel and ending the armed struggle. To take a more recent example, Israelis perceived Prime Minister Barak's offer to the Palestinian side at the 2000 Camp David talks as very generous, because his concessions went considerably further than those made by any previous Israeli government. Palestinians, however, perceived the offer as inadequate, because it did not meet their minimal requirements for a viable Palestinian state and for a final settlement of the conflict (Kelman, 2007a).

Not only do parties in conflict—starting from different reference points—find it difficult to perceive change in the enemy, they often believe that there will not and cannot be any change in the enemy's position. They give greater credence to history and formal documents than to the ongoing and evolving political process. They therefore consider it dangerous or even treasonous to propose that the enemy has changed or will change, and see no way to exert influence and encourage change other than by force—"the only language the enemy understands." Such beliefs are not easily penetrated by new information suggesting that there has been change in the enemy camp and that further changes are in the offing.

Despite all the reasons why conflict images are particularly resistant to contradictory information, they are not immutable. Social-psychological evidence suggests that they can change, and historical evidence shows that they do change. The challenge for scholars and practitioners of international conflict resolution is to devise the means to overcome their resistance to change.

CONCLUSION

The analysis provided in this chapter supports the assertion that perceptual and cognitive processes play a critical role in the escalation and intractability of destructive intergroup and international conflict. In particular, the various cognitive mechanisms and biases enumerated here contribute both to the development of inaccurate and exaggerated mirror images and to the high degree of resistance of conflict images to disconfirming information. It is clear that human social groups are therefore limited in their capacity to effectively manage intense conflict that threatens their well-being and existence. At the same time, several caveats should be offered in making the case for the importance of social-psychological processes in the causation and escalation of destructive and intractable conflict. First, it is acknowledged that a considerable amount of theorizing and research in social psychology suffers from a number of limitations, essentially that the discipline operates largely at the individual level of analysis with a focus on cognitive processes, rather than motivational or emotional ones, and typically ignores or downplays the broader social or system context in which the individual functions. This concern is reinforced by the limited external validity of the common research designs, using laboratory experiments or questionnaire studies with a restricted population largely composed of American and European university students. A further qualification relates to the cultural generalizability of theories and findings developed primarily in a limited cultural milieu. Given that each culture possesses it own unique view of conflict and methods for dealing with it, a considerable amount of caution must be invoked in applying concepts and processes beyond their domain of origin. Nonetheless, if assertions are offered as hypotheses to be assessed in a variety of cases, as found in the illustrations provided here, then some gains in understanding and amelioration may accrue.

Social-psychological processes more generally—including the perceptual processes we have described, as well as the normative processes that typically prevail in conflicting societies (Kelman, 2007b)—contribute to resistances that entrap parties in a pattern of interaction with an escalatory, self-perpetuating dynamic. A social-psychological approach provides insight into how change comes about in group, national, and international systems, by illuminating how publics and leaders frame issues, define interests, and develop a collective readiness to pursue war or peace. Creating the conditions for change in a peaceful direction requires a reversal of the social-psychological processes that promote conflict through changes in the habitual ways of thinking, acting, and interacting. In light of the analysis in this chapter, it is especially important to develop communication patterns that allow new information to challenge conflict-related images and to help break the conflict spirals that are initiated and supported by these images. Overcoming the barriers to conflict resolution requires the promotion of a different kind of interaction that is capable of reversing the conflict dynamic.

At the micro level, interactive conflict resolution and its prototype, the problem-solving workshop, along with similar approaches, are designed to encourage influential members of the conflicting parties to penetrate each other's perspective, to differentiate their enemy images, to develop initiatives for mutual reassurance, and to generate ideas for resolving the conflict that address the collective needs and fears on both sides (Fisher, 1997; Kelman, 1986, 2002). At the macro level, it is necessary to establish a different discourse between the parties that shifts from reliance on the coercive use of power to mutual responsiveness and reciprocity in the context of an open and cooperative relationship. An understanding of the perceptual and cognitive dynamics of conflict relationships is essential to such efforts to de-escalate and resolve intergroup and international conflict.

REFERENCES

Alexander, M. G., Brewer, M. B., & Herrmann, R. (1999). Images and affect: A functional analysis of out-group stereotypes. *Journal of Personality and Social Psychology, 77*(1), 78–93.

Bar-Tal, D., Chernyak-Hai, L., Schori, N., & Gundar, A. (2009). A sense of self-collective victimhood in intractable conflicts: Nature, antecedents, functions, and consequences. *International Red Cross Review, 91*, 229–258.

Bar-Tal, D., & Geva, N. (1986). A cognitive basis of international conflicts. In S. Worchel & W. G. Austin (Eds.), *Psychology of intergroup relations* (2nd ed., pp. 118–133). Chicago: Nelson-Hall.

Bar-Tal, D., & Teichman, Y. (2005). *Stereotypes and prejudice in conflict: Representations of Arabs in Israeli Jewish society*. Cambridge, UK: Cambridge University Press.

Betancourt, H. (1990). An attributional approach to intergroup and international conflict. In S. Graham & V. S. Folkes (Eds.), *Attribution theory: Applications to achievement, mental health, and interpersonal conflict* (pp. 205–220). Hillsdale, NJ: Lawrence Erlbaum.

Bronfenbrenner, U. (1961). The mirror image in Soviet-American relations: A social psychologist's report. *Journal of Social Issues, 17*(3), 45–56.

Burton, J. W. (Ed.). (1990). *Conflict: Human needs theory*. New York: St. Martin's Press.

Cairns, E., Mallet, J., Lewis, C., & Wilson, R. (2003). *Who are the victims? Self-assessed victimhood and the Northern Irish conflict* (NIO Research & Statistical Series: Report No. 7). Belfast: Northern Ireland Office, Northern Ireland Statistics and Research Agency.

Coleman, P. T. (2003). Characteristics of protracted, intractable conflict: Towards the development of a metaframework—I. *Peace and Conflict: Journal of Peace Psychology*, 9, 1–38.

Coleman, P. T. (2006). Intractable conflict. In M. Deutsch, P. T. Coleman, & G. E. Marcus (Eds.), *The handbook of conflict resolution* (2nd ed., pp. 533–559). San Francisco, CA: Jossey-Bass.

Dovidio, J. F., Maruyama, G., & Alexander, M. G. (1998). A social psychology of national and international group relations. *Journal of Social Issues*, 54(4), 831–846.

Festinger, L. (1957). *A theory of cognitive dissonance*. Stanford, CA: Stanford University Press.

Festinger, L., Pepitone, A., & Newcomb, T. (1952). Some consequences of deindividuation in a group. *Journal of Abnormal and Social Psychology*, 47, 382–389.

Fisher, R. J. (1990). *The social psychology of intergroup and international conflict resolution*. New York: Springer-Verlag.

Fisher, R. J. (1997). *Interactive conflict resolution*. Syracuse, NY: Syracuse University Press.

Fisher, R. J. (2001). Cyprus: The failure of mediation and the escalation of an identity-based conflict to an adversarial impasse. *Journal of Peace Research*, 38, 307–326.

Fisher, R. J. (2008). An overview of selected social-psychological contributions to international conflict resolution: Social cognition, decision making and escalation. Paper presented at the *49th Annual Convention of the International Studies Association*, San Francisco, CA, March 26–29, 2008.

Fiske, S. (1998). Stereotyping, prejudice, and discrimination. In D. T. Gilbert & S. T. Fiske (Eds.), *The handbook of social psychology* (4th ed., Vol. 1, pp. 357–441). New York: McGraw-Hill.

Hamilton, D. L. (1979). A cognitive-attributional analysis of stereotyping. In L. Berkowitz (Ed.), *Advances in experimental social psychology* (Vol. 12, pp. 53–84). New York: Academic Press.

Hamilton, D. L. (Ed.). (1981). *Cognitive processes in stereotyping and intergroup behavior*. Hillsdale, NJ: Erlbaum.

Hamilton, D. L., Stroessner, S. J., & Driscoll, D. M. (1994). Social cognition and the study of stereotyping. In P. G. Devine, D. L. Hamilton, & T. M. Ostrom (Eds.), *Social cognition: Impact on social psychology* (pp. 291–321). San Diego, CA: Academic Press.

Haque, A. (1973). Mirror image hypothesis in the context of the Indo-Pakistan conflict. *Pakistan Journal of Psychology*, 6, 13–22.

Haque, A., & Lawson, E. D. (1980). The mirror image phenomenon in the context of the Arab–Israeli conflict. *International Journal of Intercultural Relations*, 4, 107–116.

Harmon-Jones, E., & Mills, J. (Eds.). (1999). *Cognitive dissonance: Progress on a pivotal theory in social psychology*. Washington, DC: American Psychological Association.

Heider, F. (1958). *The psychology of interpersonal relations*. New York: Wiley.

Heradstveit, D. (1981). *The Arab–Israeli conflict: Psychological obstacles to peace* (2nd ed.). Oslo: Universitetsforlaget.

Herrmann, R. (2003). Image theory and strategic interaction in international relations. In D. O. Sears, L. Huddy, & R. Jervis (Eds.), *Oxford handbook of political psychology* (pp. 285–314). Oxford: Oxford University Press.

Herrmann, R., & Fischerkeller, M. P. (1995). Beyond the enemy image and spiral mode: Cognitive-strategic research after the cold war. *International Organization*, 49(3), 415–450.

Hewstone, M. (1988). Attributional bases of intergroup conflict. In W. Stroebe, A. W. Kruglanski, D. Bar-Tal, & M. Hewstone (Eds.), *The social psychology of intergroup conflict*. New York: Springer-Verlag.

Hewstone, M. (1990). The 'ultimate attribution error'? A review of the literature on intergroup causal attribution. *European Journal of Social Psychology*, 20, 311–335.

Hunter, J. A., Stringer, M., & Watson, R. P. (1991). Intergroup violence and intergroup attributions. *British Journal of Social Psychology*, 30(3), 261–266.

Jervis, R. (1976). *Perceptions and misperceptions in international politics*. Princeton, NJ: Princeton University Press.

Jervis, R. (1988). War and misperception. *Journal of Interdisciplinary History*, 18, 675–700.

Jones, E. E., & Nisbett, R. E. (1971). The actor and the observer: Divergent perceptions of the causes of behavior. In E. E. Jones, D. E. Kanouse, H. H. Kelley, R. E. Nisbett, S. Valins, & B. Weiner (Eds.), *Attribution: Perceiving the causes of behavior* (pp. 79–94). Morristown, NJ: General Learning Press.

Jussim, L. (1986). Self-fulfilling prophecies: A theoretical and intergrative review. *Psychological Review*, 93, 429–445.

Katz, D. (1960). The functional approach to the study of attitudes. *Public Opinion Quarterly*, 24, 163–204.

Katz, D., & Braly, K. (1935). Racial prejudice and racial stereotypes. *Journal of Abnormal and Social Psychology*, 30, 175–193.

Kelman, H. C. (1973). Violence without moral restraints: Reflections on the dehumanization of victims and victimizers. *Journal of Social Issues*, 29(4), 25–61.

Kelman, H. C. (1978). Israelis and Palestinians: Psychological prerequisites for mutual acceptance. *International Security*, 3, 162–186.

Kelman, H. C. (1986). Interactive problem solving: A social-psychological approach to conflict resolution. In W. Klassen (Ed.), *Dialogue: Toward interfaith understanding* (pp. 293–314). Tantur, Jerusalem: Ecumenical Institute for Theological Research.

Kelman, H. C. (1987). The political psychology of the Israeli–Palestinian conflict: How can we overcome the barriers to a negotiated solution? *Political Psychology*, 8, 347–363.

Kelman, H. C. (2002). Interactive problem solving: Informal mediation by the scholar-practitioner. In J. Bercovitch (Ed.), *Studies in international mediation: Essays in honor of Jeffrey Z. Rubin* (pp. 167–193). New York: Palgrave Macmillan.

Kelman, H. C. (2007a). The Israeli–Palestinian peace process and its vicissitudes: Insights from attitude theory. *American Psychologist*, 62, 287–303.

Kelman, H. C. (2007b). Social-psychological dimensions of international conflict. In I. W. Zartman (Ed.), *Peacemaking in international conflict: Methods and techniques* (rev. ed., pp. 61–107). Washington, DC: United States Institute of Peace.

Kelman, H. C. (Ed.). (1965). *International behavior: A social-psychological analysis*. New York: Holt, Rinehart and Winston.

Kelman, H. C., & Fisher, R. J. (2003). Conflict analysis and resolution. In D. O. Sears, L. Huddy, & R. Jervis (Eds.), *Oxford handbook of political psychology* (pp. 315–353). Oxford: Oxford University Press.

LeVine, R. A., & Campbell, D. T. (1972). *Ethnocentrism: Theories of conflict, ethnic attitudes and group behavior*. New York: Wiley.

Levy, J. S. (2003). Political psychology and foreign policy. In D. O. Sears, L. Huddy, & R. Jervis (Eds.), *Oxford handbook of political psychology* (pp. 253–284). Oxford: Oxford University Press.

Maoz, I., & McCauley, C. (2008). Threat, dehumanization, and support for retaliatory aggressive policies in asymmetric conflict. *Journal of Conflict Resolution*, 52(1), 93–116.

Mitchell, C. R. (1981). *The structure of international conflict*. London: Macmillan.

Newcomb, T. (1947). Autistic hostility and social reality. *Human Relations, 1*, 69–86.

Pettigrew, T. F. (1979). The ultimate attribution error: Extending Allport's cognitive analysis of prejudice. *Personality and Social Psychology Bulletin, 5*, 461–476.

Pruitt, D. G., & Kim, S. H. (2004). *Social conflict: Escalation, stalemate, and settlement* (3rd ed.). New York: McGraw-Hill.

Rosati, J. A. (2001). *The power of human cognition in the study of world politics*. Malden, MA: Blackwell Publishers.

Rosenberg, S. W., & Wolfsfeld, G. (1977). International conflict and the problem of attribution. *Journal of Conflict Resolution, 21*, 75–103.

Rosenthal, R., & Jacobson, L. (1968). *Pygmalian in the classroom*. New York: Holt, Rinehart & Winston.

Ross, L. (1977). The intuitive psychologist and his shortcomings. In L. Berkowitz (Ed.), *Advances in experimental social psychology* (Vol. 10, pp. 173–220). New York: Academic Press.

Ross, L., & Ward, A. (1995). Psychological barriers to dispute resolution. In M. P. Zanna (Ed.), *Advances in experimental social psychology* (Vol. 27, pp. 255–304). New York: Academic Press.

Rothbart, M. (1993). Intergroup perception and social conflict. In S. Worchel & J. A. Simpson (Eds.), *Conflict between people and groups: Causes, processes and resolutions* (pp. 93–109). Chicago, IL: Nelson-Hall.

Rothbart, M., Evans, M., & Fulero, S. (1979). Recall for confirming events: Memory processes and the maintenance of social stereotypes. *Journal of Experimental Social Psychology, 15*, 343–355.

Rothbart, M., & Lewis, S. H. (1994). Cognitive processes and intergroup relations: A historical perspective. In P. G. Devine, D. L. Hamilton, & T. M. Ostrom (Eds.), *Social cognition: Impact on social psychology* (pp. 347–382). San Diego, CA: Academic Press.

Rouhana, N. N. (1997). *Palestinian citizens in an ethnic Jewish state: Identities in conflict*. New Haven, CT: Yale University Press.

Rouhana, N. N., & Fiske, S. T. (1995). Perceptions of power, threat, and conflict intensity in asymmetric intergroup conflict. *Journal of Conflict Resolution, 39*, 49–81.

Schneider, D. J. (2004). *The psychology of stereotyping*. New York: The Guilford Press.

Scott, W. A. (1965). Psychological and social correlates of international images. In H. C. Kelman (Ed.), *International behavior: A social-psychological analysis* (pp. 71–103). New York: Holt, Rinehart & Winston.

Sherif, M. (1966). *In common predicament: Social psychology of intergroup conflict and cooperation*. Boston: Houghton-Mifflin.

Silverstein, B., & Flamenbaum, C. (1989). Biases in the perception and cognition of the actions of enemies. *Journal of Social Issues, 45*(2), 51–72.

Snyder, M. (1984). When belief creates reality. In L. Berkowitz (Ed.), *Advances in experimental social psychology* (Vol. 18, pp. 248–306). New York: Academic Press.

Snyder, M., Tanke, E. D., & Berscheid, E. (1977). Social perception and interpersonal behavior: On the self-fulfilling nature of social stereotypes. *Journal of Personality and Social Psychology, 35*, 656–666.

Stein, J. G. (2001). Image, identity, and the resolution of violent conflict. In C. A. Crocker, F. O. Hampson, & P. Aall (Eds.), *Turbulent peace: The challenges of managing international conflict* (pp. 189–208). Washington, DC: United States Institute of Peace.

Taber, C. S. (2003). Information processing and public opinion. In D. O. Sears, L. Huddy, & R. Jervis (Eds.), *Oxford handbook of political psychology* (pp. 433–476). Oxford: Oxford University Press.

Tajfel, H. (Ed.). (1982). *Social identity and intergroup relations*. Cambridge, UK: Cambridge University Press.

Tajfel, H., & Turner, J. C. (1986). The social identity theory of intergroup behavior. In S. Worchel & W. G. Austin (Eds.), *Psychology of intergroup relations* (2nd ed., pp. 7–24). Chicago, IL: Nelson-Hall.

Tetlock, P. E., & McGuire, C. B. (1985). Cognitive perspectives on foreign policy. In S. Long (Ed.), *Political behavior annual* (Vol. 1, pp. 255–273). Boulder, CO: Westview.

Triandis, H. C., & Vassiliou, V. (1967). Frequency of contact and stereotyping. *Journal of Personality and Social Psychology, 7*, 316–328.

White, R. K. (1965). Images in the context of international conflict: Soviet perceptions of the U.S. and the U.S.S.R. In H. C. Kelman (Ed.), *International behavior: A social-psychological analysis* (pp. 238–276). New York: Holt, Rinehart and Winston.

White, R. K. (1970). *Nobody wanted war: Misperception in Vietnam and other wars.* Garden City, NY: Doubleday.

White, R. K. (2004). Misperception and war. *Peace and Conflict: Journal of Peace Psychology, 10*(4), 399–409.

3

Emotion and Emotion Regulation in Intergroup Conflict
An Appraisal-Based Framework

ERAN HALPERIN, KEREN SHARVIT, and JAMES J. GROSS

"The sheer passion expended in pursuing ethnic conflict calls out for an explanation that does justice to the realm of feelings ... A bloody phenomenon cannot be explained by a bloodless theory."

(Horowitz, 1985, p. 140)

Scholars who study international relations and ethnic conflicts have long recognized the central role played by emotions in conflict escalation, de-escalation, and resolution (Horowitz, 1985; Lindner, 2006; Petersen, 2002). This suggests that psychological research has much to contribute to the understanding of large-scale protracted conflicts, which are the ones typically addressed in the international relations literature. Surprisingly, however, psychologists have devoted relatively little attention to the role of emotion and emotion regulation in such intense conflicts.

Our goal in this chapter is to present a general framework for examining emotion and emotion regulation in intergroup conflict situations. Our focus is on intense intractable conflicts. However, given the paucity of psychological research on the role of emotions in such conflicts, we draw upon findings from the broader domain of emotions and intergroup relations. We begin our chapter by defining key concepts in the study of emotion, emotion regulation and the psychology of intergroup conflicts. We then introduce a conceptual framework for examining how emotion and emotion regulation affect individuals' beliefs, attitudes and behaviors regarding the conflict. Next, based on a review of the literature, we apply our framework to three stages of intergroup conflicts—conflict outbreak, de-escalation, and reconciliation. We conclude by discussing ideas for future research.

BASIC DEFINITIONS AND CONCEPTS

Emotions

Despite spectacular growth in the field of emotion (Lewis, Haviland-Jones, & Barrett, 2008), a consensual definition of the concept is still elusive. Part of the difficulty here is that there are fundamental disagreements regarding the theoretical boundaries of the field. Because the term "emotion" is drawn from common usage, there remains disagreement about the phenomena that require explanation (e.g., emotional words, emotional experience, emotional expressions, or emotional behavior; see Frijda, 2004; Niedenthal, Krauth-Gruber, & Ric, 2006).

In this chapter, we adopt William James's (1884) classical perspective on emotions as response tendencies. According to this view, emotions are flexible response sequences (Frijda, 1986; Scherer, 1984) that are called forth whenever an individual evaluates a situation as offering important challenges or opportunities (Tooby & Cosmides, 1990). In other words, emotions transform a substantive event into a motivation to respond to it in a particular manner (Zajonc, 1998).

Core components of emotion include subjective feelings, bodily changes, facial expressions, and other physiological reactions. These components help to distinguish emotions from other phenomena such as attitudes or beliefs (Cacioppo & Gardner, 1999). However, our perspective on emotions highlights the role of two additional components—cognitive appraisals and response tendencies—which we see as central to the understanding of the role of emotions in intergroup conflicts.

Recognition of the symbiotic relations between emotion and cognition has led to extensive research on the cognitive aspects of discrete emotions (Lazarus, 1991; Roseman, 1984; Scherer, 2004; Smith & Ellsworth, 1985). It is now well established that in most situations, emotions include a comprehensive evaluation of the emotion-eliciting stimulus (which may be conscious or unconscious). Despite differences in terminology, it is possible to identify several appraisal dimensions that are common in the writings of most scholars. These include pleasantness, anticipated effort, attentional activity, certainty, perceived obstacles, responsibility attribution (to the self, other, or situation), and relative strength (controllability).

In addition to the appraisal component, Arnold (1960) suggested that each emotion is related to a specific action tendency. More recently, Frijda (1986) identified specific types of action readiness that characterize 17 discrete emotions. Roseman (1984) and Roseman, Wiest, and Swartz (1994) has distinguished between actions, action tendencies, and emotional goals. While general motives or goals are inherent components of each emotion, and thus can be predicted by specific emotions, the transformation of these motives into context-specific response tendencies and actual behavior depends on numerous external factors and is therefore quite flexible (Frijda, Kuipers, & ter Schure, 1989; Roseman, 2002). The classic example is of this pluripotentiality is seen with fear, which is related to the general motive of creating a safer environment, but can take the form of either fight or flight response tendencies, depending on the situation.

Emotions, Moods, Sentiments, and Group-Based Emotions

Emotions represent just one of several types of affective responses (Gross, 2007). For our purposes in this chapter, it is important to distinguish among emotions, sentiments, and moods. As we have seen, emotions are multicomponential responses to specific events. Sentiments, by contrast, are enduring configurations of emotions (Arnold, 1960; Ekman, 1992; Frijda, 1986). According to this view, an emotional sentiment is a temporally stable emotional disposition toward a person, group, or symbol (Halperin, in press). Emotional sentiments differ from moods in that moods typically do not have well-defined objects, whereas emotional sentiments do.

In recent years, there has been growing interest in the concept of group-based emotions, which refers to emotions that are felt by individuals as a result of their membership in or identification with a certain group or society (Mackie, Devos, & Smith, 2000; Smith, 1993; Smith & Mackie, 2008). Accordingly, research has shown that individuals may experience emotions not only in response to personal life events and activities, but also in response to events that affect other members of a group with which they identify (Mackie et al., 2000; Wohl, Branscombe, & Klar, 2006; Yzerbyt, Dumont, Wigboldus, & Gordin, 2003). Group-based emotions are personal experiences that can be targeted at events, individuals or social groups. In the later case, they are defined as intergroup emotions, that is, emotions that are felt as a result of the felt belongingness to a certain group, and targeted at another group (Smith, Seger, & Mackie, 2007).

On the societal level of analysis, when intergroup emotions are shared and felt simultaneously by large numbers of individuals in a certain society, they are defined as collective emotions (Bar-Tal, 2001; Stephan & Stephan, 2000). De Rivera (1992) introduced a related concept, emotional climate. He suggested that emotional climate is not the aggregate of the emotional experiences of individual society members, but rather a characteristic of the society that maintains its identity and unity. Although most of the current chapter focuses on the individual, not the societal level of analysis, it is worth noting that individual experiences of emotions occur within a certain societal context. Hence, the collective configuration of emotions—or emotional climate—is important to the understanding of the role of individualistic emotions in the context of intergroup conflicts (Bar-Tal, Halperin, & de Rivera, 2007).

Emotion Regulation

In recent years, scholars in the emerging field of emotion regulation have taken up the issue of how emotions may be altered or influenced. Typically, their focus has been individuals and interpersonal relations (Gross, 2007). This approach is grounded in previous work on psychological defenses (Freud, 1926/1959), stress and coping (Lazarus, 1966), attachment (Bowlby, 1969), and self-regulation (Mischel,

Shoda, & Rodriguez, 1989). We would argue that some of the insights that have been gained from studies of emotion regulation may be applied to the intergroup context.

At the individual level, emotion regulation refers to processes that are engaged when individuals try to influence the type or amount of emotion they (or others) experience, when they (or others) have them, and how they (or others) experience and express these emotions (Gross, 1998). Emotion regulation may be automatic or controlled, conscious or unconscious, and may have its effects at one or more points in the emotion generative process. Emotion regulation may change the degree to which emotion response components cohere as the emotion unfolds, such as when large changes in emotion experience and physiological responding occur in the absence of facial behavior.

The current literature points out five families of emotion regulation processes: situation selection, situation modification, attentional deployment, cognitive change, and response modulation (Gross, 1998). These families are distinguished by the point in the emotion-generative process at which they have their primary impact (Gross & Thompson, 2007). For example, the "situation selection" strategy occurs very early in the process and involves actions that make it more (or less) likely that one will end up in situations that are expected to give rise to desirable (or undesirable) emotions. In contrast, the "response modulation" strategy occurs late in the emotion-generative process, after response tendencies have been initiated. Despite the importance of all other regulatory strategies, our focus in this chapter is on processes of cognitive change. The main reason for this selection is the expected applicability of this strategy to large-scale intergroup conflicts. In particular, we focus on attempts to reappraise the ongoing events in order to up- or downregulate certain intergroup emotions.

Intractable Intergroup Conflicts

Social conflicts are usually defined as situations where "two or more persons or groups manifest the belief that they have incompatible objectives" (Kriesberg, 2007, p. 2; Mitchell, 1981; Rubin, Pruitt, & Kim, 1994). From a psychological perspective, the appearance of a belief regarding contradictory goals or interests is always a dual-stage process. The first stage involves subjective evaluations regarding the in-group's goals, the other group's goals and the interaction between them. In the second stage, the evaluation is expressed in a motivation and readiness to act in a certain way. Hence, cognitive appraisals and response tendencies, both embedded within the structure of emotions, are an integral part of the most basic definition of conflict, attesting to their importance.

Different scholars refer to different stages of conflicts (Mitchell, 1981). Kriesberg (2007) provided a recent notable example, which described the three main stages for each conflict: (1) the emergence, outbreak or manifestation of the conflict; (2) the escalation of the conflict; and (3) its de-escalation and settlement. Other scholars have recently discussed another important stage of conflict, namely reconciliation (Gibson, 2006). In the present chapter, we examine the role of emotion and emotion regulation in three stages of intergroup conflict: conflict outbreak and escalation, conflict de-escalation and reconciliation.

The current chapter adopts a bottom-up perspective, according to which, emotions, attitudes and actions of individuals and groups influence the course of the conflict. This psychology of the "people" is even more important in intractable conflicts than in other contexts, because intractable conflicts are so often violent and protracted, demand extensive investment, play a central role in the lives of the involved societies, and are perceived as total, irresolvable and being zero-sum (Bar-Tal, 1998; Kriesberg, 1993). According to Bar-Tal (2007), societies that are involved in these kinds of conflicts develop a unique psychological repertoire, which includes a system of conflict-related societal beliefs (i.e., "ethos of conflict"), a biased collective memory of the history of the conflict, and a highly negative "collective emotional orientation" toward the opponent (Bar-Tal & Halperin, Chapter 9, this volume).

The role that the emotional component of this repertoire plays in maintaining the conflict is central to the current framework. The nature of long-term, intractable conflicts creates a fertile ground for the continuation and aggregation of emotions beyond the immediate time frame. Some major conflict-related events, which may be accompanied by repeated dissemination of specific information about the conflict, may produce stable group-based emotional sentiments toward the opponent and the conflict. As a result, stable negative intergroup emotions such as fear, anger and hatred become an inherent part of the standing psychological context of individuals in such conflicts (Kelman, 1997). The interaction between these emotional sentiments and the emotions that arise in response to conflict-related events, as well as their joint influence on attitudes and actions, stands at the center of our proposed appraisal-based framework.

EMOTIONS AND EMOTION REGULATION IN INTERGROUP CONFLICT: AN APPRAISAL-BASED FRAMEWORK

Despite increased interest in the role of emotion in conflicts, we are aware of no comprehensive framework for understanding how emotions influence individual and collective beliefs, attitudes and behaviors regarding war and peace. In the following section, we introduce a new appraisal-based framework that captures key aspects of this process, and may therefore be useful as a theoretical platform for future empirical work in the field. The first part of our appraisal-based framework (bold circles in Figure 3.1) describes the sequence of processes by which emotional sentiments and emotions contribute to the formation of specific attitudinal and behavioral responses to conflict related events.

The process begins with the occurrence of a new event and/or appearance of new information related to the conflict and/or recollection of a past conflict related event. The event or information can be negative (e.g., war, terror attack, and rejection of a peace offer) or positive (e.g., a peace gesture and willingness to compromise), but it must be appraised as meaningful. Although events can be experienced personally, in most cases they are experienced directly by few group members and transmitted to other group members through the mediation of leaders, the mass media or other individuals. In these cases, if individuals identify with the same

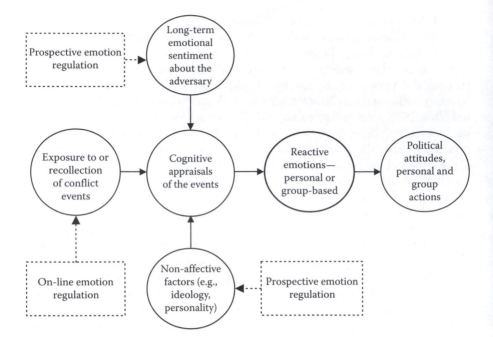

Figure 3.1   An appraisal-based framework for emotions and emotion regulation in conflicts.

group as the directly exposed individuals, they would experience group-based emotions (Mackie et al., 2000; Smith, 1993).

Such short-term events will elicit individual and group-based emotions and the ensuing political response tendencies, depending on the manner in which they are appraised. For example, a violent act committed by out-group members toward the in-group that is appraised as unjust and is accompanied by the evaluation of the in-group as strong would induce anger (Halperin, 2008; Huddy, Feldman, & Cassese, 2007). Hence, the subjective appraisal of an event is a crucial factor in determining the kind of emotion that will result from the event.

According to the proposed framework, in the context of long-term conflicts, the appraisal of events is influenced by three main factors. First, the event may be framed in a certain way, and this framing influences individuals' appraisal of the event (Halperin, in press). Different frames for the same event may lead to different cognitive appraisals, which, in turn, will lead to different emotional responses (Gross, 2008). For example, if a military action by the opponent is framed as a defensive response to previous militant actions by one's own side, it may elicit fear or possibly sadness. But if framed as an aggressive action with no justified causes, it may lead to extreme anger or even hatred.

Second, the appraisal of the event will be influenced by a relatively wide range of nonaffective factors. An extensive review of these factors is beyond the scope of the current chapter, but a nonexhaustive list of them would include personality factors (e.g., authoritarianism, need for structure, and implicit theories), adherence to moral values, socio-economic status, and long-term ideology about the conflict and the opponent (Halperin, in press; Sharvit, Halperin, & Rosler, 2008).

Finally, and most relevant, our appraisal-based framework assumes that long-term emotional sentiments will bias the cognitive appraisals of specific events (Halperin & Gross, in press). This premise is based upon the appraisal tendency framework (Lerner & Keltner, 2000), according to which each emotion activates a cognitive predisposition to interpret events in line with the central appraisal dimensions that triggered the emotion. For example, long-term external threat to the group will make society members more attuned to threatening cues and will lead to higher appraised danger that will elicit, in turn, more frequent fear responses (Bar-Tal et al., 2007).

We suggest that the occurrence of a new event, integrated with these three groups of factors, will shape the cognitive appraisal of the event, which will provide the basis for the development of corresponding discrete emotions. In turn, these discrete emotions, and particularly the emotional goals and response tendencies embedded within them, will dictate the behavioral and political responses to the event (Halperin, in press).

The first part of the proposed framework considers the central role of discrete emotions in determining reactions to conflict related events. In the second part of the framework (striped lines boxes in Figure 3.1) we describe two possible paths for the regulation of these emotions in the context of intergroup conflicts through their various phases. It is worth noting that, to the best of our knowledge, strategies of emotion regulation have never been empirically tested in the context of inter-group relations and conflict resolution. Hence, this part of the framework is specu-lative and requires empirical validation.

As noted, prior work on emotion regulation at the individual level has focused on several strategies that may be used to regulate emotions (Gross, 1998). We believe that the most relevant strategy in the context of protracted intergroup conflicts is emotion regulation through cognitive change and, more specifically, reappraisal. Reappraisal involves changing a situation's meaning in a way that alters its emotional impact (Gross, 2002). The most direct way to create cognitive change is to ask individuals to reappraise, consider alternative perspectives or rethink their interpretation of events or information (Ochsner & Gross, 2008). Although this procedure was quite successful in reducing negative emotions in individual and inter-personal settings, it is not as clearly applicable to the context of intergroup conflict. The main reason is that the psychological repertoire of the conflict is often so deeply entrenched (Bar-Tal, 2007) that individuals are unlikely to be willing to change it upon request. Hence, we would argue that creating cognitive change in such a context is most likely to be achieved by using indirect ways. In particular, we believe that it is important to distinguish between two types of reappraisal: online reappraisal and prospective reappraisal.

Online reappraisal refers to "the attempt to change emotion that starts and con-tinuously operates while the emotion-triggering event unfolds" (Sheppes & Meiran, 2007, p. 1518). In the context of intergroup conflict, this process pertains to cognitive change that may be caused by altering the manner in which events are presented to the public or framed. This process can begin only after the occurrence of an event, and would be effective mainly if the process of reappraisal begins very soon after the triggering event (Sheppes & Meiran, 2007). Hence, the dissemination of a desired interpretation or frame of the event to the public should start immediately after the occurrence of the event. Such a frame should highlight specific appraisals that correspond with emotions that serve constructive purposes while avoiding the use of appraisals that are associated with destructive emotions. For example, in order to upregulate group-based guilt in response to the failure of a peace summit, the media reports may immediately highlight the in-group's responsibility for the failure, since appraisal of in-group responsibility is important for the emotional experience of group-based guilt (Wohl et al., 2006).

But successful regulation of emotions in long-term conflicts should not begin only after the appearance of a triggering event. Previous findings have demonstrated the effectiveness of reappraisal when it is initiated in advance of emotion-triggering events (Gross & Levenson, 1997). Therefore, our framework introduces a new strategy of emotion regulation through cognitive change, namely prospective reappraisal. The logic underlying prospective reappraisal is that significant changes in the long-term emotional sentiments and beliefs of members of groups that are involved intergroup conflicts will alter their appraisals and resulting emotional reactions to specific events. Specifically, the reduction of negative intergroup sentiments or the moderation of long-term negative beliefs prior to the events can alter the manner in which individuals will eventually interpret the events. For example, the manner in which individuals appraise a new peace proposal by the opponent may be highly dependent on the levels of long-term hatred they feel toward that opponent. Hence, reducing levels of long-term hatred may create a fertile ground for more constructive emotional responses to positive as well as negative conflict-related events. This strategy is highly suitable to the unique context of intergroup conflict, because it overcomes the difficulties in "real time" regulation of emotions among large populations.

An additional advantage of prospective reappraisal is its ability to affect the type of response tendencies that will arise once an emotion is elicited. In other words, prospective reappraisal may bring about both quantitative (e.g., lower levels of fear) or qualitative (e.g., "flight" instead of "fight" response tendencies to fear) change in the experienced emotion. This strategy of emotion regulation seems more applicable (e.g., through educational channels), yet changing such long-term emotions and beliefs may be very difficult (Bar-Tal & Halperin, Chapter 9, this volume).

APPLYING THE MODEL IN DIFFERENT STAGES OF THE CONFLICT

Our appraisal-based framework captures the four-step process of event → emotional-response → emotion regulation → political-position/behavior. We believe that this framework may usefully be applied to three major stages of intergroup conflicts: conflict outbreak and escalation, conflict de-escalation, and reconciliation. In the following sections, we review findings from research conducted in different conflicts in order to highlight the roles played by emotion and emotion regulation at each conflict phase. We divide the discussion of each stage into two parts. The first part focuses on the role of emotions in a given stage, and is descriptive in its nature. The second part considers how online and prospective reappraisal may be used to diminish conflict, and takes a normative approach.

It should be noted that most empirical studies to date have focused solely on the specific link between emotions and political positions/behavior regarding the conflict, and have not incorporated other aspects of the model (e.g., appraisals and emotion regulation). Hence, since our aim is to propose a model that is broader than the ones previously tested, we use our comprehensive framework to evaluate previous empirical studies and to generate predictions for future investigations.

Conflict Outbreak and Escalation

This stage refers to the manifestation or transformation of latent disagreements into a violent conflict. It involves decision-making processes by leaders, which, in democratic societies, must be backed up by public support. This kind of support is essential due to the high risk and potential sacrifices required from the people involved. The degree to which society members support various courses of aggressive collective action may largely depend on their emotions.

Emotions and the Outbreak/Escalation of Conflicts   The emotion that has been most frequently studied with respect to this stage of the conflict is anger. Anger is evoked by events in which the individual perceives the actions of others as unjust, unfair or as deviating from acceptable societal norms (Averill, 1982). In addition, it involves appraisals of relative strength and high coping potential (Mackie et al., 2000). The integration of these two characteristics often creates a tendency to confront (Berkowitz, 1993; Mackie et al., 2000), hit, kill or attack the anger evoking target (Roseman et al., 1994).

In line with its characteristics, previous studies conducted in the context of real-world conflicts have consistently found a clear and direct association between anger and attribution of blame to the out-group (Halperin, 2008; Small, Lerner, & Fischhoff, 2006). Other studies found that individuals who feel angry appraise future military attacks as less risky (Lerner & Keltner, 2001) and forecast more positive consequences of such attacks (Huddy et al., 2007). Accordingly, studies conducted in the United States following the 9/11 attacks found that angry individuals were highly supportive of an American military response in Iraq and elsewhere (Cheung-Blunden & Blunden, 2008; Huddy et al., 2007; Lerner, Gonzalez, Small, & Fischhoff, 2003; Skitka, Bauman, Aramovich, & Morgan, 2006). This type of reaction is exactly the kind that promotes escalation of conflicts.

Fortunately, in most cases, anger is not the only emotion triggered by the opponent's provocations, aggressive statements or military actions. Other emotional reactions, such as fear, may tone down the response tendencies of anger. Fear arises in situations of perceived threat and danger to individuals and/or their environment or society, and enables adaptive responses (Gray, 1989). Fear is associated with an appraisal of low strength and low control over the situation (Roseman, 1984), as well as increased risk estimates and pessimistic predictions (Lerner & Keltner, 2001). Behaviorally, fear is related to avoidance tendencies and a desire to create a safe environment (Frijda et al., 1989; Roseman et al., 1994). Therefore, at this stage of the conflict, fear may discourage group members from engaging in violent military activities, due to elevated risk estimates and avoidance tendencies. Indeed, several studies have found that fear reactions among Americans to the 9/11 terror attacks increased estimated risks of terrorism and war (Huddy et al., 2007; Lerner et al., 2003) and decreased support for military activities and the war in Iraq (Huddy et al., 2007).

As suggested by our proposed theoretical model, short-term emotions develop in a context of more enduring emotional sentiments toward the out-group. The most destructive emotional sentiment that influences beliefs, attitudes and behaviors at the stage of conflict outbreak is hatred. Hatred is a secondary, extreme, negative emotion (Royzman, McCauley, & Rosin, 2005; Sternberg & Sternberg, 2008) with a potentially destructive impact on intergroup relations (Halperin, 2008; Petersen, 2002; Volkan, 1997). It is directed at a particular individual or group and denounces them fundamentally and all inclusively (Sternberg, 2003). In most cases, hatred involves appraisal of the behavior of an out-group as stemming from a deep-rooted, permanent evil character. As a result, hatred is associated with very low expectations for positive change, and with high levels of despair.

The evaluation of short-term conflict-related events through the lens of hatred automatically increases support for initiating violent actions and for escalating the conflict (Staub, 2005). If one is convinced of the destructive intentions of the out-group and feels total despair regarding the likelihood of the out-group changing its ways, the violent alternative may seem as the only reasonable one. A recent study conducted in Israel at the eve of the Annapolis peace summit in 2007 found that above and beyond any other emotion, sentimental hatred increased the tendency of Israelis to support extreme military action toward Palestinians (Halperin, in press).

Corresponding with the proposed framework, we suggest that the level of long-term hatred may also influence the behavioral manifestations of anger. Anger that occurs in the presence of high levels of hatred will most likely bring about an extreme aggressive reaction. In contrast, anger that occurs in the presence of low levels of hatred may lead to more constructive approach tendencies (Fischer & Roseman, 2007). If one believes that the opponent group can change its behavior and that its intentions are defensive or innocent (i.e., low levels of hatred), the "high strength" appraisal embedded in anger may create a tendency to engage in constructive problem solving and crisis management, instead of the more common violent reaction (Halperin, 2008, in press).

Emotion Regulation and the Outbreak/Escalation of Conflicts   If one wish to avoid escalation of the conflict, emotion regulation should play a crucial role in the stage of decision making regarding possible offensive actions. Strategies of online reappraisal can be used in order to up-regulate levels of reactive fear and down regulate anger. For these purposes, the framing of events and the assessments of possible responses to them should highlight the high risks involved in initiating military action. This should be done by emphasizing the strengths of the opponent and the weaknesses of one's own side. In addition, the

conveyed message should be as balanced as possible regarding the responsibility of both sides to the situation. Such information may reduce the levels of appraised unfairness and injustice and therefore reduce levels of anger.

Strategies of prospective reappraisal should focus on attempts to reduce levels of long-term hatred toward the opponent and despair about the situation. These attempts should emphasize humanness and heterogeneity of the out-group as well as the ability of individuals and groups to change their characteristics, moral-values, positions, and behavior (Dweck, Chiu, & Hong, 1995). In addition, strategies of perspective taking can be used, in order to increase understanding regarding the motives and goals of the adversary (Galinsky & Moskowitz, 2000). We propose that such long-term processes, disseminated through education channels, cultural products and other societal mechanisms, will alter the behavioral manifestations of reactive negative emotions, which are themselves natural and legitimate responses to offensive acts or provocations.

De-escalation of the Conflict

This stage involves attempts to achieve some sort of conflict resolution or even a formal peace agreement. In most cases de-escalation is a nonlinear, long and difficult process. It involves breaking such well-established taboos as negotiating with enemies, who had been formerly considered "murderers" or "terrorists." In addition, it requires a difficult process of compromises on important interests or even ideological beliefs. Public views play a central role in inhibiting or encouraging these processes.

Emotions and De-escalation   As a result of the drawn-out nature of this process, long-term emotional sentiments play a pivotal role. Two contradictory and powerful sentiments dominate this process—fear and hope (Jarymowicz & Bar-Tal, 2006). Any step toward peaceful resolution of intergroup conflicts requires willingness to take risks. Therefore, the emotional sentiment of fear, which hinders the willingness to take risks, is frequently considered as the most significant barrier to resolution.

In contrast to the restraining role of reactive fear at the escalation stage, once violent conflict is already in motion, sentimental fear may stabilize the violent situation and prevent mutual attempts to negotiate. More specifically, research suggests that experiences of threat and fear increase conservatism, prejudice, ethnocentrism, and intolerance (Duckitt & Fisher, 2003; Feldman & Stenner, 1997; Jost, Glaser, Kruglanski, & Sulloway, 2003; Stephan & Stephan, 2000). Due to recurring experiences of threat and danger resulting from the conflict, society members may become over-sensitized to cues that signal danger and exist in a state of constant readiness to defend themselves (Jarymowicz & Bar-Tal, 2006).

The other important sentiment in the stage of conflict de-escalation is hope. Hope involves expectation and aspiration for a positive goal, as well as positive feelings about the anticipated outcome (Staats & Stassen, 1985). Hope facilitates goal-setting, planning, use of imagery, creativity, cognitive flexibility, mental exploration of novel situations, and even risk taking (Breznitz, 1986; Snyder, 1994).

Consequently, hope allows members of groups that are involved in violent conflicts to imagine a future that is different from the past and to come up with creative solutions to the disputes at the core of the conflict (Jarymowicz & Bar-Tal, 2006). The belief that peaceful resolution of the conflict is possible is an essential step toward taking risks and compromising. Indeed, a study conducted in Northern Ireland found that hope was positively related to the dissipation of the desire to retaliate, which, in turn, was positively related to willingness to forgive the adversary (Moeschberger, Dixon, Niens, & Cairns, 2005).

Regarding the negative emotions, it would be rather tempting to suggest that emotions like anger or hatred, which contribute to the outbreak and escalation of conflicts, also play a role in the continuation and maintenance of the conflict. As far as hatred is concerned, this prediction has proven valid. One recent study found that individuals who experienced short-term episodes of hatred in times of negotiations in the Middle East tended to reject any positive information about the opponent, and oppose continuation of negotiations, compromise and reconciliation (Halperin, in press).

In the case of anger, however, research presents a mixed picture regarding its role in efforts to de-escalate conflicts. At this stage, anger may result from perceived regression in the willingness of the other side to achieve peace or from violent actions of extremists during negotiations. Studies conducted in Northern Ireland and in Spain regarding the conflict in the Basque country have demonstrated that anger toward the opponent may constitute a significant emotional barrier in the face of potential compromises, consistent with its role at the escalation stage (Paez, 2007; Tam et al., 2007). Yet in other cases, anger appears to increase support for risk-taking in negotiations, and consequently may contribute to the peaceful resolution of conflicts (Halperin, in press; Reifen, Halperin, & Federico, 2008). We suggest that anger always activates an approach tendency, but the nature of the actual response (i.e., constructive versus destructive) may be determined by concomitant levels of sentimental fear, hatred and hope.

Another important category of emotions that may contribute to processes of de-escalation of conflicts are moral emotions targeted at the in-group (Rozin, Lowery, Imada, & Haidt, 1999). During the process of negotiation toward conflict resolution, certain events or new information about the in-group's actions (e.g., attacks against noncombatants) may bring about severe threat to the positive self image of group members. Such threat may give rise to group-based moral emotions, which are defined as emotional reactions to a behavior that is appraised as violating basic moral values in which one believes (for a recent review see Tangney, Stuewig, & Mashek, 2007). The most frequently studied moral emotions in the context of conflicts are group-based guilt and shame.

Group-based guilt is associated with an appraisal that one's in-group is responsible for actions that violate norms or values to which the group is committed (Branscombe, 2004). Guilt is focused on the wrongdoing itself and not on the characteristics of the violator (Tangney, Wagner, Fletcher, & Gramzow, 1992). Consequently, it motivates group members to rectify the wrongdoing and to compensate the victims (Doosje, Branscombe, Spears, & Manstead, 1998; Iyer, Leach, & Crosby, 2003).

Numerous studies conducted in the contexts of various conflicts (e.g., Bosnia, South-Africa, and Middle East) have demonstrated that individuals who recognize their own group's responsibility for the harm caused to the opponents and experience collective guilt, are motivated to compensate and offer reparations to the victims of their own group's actions (Brown & Cehajic, 2008; Brown, González, Zagefka, & Cehajic, 2008; Klandermans, Werner, & van Doorn, 2008; Pagano & Huo, 2007; Sharvit et al., 2008; Wohl et al., 2006). As such, guilt may contribute to improving the relations between opponent groups and facilitate the process of conflict resolution.

Group-based shame is also associated with an appraisal of improper behavior on the part of in-group members (Lazarus, 1999). Yet unlike guilt, shame implies that the wrongdoing reflects on the general character of the perpetrators (Tangney et al., 1992). Consequently, the response tendencies associated with shame are targeted toward the self. Therefore, the contribution of shame to the peaceful resolution of the conflicts is less clear. Although evidence exists for positive effects of shame on constructive political tendencies (Brown & Cehajic, 2008; Brown et al., 2008), in most cases shame only leads to a desire to distance the in-group from the shame-invoking situation (Iyer, Schmader, & Lickel, 2007; Sharvit et al., 2008).

De-escalation and Emotion Regulation

In order to facilitate conflict de-escalation and resolution, online efforts should be made to upregulate group-based guilt, while avoiding the up-regulation of shame. For these purposes, knowledge of the in-group's wrongdoings (e.g., torture, oppression, and killing of innocents) should be disseminated to the public on a frequent basis, in order to give rise to perceptions of threat to the group's positive image and induce appraisals of collective responsibility for the wrongdoings. This information should be framed in a way that does not reflect negatively on the appraised dispositions of group members. In other words, in order to give rise to group-based guilt and not shame, group members must believe that they have the ability to change their behavior and improve their image by turning to the path of peace.

Prospective emotion regulation efforts at this stage should focus on down-regulation of long-term fear. Previous research has shown that in early stages of intergroup conflict (i.e., the escalation stage), emphasizing the relative strength of the in-group may reduce levels of fear and lead to confrontation tendencies (Mackie et al., 2000). We suggest that during the de-escalation stage, the same regulatory process (i.e., highlighting in-group strengths and out-group weaknesses) may reduce the fear of risk-taking in attempts to achieve peace, and hence increase support for negotiations with the opponent and for compromises.

The long-term efforts to reduce fear should be accompanied by consistent attempts to establish sentiments of hope about the future of the conflict. Inducing hope in long-term conflicts poses a considerable challenge mainly because many members of the societies involved in these conflicts have never experienced a peaceful situation, and hence cannot imagine the benefits of peace. Therefore, efforts to induce hope should highlight realistic and concrete goals and allow the generation of pragmatic means of achieving such goals (Halperin, Bar-Tal, Nets-Zehngut, &

Almog, 2008). A nonexhaustive list of possible means of stimulating such a process may include frequent presentation of positive changes that took place in other similar conflicts around the world, emphasizing incremental theories about change-ability in groups' characteristics and behaviors (Rydell, Hugenberg, Ray, & Mackie, 2007) and highlighting the moderate segments within the opponent group.

Reconciliation

The end of violence and even formal resolution of the conflict do not necessarily result in genuinely peaceful relations among the parties (Kriesberg, 1998; Lederach, 1997). Often, a longer process of reconciliation is required in order to allow stable, peaceful relations between the groups. Reconciliation involves a deep psycho-logical and cultural transformation that goes beyond a formal resolution of the conflict (Bar-Tal, 2008; Kelman, 1997; Lederach, 1997). Such process requires perspective change, as well as change in everyday activities of group members.

Emotions and Reconciliation   The two most prominent emotions in the stage of reconciliation are forgiveness and empathy. Forgiveness is usually defined as an emotional process that involves letting go of past anger and resentment (Baumeister, Exline, & Sommer, 1998; Enright & Fitzgibbons, 2000). Accordingly, two studies conducted among Protestants and Catholics in Northern Ireland revealed that anger toward the opponent group was negatively related to willing-ness to forgive (Tam et al., 2007; Tam et al., 2008a, 2008b). What follows is that a process aimed at promoting forgiveness should involve acknowledgment of mutual responsibility for atrocities committed during the conflict and increasing the understanding of the out-group's past motives and interests.

Another emotional process that is important for reconciliation is empathy, which is an other-oriented emotional state that stems from the perceived affective state of others and is congruent with their perceived welfare (Batson, Ahmad, Lishner, & Tsang, 2005). Behaviorally, empathy induces a desire to help others and do justice to them (Zhou, Valiente, & Eisenberg, 2003). Several studies conducted in the postconflict settings of Northern Ireland (Moeschberger et al., 2005; Tam et al., 2008b) and Bosnia (Cehajic, Brown, & Castano, 2008) reveal a positive relationship between empathy and willingness to forgive the opponents. Another study conducted in Israel found that empathy felt by Arab children toward Jewish children was negatively related to support for violence (Shechtman & Basheer, 2005). Nadler and Liviatan (2006) suggested that exposure to expressions of empathy by an adversary may also facilitate willingness to reconcile.

Emotion Regulation and Reconciliation   One may consider the entire process of reconciliation as a process of regulation of intergroup emotions that follows the formal resolution of the conflict. Throughout this process both parties to the conflict face the tremendous challenge of down regulating such long-term negative emotions as fear, hatred and anger, which have gradually built up and aggregated over years of conflict. We suggest that the process of reconciliation inherently involves emotion regulation through reappraisal of past events. In other words, contrary to the two previous stages of the conflict, which were character-ized by emotional reactions to new conflict related events, the main challenge of the stage of reconciliation is to create conditions that allow constructive coping with recollections of past atrocities committed by both parties.

For these purposes, most regulatory efforts in the stage of reconciliation should focus on long-term (prospective) attempts to increase empathy toward the out-group. It appears that the dynamic of reducing intergroup hatred has much in common with inducing intergroup empathy. Hence, very similar to the strategy of reducing hatred, the central route to intergroup empathy involves efforts to encour-age members of each side to adopt the perspective of the other side (Davis, 1994) and to imagine how the opponents feel (Batson, Early, & Salvarani, 1997).

A recent study conducted among Catholics and Protestants in Northern Ireland (Tam et al., 2008a) found that the opportunity to create intergroup friendships was a major antecedent of perspective taking and empathy. These results and the more general findings regarding the positive effect of contact on intergroup relations (Pettigrew & Tropp, 2006) stress the need to institutionalize occasions for inter-group contact at this stage of the conflict beyond sporadic, random intergroup encounters.

Another recent study conducted in two different postconflict contexts—indigenous–nonindigenous relations in Chile and the mid-1990s war in Bosnia—found that reminders of in-group responsibility for past wrongdoings, combined with re-humanization of the previously de-humanized out-group, significantly elevated levels of out-group empathy (Cehajic, Brown, & González, 2008). We suggest that regulation of the abovementioned antecedents of empathy is a long and difficult educational process that should include a coordinated effort of NGOs, academia, formal education systems and even the mass-media.

DIRECTIONS FOR FUTURE RESEARCH

Intractable intergroup conflicts are saturated with negative emotions such as anger and fear. They also involve high levels of negative sentiments such as hatred and despair. These negative emotions and sentiments powerfully influence the manner in which ongoing events are appraised and the responses to them. Hence, any comprehensive psychological explanation to the development and potential resolution of such conflicts must take into account the central role of emotions in these processes.

In this chapter we have introduced a new conceptual framework for the role of emotions and emotion regulation in intergroup conflict. According to the descriptive part of the model, framing processes, long-term sentiments toward the out-group and deep rooted beliefs about the conflict and the out-group shape group members' appraisals of conflict-related events. These appraisals, in turn, give rise to emotions, which widely influence individuals' political and behavioral responses to events.

From a prescriptive perspective, we have proposed two different paths of emotion regulation that may mitigate the impact of destructive emotions in intergroup conflicts while intensifying the effect of constructive emotions, thus contributing to processes of conflict resolution and reconciliation. The incorporation of emotion regulation theory introduces a new perspective to the study of emotions in conflict. The main assumption underlying this perspective is that the potent effect of emotions in intergroup conflicts can and should be utilized for purposes of building viable peace and reconciliation. As described in the chapter, sensitive regulation of emotions among group members can greatly contribute to this important but difficult process.

Despite important developments in recent years, the study of emotions in conflict is still in its initial stages. Further theoretical work is needed in order to elaborate key aspects of the proposed framework. In addition, specific predictions of the proposed framework should be empirically tested in different contexts and conflicts around the world. These future efforts should be based upon a theoretical and empirical integration of all relevant sub-fields, namely, the study of international conflicts, the study of emotions and the study of emotion regulation.

The framework we introduced paves the route toward such integration and suggests several directions for future studies. First, further research may identify the specific roles of discrete emotions in different stages of conflicts. This research must address the unique interaction between long-term and short-term emotions and their confluence on conflict related political processes. Yet, such efforts will not be satisfactory unless they are followed by attempts to discover means of regulating these emotions in the unique context of conflict. In a way, one of the most important challenges of our field would be to identify ways in which large-scale strategies of emotion regulation might transform the destructive power of intergroup emotions in conflicts into a more constructive one.

REFERENCES

Arnold, M. B. (1960). *Emotion and personality* (Vols. 1 and 2). New York: Columbia University Press.

Averill, J. R. (1982). *Anger and aggression: An essay on emotion.* New York: Springer-Verlag.

Bar-Tal, D. (1998). Societal beliefs in times of intractable conflict: The Israeli case. *International Journal of Conflict Management, 9,* 22–50.

Bar-Tal, D. (2001). Why does fear override hope in societies engulfed by intractable conflict, as it does in the Israeli society? *Political Psychology, 22,* 601–627.

Bar-Tal, D. (2007). Societal-psychological foundations of intractable conflicts. *American Behavioral Scientist, 50,* 1430–1453.

Bar-Tal, D., (2008). Reconciliation as a foundation of culture of peace. In J. de Rivera (Ed.), *Handbook on building cultures for peace* (pp. 363–377). New York: Springer.

Bar-Tal, D., Halperin, E., & de Rivera, J. (2007). Collective emotions in conflict: Societal implications. *Journal of Social Issues, 63,* 441–460.

Batson, C. D., Ahmad, N., Lishner, D. A., & Tsang, J. A. (2005). Empathy and altruism. In C. R. Snyder & S. J. Lopez (Eds.), *Handbook of positive psychology* (pp. 485–498). Oxford: Oxford University Press.

Batson, C. D., Early, S., & Salvarani, G. (1997). Perspective taking: Imagining how another feels versus imagining how you would feel. *Personality and Social Psychology Bulletin, 23,* 751–758.

Baumeister, R., Exline, J. J., & Sommer, K. L. (1998). The victim role, grudge theory, and two dimensions of forgiveness. In E. L. Worthington (Ed.), *Dimensions of forgiveness: Psychology research and theoretical perspectives* (pp. 79–104). Philadelphia: Templeton Foundation Press.

Berkowitz, L. (1993). *Aggression: Its causes, consequences and control*. Philadelphia: Temple University Press.

Bowlby, J. (1969). *Attachment and loss: Attachment*. New York: Basic Books.

Branscombe, N. R. (2004). A social psychological process perspective on collective guilt. In N. R. Branscombe & B. Doosje (Eds.), *Collective guilt: International perspectives* (pp. 320–334). New York: Cambridge University Press.

Breznitz, S. (1986). The effect of hope on coping with stress. In M. H. Appley & R. Trumbull (Eds.), *Dynamics of stress: Physiological, psychological and social perspectives* (pp. 295–306). New York: Plenum Press.

Brown, R., & Cehajic, S. (2008). Dealing with the past and facing the future: Mediators of the effects of collective guilt and shame in Bosnia and Herzegovina. *European Journal of Social Psychology, 38*, 669–684.

Brown, R., González, R., Zagefka, H., & Cehajic, S. (2008). Nuestra Culpa: collective guilt and shame as predictors of reparation for historical wrongdoing. *Journal of Personality and Social Psychology, 94*, 75–90.

Cacioppo, J. T., & Gardner, W. L. (1999). Emotion. *Annual Review of Psychology, 50*, 191–214.

Cehajic, S., Brown, R., & Castano, E. (2008). Forgive and Forget? Antecedents and consequences of intergroup forgiveness in Bosnia and Herzegovina. *Political Psychology, 29*, 351–367.

Cehajic, S., Brown, R., & González, R. (2008). What do I care? Perceived ingroup responsibility and dehumanization as predictors of empathy felt for the victim group. (Unpublished manuscript).

Cheung-Blunden, V., & Blunden, B. (2008). The emotional construal of war: Anger, fear and other negative emotions. *Peace and Conflict—Journal of Peace Psychology, 14*, 123–150.

Davis, M. H. (1994). *Empathy: A social psychological approach*. Wisconsin: Brown & Benchmark.

de Rivera, J. (1992). Emotional climate: Social structure and emotional dynamics. In K. T. Strongman (Ed.), *International review of studies on emotion* (Vol. 2, pp. 199–218). New York: John Wiley.

Doosje, B., Branscombe, N. R., Spears, R., & Manstead, A. S. R. (1998). Guilty by association: When one's group has a negative history. *Journal of Personality and Social Psychology, 75*, 872–886.

Duckitt, J., & Fisher, K. (2003). The impact of social threat on worldview and ideological attitudes. *Political Psychology, 24*, 199–222.

Dweck, C. S., Chiu, C., & Hong, Y. (1995). Implicit theories: Elaboration and extension of the model. *Psychological Inquiry, 6*, 322–333.

Ekman, P. (1992). Facial expression of emotion: New findings, new questions. *Psychological Science, 3*, 34–38.

Enright, R. D., & Fitzgibbons, R. P. (2000). *Helping clients forgive*. Washington, DC: American Psychological Association.

Feldman, S., & Stenner, K. (1997). Perceived threat and authoritarianism. *Psychological Psychology, 18*, 741–770.

Fischer, A. H., & Roseman, I. J. (2007). Beat them or ban them: The characteristics and social functions of anger and contempt. *Journal of Personality and Social Psychology, 93*, 103–115.

Freud, S. (1959). Inhibitions, symptoms and anxiety. In 3. Strachey (Ed. and Trans.), *The standard edition of the complete psychological works of Sigmund Freud* (Vol. 20, pp. 77–175). London: Hogarth Press. (Original work published 1926).

Frijda, N. H. (1986). *The emotions*. Cambridge: Cambridge University Press.

Frijda, N. H. (2004). Emotions and action. In A. S. R. Manstead, N. Frijda, & A. Fischer (Eds.), *Feeling and emotions: The Amsterdam symposium* (pp. 158–173). Cambridge: Cambridge University Press.

Frijda, N. H., Kuipers, P., & ter Schure, E. (1989). Relations among emotion, appraisal and emotional action readiness. *Journal of Personality and Social Psychology*, 57, 212–228.

Galinsky, A. D., & Moskowitz, G. B. (2000). Perspective taking: Decreasing stereotype expression, stereotype accessibility, and ingroup favoritism. *Journal of Personality and Social Psychology*, 78, 708–724.

Gibson, J. (2006). The contribution of truth to reconciliation: Lessons from South Africa. *Journal of Conflict Resolution*, 50, 409–432.

Gray, J. A. (1989). *The psychology of fear and stress* (2nd ed.). Cambridge: Cambridge University Press.

Gross, J. J. (1998). The emerging field of emotion regulation: An integrative review. *Review of General Psychology*, 2, 271–299.

Gross, J. J. (2002). Emotion regulation: Affective, cognitive, and social consequences. *Psychophysiology*, 39, 281–291.

Gross, J. J. (2007). *Handbook of emotion regulation*. New York: Guilford Press.

Gross, J. J., & Levenson, R. W. (1997). Hiding feelings: The acute effects of inhibiting positive and negative emotions. *Journal of Abnormal Psychology*, 106, 95–103.

Gross, J. J., & Thompson, R. A. (2007). Emotion regulation: Conceptual foundations. In J. J. Gross (Ed.), *Handbook of emotion regulation* (pp. 3–24). New York: Guilford Press.

Gross, K. (2008). Framing persuasive appeals: Episodic and thematic framing, emotional response, and policy opinion. *Political Psychology*, 29, 169–192.

Halperin, E. (2008). Group-based hatred in intractable conflict in Israel. *Journal of Conflict Resolution*, 52, 713–736.

Halperin, E. (in press). Emotional barriers to peace: Negative emotions and public opinion about the peace process in the Middle East. *Peace and Conflict: Journal of Peace Psychology*.

Halperin, E., & Gross, J. J. (in press). Intergroup anger in intractable conflict: Long-term sentiments predict anger responses during the Gaza war. *Group Processes and Intergroup Relations*.

Halperin, E., Bar-Tal, D., Nets-Zehngut, R., & Almog, E. (2008). Fear and hope in conflict: Some determinants in the Israeli–Jewish society. *Peace and Conflict: Journal of Peace Psychology*, 14, 1–26.

Horowitz, D. L. (1985). *Ethnic groups in conflict*. Berkeley, CA: University of California Press.

Huddy, L., Feldman, S., & Cassese, E. (2007). On the distinct political effects of anxiety and anger. In A. Crigler, M. MacKuen, G. Marcus, & W. R. Neuman (Eds.), *The dynamics of emotion in political thinking and behavior* (pp. 202–230). Chicago, IL: Chicago University Press.

Iyer, A., Leach, C. W., & Crosby, F. J. (2003). White guilt and racial compensation: The benefits and limits of self-focus. *Personality and Social Psychology Bulletin*, 29, 117–129.

Iyer, A., Schmader, T., & Lickel, B. (2007). Why individuals protest the perceived transgressions of their country: The role of anger, shame, and guilt. *Personality and Social Psychology Bulletin*, 33, 572–587.

James, W. (1884). What is an emotion? *Mind*, 19, 188–204.

Jarymowicz, M., & Bar-Tal, D. (2006). The dominance of fear over hope in the life of individuals and collectives. *European Journal of Social Psychology*, *36*, 367–392.

Jost, J. T., Glaser, J., Kruglanski, A., & Sulloway, F. J. (2003). Political conservatism as motivated social cognition. *Psychological Bulletin*, *129*, 339–375.

Kelman, H. C. (1997). Group processes in the resolution of international conflicts: Experiences from the Israeli-Palestinian case. *American Psychologist*, *52*, 212–220.

Klandermans, B., Werner, M., & van Doorn, M. (2008). Redeeming Apartheid's legacy: Collective guilt, political ideology, and compensation. *Political Psychology*, *29*, 331–349.

Kriesberg, L. (1993). Intractable conflict. *Peace Review*, *5*, 417–421.

Kriesberg, L. (1998). Coexistence and the reconciliation of communal conflicts. In E. Weiner (Ed.), *The handbook of interethnic coexistence* (pp. 182–198). New York: The Continuum Publishing Company.

Kriesberg, L. (2007). *Constructive conflicts: From escalation to resolution* (3rd ed.). New York: Rowman and Littlefield Publishers.

Lazarus, R. S. (1966). *Psychological stress and the coping process*. New York: McGraw-Hill.

Lazarus, R. S. (1991). *Emotion and adaptation*. New York: Oxford University Press.

Lederach, J. P. (1997). *Building peace: Sustainable reconciliation in divided societies*. Washington, DC: United States Institute of Peace Press.

Lerner, J. S., & Keltner, D. (2000). Beyond valence: Toward a model of emotion-specific influences on judgment and choice. *Cognition and Emotion*, *14*, 473–493.

Lerner, J. S., Gonzalez, R. M., Small, D. A., & Fischhoff, B. (2003). Effects of fear and anger on perceived risk of terrorism: A national field experiment. *Psychological Science*, *14*, 144–150.

Lerner, J. S., & Keltner, D. (2001). Fear, anger and risk. *Journal of Personality and Social Psychology*, *81*, 1146–1159.

Lewis, M., Haviland-Jones, J. M., & Barrett, L. F. (Eds.). (2008). *Handbook of emotions* (3rd ed.). New York, NY: Guilford.

Lindner, E. G. (2006). Emotion and conflict: Why it is important to understand how emotions affect conflict and how conflict affects emotions. In M. Deutch, P. T. Coleman, & E. C. Marcus (Eds.), *The handbook of conflict resolution* (2nd ed., pp. 268–293). San Francisco: Jossey-Bass.

Mackie, D. M., Devos, T., & Smith, E. R. (2000). Intergroup emotions: Explaining offensive actions in an intergroup context. *Journal of Personality and Social Psychology*, *79*, 602–616.

Mischel, W., Shoda, Y., & Rodriguez, M. L. (1989). Delay of gratification in children. *Science*, *244*, 933–938.

Mitchell, C. R. 1981. *The structure of international conflict*. Basingstoke and London: The Macmillan Press.

Moeschberger, S. L., Dixon, D. N., Niens, U., & Cairns, E. (2005). Forgiveness in Northern Ireland: A model for peace in the midst of the "Troubles". *Peace and Conflict: Journal of Peace Psychology*, *11*, 199–214.

Nadler, A., & Liviatan, I. (2006). Intergroup reconciliation: Effects of adversary's expressions of empathy, responsibility, and recipients' trust. *Personality and Social Psychology Bulletin*, *32*, 459–470.

Niedenthal, P. M., Krauth-Gruber, S., & Ric, F. (2006). *Psychology of emotion: Interpersonal, experiential, and cognitive approaches*. New York: Psychology Press.

Ochsner, K. N., & Gross, J. J. (2008). Cognitive emotion regulation: Insights from social cognitive and affective neuroscience. *Current Directions in Psychological Science*, *17*, 153–158.

Paez, D. (2007). Emotional responses and attitudes to the talks with E.T.A. (Unpublished manuscript).

Pagano, S. J., & Huo, Y. J. (2007). The role of moral emotions in predicting support for political actions in post-war Iraq. *Political Psychology, 28*, 227–255.

Petersen, R. D. (2002). *Understanding ethnic violence: Fear, hatred, and resentment in twentieth-century Eastern Europe*. Cambridge: Cambridge University Press.

Pettigrew, T. F., & Tropp, L. R. (2006). A meta-analytic test of intergroup contact theory. *Journal of Personality and Social Psychology, 90*, 751–783.

Reifen-Tagar, M., Federico, C., & Halperin, E. (2008). *The positive effect of negative emotions in protracted conflict: The case of anger*. Paper presented at the ISPP Annual meeting, Dublin, July 2009.

Roseman, I. J. (1984). Cognitive determinants of emotions: A structural theory. In P. Shaver (Ed.), *Review of Personality and Social Psychology* (Vol. 5, pp. 11–36). Beverly Hills, CA: Sage Publications.

Roseman, I. J. (2002). Dislike, anger, and contempt: Interpersonal distancing, attack, and exclusion emotions. *Emotion Researcher, 16*, 5–6.

Roseman, I. J., Wiest, C., & Swartz, T. S. (1994). Phenomenology, behaviors, and goals differentiate discrete emotions. *Journal of Personality and Social Psychology, 67*, 206–221.

Royzman, E. B., McCauley, C., & Rosin, P. (2005). From Plato to Putnam: Four ways to think about hate. In R. J. Sternberg (Ed.), *The psychology of hate* (pp. 3–36). Washington, DC: American Psychological Association.

Rozin, P., Lowery, L., Imada, S., & Haidt, J. (1999). The CAD triad hypothesis: A mapping between three moral emotions (contempt, anger, disgust) and three moral codes (community, autonomy, divinity). *Journal of Personality and Social Psychology, 76*, 574–586.

Rubin, J. Z., Pruitt, D. G., & Kim, S. H. (1994). *Social conflict*. New York: McGraw-Hill.

Rydell, R. J., Hugenberg, K., Ray, D., & Mackie, D. M. (2007). Implicit theories about groups and stereotyping: The role of group entitativity. *Personality and Social Psychology Bulletin, 33*, 549–558.

Scherer, K. R. (1984). Emotion as a multicomponent process: A model and some cross-cultural data. *Review of Personality and Social Psychology, 5*, 37–63.

Scherer, K. R. (2004). Feeling integrate the central representation of appraisal-driven response organization in emotion. In A. S. R. Manstead, N. Frijda, & A. Fischer (Eds.), *Feeling and emotions: The Amsterdam symposium* (pp. 136–157). Cambridge: Cambridge University Press.

Sharvit, K., Halperin, E., & Rosler, N. (2008). *Forces of stability and change in prolonged occupation: Image threat, emotions, and justifying beliefs*. Paper presented at the 31st annual scientific meeting of the International Society of Political Psychology, in Paris, France.

Shechtman, Z., & Basheer, O. (2005). Normative beliefs supporting aggression of Arab children in an intergroup conflict. *Aggressive Behavior, 31*, 324–335.

Sheppes, G., & Meiran, N. (2007). Better late than never? On the dynamics of online regulation of sadness using distraction and cognitive reappraisal. *Personality and Social Psychology Bulletin, 33*, 1518–1532.

Skitka, L. J., Bauman, C. W., Aramovich, N. P., & Morgan, G. C. (2006). Confrontational and preventative policy responses to terrorism: Anger wants a fight and fear wants "them" to go away. *Basic and Applied Social Psychology, 28*, 375–384.

Small, D. A., Lerner, J. S., & Fischhoff, B. (2006). Emotion priming and attributions for terrorism: Americans' reactions in a national field experiment. *Political Psychology, 27*, 289–298.

Smith, E. R. (1993). Social identity and social emotions: Toward new conceptualization of prejudice. In D. M. Mackie & D. L. Hamilton (Eds.), *Affect, cognition and stereotyping: Interactive processes in group perception* (pp. 297–315). San Diego, CA: Academic Press.

Smith, C. A., & Ellsworth, P. C. (1985). Patterns of cognitive appraisal in emotion. *Journal of Personality and Social Psychology, 48,* 813–838.

Smith, E. R., & Mackie, D. M. (2008). Intergroup emotions. In M. Lewis, J. M. Haviland-Jones, & L. F. Barrett (Eds.), *Handbook of emotions* (3rd ed., pp. 428–439). New York, NY: Guilford.

Smith, E. R., Seger, C. R., & Mackie, D. M. (2007). Can emotions be truly group level? Evidence for four conceptual criteria. *Journal of Personality and Social Psychology, 93,* 431–446.

Snyder, C. R. (1994). *The psychology of hope.* New York: Free Press.

Staats, S. R., & Stassen, M. A. (1985). Hope: An affective cognition. *Social Indicators Research, 17,* 235–242.

Staub, E. (2005). The origins and evolution of hate, with notes on prevention. In R. J. Sternberg (Ed.), *The psychology of hate* (pp. 51–66). Washington, DC: American Psychological Association.

Stephan, W. G., & Stephan, C. W. (2000). An integrated threat theory of prejudice. In S. Oskamp (Ed.), *Reducing prejudice and discrimination* (pp. 23–45). Mahwah, NJ: Lawrence Erlbaum.

Sternberg, R. J. (2003). A duplex theory of hate: Development and application to terrorism, massacres and genocide. *Review of General Psychology, 7,* 299–328.

Sternberg, R., & Sternberg, K. (2008). *The nature of hatred.* New York: Cambridge University Press.

Tam, T., Hewstone, M., Cairns, E., Tausch, N., Maio, G., & Kenworthy, J. (2007). The impact of intergroup emotions on forgiveness in Northern Ireland. *Group Processes and Intergroup Relations, 10,* 119–135.

Tam, T., Hewstone, M., Kenworthy, J., Cairns, E., Marinetti, C., Geddes, L., & Parkinson, B. (2008a). Postconflict reconciliation: Intergroup forgiveness and implicit biases in Northern Ireland. *Journal of Social Issues, 64,* 303–320.

Tam, T., Hewstone, M., Kenworthy, J., Voci, A., Cairns, E., & Van-Dick, R. (2008b). *The role of intergroup emotions and empathy in contact between Catholics and Protestants in Northern Ireland* (Unpublished manuscript).

Tangney, J. P., Stuewig, J., & Mashek, D. J. (2007). Moral emotions and moral behavior. *Annual Review of Psychology, 58,* 345–372.

Tangney, J. P., Wagner, P. E., Fletcher, C., & Gramzow, R. (1992). Shamed into anger? The relation of shame and guilt to anger and self-reported aggression. *Journal of Personality and Social Psychology, 62,* 669–675.

Tooby, J., & Cosmides, L. (1990). The past explains the present: Emotional adaptations and the structure of ancestral environments. *Ethology and Sociobiology, 11,* 375–424.

Volkan, V. (1997). *Bloodlines: From ethnic pride to ethnic terrorism.* New York: Farrar, Straus and Giroux.

Wohl, M. J. A., Branscombe, N. R., & Klar, Y. (2006). Collective guilt: Emotional reactions when one's group has done wrong or been wronged. *European Review of Social Psychology, 17,* 1–37.

Yzerbyt, V., Dumont, M., Wigboldus, D., & Gordin, E. (2003). I feel for us: The impact of categorization and identification on emotions and action tendencies. *British Journal of Social Psychology, 42,* 533–549.

Zajonc, R. B. (1998). Emotions. In D. Gilbert, S.T. Fiske, & G. Lindzey (Eds.), *The handbook of social psychology* (4th ed., Vol. 1, pp. 591–632). Boston: McGraw-Hill.

Zhou, Q., Valiente, C., & Eisenberg, N. (2003). Empathy and its measurement. In S. J. Lopez & C. R. Snyder (Eds.), *Positive psychological assessment: A handbook of models and measures* (pp. 269–284). Washington: American Psychological Association.

4

Collective Memory of Conflicts

DARIO R. PAEZ and JAMES HOU-FU LIU

*T*his chapter examines the processes by which collective remembering of conflict's past affects the course of current conflicts. Memory of collective violence that has been experienced in the past often burdens the present conflict with aggressive forms of in-group favoritism, a duty of retaliation, generalized hatred, and makes the current situation appear as a repetition of previous violent conflicts. Recently, there have been many examples where the collective remembering of historical warfare, like the Field of Blackbirds near Kosovo, became a tool for fueling civil war and a justification for a current conflict. Emotionally loaded collective memory (CM) of past conflicts, wars in particular, can make it virtually impossible to negotiate a compromise solution, by sewing seeds of fear and mistrust (Bar-Tal, 1998, 2007). This chapter briefly summarizes what CM is, and describes factors related to the creation, maintenance and reactivation of collective memories of past conflicts. Then, it discusses societal beliefs or social representations of past warfare, focusing on the World Wars and various civil wars, elaborating how different forms of representing past warfare reinforce or weaken proconflict attitudes. Finally, processes of collective remembering that can help to overcome intense violent past conflicts, such as changes in war representations and transitional justice rituals like truth and reconciliation commissions, are examined.

DEFINITION OF COLLECTIVE MEMORY

CM is a widely shared knowledge of past social events that may not have been personally experienced but are collectively constructed through communicative social functions (Schuman & Scott, 1989). These social representations, or shared knowledge about the past, are elaborated, transmitted and conserved in a society through both interpersonal and institutional communications. Social representations of the past are helpful to people for a variety of reasons. First, they maintain a positive image of the group to which they belong. Second, they preserve a sense of continuity of the group, able to endure through time (Bellelli, Bakhurst, & Rosa, 2000). Third, they provide guidance to group values and norms by prescribing behaviors and contributing to what characterizes or should characterize the group (Olick & Robbins, 1998). Fourth, collective memories are a symbolic resource that can be mobilized politically to legitimize political agenda for the present and future (Liu & Hilton, 2005).

Some scholars argue that CM is a reification of individual process and an example of the inappropriate application of personal features to collective processes (Winter, 2006). It is argued that in the social discourse, there is a frequent use of metaphors, such as "the nation never forgets" or "repressed events reemerge in the collective mind" or "a nation suffering from a negative past needs to express feelings to heal and deal with this past". From this point of view, CM is a juxtaposition of personal and national processes where societies are conceived as king size psyches or personalities writ large (Hamber & Wilson, 2003). We do not subscribe to this strong version of CM where a collective mind is assumed to exist above individual minds. We rather hold with those who favor a distributed view of CM where representations of the past are distributed and emerge through interactions among members of a group, including institutionally mediated interactions like public education or commemoration (Wertsch, 2002). We emphasize the processes through which people and institutions engage in collective acts of remembrance.

CM is an explicit, if informal, transmission of meaning and identities from the historical past of a group. It is common to differentiate between formal or institutional memories and informal or popular ones. At the formal level, carriers of CM include official histories and textbooks as well as commemoration, monuments and rituals. At the popular level, processes of CM include magazines, newspapers, television, and film, whereas at the informal level, conversations, letters, and diaries are included (Olick & Levy, 1997). If we focus on process, CM encompasses the cross-generational oral transmission of events important for the group (Vansina, 1985). Core characteristics of CM are group dynamics in remembering and forgetting—oral stories, rumors, gestures, or cultural styles, in addition to written stories and institutionalized cultural activities (Halbwachs, 1950/1992). Following Assman's (1992, quoted in László, 2003) argument, a distinction between communicative and cultural memory is needed. According to Assman, communicative memory is mainly related to the oral transmission of vivid "first-hand" information about an event while cultural memory is the semantic knowledge that the culture affords (e.g., knowledge about nineteenth century wars). A characteristic example of communicative memory is generational memory (Schuman & Scott, 1989), which spans about 80–100 years (or three or four generations). Generational communicative memory explains why World War II (WW2) and the other recent wars are important events for CM; because there are living grandparents still talking about these events. In this case, memory is lived, and as such tends to be more influential in public discourse and personal behavior.

Cultural memory, on the other hand, is usually institutionally mediated, through such societal functions like commemoration or public education regarding history. This aspect of collective remembering appears to be the province of sociologists and historians rather than psychologists. However, CM in our view needs to examine the interplay between institutional or cultural and informal or communicative modes of remembering. Conflict between different memories of the same events and between institutional and informal memory are frequent. For instance, in the case of Germany, the official or institutional position assumes the responsibility of the nation for WW2 crimes. However, in a 2000 survey, only 30% of Germans agreed with the statement that "German citizens supported the Nazis and were involved" (Langenbacher, 2003), whereas 40% believed that Germans were passive bystanders and 23% believed they were victims of Nazis. A majority (51%) agreed with putting a line over the past putting it behind (Langenbacher, 2003). In spite of institutional self-criticism, trials by German judges, and laws against the denial of Holocaust, current public opinion in Germany tends to reject collective guilt and agrees with forgetting the negative past (Dresler-Hawke & Liu, 2006).

THE CONSTRUCTION OF COLLECTIVE MEMORY

CM, considered as shared memories of relevant public events with their important psychosocial functions, usually results from a few markedly positive but more often negative events that are unexpected or extraordinary (Wagner, Kronberger, & Seifert, 2002). CM evolves from events that affect collectively a large number of people, either as members of a national community or a political group. These events could be specific, like John F. Kennedy's (JFK) assassination, or chronic, like the Stalinist terror or the Great Depression. Studies show that people remember more events that are relevant for their social identity. For instance, 54% of African Americans recalled the Civil Rights movement as an important historical national event and 4% WW2, versus 10% and 23% of Whites, respectively. Similarly, memories of the Martin Luther King assassination were more common among African Americans than among Euro-Americans (Gaskell & Wright, 1997).

Moreover, CM relates to important changes in the social fabric or to important threats to social cohesion and values. CM rests on events which have had an impact on collectives and have driven them to modify their institutions, beliefs and values; as such, they are often still relevant today (Sibley, Liu, Duckitt, & Khan, 2008). Connerton (1989) analyzes how even though the killing of French kings was not unusual in French history, the execution of Louis XVI during the French bourgeois revolution of 1793 had a very strong impact and is remembered today because it altered the social landscape. For the United States, the American Revolution, Civil War, WW2, and Vietnam War are largely institutionally commemorated or recalled in polls as important events, while the War of 1812, 1847 Mexican–American War, the Philippines War of Independence, and the Korean War are largely forgotten (Neal, 2005; Phieler 2008). Vietnam and WW2 were associated with high impact on institutions and subsequent societal change, whereas the Philippines or Korea were less socially relevant wars for Americans (but not for Filipinos and Koreans). American casualties in the Korean War were similar to those suffered in Vietnam or in the entire Pacific during WW2. However, as American objectives were achieved and the necessity of engagement in Korea was perceived as consensual within American society, the Korean War has not formed an enduring part of American CM (Neal, 2005).

Events such as collective triumphs or, at the opposite, attacks, disasters, political assassinations and crises all provoke shared emotions such as surprise, interest and pride, or, at the opposite, sadness, anger, fear and anxiety in rank order, when the group is the target of events like September 11, 2001 (Conejeros & Etxeberria, 2007). Reported emotionality counts are among the predictors of long term sustained memories, such as the memories of JFK's assassination (Luminet & Curci, 2009; Rimé, 1997).

Finally, because of its impact on the social fabric and group identity, unexpected and emotionally loaded events provoke intense social rehearsal through mass media and interpersonal communication. A majority of people initially learned about CM events from mass media, and then kept following news about these events subsequently, often sharing them with others. The case of JFK's assassination offered a paradigmatic example of such collective sharing and rehearsal. According to Neal (2005), "the nation was engrossed in television coverage of the funeral ceremony ... and the subsequent funeral procession to Arlington" (p. 108). More generally, Wagner, Kronberger, and Seiferth (2002) consider symbolic coping to be a major driver of the creation of societal beliefs.

CM influences the development and course of present-day conflicts. First, CM of past conflict can reinforce categorization or differentiation and enhance in-group superiority. CM of past conflict could amplify present intergroup conflict by influencing categorization processes, such as reinforcing the intensity of in-group identification (which strengthens the in-group boundaries salience), increasing perceived dissimilarity between out-group and in-group beliefs, questioning superordinate categories' increasing cues to category membership, and diluting or eliminating crosscutting categories (Messick & Smith, 2002). For instance, collective remembering of ancient battles between Turks and Christians in Kosovo were revived by Serbian leaders to clearly differentiate between present day Serbs and Muslims by marking Kosovo's Muslim successors as heirs to the Ottoman Turks. CM of past trauma increases cues for identity and "forgetting" or ignoring the superordinate categorization, Nationalist Serbian narratives omitted the existence of multiethnic periods and states (like Tito's Yugoslavia). Serbian nationalist CM criticized Croatians and Albanians. Both groups were associated to fascist and collaborationist militias that killed thousand of Serbs in WW2. Serbs omitted their own repression of Croatians within Serb dominated Yugoslavia, and downplayed the existence of crosscutting social types such as the nonfascist Croatian Marshall Tito, who was in fact a communist Croatian (Jones, 2006).

Second, CM of past conflict plays a cognitive–perceptual role by shaping the perception of interest, threat and others intentions (Bar-Tal, 2007). Perceived or real threat is an important factor in conflicts. When remembering past conflicts, groups often perceive their present-day security to be endangered, and might even be afraid of extinction through violence or assimilation. Such fear inevitably destroys any trust the group might have toward the out-group, and, in consequence, even conciliatory gestures from the out-group may be misinterpreted as menacing. For instance, when remembering past slaughters during recent Balkan's wars,

Serbs perceived the conflict as an extreme one and believed that Croatian and Albanian atrocities could be repeated (Jones, 2006).

Third, CM of past conflicts has a motivational function for collective behavior, as it stimulates groups to act collectively, and justify actions of the in-group toward the out-group (Liu & Hilton, 2005). With respect to the motivational function, fear related to the past threat and anger stemming from the revival of past atrocities motivates people to fight against historical enemies and justify a preventive war needed to "eliminate the danger," and this motivates and justifies current conflict. Some studies confirm the existence of the justificatory function of CM. These studies analyzed the consequences of remembering past collective traumas or historical victimization for reactions to a current adversary. Jews who were reminded of the Holocaust were more inclined to accept their group's harmful actions toward the Palestinians than those not reminded of their in-group's past victimization. Americans justify more (i.e., experience less collective guilt) the harms committed by their in-group in Iraq following reminders of the September 11, 2001 attacks or the 1941 Japanese attack on Pearl Harbor (Wohl & Branscombe, 2008).

Collective memories that reinforce extreme conflicts have some specific features, such as: (a) they are usually associated with contempt, hatred and anger directed toward an out-group; (b) there are rituals or current circumstances that maintain or revive the past traumatic event in the present; (c) they are based on chosen traumas that are simultaneously a chosen glory, which makes it difficult to mourn the loss; and (d) often deny important aspects of the history. Chosen glories are important, usually idealized achievements that took place in the past and chosen traumas are losses, defeats or humiliations, also mythologized and usually difficult to mourn (Pick, 2001).

A prototypical historical example is the "myth of the knife in the back": the German Army was supposed to have lost World War I (WW1) because Germans were betrayed by communists, socialists, liberals and Jews (the trauma facet) after a victorious campaign (the glorious facet). These representations of the past were historically baseless but widely believed. German CM in the thirties also was based on claims of innocence in 1914 and emphasized wrongful oppression in the aftermath of WW1. Economic compensation to allies and the economic crisis reactivated those representations of *betrayed innocence* and played a role in the rise of Nazism and the outbreak of WW2 (Pick, 2001; see Sen & Wagner, 2005 for an example from India using more psychological interpretations).

As we have seen, social factors are involved in the processes which explain why certain past conflicts are better maintained and more easily reactivated by society members, both at formal or institutional remembering level and at informal or "popular" memory level. Important factors in the maintenance and reactivation of CM include the existence of ritual or intensity of formal and informal acts of remembering and relevance to current social issues. Other more generic factors affecting CM processes are intergroup power relations, tendency to enhance collective self esteem, level of experience and involvement in collective events and cultural values. These factors will be reviewed with respect to the CM of past wars examples because of their relevance for current social conflicts.

FACTORS IN THE MAINTENANCE AND REACTIVATION OF COLLECTIVE MEMORIES

Events that create CM often also provoke participation in collective behaviors and rituals, such as political demonstrations, public worship, funerary rituals, and so on (De Rivera & Paez, 2007). In time, these can become institutionalized through commemoration, museum exhibits, and historical textbooks and finally form part of (in Assman's vocabulary) cultural memories. The frequency and content of institutional and informal rituals and acts of remembering are an important factor in the maintenance and activation of memories of past conflicts. For instance, Japanese remember the end of WW2 better than Germans. In Japan "Surrender Day" is also a day of ritual remembering of fallen soldiers by the nation while no ritual related to Surrender Day exists in Germany (Schuman, Akiyama, & Knaüper, 1998).

A survey (1995) showed that Germans reported the lowest historical pride (to the question, "Do you feel proud of your nation's history?" 8% of Germans responded "yes" vs. a 34% general mean) among a sample of 23 European, American, and Asian nations. Austrian and Japanese samples showed a medium level of historical pride (40% and 33%), suggesting a lower level of collective guilt and shame (UNESCO, 2000). Cultural explanations of German learning versus Japanese "amnesia" refer to a dichotomy between cultures of shame, focused on public image and external punishment, and cultures of guilt, related to internalized self-critic (Conrad, 2003). However, this argument does not explain the case of Austria.

One plausible explanation for lower historical guilt is lower levels of institutional self-criticism facilitated by allied political decisions (Liu & Atsumi, 2008). Emperor Hirohito was never judged as a war criminal despite his involvement in Japanese Army decisions leading to war crimes. Austria was recognized as a victim of Nazi Germany in spite of widespread support from the population for Nazism. Trials were larger in Germany than in Japan and Austria—the ratio of war crime death penalties by millions of inhabitants was higher in Germany (20) than in Japan (12.4) and both were higher than in Austria (5.8) (Dower, 1991; Rousso, 1992).

Changes in formal education and political context also influence how people remember historical events. Older Russians emphasize the positive military role of Stalin in WW2. Younger Russians, educated under postSoviet systems of education, evaluated Stalin negatively and blamed his leadership for the early failures against the German Army (Emelyanova, 2002; Merridale, 2003). In 1945, a poll found that 57% of French believed the Red Army was the most important factor in defeating Germany in WW2. Sixty years later, after the Cold War, the USSR collapse and dozens of movies showing the role of the US and UK armies, only 20% agreed with this idea (Lacroix-Riz, 2005).

Finally, the creation of a state strongly influences collective remembering (Olick & Robbins, 1998). For example, a recent study has found that virtually every single event nominated by East Timorese as important in world history was relevant to the creation of the new Timorese state, including the invasions by Indonesia, the intervention by the United Nations based on human rights legislation, and so on; similar, though less, extreme effects were found in Indian and Chinese ancient civilizations where collective remembering is now focused on the history of the contemporary state (Liu et al., 2009).

Usually, formal and institutional memories enhance collective self-esteem, self-efficacy, collective cohesion, and the distinctiveness of the national group. Even in the case of negative events, in-group favoritism is frequent. A good example is the war of 1812 between the United States and Great Britain; for Americans, most confrontations ended in defeat and efforts to invade Canada proved to be embarrassing. However, in the aftermath of the war (and American historical texts today) collective remembering has focused on a few great triumphs and the exploits of Andrew Jackson, selectively ignoring the general failures (Phieler, 1995). At the informal level, studies show that national and ethnic belongingness and identification are related to elevated levels of free recall of in-group favoring and relevant political events. For instance, when asked to mention important historical events of the twentieth century, highly identified Basque respondents recalled more frequently events such as the political struggle against fascist repression, the transition from Franco's dictatorship to democracy, and the emergence of the Basque Country autonomy (Bellelli, Bakhurst, & Rosa, 2000).

However, studies do not always find that social identity is related to selective and in-group favoring remembering. For instance, a study conducted in Ireland did not find that Catholics remembered better events related to political conflict than Protestants, and another survey showed that both Catholic and Protestants mentioned the IRA's ceasefire as an important event in 1995 (McLernon, Cairns, Lewis, & Hewstone, 2003). Both leftist and rightist people in Spain mentioned the Spanish Civil War as an important historical event of the twentieth century (Bellelli, Bakhurst, & Rosa, 2000). These examples suggest that some events are remembered because of their importance, mass media coverage and formal commemoration rather than simply being group relevant.

A case in point is WW2. Different studies have found that across Eastern and Western societies, young people overwhelmingly remember war and to a lesser extent politics as the most important events in world history, with WW2 being the most important event in virtually all samples, and more events nominated from Europe than Asia even for Asian samples (Liu et al., 2005, 2009; Pennebaker et al., 2006). Across cultures, social representations of history were overwhelmingly about politics and wars. The overall pattern was more eurocentric than ethnocentric. These representations attest to the power of Western nations, and their disproportionate control of the world's wealth, power, and resources (Liu et al., 2005, 2009).

In-group favoritism organized by the state is constrained by relationships with other states. History can be contested between states and by supra-national institutions as well as by ethnic or other groups within states. Liu and Hilton (2005), for example, note how the problem of misconduct during WW2 was much more of an issue for Germany, located at the center of Europe and the object of countless Hollywood movies, than it was for Japan, an island nation that surrendered to the United States rather than to its Asian neighbors against whom it committed its most serious war crimes (Liu & Atsumi, 2008).

COLLECTIVE MEMORIES OF WARS AND THEIR RELATIONSHIP WITH IDENTITY AND CONFLICT

In many countries, wars of independence or other instances of collective violence are among the foundational events for narratives of national identity (Huang, Liu, & Chang, 2004). Moreover, representations of war associated with the nobility of arms, the cleansing effects of combat, and the redemptive and manly character of sacrifice have played an important role in the legitimization of national institutions and social identity (Winter, 2006). Societies involved in intractable conflict cope using collective memories, usually associated with a societal ethos that emphasizes collective emotions of hatred, fear, anger, and pride (Bar-Tal, 2007; see also Chapter 3). From the perspective of formal memory, institutional narratives of heroism and romantic notions of war were widespread before WW1 but even today are used to reinforce conflicts. Rosoux (2001), focusing on Germany and France in the nineteenth and early twentieth century, found the following common features of institutionalized representations of past wars (Bar-Tal, 2007):

(a) They explain and justify the outbreak of the conflict and the course of its development. Ontological differences existed between France and Germany, with intergroup relationships marked by natural hostility and mistrust, and each country portrayed as the natural and hereditary enemy of the other.

(b) They present the in-group in a positive light. Memorials, monuments and textbooks often gloss over the tragedies of collective violence, and the horrors of war are displaced by emphasis on heroes, glory, and justification of sacrifices. Death and destruction are reevaluated within the sacred task of defending the nation. "Our" shameful past war episodes are concealed. "Our" heroes, martyrs and epic battles are remembered. No references to others as victims appear.

(c) They describe the out-group in delegitimizing ways (Bar-Tal, 1990). A negative image of the out-group justifies violence (see Chapter 2, this volume). For instance, the Germans were called the Huns in WW1—an image of barbarians. Negation of the enemy as human being, an image of being inferior or with animal traits, low or deficient in morality, is associated to high death tolls in the Mexican–American war, war with Native Americans, colonial wars, Pacific and Eastern front in WW2, by comparison with the American Civil War or the Western front in WW2 (Neely, 2007).

(d) They portray the in-group as a victim of the opponent. Recalling past persecutions and martyrs imposes the duty of fidelity and justifies revenge against evil-doers. Aggression against enemies is portrayed as a means to avenge injuries suffered by the nation (Rosoux, 2001; see Chapter 2, this volume).

A group's representation of its history can explain how its world has come to be the way it is and justify its responses to current challenges (Liu & Hilton, 2005). In the case of victorious nations, like the United States and Russia, WW2 is represented as a Just War, or a "Great Patriotic War" (Wertsch, 2002) and this representation reinforces attitudes favorable to participation in a new war. Páez et al. (2008) found that at the national level, young people in victorious nations reported higher recall of WW2 memories, a less negative evaluation of this event and expressed more willingness to fight in a new war for the motherland; on the other hand, belonging to the Axis powers was related to a relatively lower mention of WW2 and its lower evaluation.

Moreover, differences in meaning related to victory appear within a nation: Russian participants mention WW2 with two different labels, WW2 (56%) and the Great Patriotic War (44%) (Pennebaker et al., 2006). Only 6% mentioned both. The mean evaluation for the first label was 2.09 and for the second 4.0. Younger Russians, educated under postSoviet systems of education, used predominantly the first label and evaluate WW2 negatively—probably because of Stalin's negative leadership, failures against the German Army and high casualties. Wertsch (2002) argues that the "Great Patriotic War" label, on the other hand, is a condensation of the important positive narrative template "triumph over alien forces" for Russia.

Even if loser nations conceal more negative aspects of their WW2 actions (e.g., denial of crimes of war by the Imperial Japanese and German Armies; Buruma, 2002), their representations of the war do not (or are not able to) reinforce a positive view of war and national warriors. As defeated nations remember war defensively, emphasizing in-group suffering, they may teach new generations about the negative effects of collective violence (Conrad, 2003). The younger generations learn that wars are "social catastrophes."

Civil wars or internal political violence after the war were unrelated to WW2 recall, evaluation, or to willingness to fight in a new war (Páez et al., 2008). This rules out direct experience of collective violence as a factor affording positive dispositions toward war. While civil wars may be just as violent as wars between states, they are rarely glorified. In fact, some authors argue that the remembering of catastrophic civil wars (e.g., the French Commune in nineteenth century) played a role in inhibiting the opposing attitudes of political elites and reducing the level of social conflict in the transition of Vichy to the 4th Republic (Rousso, 1992). A similar social representation of the Spanish Civil War was constructed in the last phase of Franco's fascist dictatorship. Some authors posit that this representation of the Spanish Civil war as a catastrophe teaches new generations the necessity of consensus and of avoiding social conflict, and helped ease a relatively peaceful transition from dictatorship to democracy after Franco's death (Barahona, Aguilar, & Gonzalez, 2001).

From the point of view of popular memory, most soldiers remember war as a negative but normalized experience—experience was mainly negative in the case of victorious armies, like the Red Army, and even more negative in the case of defeated armies, like the German Army (Bourke, 2001). Both in the case of victorious nations, like USSR (Merridale, 2006) and in defeated nations, like Germany and Japan after WW2, people remember their own suffering but conceal, silence or ignore other's suffering (Dower, 1991; Wette, 2006). Only a minority of war veterans recalled and narrated the brutal nature of combat and talked about the violence and crimes in which they played a role as actors; more of them were willing to talk about comradeship (Phieler, 1995).

The collective suffering of WW1 and WW2 was too much to sanitize. Direct remembrances of large-scale collective suffering, together with changes in cultural values, progressively eroded representations of war as heroic, epic and positive events. Highly idealized portraits of soldiers, characterized by stoicism, leadership and voluntary sacrifice for a meaningful cause were changed by heavy civilian casualties, traumatized war veterans, and by the failure of ideological goals. WW1 was called the last war as a symbol of a social catastrophe. Even if WW2 retains a better image, victims of genocide and the Holocaust are their current dominant symbols, more than heroic combatants (Bourke, 2001), leading to a collective learning of disenchantment with warfare (Winter, 2006). Antiromantic representations of war and full conscience of the evils of collective violence became dominant—even if romantic and positive representations were still important and supported by national institutions. It is important to notice that currently, even among victorious WW2 nations, mean evaluations are not positive, but rather neutral or less negative than in defeated nations (Páez et al., 2008).

REPRESENTATIONS OF PAST COLLECTIVE CONFLICTS AND IMPROVING CURRENT INTERGROUP RELATIONSHIPS

How to deal with and remember past collective crimes is a frequent problem (for negotiation and reconciliation in the case of intergroup conflict in general; see Chapters 10 through 13). We will review two forms of overcoming the negative effects of past wars and collective violence: Changes in the representation of wars and rituals of transitional justice aiming at the creation of CM of past conflicts.

As we have seen, painting representations of past wars as a social catastrophe can help to overcome prolonged conflicts. On the other hand, the reconstruction of social representations of the past can help to overcome the past of intense and violent intergroup conflict (Bar-Tal, 2008). One example, though controversial, is the commemoration of the American civil war at the end of nineteenth century. Commemoration focused on the battlefield and the heroic qualities and suffering soldiers' experiences on both sides, avoiding political issues and minimizing the causal role of slavery and the participation of black soldiers in the conflict. Monuments, memorials and commemorations mourned the dead, remaining free of symbolism arousing polemical displays of emotions. Official memory promoted reconciliation, honored the sacrifice of all who fought in the civil war, glossed over the causes of conflict, and the brutality and anger of war was ignored by creators of Civil war memorials (Phieler, 1995). Despite this, celebration of the American centennial in 1876 was primarily a North-eastern project, and relatively ignored in the South, where the wounds were still raw (Spillman, 1997). It took a hundred years for Abraham Lincoln to be transformed from *protector of the union* to a symbol of racial equality (Schwartz, 1997).

Another example of reconstruction is the representation of WW1 and WW2 in official German and French memory. The meaning of great battles, like Verdun with a quarter million victims, was patriotic and nationalist in the aftermath of WW1. Verdun was construed on both German and French sides as a manifestation of heroism, glory, and the fighting spirit of combatants. After WW2, battles like Verdun became a symbol of the slaughter with a similar meaning for combatants on both sides. Soldiers who fought in opposite camps gathered in a common tribute. This representation was enacted when Mitterrand and Kohl, the French president and German prime minister, stood hand- in-hand in front of a French ossuary of dead soldiers (Rosoux, 2004).

These experiences suggest that the acceptance of events is a first step toward the negotiation of a shared representation of the past. Acceptance of real facts, including others' suffering, is essential for reconciliation. What is important is to acknowledge the reality of the suffering and victims, "to keep it from happening again ..." but to forget the emotions of hate (Hayner, 2001; Rosoux, 2001). As a former French Prime Minister said, "memory should be considered not as a way of awakening ancient sufferings, but as a tool allowing people to make peace with the past, without forgetting previous wounds" (Rosoux, 2004, p. 107). The narrative grasping or configuring of facts within a narrative that offers a place for both sides without completely sanitizing the conflict could complete the cycle of healing (Liu & László, 2007; Wertsch, 2002).

Public apologies and expression of repentance can help to restore better inter-group relationships, the prototypical case being the former German anti-Nazi fighter and Prime Minister Willy Brandt asking for pardon nonverbally by kneeling in front of the Warsaw ghetto insurrection monument. However, usually these rituals are perceived as having positive effects at the societal level but not helping to overcome the suffering of victims (Lillie & Janoff-Bulman, 2007). Direct victims with proximity to the violence, are associated with dismissing or not accepting such apologies—"too few and too late" is a common critique that these apologies arouse in different contexts, from America to Europe, New Zealand, and Africa. Vicarious perpetrators or members of the group responsible of past collective violence agree more with the efficacy of apologies, while direct and indirect victims are more reluctant to accept apologies (Ferguson et al., 2007; Manzi & Gonzalez, 2007).

Truth, justice and reparation commissions, like the South African Truth and Reconciliation Commission (TRC) are a common response to deal with and remember past collective crimes. There have been more than 30 official truth commissions established around the world since the 1970s (Hayner, 2001). Truth commissions may serve long-term societal goals such as prevention of cycles of revenge and prevention of new crimes of war and collective violence. Commissions and trials are supposed to reinforces the rule of law, including the accountability of holders of government, army, police and armed political factions, and the respect of political rights. They could contribute to strengthening social norms and reduce future human rights violations. A central aspect of these rituals is the construction of shared and inclusive CM. This memory of past conflict reinforces intergroup reconciliation as it documents factual atrocities committed by all sides involved, asserting that all groups are to blame and "have dirty hands" (a representation similar to current view of the American civil war). Sharing blame and victimhood prevents selective victimization, in-group idealization and opens a space toward dialogue (Gibson, 2004). Public rituals of transitional justice (e.g., truth commission) which incited the reconstructing of CM of suffering did not achieve a "therapeutic" goal at the individual level and, on the contrary, reinforced negative emotions. For instance, two-thirds of a South African national poll perceived that the revelations of the TRC had made people angrier and complicated intergroup relationships (Gibson, 2004). However, these rituals of CM construction and reconstruction are perceived to have other positive effects at the individual and the macro-social or national level, fortifying in-group cohesion and reconciliation in a long-term process (Lillie & Janoff-Bulman, 2007). Gibson's (2004) study in South Africa found that people who were more willing to accept the TRC's version of the truth, that is, to accept CM declaring that all sides are to blame and "have dirty hands," agreed more with reconciliation, even if this "truth effect" was stronger for dominant and vicarious perpetrator groups: the correlation between truth acceptance and reconciliation was 0.23 among Africans and 0.53 among Whites. Of course, reality constraints imposed limitations on this "relativistic" reconstruction of the past. In some cases rates of mortality and misdeeds were similar in both groups, in the other cases there was a clear victimized and perpetrator group.

Evidence suggests that truth commissions, which give rise to shared and accepted CM of past suffering and of collective guilt and responsibility, have a positive psycho-social impact. This type of CM not only fails to reinforce conflicts, as exemplified with those cases when it becomes commonly accepted that "all groups have dirty hands" and suffering was common in both groups, but also decreases current conflicts because: (a) it is associated with sadness and with a limited degree of anger directed at a small number of individuals, not large out-groups; (b) there are no rituals or events that maintain or revive the traumatic collective experience; (c) is based on unambiguously chosen traumas that are not simultaneously a chosen glory, and therefore easier to mourn; and (d) finally, the degree of denial of the history is mild. An example of this type of CM is the current representation of the American Civil War or the Franco-German representation of the WW1. The lose of life during battle is not denied, there is no chosen glory aspect of the event, there is no emphasis on anger or on hatred of enemies, and there are no rituals perpetuating hatred towards the enemy and revitalizing the desire for revenge (Pick, 2001).

CONCLUSIONS

Collective events have the highest probability of leading to a long-lasting CM, or set of social representations concerning the past, when they: (1) influence social change in the long run and are socially relevant in the present; (2) are emotionally loaded; (3) elicit abundant social sharing; (4) are socially rehearsed by mass media; and (5) are associated with collective behavior and commemoratives rituals, that can be narrated coherently by institutions and individuals.

In all types of cultures, people have mythologized their own war dead, and forgotten their out-group victims. Because societies tend to remember their own heroes and soldiers and forget their crimes and misdeeds, social representations of history can feed violent conflicts, where there is rumination on in-group suffering that represents the in-group as a victim, and where the target out-group is defined as an aggressor or perpetrators. In this way, violence is construed as a legitimate form of retaliation. Social representations of the past can reinforce aggressive actions, where war and collective violence is seen as a rational and justified response to the past aggression of out-groups and generates a cycle of competitive victimhood.

With respect to collective ways of dealing with negative historical events associated to violent conflicts, we offer the following tentative conclusions. First, humanization of the other side and acknowledging their sufferings are an important step forward. Acknowledgment does not necessarily imply an agreement as to the meaning of events, but at least allows the coexistence of different representations of a shared truth. Second, the absence of personal and collective guilt is a modal response for perpetrators of collective crimes and violence (Marques, Paez, Valencia, & Vincze, 2006). Hence, it is not realistic to think that a majority of perpetrators should feel guilt and react with reparative and compensation behaviors toward victims. Denial, justification, and other forms of cognitive coping, allow perpetrators to share a positive collective identity and reject criticism about human right violations (Branscombe & Doosje, 2004; Sibley et al., 2008). Only a minority feel guilt, whereas a majority might display public guilt and shame, but only as compliance to institutionalized norms. The third generation descended from a perpetrator group could paradoxically be more able to feel collective guilt, shame and responsibility than the generation involved in war crimes because the emotional distance allows somewhat greater acceptance (Dresler-Hawke & Liu, 2006). Even in this case, it is reasonable to expect the presence of "defence mechanisms" oriented toward negation, minimization and positivistic reconstruction of past criminal collective behavior (Marques et al., 2006; Sibley et al., 2008).

Third, internal procedures may be more important for public opinion than external trials and procedures. In Germany, the Nuremberg Trials had a lower impact on public opinion than the normal action of German justice on human rights violations (Evans, 2003). Credible local or in-group leaders are more able to gain the population's adherence to social representations of past that accept responsibility for past crimes and errors, and, furthermore, can reinforce truth and reconciliation trends—like Mandela and Archbishop Tutu in South Africa (Rosoux, 2001). When dealing with the evidence of collective negative past behavior, people tend to question the credibility of the sources. They engage cognitive coping mechanisms that minimize emotional reaction and question the relevance of events—these are old stories, they are not important in the present (Sibley et al., 2008). They reframe in-group criminal behavior as more understandable in the historical context, attribute negative and criminal behavior to a minority of black sheep—extreme atypical members of the nation—and minimize the frequency of criminal behaviors.

Fourth, the tendency to punish a minority of criminals appears correlated with a global positive reconstruction that denies the reality of general apathy and diffuses global responsibilities (Marques et al., 2006). Official reports should be able to overcome these collective defence mechanisms. In these cases, self-criticism by high status in-group sources is important for the perpetrator group.

However, these public apologies have a limited effect for direct or indirect victims of past collective violence. Public rituals of transitional justice (e.g., truth commissions or trials on crimes like Gacaca) do not help to overcome suffering at the individual level and usually reinforce negative emotions. However, these rituals have some positive effects at the individual level, empowering victims, reinforcing the truth of accounts of past violence, and this in turn reinforces reconciliation, improving intergroup relationships. Transitional rituals have macro-social or national level positive effects, reinforcing cohesion and reconciliation, and respect for human rights.

In final summary, there appear to be several basic narratives used with varying degrees of effect to reconcile bloody past conflict. The first, rarest, and most powerful form is a complete cognitive reconfiguration of the meaning of national identity. This has been attempted in Germany and New Zealand to handle the Holocaust and the bitter fruits of colonization for indigenous peoples respectively. More common is a sanitization of past conflict in order to overcome intractable differences in the meaning of war. This was undertaken in the United States following its Civil War, and appears characteristic of accounts in Latin America as well; in Moscovici's (1988) terms, these are emancipated representations that mutually intersect but also agree to disagree. The danger of this form is that because of incomplete narration, the past can rear its ugly head and lead to a fresh cycle of recrimination and vengeance, as in the Balkans for example. Most common is denial, emphasis on own victimhood, and in-group favoritism. This form rests on having the power to repress or ignore alternative accounts. While this is the most palatable form psychologically for the perpetrator group, it is very risky when a former victim, like China in the case of the Sino-Japanese War, becomes powerful enough to contest the denial. In this case, active mediation by political elites on both sides is necessary to prevent the reinvigoration of conflict (Liu & Atsumi, 2008).

The narration reconfiguration and CM of conflict is one of the most promising future avenues for psychology to contribute to global peacemaking, precisely because it delineates the flaws and foibles of our human inheritance as meaning making beings.

REFERENCES

Barahona, A., Aguilar, P., & Gonzalez, C. (2001). *The politics of memory: Transitional justice in democratising societies.* Oxford: Oxford University Press.

Bar-Tal, D. (1990). Causes and consequences of delegitimization: Models of conflict and ethnocentrism. *Journal of Social Issues, 46*(1), 65–81.

Bar-Tal, D. (1998). Societal beliefs in times of intractable conflict: The Israeli case. *International Journal of Conflict Management, 9,* 22–50.

Bar-Tal, D. (2003). Collective memory of physical violence: its contribution to the culture of violence. In E. Cairns & M. D. Roe (Eds.), *The role of memory in ethnic conflict* (pp. 75–93). London: Palgrave McMillan.

Bar-Tal, D. (2007). Sociopsychological foundations of intractable conflicts. *American Behavioral Scientist, 50,* 1430–1453.

Bar-Tal, D. (2008). Reconciliation as a foundation of culture of peace. In J. de Rivera (Ed.), *Handbook on building cultures for peace* (pp. 363–377). New York: Springer.

Bellelli, G., Bakhurst, D., & Rosa, A. (Eds.). (2000). *Trace: Studi sulla memoria collective*. Napoli: Liguori. (*Studies on collectives memories*).

Bourke, J. (2001). *The Second World War. A people's history*. Oxford: Oxford University Press.

Branscombe, N. R., & Doosje, B. (2004). *Collective guilt: International perspectives*. Cambridge: Cambridge University Press.

Buruma, I. (2002). *The wages of guilt: Memories of war in Germany and Japan*. London: Phoenix Paperback.

Candau, J. (2005). *Anthropologie de la mémoire*. Paris: Armand Colin. (*Anthropology of memory*).

Conejeros, S., & Etxeberria, I. (2007). The impact of Madrid bombing on personal emotions, emotional atmosphere and emotional climate. *Journal of Social Issues*, 63, 273–288.

Connerton, P. (1989). *How societies remember*. Cambridge: Cambridge University Press.

Conrad, S. (2003). Entangled memories: Versions of the past in Germany and Japan, 1945–2001. *Journal of Contemporary History*, 38, 85–99.

De Rivera, J., & Paez, D. (2007). Emotional climate, human security and cultures of peace. *Journal of Social Issues*, 63, 233–253.

Dower, J. W. (1991). *Embracing defeat: Japan in the wake of World War II*. New York: Norton & Company.

Dresler-Hawke, E., & Liu, J. H. (2006). Collective shame and the positioning of German national identity. *Psicologia Politica*, 32, 131–153.

Emelyanova, T. (2002). Les Représentations Sociales des événements historiques: le cas de la Deuxième Guerre Mondiale. In S. Laurens & N. Roussiau (Eds.), *La mémoire Sociale* (pp. 259–268). Rennes: Presses Universitaires de Rennes. (*Social representations of historical events: The case of the Second World War. In social memory*).

Evans, R. J. (2003). Introduction. Redesigning the past: History in political transitions. *Journal of Contemporary History*, 38, 5–12.

Ferguson, N., Binks, E., Roe, M. D., Brown, J. N. et al. (2007). The IRA Apology of 2002 and forgiveness in Northern Ireland troubles: A cross national study of Printed Media. *Peace and Conflict*, 13, 93–114.

Gaskell, G. D., & Wright, D. (1997). Group differences in memory for a political event. In J. Pennebaker, D. Paez, & B. Rimé (Eds.), *Collective memory of political events* (pp. 175–190). Mahaw, NJ: Lawrence Erlbaum.

Gibson, J. L. (2004). *Overcoming apartheid: Can truth reconcile a divided nation?* New York: Russell Sage Foundation.

Halbwachs, M. (1950/1992). *On collective memory*. Chicago: The University of Chicago Press.

Hamber, B., & Wilson, R. A. (2003). Symbolic closure through memory, reparation and revenge in post-conflicts societies. In E. Cairns & M. D. Roe (Eds.), *The role of memory in ethnic conflict* (pp. 144–168). London: Palgrave McMillan.

Hayner, P. B. (2001). *Unspeakable truths: Confronting state terror and atrocity*. New York: Routledge.

Huang, L. L., Liu, J. H., & Chang, M. L. (2004). The double identity of Chinese Taiwanese: A dilemma of politics and identity rooted in history. *Asian Journal of Social Psychology*, 7(2), 149–189.

Inglehart, R., & Baker, W. E. (2000). Modernization, cultural change and the persistence of traditional values. *American Sociological Review*, 65, 19–51.

Jones, L. (2006). *Then they started shooting*. Harvard: Harvard University Press.

Lacroix-Riz, A. (2005). L'Union Sovietique par perte and profits. *Le Monde Diplomatique*, 52(614), 24–25. [Soviet Union loss and benefits.]

Langenbacher, E. (2003). *Memory regimes in contemporary Germany*. Paper for ECPR Joint Session, Edinburgh 2003. Workshop 16: Politics and Memory.

László, J. (2003). History, identity and narratives. In J. László & W. Wagner (Eds.), *Theories and controversies in societal psychology* (pp. 180–182). Budapest: New Mandate Publishers.

Lillie, C., & Janoff-Bulman, R. (2007). Macro versus microjustice and perceived fairness of truth and reconciliation commissions. *Peace and Conflict, 13*, 221–236.

Liu, J. H. (2005). History and identity: A systems of checks and balances for Aotearoa/New Zealand. In J. H. Liu, T. McCreanor, T. McIntosh, & T. Teaiwa (Eds.), *New Zealand identities: Departures and destinations* (pp. 69–87). Wellington, NZ: Victoria University Press.

Liu, J. H., & Atsumi, T. (2008). Historical conflict and resolution between Japan and China: Developing and applying a narrative theory of history and identity. In T. Sugiman, K. J. Gergen, W. Wagner, & Y. Yamada (Eds.), *Meaning in action: Constructions, narratives, and representations* (pp. 327–344). Tokyo: Springer-Verlag.

Liu, J. H., Goldstein-Hawes, R., Hilton, D. J., Huang, L. L., Gastardo-Conaco, C., Dresler-Hawke, E., et al. (2005). Social representations of events and people in world history across twelve cultures. *Journal of Cross Cultural Psychology, 36*, 171–191.

Liu, J. H. & Hilton, D. (2005). How the past weights on the present: Social representations of history and their impact on identity politics. *British Journal of Social Psychology, 44*, 537–556.

Liu, J. H., Páez, D., Slawuta, P., Cabecinhas, R., Techio, E., Kokdemir, D. et al. (2009). Representing world history in the 21st century: The impact of 9/11, the Iraq war, and the nation-state on the dynamics of collective remembering. *Journal of Cross-Cultural Psychology, 40*, 667–692.

Liu, J. H., & László, J. (2007). A narrative theory of history and identity: Social identity, social representations, society and the individual. In G. Moloney & I. Walker (Eds.), *Social representations and identity: Content, process and power* (pp. 85–107). London: Palgrave Macmillan.

Liu, J. H., Wilson, M. S., McClure, J., & Higgins, T. R. (1999). Social Identity and the perception of history: Cultural representations of Aotearoa/New Zealand. *European Journal of Social Psychology, 29*, 1021–1047.

Luminet, O., & Curci, A. (Eds.). (2009). *Flashbulb memories: New issues and new perspectives*. London: Psychology Press.

Marques, J., Paez, D., Valencia, J., & Vincze, O. (2006). Effects of group membership on the transmission of negative historical events. *Psicologia Politica, 32*, 79–105.

Manzi, J., & Gonzalez, R. (2007). Forgiveness and reparation in Chile. *Peace and Conflict, 13*, 71–92.

McLernon, F., Cairns, E., Lewis, C. A., & Hewstone, M. (2003). Memories of recent conflict and forgiveness in Northern Ireland. In E. Cairns & M. D. Roe (Eds.), *The role of memory in ethnic conflict* (pp. 125–143). London: Palgrave McMillan.

Merridale, C. (2003). Redesigning history in contemporary Russia. *Journal of Contemporary History, 38*(1), 13–28.

Merridale, C. (2006). *Ivan's war*. Washington: Metropolitan Books.

Messick, D. M., & Smith, E. R. (2002). *From Prejudice to Intergroup Emotions*. New York: Psychology Press.

Moscovici, S. (1988). Notes towards a description of social representations. *European Journal of Social Psychology, 18*, 211–250.

Neal, A. G. (2005). *National trauma and collective memory* (2nd ed.). Armonk, NY: M.E. Sharpe.

Neely, M. E. (2007). *The Civil War and the limits of destruction*. Harvard: Harvard University Press.

Olick, J. K., & Levy, D. (1997). Collective memory and cultural constraint: Holocaust myth and rationality in German politics. *American Sociological Review*, 62, 921–936.

Olick, J., & Robbins, J. (1998). Social memory studies: From "collective memory" to the historical sociology of mnemonic practices. *Annual Review of Sociology*, 24, 105–140.

Páez, D., Liu, J. H., Techio, E., Slawuta, P., Zlobina, A., & Cabecinhas, R. (2008). Remembering World War II and willingness to fight: Socio-cultural factors in the social representation of historical warfare across 22 societies. *Journal of Cross Cultural Psychology*, 39, 373–380.

Pennebaker, J., Paez, D., & Rimé, B. (1997). *Collective memory of political events*. Mahaw, NJ: Lawrence Erlbaum.

Pennebaker, J. W., Rentfrow, J., Davis, M., Paez, D., Techio, E., Slawuta, P. et al. (2006). The social psychology of history: Defining the most important events of world history. *Psicología Política*, 7, 15–32.

Pick, T. M. (2001). The myth of trauma/ The trauma of myth. *Peace and Conflict: Journal of Peace Psychology*, 7, 201–226.

Phieler, G. K. (1995). *Remembering war the American way*. Washington: Smithsonian Books.

Phieler, G. K. (2008). *Remembering war the American way* (2nd ed.). Washington: Smithsonian Books.

Rimé, B. (1997). How individual emotional episodes feed collective memory. In J. W. Pennebaker, D. Paez, & B. Rimé (Eds.), *Collective memory of political events* (pp. 131–146). Mahwah, NJ: Lawrence Erlbaum.

Rosoux, V. (2001). National identity in France and Germany: From mutual exclusion to negotiation. *International Negotiation*, 6, 175–198.

Rosoux, V. (2004). Human rights and the work of memory in international relations. *International Journal of Human Rights*, 3, 159–170.

Rousso, H. (1992). *Vichy: L'evenement, la memoire et l'histoire*. Paris: Gallimard. (*Vichy: the event, memory and history*).

Schuman, H., Akiyama, H., & Knäuper, B. (1998). Collective memories of Germans and Japanese about the first half century. *Memory*, 6, 427–454.

Schuman, H., & Rodgers, W. L. (2004). Cohorts, chronology, and collective memories. *Public Opinion Quaterly*, 68, 217–254.

Schuman, H., & Scott, J. (1989). Generations and collective memory. *American Sociological Review*, 54, 359–381.

Schwartz, B. (1996). Memory as a cultural system: Abraham Lincoln in World War II. *American Sociological Review*, 61, 908–927.

Schwartz, B. (1997). Collective memory and history: How Abraham Lincoln became a symbol of racial equality. *The Sociological Quarterly*, 38, 469–496.

Schwartz, S. (1994). Beyond individualism/collectivism: New cultural dimensions of values. In U. Kim, H. C. Triandis, C. Kagitcibasi, S. Choi, & G. Yoon (Eds.), *Individualism and collectivism* (pp. 85–119). Thousands Oaks, CA: Sage.

Scott, J., & Zac, L. (1993). Collective memories in Britain and the United States. *Public Opinion Quarterly*, 57, 315–351.

Sen, R., & Wagner, W. (2005). History, emotions and hetero-referential representations in inter-group conflict: The example of Hindu–Muslim relations in India. *Papers on Social Representations*, 14, 2.1–2.23.

Sibley, C. S., & Liu, J. H. (2007). New Zealand=bicultural? Implicit and explicit associations between ethnicity and nationhood in the New Zealand context. *European Journal of Social Psychology*, 37, 1222–1243.

Sibley, C. S., Liu, J. H., Duckitt, J., & Khan, S. S. (2008). Social representations of history and the legitimation of social inequality: The form and function of historical negation. *European Journal of Psychology*, *38*, 542–565.

Spillman, L. (1997). *Nation and Commemoration: Creating national identity in the USA and Australia*. Cambridge: Cambridge University Press.

UNESCO (2000). *World culture report*. Paris: UNESCO Press.

Vansina, J. (1985). *Oral tradition as history*. London: Academic Press.

Wagner, W., Kronberger, N., & Seifert, F. (2002). Collective symbolic coping with new technology: Knowledge, images and public discourse. *British Journal of Social Psychology*, *41*, 323–343.

Wertsch, J. (2002). *Voices of collective remembering*. Cambridge: Cambridge University Press.

Wette, W. (2006). *La wehrmacht*. Barcelona: Critica. (*The German Army*).

Winter, J. (2006). *Remembering war.* New Haven, CT: Yale University Press.

Wohl, M. J. A., & Branscombe, N. R. (2008) Remembering historical victimization: Collective guilt for current ingroup transgressions. *Journal of Personality and Social Psychology*, *94*, 988–1006.

Zerubavel, Y. (1995). *Recovered roots: Collective memory and the making of Israeli national tradition*. Chicago: University of Chicago Press.

5

Identity and Conflict

MARILYNN B. BREWER

"All of the massacres that have taken place in recent years, like most of the bloody wars, have been linked to complex and long-standing 'cases' of identity … for people directly involved in conflicts arising out of identity, for those who have suffered and been afraid, nothing else exists except 'them' and 'us,' the insult and the atonement."

In the Name of Identity
(Maalouf, 1996/2003, p. 33)

As illustrated by this quote from Lebanese–French author, Amin Maalouf, identity—more specifically, group identity or collective identity—has often been implicated in the origin and maintenance of intergroup conflict. There are at least two ways in which identity can be seen as playing a significant role in determining the course of intergroup relations. The first arises out of the identification process itself, at the level of the individual. Identification (i.e., social identity) involves the attachment of one's sense of self and self-interest to the collective as a whole. When a group identity is both important and salient, the individual is motivated to enhance group welfare and protect group interests, including defending the group boundaries from encroachment, protecting group values from dilution, and preserving group integrity. To the high identifier, any perceived threat to the group as a whole is seen as a threat to the self, even if the existence or welfare of the individual self is not directly endangered.

The second way in which identity concerns become implicated in intergroup conflict arises out of the symbolic meaning attached to the collective and the need for recognition and legitimization of group symbols and identity narratives (i.e., collective identity). Concerns for symbolic threats to group values and icons or lack of respect and recognition are often conceptualized as the subjective "irrational" bases of intergroup hostility and fear, posed in opposition to concerns for objective or "realistic" threats to material welfare and group existence as posited by rational actor theories of group behavior. But objective assessments of conflict of interest and subjective perceptions of identity threat are inextricably intertwined. Especially in the modern world, competition over resources (e.g., land and power) has as much to do with the identity meaning of those resources as it does actual group survival (Ledgerwood, Liviatan, & Carnevale, 2007; Rothman, 1997).

The purpose of this chapter is to explicate the roles of social identity and collective identity in intergroup conflict. First, I will review briefly the major theories of group identification as a fundamental feature of human nature. Then I will discuss how perceived material and symbolic threat to shared identity plays a critical role in initiating and sustaining destructive intergroup conflict. Finally, I will discuss how identity dynamics might be captured in the service of conflict reduction and reconciliation.

THEORIES OF GROUP IDENTIFICATION

Within social psychology, the study of identification with groups is associated primarily with social identity theory (Tajfel & Turner, 1979). But the recognition that group identity is a fundamental characteristic of human psychology is represented in anthropology, psychodynamic theory, symbolic interactionism, and developmental psychology as well. Collectively, these different disciplinary perspectives underscore the conceptualization of group identification as a feature of human psychology that serves to regulate and maintain the essential relationship between individuals and their social groups.

Ethnocentrism: The In-group and the Self

The apparently universal tendency for human beings to differentiate themselves according to group membership was documented in rich anthropological observations compiled by Sumner (1906). Sumner adopted the terms in-group and out-group to refer to social groupings to which a particular individual belongs or does not belong, respectively. In-groups could be of many different types, ranging from small, face-to-face groupings of family and friends, to large social categories such as gender, religion, and nationality. The psychological meaning of group membership does not seem to be restricted by group size or direct interaction with fellow group members. In-group membership is more than mere cognitive classification—it carries emotional significance as well. Attachment to in-groups and preference of in-groups over out-groups may be a universal characteristic of human social life. Sumner (1906) coined the term ethnocentrism to refer to this social psychological phenomenon:

> .... a differentiation arises between ourselves, the we-group, or in-group, and everybody else, or the others-groups, out-groups. The insiders in a we-group are in a relation of peace, order, law, government, and industry, to each other .... Ethnocentrism is the technical name for this view of things in which one's own group is the center of everything, and all others are scaled and rated

with reference to it .... Each group nourishes its own pride and vanity, boasts itself superior, exalts its own divinities, and looks with contempt on outsiders ... (pp. 12–13).

Evidence for the pervasiveness of in-group preference extends beyond the literature on ethnic and national identity. Experimental social psychologists have demonstrated that even classifying individuals into arbitrary categories in the laboratory can elicit in-group–out-group feelings (Brewer, 1979; Tajfel, Billig, Bundy, & Flament, 1971; Turner, 1978). And there is experimental evidence that the concepts "we" and "us" carry positive emotional significance that is activated automatically and unconsciously (Perdue, Dovidio, Gurtman, & Tyler, 1990).

Evolutionary Psychology

Theories of human evolution must take into account the overwhelming evidence that the human species evolved in the context of group living (Caporael & Brewer, 1991). Much of the speculation about species-specific traits and abilities derives from analysis of the survival requirements associated with living in hunter–gatherer societies (Buss, 1991). Sociobiological models of the evolution of human social behavior rest heavily on the notion of inclusive fitness. These models assume that the gene is the basic unit of selection, and that selection favors genes that produce behavior benefiting anyone who carries those genes, including other individuals who possess the same genes by common descent or kin relationships (Archer, 1991).

One implication of this model of evolution is that there is a genetic disposition to behave differently toward "insiders" (kin and extended family likely to share common genes) and "outsiders" (nonkin, out-groups). This idea is the basis for a "sociobiology of ethnocentrism" (Reynolds, Falger, & Vine, 1987; van den Berghe, 1981), which holds that ethnocentric behavior derives from self-interested pursuit of inclusive genetic fitness. Cooperation between individuals will occur only to the extent that they have a high proportion of shared genes, since helping close relatives perpetuates one's own genes. Conversely, the likelihood of conflict between individuals or groups of individuals increases as the proportion of shared genes decreases (van den Berghe, 1981, p. 7).

According to the sociobiological view, the primal ethnic group is the small band of 100–200 related individuals, within which the human propensity for cooperative social arrangements is presumed to have evolved. Ethnocentric preference is extended to larger social groups through the development of "markers" (skin pigmentation, hair and facial features, mannerisms, etc.) which signal genetic relatedness among unfamiliar individuals (Johnson, 1989). One model goes so far as to postulate an evolved "identification mechanism" that provides for selective attachment to large groups that best promote the interests of the nucleus (kin-based) ethnic group (Shaw & Wong, 1989). More recent evolutionary treatments give greater attention to the survival value of intragroup cooperation in an environment of intense selective pressure (Brewer & Caporael, 2006) or intergroup conflict (van Vugt & Park, 2010) as factors shaping ethnocentrism and in-group bias in humans.

Psychodynamic Theories

Freudian theory departs somewhat from evolution-based biological models in assigning a greater role to experience and development in the origin of ethnocentric identification. Freud's own theory of group identification centered on the role of the group leader as the object of identification (Freud, 1921/1960). Neo-Freudian "object relations theory" (Ashbach & Schermer, 1987; Klein, 1975) extended the theory to incorporate all symbolic representations of the group as objects of identification. According to this view, social identity is the product of projection of the self onto external objects and introjection/incorporation of objects into the sense of self.

Freud also coined the phrase "narcissism of minor differences" to refer to the apparent preoccupation of group members with small or trivial distinctions that maintain differentiation between groups (Freud, 1912/1957). Volkan (1988) used this as a basis for a theory of identity formation that holds that individual identity is achieved through a universal process of defining "allies" and "enemies." The process begins in the first few months of life as the infant bonds with the primary caretaker and learns to distinguish familiar others from strangers. This process of we–they differentiation (along with associated affect) continues as a basis for achieving a stable definition of self.

A recent extension of psychoanalytic approaches to understanding group identity is terror management theory (Solomon, Greenberg, & Pyszczynski, 1991) which is based on the idea that when human beings evolved the capacity for self-awareness, this included awareness of mortality and the inevitability of one's own death. Given the universal instinct for self-preservation, this awareness creates a high level of anxiety which could lead to paralyzing fear if not sufficiently suppressed. According to the theory, human societies have evolved shared world views and cultural values as an adaptation to cope with this anxiety over death. By subscribing to this worldview and living up to cultural values, individuals achieve a sense of validation, self-worth, and a type of psychological immortality that serves to suppress mortality terror.

One implication of terror management theory is that if thoughts of mortality are made salient, an individual will respond by reaffirming his or her own cultural worldview, with intolerance toward different values or cultural views. A number of experiments have demonstrated just such a relationship between mortality salience and in-group bias (Greenberg, Simon, Pyszczynski, Solomon, & Chatel, 1992; Harmon-Jones, Greenberg, Solomon, & Simon, 1996; Nelson, Moore, Olivetti, & Scott, 1997). When participants in these studies are induced to think about the prospect of their own death (as compared to other possible negative experiences, such as a painful dental procedure), in-group preference, intolerance of others, and intergroup bias are significantly increased.

Social Identity and Self-Categorization Theory

As originally articulated by Tajfel and Turner (Tajfel, 1981; Tajfel & Turner, 1979; Turner, 1975), the basic premise of social identity theorists is that in-group out-group distinctions arise from social categorization processes. Social identity theory represents the convergence of two traditions in the study of intergroup attitudes and behavior—social categorization and social comparison. The theoretical perspective rests on the following two basic premises:

1. Individuals organize their understanding of the social world on the basis of categorical distinctions that transform continuous variables into discrete classes; categorization has the effect of minimizing perceived differences within categories and accentuating intercategory differences.
2. As individual persons are themselves members of some social categories and not others, social categorization carries with it implicit in-group–out-group (we–they) distinctions; because of the self-relevance of social categories, the in-group–out-group classification is a superimposed category distinction with affective and emotional significance. Accentuation of category differences, combined with a need for positive distinctiveness (intergroup social comparison), results in in-group favoritism or ethnocentrism.

Further elaboration of the cognitive underpinnings of group formation and in-group preference is represented by Turner's self-categorization theory (SCT) (Turner, 1985; Turner, Hogg, Oakes, Reicher, & Wetherell, 1987). From this perspective, personal and social identities differ in that they represent different levels of abstraction (inclusiveness) for self-categorization. Self-categorization at the group level (social identity) is incompatible with categorization at the personal level because it entails a "depersonalization" of self-perception, perceiving oneself as a representative of the in-group category possessing those characteristics that distinguish the in-group from relevant out-groups. According to SCT, it is this depersonalization of self-perception that underlies basic group phenomena, including ethnocentrism, cooperation, emotional contagion, and conformity to group norms (Turner et al., 1987).

Motivational Theories of Social Identification

Self-categorization theory has been influential as a perspective on the underlying nature of group identification, but for many social psychologists, the idea that social identification—with all its significant emotional and behavioral concomitants—is based solely on processes of cognitive categorization was intuitively incomplete. Because group identity sometimes entails self-sacrifice in the interests of group welfare and solidarity, understanding why and when individuals are willing to relegate their sense of self to significant group identities requires motivational as well as cognitive analysis.

Self Esteem   The motivational concept most associated with social identity theory is that of self-esteem enhancement. And it is true that initial development of social identity theory (Tajfel & Turner, 1979; Turner, 1975) implicated self-esteem in postulating a need for "positive distinctiveness" in in-group–out-group

related, empirical research demonstrates little consistent relation between the two. Indeed, results from both laboratory experiments and field studies indicate that variations in in-group positivity and social identification do not systematically correlate with degree of bias or negativity toward out-groups (Brewer, 1979; Hinkle & Brown, 1990; Kosterman & Feshbach, 1989; Struch & Schwartz, 1989). Even for those who are highly identified with a particular social group, attitudes toward relevant out-groups can range from negativity, to indifference, to positivity, depending on the nature of the intergroup context (Duckitt, Callaghan, & Wagner, 2005). It is possible to have in-group loyalty and attachment in the absence of conflict with out-groups.

In order to understand how in-group identification plays a role in intergroup conflict and hostility, it is necessary to identify the conditions under which the survival and welfare of the in-group become associated with specific out-groups. To justify out-group hate and intergroup conflict, the very existence of the out-group, or its goals and values, must be seen as a threat to the maintenance of the in-group and to one's own social identity. Thus, understanding the relationship between in-group identification and out-group hostility requires understanding how the interests and identity of the in-group and those of the out-group come to be perceived as in conflict.

Identification and Intergroup Threat

The many functions that in-group membership and attachment serve for individual security and well-being means that perceived threats to the in-group's existence, welfare, integrity, or distinctiveness have strong emotional significance for identified group members. When the perceived intentions, motives, or interests of a specific out-group are interpreted as posing a threat to the in-group, identification with the in-group and attitudes and behaviors toward that out-group become intertwined. According to the integrated threat theory of intergroup relations (Stephan & Stephan, 2000; Stephan & Renfro, 2002) there are two broad categories of group-level threat—realistic threats and symbolic threats.° Realistic threats are threats to the tangible material, economic, and political welfare of the group, including land, resources, power, and physical well-being. Symbolic threats are nontangible—challenges to the in-group's values, shared beliefs, and worldview including, importantly, collective identity. When group members perceive that their shared sense of who they are and their claims to distinct identity have been denied or disrespected by an out-group, this constitutes a form of symbolic threat that can have impact equivalent to that of more tangible material threat to in-group well-being.

Once an out-group has been perceived as a threat to the integrity of the in-group—whether material or symbolic—the seeds of intergroup conflict have been sown. Of course, a large number of both external and internal factors are

---

° Note that "realistic threat" here refers to the type of threat perceived, not necessarily its objective validity. In either case, what is being referred to is subjective perceptions of threat.

implicated in progressing from intergroup antagonism to overt conflict, but the intimate link between group identification and intergroup threat plays a role in both the onset and perpetuation of intergroup conflict.

Role of Identification in Perceived Threat

Although not all intergroup threats are identity threats, the level of identification among in-group members with the collective as a whole influences the dynamics of perceived intergroup threat in at least two ways. First of all, strength of identification determines how much a threat to the in-group matters to individuals and how likely they are to mobilize in defense of in-group interests (Branscombe, Ellemers, Spears, & Doosje, 1999). The degree of emotional response to collective threats—whether anger or fear or some combination of both—is closely linked to the strength of group identification (Doosje et al., 1998; Smith, Seger, & Mackie, 2007).

Second, strength of in-group identification influences whether intergroup threats are perceived in the first place. For individuals who are highly identified with a group, group interests and personal well-being are intimately linked. Such individuals are more likely than low identifiers to appraise out-group goals and actions in terms of their implications for in-group interests and to be more sensitive to symbolic challenges to in-group identity or values (Smith et al., 2007). In effect, high identification means that the threshold for perceived threat is lowered, and the distinction between symbolic and material, realistic threats may become blurred.

Role of Identification in Justifying Aggression

Although perceived threat may provide sufficient justification to motivate offensive or defensive aggression against the threatening out-group to begin with, the escalation of violence and aggressive actions associated with protracted intergroup conflict may require further collective cognitive effort to justify perpetuating conflict. Again, group identification processes play an important role here. Social psychological research indicates that high identifiers perceive in-group aggression against an out-group as more justified, are more likely to feel satisfaction rather than guilt in response to such intergroup aggression and, in turn, to increase support for further aggression (Maitner, Mackie, & Smith, 2007). Justifying cognitions include attributions to external circumstances or blaming the out-group for bringing it on themselves, downplaying the severity of the harm (Branscombe & Miron, 2004), and dehumanization and moral exclusion of the out-group (Bar-Tal, 1990; Castano & Giner-Sorolla, 2006; Staub, 1990).

Further research suggests that it is a particular type of strong in-group identification that is implicated in the spiral of justifying in-group aggression, especially for particularly brutal or inhumane aggressive actions that might violate moral principles. Group identification actually has a paradoxical relationship to emotional reactions to in-group moral violations. On the one hand, high identification is associated with taking responsibility for in-group actions, a precondition for collective guilt. On the other hand, those who are highly identified are most motivated to maintain and defend a positive in-group identity and hence most likely to seek to justify in-group behaviors. In considering this inherent contradiction, Roccas, Klar, and Liviatan (2006) proposed that identification per se does not necessarily motivate defensive justification for in-group wrongdoing, but only the form of in-group attachment that they termed "glorification" (similar to Staub's (1997) concept of "blind patriotism"). Consistent with their hypothesis, a study of Israeli national identity found that glorification of the national group was associated with endorsement of justifying cognitions in response to a story of an in-group atrocity and negatively related to collective guilt. Controlling for glorification, attachment to the in-group was associated with less justification and more guilt. However, when combined with beliefs in in-group superiority and intense attachment to in-group identity symbols, national identification contributed to a psychology of escalation of intergroup conflict and violence.

THE ROLE OF COLLECTIVE IDENTITY IN INTRACTABLE CONFLICTS

Although perceived threat from specific out-groups fuels intergroup antagonism and hostility, many of these antagonisms never erupt in overt conflict or, if they do, the conflict is relatively quickly resolved through military action or diplomatic negotiation. Of special concern are so-called "intractable conflicts," in which the same two parties are engaged in a persistent state of conflict, including violent clashes and military action, over long periods of time. Intractable conflicts are most often associated with national, ethnic, or religious identity groups (within or between nations), but have also been observed within organizations and small communities (Fiol, Pratt, & O'Connor, 2009; Rothman, 1997).

The central characteristic of intractable conflicts is that they are long standing (Coleman, 2003; Rouhana & Bar-Tal, 1998; Zartman, 2005), lasting for years or even generations. Intractable conflicts are also highly central or chronically salient to those involved in the conflicts (Bar-Tal, 2007; Coleman, 2003). Many researchers view identity as being implicated in intractable conflicts. Research on how intractable conflicts develop suggests that intractable conflicts often begin when a group's identity is denied or invalidated by another party (Kriesberg, 2005; Northrup, 1989; Zartman, 2005). Since identity is central to how people make sense of the world, this invalidation is followed by a distortion of information to fit prior beliefs (Bar-Tal, 2007; Northrup, 1989). Given the central and protracted nature of such conflicts, beliefs about the causes and justification for the antagonism become deeply embedded shared societal beliefs (Bar-Tal, 1998; Rouhana & Bar-Tal, 1998) which include a conviction about the rightness of the in-group's motives and goals, delegitimization of the out-group's position, extreme ethnocentric self-perceptions, and victimization beliefs. As shared beliefs, these conceptualizations of the self and other become incorporated in the narratives of collective identity and group history by both parties (Hammack, 2006).

The role of identity concerns in sustaining intractable conflicts is of particular importance because the costs of extensive and protracted conflict in terms of material resources and human lives defy rational choice theories of group behavior.

With the possible exception of a few individuals who benefit personally (in terms of material wealth or political power) from the ongoing conflict, members of both groups generally recognize that they would be collectively better off if the conflict were resolved. Yet deeply held identity concerns stand as a barrier to negotiated resolution (Kelman, 1999, 2001). Two aspects of collective identity that have been implicated in the perpetuation of destructive conflicts are the perception of the in-group as victim and the development of zero-sum oppositional identities.

Victim Identity

The perception of the in-group as the victim of unfair treatment or aggression from the out-group enemy is a complement to the perception of threat and other justifying cognitions that sustain intergroup conflict. Seeing the self as the victim places the in-group on the moral high ground at the same time that it serves to justify inflicting harm on the out-group. There are at least two ways in which perceived victimization (and associated moral outrage) might become a component of collective identity. The first is the representation of a specific historical event (or period of time) in which members of the in-group were subjected to massacre or humiliation, which becomes part of the collective memory, passed on through generations to the point of becoming a symbol of in-group identity—what Volkan (2007) refers to as *the chosen trauma*, or what Staub (1999) calls *the unhealed wound*. As an element of the shared belief system, the remembered victimization can be activated at any time to mobilize feelings of vulnerability, in-group defense, and moral righteousness in response to perceived contemporary threats, even if the current target out-group is not the same as the historical perpetrator (Kelman, 1999).

The second route by which victimization becomes part of in-group identity occurs in the course of ongoing conflict. Seeing the in-group as victim of the out-group's aggressive intents is often an essential element of the shared beliefs that justify continued hostilities (Rouhana & Bar-Tal, 1998). The focus of such beliefs is on the harm and atrocities perpetrated by the out-group against the in-group, which justify retaliatory actions that perpetuate conflict. In many protracted conflicts, both sides see themselves as the victims of the adversary's aggression, and the perception of in-group as victim becomes a central component of collective identity. In such cases, identities of the conflicting groups become truly oppositional, in the sense that elements of one group's identity negates critical elements of the other's identity and collective narrative.

Oppositional or Zero-Sum Identities

As illustrated by mutual perceptions of victimization, intractable conflicts are characterized by zero-sum conceptualizations of identity (Coleman, 2003; Fiol et al., 2009 Kelman, 1999, 2001; Zartman, 2005). The identities of parties in intractable conflicts are negatively interdependent, such that a key component of each group's identity is based on negation of the other (Kelman, 1999). Further, for one group to maintain its legitimacy, it must delegitimize the other. As a case in point, Kelman

(1999) describes the *psychological core* of the Israeli–Palestinian conflict as "the perception by both parties that it is a zero-sum conflict, not only with respect to territory, but, most importantly, with respect to national identity and national existence" (p. 588). Under such a zero-sum conceptualization, each holds the perception than only one can be legitimately recognized as a nation, that one can acquire national identity only at the expense of the other's claim to nationhood.

A related conceptualization of oppositional identities is represented by Staub (1999) as the "ideology of antagonism"—the perception of the other as an enemy and an in-group identity in which enmity to the other has become an integral component (p. 183). That is, for Groups A and B, a salient part of Group A's identity is not being a member of Group B, and vice versa. When collective identities are oppositional in this sense, successes or achievements of the out-group are interpreted as threats to the in-group and in-group welfare is defined in terms of relative advantage over the out-group. "What sustains the identity of one threatens the identity of the other" (Kelman, 1999, p. 592). Such mutually oppositional or zero-sum conceptions of in-group identity are quintessential elements of intractable conflicts and contribute substantially to what makes such conflicts intractable. As Kelman (1999) puts it, "this negative interdependence not only creates obstacles to conflict resolution and ultimate reconciliation but also makes it more difficult and costly for each group to establish its own identity. It is not enough to demonstrate … its own legitimacy … as a national group; it also has the additional burden of demonstrating the illegitimacy … of the other" (p. 589).

THE ROLE OF IDENTITY IN CONFLICT REDUCTION

As Rothman (1997) noted, "when people's essential identities, as expressed and maintained by their primary group affiliations, are threatened or frustrated, intransigent conflict almost inevitably follows. For such conflicts, conventional methods of conflict management are usually inadequate and may even exacerbate the problem" (p. 5). This epitomizes the view that once intergroup conflicts become defined as "identity conflicts," conflict resolution becomes particularly problematic.

Conflict Resolution as Identity Change

When conflicts take on the characteristics of mutual zero-sum representations of identities by the conflicting parties, prospects for peace and reconciliation require nothing short of collective identity change. In his analysis of the Israeli–Palestinian conflict in particular, Kelman (1999, 2004) emphasizes the need to negotiate a *transcendent identity* as essential to the prospects for peace, but at the same time recognizes the deep-rooted resistance to such identity transformation. Once a longstanding conflict has become incorporated into a group's identity, there is a psychological commitment that becomes a major barrier to change in the conflict relationship. Going from negational identities to shared identity is a Herculean leap. Hence Kelman recognizes the need for transcendent, superordinate identity to develop *alongside* of particularistic identities whereby the distinctive identities of the component subgroups is acknowledged and maintained.

Although nested dual identities have frequently been proposed as a solution to intergroup conflict (Gaertner & Dovidio, 2000; Hornsey & Hogg, 2000), a great deal of social psychological research suggests that an effective balance of dual identification between subgroups and superordinate identity is difficult to achieve or maintain (Brewer, 2000; Mummendey & Wenzel, 1999). For both cognitive and motivational reasons, identification and loyalty to subgroups are likely to take priority over loyalty to the superordinate when interests conflict. Thus, the dual identity strategy for intergroup conflict resolution is a vulnerable one.

Identity Complexity and Conflict Reduction

Given the shared nature of collective identity, identity change is a difficult, extended process, perhaps rarely successfully accomplished by direct, explicit intention. In the face of overt intergroup conflict, more indirect methods of altering identity dynamics may prove to be more fruitful.

Returning to the insights of Maalouf (2000) with which this chapter began, he makes the point that the nemesis is not group identity per se, but rather the focus on singular identity that reduces the complexity of individual attachments and affiliations to a single, central us–them distinction. "People often see themselves in terms of whichever one of their allegiances is most under attack ... And then, whether it relates to color, religion, language or class, it invades the person's whole identity." (Maalouf, 2000, p. 26). Once a people feels wronged or humiliated, they are vulnerable to political leaders or demogogs who exploit the sense of fear, humiliation, and victimization to define themselves in terms of this offended identity, suppress other allegiances, inflame vengeance against the offending "other" and set the stage for war and lethal violence.

In contrast to this singular view of social identity, Maalouf (2000) then goes on to note the consequences of recognizing identity complexity ...

> On the other hand, when one sees one's own identity as made up of a number of allegiances, some linked to an ethnic past and others not, some linked to a religious tradition and others not ... then one enters into a different relationship both with other people and with one's own 'tribe.' It's no longer just a question of 'them' and 'us' .... From then on there are people on 'our' side with whom I ultimately have little in common, while on 'their' side there are some to whom I might feel very close ... (p. 31)

What Maalouf is alluding to here is what social scientists refer to as cross-cutting ties or category memberships. Many bases of social category differentiation—gender, age, religion, ethnicity, occupation—represent cross-cutting cleavages. In contrast to nested social category identities, cross-cutting categorizations involve only partial overlap between membership in two different in-groups; one in-group is not full subsumed within the other. Instead, from the standpoint of a particular person, other individuals may be fellow in-group members on one dimension of category differentiation but out-group members on another.

Evidence from both anthropology (Gluckman, 1955) and political sociology (Coser, 1956) has long suggested that societies characterized by cross-cutting loyalty structures are less prone to schism and internal intergroup conflict than societies characterized by a single hierarchical loyalty structure. More recently, social psychologists have also begun to consider the implications of such multiple cross-cutting social identities for reduction of in-group bias at the individual level (Deschamps & Doise, 1978; Crisp & Hewstone, 2007; Marcus-Newhall, Miller, Holtz, & Brewer, 1993; Roccas & Brewer, 2002). A number of mechanisms have been proposed for why crosscutting group memberships would decrease in-group bias and intergroup discrimination. For one thing, the increased complexity of a multiple social categorizations reduces the salience or degree of differentiation associated with any one in-group–out-group distinction. Beyond the cognitive effects of category complexity, motivational factors also enter in to reduce the likelihood of intense in-group–out-group discrimination. First, the presence of multiple group loyalties potentially reduces the importance or significance of any one social identity for self definition or belonging. Further, cross-category connections and consistency (balance) motives mitigate against negative attitudes toward out-groups that contain members who are fellow in-groupers on some other category dimension. Finally, cross-cutting category memberships increase the degree of interpersonal interaction and contact across any particular category boundaries (Brewer, 2000).

The implication of identity complexity for intergroup relations is that, as individuals, members of conflicting identity groups may belong to other identity groups in which they share membership with some members of the enemy out-group (e.g., farmers, scientists, Christians, etc.). Capitalizing on these cross-cutting identity structures may provide an avenue for mitigating the intensity of singular identity conflicts while not requiring significant identity transformations, at least not all at once. Further, there is evidence that cross-categorization may facilitate the development of transcendent superordinate identities, and, conversely, that the benefits of cross-categorization may be enhanced when both category distinctions are embedded in a common superordinate group identity (Crisp, Walsh, & Hewstone, 2006). Thus, crossed categorization and common in-group identities may work together to produce enhanced inclusiveness and reduced intergroup conflict.

IDENTITY AND CONFLICT: A SUMMARY

As indicated at the start of this chapter, many intractable intergroup conflicts have been designated as "identity conflicts." The purpose of this chapter has been to explicate the multiple different routes by which group identity may be implicated in why conflicts originate and why and how they are sustained. More specifically, I distinguished between processes associated with group identification (social identity) at the individual level and processes associated with the maintenance of shared collective identity at the group level. Of course, social identity and collective identity are inextricably intertwined. Shared values, norms, and a common understanding of collective history and definition of the "we" are essential to establish and maintain the perception of a meaningful group entity that engages identification among group members. Identification, in turn, means that the collective identity is incorporated in the individual's sense of self and continuity across time (Hammack, 2008). Thus, as identification increases, the importance of maintaining a consistent and agreed-upon collective narrative is increased, and as the salience of a consensual collective identity is increased (though incorporation in group institutions, practices, and discourse), identification is furthered increased, and so on.

This reciprocal relationship between collective identity content and social identification processes explains why intergroup conflicts that become imbued with identity significance are so likely to be intractable—especially if the conflict becomes part of the collective identity itself (Bar-Tal, 2007). And conflict also reinforces and strengthens the linkage between collective and social identity and between individual and group survival. The reciprocal relationship between collective and social identity also explains why identity change is so difficult, because it requires breaking the mutually reinforcing ties between shared definitions of the collective and strength of identification with the group and its preservation. It is for this reason that I have suggested that more indirect strategies that capitalize on alternative social identities and cross-cutting ties may provide the key to breaking the vicious cycle of identity conflicts.

REFERENCES

Archer, J. (1991). Human sociobiology: Basic concepts and limitations. *Journal of Social Issues, 47*(3), 11–26.

Ashbach, C., & Schermer, V. (Eds.). (1987). *Object relations, the self, and the group.* London: Routledge & Kegan Paul.

Bar-Tal, D. (1990). Causes and consequences of delegitimization: Models of conflict and ethnocentrism. *Journal of Social Issues, 46,* 65–81.

Bar-Tal, D. (1998). Societal beliefs in times of intractable conflict. The Israeli case. *International Journal of Conflict Management, 9,* 22–50.

Bar-Tal, D. (2007). Sociopsychological foundations of intractable conflicts. *American Behavioral Scientist, 50,* 1430–1453.

Baumeister, R. F., & Leary, M. R. (1995). The need to belong: Desire for interpersonal attachments as a fundamental human motivation. *Psychological Bulletin, 117,* 497–529.

Branscombe, N. R., Ellemers, N., Spears, R., & Doosje, B. (1999). The context and content of social identity threat. In N. Ellemers, R. Spears, & B. Doosje (Eds.), *Social identity: Context, commitment, content* (pp. 35–58). Oxford: Blackwell.

Branscombe, N. R., & Miron, M. (2004). Interpreting the ingroup's negative actions toward another group: Emotional reactions to appraised harm. In L. Tiedens & C. Leach (Eds.), *The social life of emotions* (pp. 314–335). New York: Cambridge University Press.

Branscombe, N. R., Schmitt, M. T., & Harvey, R. D. (1999). Perceiving pervasive discrimination among African-Americans: Implications for group identification and well-being. *Journal of Personality and Social Psychology, 77,* 135–149.

Brewer, M. B. (1979). In-group bias in the minimal intergroup situation: A cognitive-motivational analysis. *Psychological Bulletin, 86,* 307–324.

Brewer, M. B. (1991). The social self: On being the same and different at the same time. *Personality and Social Psychology Bulletin, 17,* 475–482.

Brewer, M. B. (1999). The psychology of prejudice: In-group love or out-group hate? *Journal of Social Issues*, 55, 429–444.

Brewer, M. B. (2000). Reducing prejudice through cross-categorization: Effects of multiple social identities. In S. Oskamp (Ed.) *Reducing prejudice and discrimination. The Claremont symposium on applied social psychology* (pp. 165–183). Mahwah, NJ: Erlbaum.

Brewer, M. B. (2007). The importance of being "we." Human nature and intergroup relations. *American Psychologist*, 62, 728–738.

Brewer, M. B., & Caporael, L. R. (2006). An evolutionary perspective on social identity: Revisiting groups. In M. Schaller, J. Simpson, & D. Kenrick (Eds.), *Evolution and social psychology* (pp. 143–161). New York: Psychology Press.

Buss, D. M. (1991). Evolutionary personality psychology. *Annual Review of Psychology*, 45, 459–491.

Caporael, L. R., & Brewer, M. B. (1991). Reviving evolutionary psychology: Biology meets society. *Journal of Social Issues*, 47(3), 187–195.

Castano, E., & Giner-Sorolla, R. (2006). Not quite human: Infrahumanization in response to collective responsibility for intergroup killing. *Journal of Personality and Social Psychology*, 90, 804–819.

Coleman, P. (2003). Characteristics of protracted, intractable conflict: Toward the development of a meta-framework-I. *Peace and Conflict: Journal of Peace Psychology*, 9, 1–37.

Coser, L. A. (1956). *The functions of social conflict*. New York: Free Press.

Crisp, R. J., & Hewstone, M. (2007). Multiple social categorization. In M. Zanna (Ed.), *Advances in experimental social psychology* (Vol. 39, pp. 163–254). Orlando, FL: Academic Press.

Crisp, R. J., Walsh, J., & Hewstone, M. (2006). Crossed categorization in common ingroup contexts. *Personality and Social Psychology Bulletin*, 32, 1204–1218.

Crocker, J., Luhtanen, R., Blaine, B., & Broadnax, S. (1994). Collective self-esteem and psychological well-being among White, Black, and Asian college students. *Personality and Social Psychology Bulletin*, 20, 503–513.

Deaux, K., Reid, A., Mizrahi, K., & Cotting, D. (1999). Connecting the person to the social: The functions of social identification. In T. Tyler, R. Kramer, & O. John (Eds.), *The psychology of the social self* (pp. 91–113). Mahwah, NJ: Erlbaum.

Deschamps, J-C., & Doise, W. (1978). Crossed category memberships in intergroup relations. In H. Tajfel (Ed.), *Differentiation between social groups* (pp. 141–158). Cambridge: Cambridge University Press.

Duckitt, J., Callaghan, J., & Wagner, C. (2005). Group identification and outgroup attitudes in four South African ethnic groups: A multidimensional approach. *Personality and Social Psychology Bulletin*, 31, 633–646.

Fiol, C. M., Pratt, M. G., & O'Connor, E. J. (2009). Managing intractable identity conflicts. *Academy of Management Review*, 34, 32–55.

Freud, S. (1912/1957). Totem and taboo. In *The standard edition of the complete works of Sigmund Freud*, Vol. 13. London: Hogarth Press.

Freud, S. (1921/1960). *Group psychology and the analysis of the ego*. New York: Bantam.

Gaertner, S. L., & Dovidio, J. F. (2000). *Reducing intergroup bias: The common ingroup identity model*. Philadelphia: Psychology Press.

Gluckman, M. (1955). *Customs and conflict in Africa*. London: Blackwell.

Greenberg, J., Simon, L., Pyszczynski, T., Solomon, S., & Chatel, D. (1992). Terror management and tolerance: Does mortality salience always intensify negative reactions to others who threaten one's worldview? *Journal of Personality and Social Psychology*, 63, 212–220.

Grieve, P. G., & Hogg, M. A. (1999). Subjective uncertainty and intergroup discrimination in the minimal group situation. *Personality and Social Psychology Bulletin*, 25, 926–940.

Hammack, P. L. (2006). Identity, conflict, and coexistence: Life stories of Israeli and Palestinian adolescents. *Journal of Adolescent Research, 21*, 323–369.

Hammack, P. L. (2008). Narrative and the cultural psychology of identity. *Personality and Social Psychology Review, 12*, 222–247.

Harmon-Jones, E., Greenberg, J., Solomon, S., & Simon, L. (1996). The effects of mortality salience on intergroup bias between minimal groups. *European Journal of Social Psychology, 26*, 677–681.

Hinkle, S., & Brown, R. (1990). Intergroup comparisons and social identity: Some links and lacunae. In D. Abrams & M. Hogg (Eds.), *Social identity theory: Constructive and critical advances* (pp. 48–70). Hemel Hempstead, UK: Harvester Wheatsheaf.

Hogg, M. A. & Abrams, D. (1993). Towards a single-process uncertainty-reduction model of social motivation in groups. In M. Hogg & D. Abrams (Eds.), *Group motivation: Social psychological perspectives* (pp. 173–190). Hemel Hempstead, UK: Harvester Wheatsheaf.

Hogg, M. A., & Mullin, B-A. (1999). Joining groups to reduce uncertainty: Subjective uncertainty reduction and group identification. In D. Abrams & M. A. Hogg (Eds.), *Social identity and social cognition* (pp. 249–279). Oxford: Blackwell.

Hornsey, M. J., & Hogg, M. A. (2000). Subgroup relations: A comparison of the mutual intergroup differentiation and common ingroup identity models of prejudice reduction. *Personality and Social Psychology Bulletin, 26*, 242–256.

Jetten, J., Branscombe, N. R., Schmitt, M. T., & Spears, R. (2001). Rebels with a cause: Group identification as a response to perceived discrimination from the mainstream. *Personality and Social Psychology Bulletin, 27*, 1204–1213.

Johnson, G. R. (1989). The role of kin recognition mechanisms in patriotic socialization: Further reflections. *Politics and the Life Sciences, 8*, 62–69.

Kelman, H. C. (1999). The interdependence of Israeli and Palestinian national identities: The role of the other in existential conflicts. *Journal of Social Issues, 55*, 581–600.

Kelman, H. C. (2001). The role of national identity in conflict resolution. In R. D. Ashmore, L. Jussim, & D. Wilder (Eds.), *Social identity, intergroup conflict, and conflict reduction* (pp. 187–212). New York: Oxford University Press.

Kelman, H. C. (2004). Reconciliation as identity change: A social-psychological perspective. In Y. Bar-Siman-Tov (Ed.), *From conflict resolution to reconciliation* (pp. 11–124). Oxford, England: Oxford University Press.

Klein, M. (1975). *Love, guilt, and reparation and other works: 1921–1945*. New York: Delta.

Kosterman, R., & Feshbach, S. (1989). Toward a measure of patriotic and nationalistic attitudes. *Political Psychology, 10*, 257–274.

Kriesberg, L. (2005). Nature, dynamics, and phases of intractability. In C. Crocker, F. Hampson, & P. Aall (Eds.), *Grasping the nettle: Analyzing cases of intractable conflict* (pp. 65–97). Washington, DC: United States Institute of Peace Press.

Ledgerwood, A., Liviatan, I., & Carnevale, P. (2007). Group-identity completion and the symbolic value of property. *Psychological Science, 18*, 873–878.

Maalouf, A. (2000). *In the name of identity*. New York: Penguin Books.

Maitner, A. T., Mackie, D. M., & Smith, E. R. (2007). Antecedents and consequences of satisfaction and guilt following ingroup aggression. *Group Processes and Intergroup Relations, 10*, 223–237.

Marcus-Newhall, A., Miller, N., Holtz, R., & Brewer, M. B. (1993). Cross-cutting category membership with role assignment: A means of reducing intergroup bias. *British Journal of Social Psychology, 32*, 125–146.

Mullin, B-A., & Hogg, M. A. (1998). Dimensions of subjective uncertainty in social identification and minimal intergroup discrimination. *British Journal of Social Psychology, 37*, 345–365.

Mummendey, A., & Wenzel, M. (1999). Social discrimination and tolerance in intergroup relations: Reactions to intergroup difference. *Personality and Social Psychology Review*, 3, 158–174.

Nelson, L. J., Moore, D. L., Olivetti, J., & Scott, T. (1997). General and personal mortality salience and nationalistic bias. *Personality and Social Psychology Bulletin*, 23, 884–892.

Northrup, T. (1989). The dynamic of identity in personal and social conflict. In L. Kriesberg, T. Northrup, & S. Thorson (Eds.), *Intractable conflicts and their transformation* (pp. 55–82). Syracuse, NY: Syracuse University Press.

Perdue, C., Dovidio, J., Gurtman, M., & Tyler, R. (1990). Us and them: Social categorization and the process of intergroup bias. *Journal of Personality and Social Psychology*, 59, 475–486.

Reynolds, V., Falger, V., & Vine, I. (Eds.). (1987). *The sociobiology of ethnocentrism*. London: Croom Helm.

Roccas, S., & Brewer, M. B. (2002). Social identity complexity. *Personality and Social Psychology Review*, 6, 88–106.

Roccas, S., Klar, Y., & Liviatan, I. (2006). The paradox of group-based guilt: Modes of national identification, conflict vehemence, and reactions to the in-group's moral violations. *Journal of Personality and Social Psychology*, 91, 698–711.

Rothman, J. (1997). *Resolving identity-based conflict in nations, organizations, and communities*. San Francisco, CA: Jossey-Bass.

Rouhana, N. N., & Bar-Tal, D. (1998). Psychological dynamics of intractable ethnonational conflicts: The Israeli–Palestinian case. *American Psychologist*, 53, 761–770.

Rubin, M., & Hewstone, M. (1998). Social identity theory's self-esteem hypothesis: A review and some suggestions for clarification. *Personality and Social Psychology Review*, 2, 40–62.

Shaw, R. P., & Wong, Y. (1989). *The genetic seeds of warfare: Evolution, nationalism and patriotism*. Boston: Unwin & Hyman.

Smith, E. R., Seger, C. R., & Mackie, D. M. (2007). Can emotions be truly group level? Evidence regarding four conceptual criteria. *Journal of Personality and Social Psychology*, 93, 431–446.

Solomon, S., Greenberg, J., & Pyszczynski, T. (1991). A terror management theory of social behavior: The psychological functions of self-esteem and cultural worldviews. In M. Zanna (Ed.), *Advances in experimental social psychology* (Vol. 24, pp. 91–159). San Diego, CA: Academic Press.

Stapel, D. A., & Marx, D. M. (2007). Distinctiveness is key: How different types of self-other similarity moderate social comparison effects. *Personality and Social Psychology Bulletin*, 33, 437–448.

Staub, E. (1990). Moral exclusion, personal goal theory, and extreme destructiveness. *Journal of Social Issues*, 46, 47–64.

Staub, E. (1997). Blind versus constructive patriotism: Moving from embeddedness in the group to critical loyalty and action. In D. Bar-Tal & E. Staub (Eds.), *Patriotism in the lives of individuals and nations* (pp. 213–228). New York: Nelson-Hall.

Staub, E. (1999). The roots of evil: Social conditions, culture, personality, and basic human needs. *Personality and Social Psychology Review*, 3, 179–192.

Stephan, W. G., & Renfro, C. L. (2002). The role of threat in intergroup relations. In D. Mackie & E. Smith (Eds.), *From prejudice to intergroup emotions* (pp. 191–207). Philadelphia, PA: Psychology Press.

Stephan, W. G., & Stephan, C. W. (2000). An integrated threat theory of prejudice. In S. Oskamp (Ed.), *Reducing prejudice and discrimination* (pp. 23–45). Mahwah, NJ: Erlbaum.

Struch, N., & Schwartz, S. H. (1989). Intergroup aggression: Its predictors and distinctness from in-group bias. *Journal of Personality & Social Psychology*, 56, 264–373.

Sumner, W. G. (1906). *Folkways.* New York: Ginn.

Tajfel, H. (1981). *Human groups and social categories*. Cambridge: Cambridge University Press.

Tajfel, H., Billig, M., Bundy, R., & Flament, C. (1971). Social categorization and intergroup behaviour. *European Journal of Social Psychology*, 1, 149–178.

Tajfel, H., & Turner, J. C. (1979). An integrative theory of intergroup conflict. In W. Austin & S. Worchel (Eds.), *Social psychology of intergroup relations* (pp. 33–47). Chicago, Nelson.

Turner, J. C. (1975). Social comparison and social identity: Some prospects for intergroup behaviour. *European Journal of Social Psychology*, 5, 5–34.

Turner, J. C. (1978). Social categorization and social discrimination in the minimal group paradigm. In H. Tajfel (Ed.), *Differentiation between social groups*. London: Academic Press.

Turner, J. C. (1985). Social categorization and the self-concept: A social cognitive theory of group behavior. In E. Lawler (Ed.), *Advances in group processes* (Vol. 2, pp. 77–122). Greenwich, CN: JAI Press.

Turner, J. C., Hogg, M., Oakes, P., Reicher, S., & Wetherell, M. (1987). *Rediscovering the social group: A self-categoriztaion theory*. Oxford: Basil Blackwell.

Turner, J. C., Hogg, M., Turner, P., & Smith, P. (1984). Failure and defeat as determinants of group cohesiveness. *British Journal of Social Psychology*, 23, 97–111.

van Vugt, M., & Park, J. (2010). The tribal instinct hypothesis: Evolution and the social psychology of intergroup relations. In S. Sturmer & M. Snyder (Eds.), *The psychology of prosocial behavior* (pp. 13–32). Chichester, UK: Wiley-Blackwell.

Volkan, V. D. (1988). *The need to have enemies and allies*. Northvale, NJ: Jason Aronson.

Volkan, V. D. (2007). *Killing in the name of identity. A study of bloody conflicts*. Charlottesville, VA: Pitchstone Publishing.

van den Berghe, P. L. (1981). *The ethnic phenomenon*. New York: Elsevier.

Vignoles, V. L., Chryssochoou, Z., & Breakwell, G. M. (2000). The distinctiveness principle: Identity, meaning, and the bounds of cultural relativity. *Personality and Social Psychology Review*, 4, 337–354.

Zartman, I. W. (2005). Analyzing intractability. In C. Crocker, F. Hampson, & P. Aall (Eds.), *Grasping the nettle: Analyzing cases of intractable conflict* (pp. 47–64). Washington, DC: United States Institute of Peace Press.

6

Ideological Conflict and Polarization
A Social Psychological Perspective

MARGARITA KROCHIK and JOHN T. JOST

"Beware
  Of entrance to a quarrel; but being in,
  Bear't that the opposed may beware of thee."

Polonius
Hamlet, Act I, Scene III

Social psychologists, among others, have long sought to understand and resolve conflicts between groups along cultural, ethnic, religious, or linguistic lines (Bar-Tal, Raviv, Raviv, & Dgani-Hirsh, 2009; Brewer & Miller, 1996; Brown, 2000; Deutsch, Coleman, & Marcus, 2006; Gaertner & Dovidio, 2000; Lewin, 1948; Prentice & Miller, 1999; Ross & Ward, 1995; Stephan & Stephan, 2001; Tajfel, 1982; Worchel, 1999). They have not, however, done much to analyze, let alone prevent, conflict along left–right (or liberal–conservative) ideological lines. There are probably several reasons for this, including relatively widespread skepticism among social and behavioral scientists about whether ordinary citizens are really motivated by ideological concerns (for a historical review see Jost, 2006). Furthermore, those researchers who have assumed that ideology is an important force in social and political life may have viewed ideological conflict as either necessary or desirable.

In this chapter we address four related questions pertaining to ideological conflict and polarization. For some, these questions have acquired additional urgency in the aftermath of the events of September 11, 2001. First, in what sense, if any, are ordinary people "ideological"? Second, is ideological conflict and polarization "real," or is it just a myth? Third, what are the social and psychological factors that would be expected to moderate the degree of ideological polarization? And fourth, what are the societal advantages and disadvantages of ideological conflict and polarization if and when it does occur? Answers to this last question may help to determine whether we should intervene in cases of ideological conflict, assuming that it is in fact possible to reduce ideological conflict through the kinds of interventions that help to diffuse other forms of intergroup conflict. It is important to point out that although ideological conflict between left and right is obviously not the same as interethnic conflict, ethnic or religious tensions often inflame ideological disputes. That is, issues of immigration, terrorism, and war tend to create ideological rifts as well as magnify the intensity of existing left-right ideological conflict within and between societies.

IN WHAT SENSE ARE PEOPLE "IDEOLOGICAL"?

For the present purposes, ideology may be defined rather simply as a socially shared belief system about how society should conduct itself (and how it conducts itself at present); such a belief system helps to structure (or organize) thoughts and feelings about the social and political world and motivate action for or against the status quo (Denzau & North, 1994; Freeden, 2003; Jost, 2006; Tedin, 1987). Although most philosophers and social scientists since the early twentieth century have assumed that the majority of citizens have at least some ideological inclinations, Converse (1964) argued that ordinary citizens are largely "innocent" of political ideology. Specifically, he used sets of pairwise correlations to argue that there was a fundamental lack of consistency or constraint among issue positions in the electorate. Drawing on public opinion data from the 1950s, Converse proposed that no more than 10–15% of the general population organized political knowledge in terms of left–right or liberal–conservative dimensions. This conclusion has exerted considerable influence over social scientists' assumptions about the motives and capacities of the electorate, as reflected in a great many treatments of the topic of ideology (inter alia, Bishop, 2005; Fiorina, Abrams, & Pope, 2006; Kinder & Sears, 1985; Luskin, 1987; McGuire, 1985).

In an attempt to synthesize research literatures in sociology, political science, and psychology, Jost (2006) questioned the notion that most people are "nonideological." Although Converse (1964) is correct that people are not perfectly consistent (or loyal) in their political attitudes, ample anecdotal and empirical evidence exists to support the idea that political attitudes and behaviors are far from randomly determined. Furthermore, the degree of consistency or structure that does exist may be attributable to psychological (rather than logical) processes. Ideology is not merely the expression of "rational" personal or collective interests; rather, it both reflects and reinforces the social and psychological needs, motives, and characteristics of individuals and groups. This proposition comports with the general social psychological assumption that an individual's motivational background shapes his or her thoughts, beliefs, and attributions (Kruglanski, 1996; Kunda, 1990).

Along these lines, Jost, Glaser, Kruglanski, and Sulloway (2003a, 2003b) conceptualized political ideology as a form of motivated social cognition. They began by suggesting that two core, relatively stable, consistent, and fundamental attitude dimensions characterize ideological differences between the left (e.g., liberalism) and the right (e.g., conservatism): (1) advocating (vs. resisting) social change, and (2) challenging (vs. accepting) social and economic inequality. Attitudes concerning more peripheral aspects of liberalism and conservatism were expected to be less stable, consistent, or "constrained." Jost et al. (2003a, 2003b) also proposed that an individual's position on the two core attitudinal dimensions (and the left–right spectrum in general) was governed in part by her or his epistemic and existential motives. In support of the foregoing, research has established a consistent empirical link between adherence to political conservatism (vs. liberalism) and psychological needs to reduce uncertainty and threat (Jost et al., 2003a, 2003b, 2007).

Bar-Tal et al. (2009) have recently argued that in certain sociopolitical contexts, such as contemporary Israeli society, a prevailing *ethos of conflict* can operate as an ideology that perpetuates a cycle of violence (refer to Chapter 9, this volume). At first blush, the "ethos of conflict" seems unrelated to left–right political orientation. However, there are several reasons to expect that it will be more prevalent among adherents to conservative or right-wing (rather than liberal or left-wing) orientation. For one thing, conservatives tend to be more patriotic and nationalistic than are liberals, and these characteristics are frequently associated with conflict orientations when it comes to international relations (Kerlinger, 1984; Kosterman & Feshbach, 1989; Rathbun, 2007). Second, conservatives are more authoritarian and dominance-oriented than are liberals (Altemeyer, 1996, 1998; Napier & Jost, 2008; Sidanius & Pratto, 1999). Third, those who identify themselves as right-wingers exhibit moral and ethnic intolerance to a greater extent than those who identify as leftists (Lipset & Raab, 1978; Napier & Jost, 2008). Fourth, conservatives are generally more isolationist in terms of their foreign policy preferences, but they are also more militarily assertive and more likely to recommend going to war when national interests are at stake (Herrmann, Tetlock, & Visser, 1999; Holsti & Rosenau, 1988, 1996; Murray, Cowden, & Russett, 1999; Rathbun, 2007). That is, on average, conservatives are more likely to be "hawks," whereas liberals are more likely to be "doves" (Liebes, Katz, & Ribak, 1991; Zaller, 1992). For all of these reasons, we would expect left–right ideological differences to correspond (at least roughly) to various ways of addressing intergroup conflict in society. The degree of polarization between liberals and conservatives also likely affects the tone and outcome of ethnic and other policy discussions, just as issues of ethnic conflict, terrorism, and war affect the terms of debate between the left and right within a given society.

Ideology as Motivated Social Cognition

According to the motivated social cognition perspective, ideological forces can inspire conviction, rouse passion, and prompt action in part because ideologies have the capacity to satisfy a wide range of human motives (Jost et al., 2003a). People crave meaning and reassurance, and ideologies fulfill these needs by providing powerful and efficient schemas that help people to explain, justify, or criticize aspects of the social and political world (Jost, 2006). On this view, then, ideologies are psychologically motivated, regardless of their specific contents (Jost et al., 2003b). Recently, Jost, Ledgerwood, and Hardin (2008) proposed that ideology is motivated not only by epistemic and existential motives but also by relational motives to maintain shared reality and foster solidarity with fellow group members. We discuss these three types of motives and their relations to political ideology in the sections to follow.

Epistemic Motives

Epistemic motives capture the human desire for knowledge and meaning, and they shape the strategies individuals employ to acquire, process, and reconcile information about their environment (Kruglanski, 1989). Reasoning processes are said to be motivated to the extent that an individual's desire to attain certain outcomes (e.g., accuracy) or reach certain conclusions (e.g., confirmation of a prior belief) constrains the ways in which he or she searches for and interprets information (Kunda, 1990). Thus, the desire for accuracy and comprehensive knowledge generally leads to a more inclusive, systematic integration of relevant information (Cacioppo & Petty, 1982; Freund, Kruglanski, Shpitzajzen, 1985; Petty & Cacioppo, 1984), whereas the need for immediate, firm, and unambiguous knowledge leads to a relatively cursory search for readily available, clear, and simple information, which is often followed by cognitive resistance to potentially important but contradictory information (Webster & Kruglanski, 1994).

Recent work on epistemic motivation demonstrates that liberals tend to score higher than conservatives on the Need for Cognition, a scale designed to measure the enjoyment of thinking in complex and abstract ways (Cacioppo & Petty, 1982; Federico & Schneider, 2007; Sargent, 2004). These results are consistent with previous studies of elite political discourse, which found that center-left politicians exhibit greater cognitive complexity (operationalized as the tendency to consider and integrate potentially conflicting pieces of information) in comparison with center-right politicians (Tetlock, 1983, 1984; Tetlock, Bernzweig, & Gallant, 1985). The tendency to "seize" and "freeze" on firm, unambiguous answers—fuelled by the epistemic drive to establish cognitive closure—is more prevalent among conservatives than liberals. Elevated scores on the Need for Closure scale (Webster & Kruglanski, 1994) have been observed among self-identified conservatives (Jost, Kruglanski, & Simon, 1999), supporters of right-wing political parties (Golec, 2001; Chirumbolo & Leone, 2008; Kemmelmeier, 1997), and individuals who endorse attitudes associated with the right, such as support for the death penalty (Jost et al., 1999) and the Iraq war (Federico, Golec, & Dial, 2005).

A meta-analysis conducted by Jost et al. (2003a, 2003b) confirmed that liberal and conservative ideologies are motivated by distinct epistemic needs. Averaging across dozens of studies, thousands of observations, and a variety of national contexts, the authors found a consistent positive relationship between conservative (or right-wing) political orientation and cognitive tendencies toward simplicity, stability, predictability, and order; liberal (or left-wing) political orientation, on the other hand, was associated with greater openness to experience and tolerance for uncertainty. These findings are also consistent with the observation that the social and political judgments of conservatives tend to be more internally consistent than those of liberals (Krochik, Jost, & Nosek, 2007), and that liberals are more likely than conservatives to engage in secondary processes of attitude correction (Skitka, Mullen, Griffin, Hutchinson, & Chamberlin, 2002; Skitka & Tetlock, 1993).

Existential Motives   Existential motives concern the human striving for safety and security (Jost et al., 2003a, 2003b). They can be understood as motives to maintain specific emotional end-states (e.g., equanimity) and to avoid threatening affective experiences, such as fear, anxiety, or lack of control (Higgins, 1996). The need for existential security is thus expressed in the individual's efforts to manage potential threats. When eliminating a threat is not possible, belief systems that provide a sense of meaning, predictability, order, or justice may serve as psychological buffers (Jost, Banaji, & Nosek, 2004; Kay, Gaucher, Napier, Callan, & Laurin, 2008; Lerner, 1975; Pyszczynski, Solomon, & Greenberg, 2003). Because ideologies offer broad, morally relevant interpretive frameworks that can be readily used to define, justify, or defuse situations that would otherwise be troubling, confusing, or anxiety-producing, we would expect people to seek out and hold fast to ideological explanations when security is either sought or threatened. According to proponents of terror management theory, people endorse stereotypes, ideologies, and "cultural worldviews" that help them to imbue their existence with meaning and to transcend chronic fears of death (Landau, Greenberg, & Rothschild, 2009; Solomon, Greenberg, & Pyszczynki, 2004).

While it may be true that a wide variety of cultural worldviews can provide some degree of existential security and purpose to their adherents, some types of belief systems are likely to confer more existential benefits than others (Jost, Fitzsimons, & Kay, 2004). Many studies suggest, for example, that individuals who are chronically or temporarily threatened are more likely to gravitate toward conservative ideologies (Bonanno & Jost, 2006; Cohen, Ogilvie, Solomon, Greenberg, & Pyszczynski, 2005; Jost et al., 2003a, 2007, 2009; Lavine, Polichak, & Lodge, 1999; Thorisdottir & Jost, in press). Individuals who score highly on measures of death anxiety and perceptions of a dangerous world are more likely to be conservative than liberal (Altemeyer, 1996; Duckitt, 2001; Jost et al., 2007; Wilson, 1973), in comparison with liberals. Studies of physiological reactivity indicate that individuals who endorse socially conservative positions on domestic and international issues (e.g., support for the death penalty, military spending, aggressive foreign policy, opposition to gay marriage, and immigration) are more sensitive to threatening visual stimuli (Oxley et al., 2008). In terms of international relations, it is easy to imagine that acts of terrorism or military aggression could contribute to a spiral of conflict in which the power and influence of hard-liners (especially right-wing extremists) are reinforced in two or more countries that are facing off (e.g., the United States and Iran), in large part because of the threat posed by the other.

Relational Motives   Subscribing to a shared belief system is also likely to satisfy relational needs, insofar as it facilitates "common ground" that can be used to build rapport, establish mutual understanding, and foster collective action (Bar-Tal, 1990; Jost, Federico, & Napier, 2009). According to Hardin and Higgins (1996), a primary goal of social interaction is to achieve shared reality with important others, thereby externally validating one's own perceptions and rendering subjective experiences more reliable and "objective" (Hardin & Conley, 2000; Turner, 1991). Because of this social validation function, sharing beliefs with relevant others may satisfy epistemic (as well as relational) needs insofar as it promotes subjective certainty and cognitive closure. For this reason and perhaps for other reasons too (Jost, Ledgerwood, & Hardin, 2008), conservatives may be somewhat more motivated than liberals to embrace consensually held beliefs, identify with relatively homogeneous groups, and endorse mainstream or conventional values, stereotypes, and norms (Graham, Haidt, & Nosek, 2009; Jost, Nosek, & Gosling, 2008; Kruglanski, Pierro, Mannetti, & De Grada, 2006).

At the same time, it is important to recognize that liberal as well as conservatives ideologies are transmitted through social channels; thus, relational motives probably underlie ideological conviction across the ideological spectrum. In contrast to theoretical perspectives that emphasize purely "top-down" processes of elite communication and thereby assume relatively passive ideological absorption by the masses, a motivated social cognitive perspective attends to the ways in which individuals actively engage with social influence processes as targets—as well as sources—of social influence (Jost, Federico, & Napier, 2009). Decades of theory and research in social psychology suggest that both direct and indirect forms of influence are facilitated when the target of influence is psychologically predisposed to respond favorably to the communication and to identify with its source (Kelman, 1958; McGuire, 1985; Moscovici, 1976; Turner, 1991). Because most people share ideological convictions with peers, friends, family members, social networks, and other reference groups (Beck & Jennings, 1975; Jennings & Niemi, 1981; Jost, Ledgerwood, & Hardin, 2008), issues of left and right can take on personal as well as interpersonal significance.

IDEOLOGICAL POLARIZATION: MYTH OR REALITY?

There is some utility in considering the development and trajectory of ideological conflict in the United States as a kind of example or case study of how an "ethos of conflict"—in this case an explicitly ideological ethos of conflict—can grip much of the nation's citizenry. We begin with the right-wing political candidate turned commentator Patrick Buchanan (2004), who—12 years after his infamous "culture war" speech during the Republican National Convention—forcefully reiterated his contention that the United States was deeply divided, writing in his *American Cause* column: "We no longer inhabit the same moral universe. We are no longer moral community. We are two countries." Buchanan was referring to the growing number of ideological differences between American liberals and conservatives that had accumulated since the civil rights movements of the 1960's. His words echoed an argument advanced by sociologist James Hunter (1991), whose examination of everyday American discourse led him to conclude that a culture war was ablaze between religious conservatives and secular progressives. Hunter argued that ideological conflict touched the lives of most Americans, embroiling families and even entire communities in a struggle over cherished (but opposing) values and potentially irreconcilable moral visions. Conflict in the Middle East has often precipitated religious and ideological polarization in the West, including the United States.

US Presidential elections since 2000 (and especially after the terrorist attacks of 9/11) have revealed what appear (to many observers) to be deep and widespread ideological divisions in the electorate. At the same time, much academic debate persists concerning the question of ideological polarization. Some researchers have argued that most Americans are politically centrist, that policy consensus is far more common than political conflict, and that what may look like polarization in the electorate is really just an artifact of relatively esoteric disputes among political elites. The most prominent voices in this camp are Fiorina et al. (2006), who wrote that:

> [W]hat we call the political class in America definitely is polarized and prob-
> ably has become more so in recent decades. But ... it is a mistake to assume
> that what is true of a fraction of Americans who are politically active also holds
> true for the great preponderance of us. In general, normal Americans are busy
> earning their livings and raising their families. They are not very well-informed
> about politics and public affairs, do not care a great deal about politics, do not
> hold many of their views very strongly, and are not ideological. (p. 19)

This general view owes much to Converse (1964), who supplied the epigram for Fiorina et al.'s (2006) book and who, as we have already seen, described the views of the average voter as being essentially devoid of ideological content and structure.

Abramowitz and Saunders (2008) have strongly challenged Fiorina et al.'s (2006) "myth of polarization" hypothesis by identifying fairly major ideological, partisan, and cultural divides using data from the American National Election Studies. They have also provided evidence against the notion that partisanship merely reflects citizens' attachments to specific social groups rather than any bona fide ideological inclinations (Cohen, 2003; Conover & Feldman, 1981; Green, Palmquist, & Schickler, 2002). Tracking party identification and ideology in the American public from 1952 to 2004, Abramowitz and Saunders observed that the correlation between partisanship and ideology has strengthened substantially since the 1970s.

Furthermore, ideological interest and sophistication have grown alongside educational gains in the US population over the last few decades (Jacoby, 1991; Tedin, 1987), enabling citizens to choose parties that more closely represent their own positions on various political issues (Abramowitz & Saunders, 2006, 2008). On the basis of American National Election Study results, Moskowitz and Jenkins (2004) concluded that the vast majority of the electorate: (a) expressed issue positions that were generally coherent and consistent; (b) organized their attitudes along three correlated dimensions (i.e., social, economic, and racial dimensions); (c) located themselves on a liberal–conservative spectrum that incorporated their positions with respect to all three of these dimensions; (d) conditioned their candidate and party preferences on the basis of this ideological self-placement; and (e) displayed overall democratic competence in terms of political deliberation.

Ideological thinking, in other words, is hardly limited to political elites, although it is true that party leaders (and media representatives) do serve a number of important "top-down" functions. These include engaging citizens in politics, clarifying party platforms, and helping people to structure their views across issues in line with their ideological leanings (Abramowitz & Saunders, 1998; Baldassari & Gelman, 2008; Layman & Carsey, 2002a, 2002b; Lodge & Hamill, 1986; Nie, Verba, & Petrocik,

1979; Zaller, 1992). In our view, however, it would be a mistake to characterize voters as simply passive recipients of information that is disseminated in a purely top-down fashion by elites. There are also "bottom-up" factors, such as personality and ideological proclivities, that determine individuals' receptiveness to the specific contents of political messages (Jost, Federico, & Napier, 2009; Jost, West, & Gosling, 2009).

Ideological polarization in the electorate has been observed with respect to social, economic, and racial issues (Brewer, 2005; Dalton, 1987). For instance, in a study of political communication, intergroup discussions of environmental issues, economic issues, and crime appeared to push liberals and conservatives further apart ideologically (Gastil, Black, & Moscovitz, 2008; Gastil & Dillard, 1999). Political scientists, too, see many cases of "conflict extension," whereby party cleavages generalize from one issue-based difference to others. For example, because the Democratic and Republican parties were already divided along racial lines, it was relatively easy to apply those differences to issues of social welfare and affirmative action to the extent that both racial and economic attitudes pertain to the government's role in promoting social and economic equality in society (Carmines & Stimson, 1989; Layman & Carsey, 2002b). In other words, as polarization (i.e., the distance between parties) grows, disagreements within the parties begin to seem insignificant, and inter-party differences on cultural, racial, welfare, and foreign policy issues draw much more attention (Layman et al., 2006).

In short, a diverse array of evidence exists to suggest that genuine psychological conflict and polarization are fairly pervasive, in the United States (see also Abramowitz & Saunders, 2006, 2008; Jost, 2006) and elsewhere (Bobbio, 1996; Fuchs & Klingemann, 1990). The findings we have cited are also consistent with the notion that both "top-down" (e.g., elite communication) and "bottom-up" (e.g., ideological) processes contribute to the incidence and intensity of ideological disputes (Jost, Federico, & Napier, 2009). We turn now to a consideration of social psychological variables that may be expected to exacerbate or attenuate ideological polarization in society.

WHAT SOCIAL PSYCHOLOGICAL FACTORS MODERATE THE DEGREE OF IDEOLOGICAL POLARIZATION?

The extant literature points to several social psychological factors that are likely to moderate the degree of ideological polarization. These include social identification, self-categorization, and conformity to prototypical in-group norms; in-group favoritism and out-group derogation; intergroup threat, competition, and struggles for dominance; naive realism and exaggerated perceptions of group differences; zero-sum thinking; stereotyping; and intergroup contact under competitive circumstances (see the first column in Table 6.1). We discuss each of these in turn.

Social Psychological Factors that Exacerbate Ideological Conflict and Polarization

Social Identification and Self-categorization Processes   Probably the most influential account of group polarization in social psychology was derived

TABLE 6.1   Social Psychological Processes Moderating the Degree of Ideological Conflict and Polarization

Processes Exacerbating Ideological Polarization	Processes Mitigating Ideological Polarization
Social identification, self-categorization, and conformity to prototypical in-group norms	Superordinate identification and the experience of common fate
In-group favoritism and out-group derogation	Decategorization and recategorization
Intergroup threat, competition, and struggles for dominance	System justification and responses to external (societal) threat
Naive realism, exaggerating group differences	Self-affirmation, reduced defensiveness
Stereotyping, category-based judgment	Self-disclosure, individual-based judgment
Zero-sum thinking, "fixed-pie" assumptions	Ideological log-rolling, trade-offs, integrative bargaining
Intergroup contact under competitive circumstances	Intergroup contact under cooperative circumstances

from self-categorization theory (Mackie, 1986; Turner, 1991; Turner, Hogg, Oakes, Reicher, & Wetherell, 1987), which is an offshoot of social identity theory (Tajfel & Turner, 1979). On this account, group members gravitate toward whatever positions they perceive to be "prototypical," or defining of the values and norms that are shared within the group (e.g., the positions that define one's political party) as well as the values that differentiate the in-group from relevant out-groups (e.g., the positions held by the opposing party). Prototypical group members (such as prominent party leaders) embody the group's ideals, norms, and values, illustrating in-group similarities and providing a contrast against which to compare relevant out-groups. The degree of influence that any group member is able to exert on the group is assumed to be contingent on his or her degree of prototypicality with respect to the group's values and beliefs (Hogg, 2001; Turner, 1991). Highly prototypical group members are more likely than less prototypical members to be liked by other group members (Hogg, 2001), to emerge as leaders of the group (Fielding & Hogg, 1997), and to enjoy greater influence over the group's agenda (van Knippenberg, Lossie, & Wilke, 1994).

An analysis of General Social Survey data by Miller and Hoffman (1999) provides empirical support for the self-categorization perspective on polarization. This analysis showed that the increased attention paid to divisive moral issues in the 1970s and 1980s resulted in greater attention to ideological labels and more self-categorization along ideological lines, as well as increased out-group derogation. These results are also consistent with the general notion of "ideological realignment" (Carmines & Stanley, 1990). As parties become more polarized and structured along a single liberal–conservative dimension, citizens are increasingly likely to identify with parties that represent their own ideological inclinations (Abramowitz & Saunders, 1998; Putz, 2002).

Processes of social identification and self-categorization appear to have substantial relevance in the context of ideological conflict. For example, Cohen (2003) conducted a series of experiments highlighting the role of political reference groups in the evaluation of social welfare policies. In this line of research, participants were presented with a welfare policy report that was relatively "stringent" (i.e., conservative) or "generous" (i.e., liberal) in terms of household allocations per child, insurance provision, term of aid, and additional benefits offered to welfare beneficiaries. Participants were then provided with evaluations of the policies allegedly provided by members of their political in-group (Democrats or Republicans) and were asked to indicate their own support for the policy. Results from four studies indicated that people were more likely to endorse a particular policy when they believed that their own party had proposed it, suggesting that social identities affect the interpretation of issue positions.

In-group Favoritism and Out-group Derogation The self-categorization account of intergroup polarization is linked to social identity processes. In-group favoritism, for example, including increased trust, cooperation, and empathy for the in-group, occurs when the self-concept shifts to accommodate the group prototype and the in-group is included in the self (Hewstone, Rubin, & Willis, 2002). When negative emotions, such as anger, disgust, and fear are present, in-group favoritism leads to out-group derogation (Mackie, Devos, & Smith, 2000). In the political sphere, then, ideological labels and partisanship serve to "organize individuals and groups around exclusive identities, thus crystallizing interests into opposing factions" (Baldassari & Gelman, 2008, p. 409). The increased salience of policy differences between Democrats and Republicans, sometimes instigated by party leaders with the willing assistance of the media, decreases intraparty divisions and increases intergroup rivalries in the electorate (Carsey & Layman, 2006; Huckfeldt & Kohfeld, 1989; Sinclair, 2006). Among legislators, too, social identity processes resulting in intergroup bias are likely to amplify divisions between the generally liberal and conservative platforms of the Democratic and Republican parties, respectively (Hetherington, 2001).

Research on individual differences reveals that right-wing authoritarianism, Protestant Work Ethic, religiosity, social dominance orientation, and political conservatism are associated with greater in-group favoritism and/or out-group rejection with respect to racial, ethnic, cultural, religious, and linguistic groups (Altemeyer, 1998; Batson & Burris, 1994; Biernat, Vescio, & Theno, 1996; Jost, Banaji, & Nosek, 2004; Nosek, Banaji, & Jost, 2009; Sidanius & Pratto, 1999). At the same time, political extremity (in general) is associated with perceptions of greater ideological disparities between the left and right. For instance, an examination of perceived ideological differences with respect to various political parties in Sweden, Great Britain, the Netherlands, and the United States showed that people who placed themselves farther away from the political center perceived greater ideological distance between opposing parties in government, as compared to their more moderate counterparts (Granberg & Brown, 1992). Of course, it is difficult to say on the basis of these data alone whether extremists' perceptions of the political parties are more or less accurate than the perceptions of centrists.

Intergroup Threat and Competition Ultimately, an extreme or exaggerated version of the prototypical group position allows group members to assert the values they share in contrast to the values of their adversaries. Thus, according to self-categorization theory, ideological polarization (as opposed to ideological dilution or convergence) is most likely to increase under conditions of intragroup cohesion and intergroup competition. Thus, liberals' and conservatives' attitudes concerning specific issues may be expected to diverge to the extent that the two groups represent competing "sides" in a struggle to decide how society should be run. In support of the self-categorization argument that the mere salience of the intergroup context fuels intergroup differentiation, research suggests that activating automatic associations with either the in-group or the out-group leads to political polarization (Ledgerwood & Chaiken, 2007). Both participants who were primed with stimuli representing their own party and those primed with words associated with the opposing party subsequently supported political statements that were prototypical of their political in-group and opposed political statements that were associated with their political out-group to a greater extent than did participants who were primed with neutral words. As the intergroup context becomes increasingly and explicitly competitive, the magnitude of this effect would be expected to increase.

The intergroup context can also induce feelings of threat, which may compound hostility and perceptions of intergroup difference and intractability of conflict (Stephan & Stephan, 2000). Although no empirical evidence to our knowledge directly links threat to interpersonal interactions between liberals and conservatives, it is reasonable to assume that encounters with conflicting worldviews are at least somewhat threatening, especially to the extent that one's beliefs about right and wrong are challenged. As Patrick Buchanan's (2004) fiery call to arms illustrates, conservative political discourse often makes explicit the threat they perceive from the political left and the policies liberals espouse as advocates of threatening minorities (e.g., Blacks, the gay community, immigrants, etc.) and purveyors of change to established ways of life. To the extent that conservatives experience interactions with liberals as threatening, their political views are likely to shift further to the right, and attitudinal polarization is likely to ensue. Similarly, liberals (or progressives) may see conservatives as standing in the way of progress and humanitarian objectives and therefore push more aggressively to enact their own political agenda. Threat leads to motivated closed-mindedness, which has been shown to increase the psychological affinity for political conservatism (Thorisdottir & Jost, in press). Given conservatives' greater sensitivity to various types of threat (Oxley et al., 2008), one might expect those affiliated with the political right to experience higher levels of threat when confronted with leftist initiatives than vice versa, all else being equal.

Consistent with the notion that conservative groups may be particularly prone to opinion homogeneity and derogation of dissimilar others, Kruglanski et al. (2006) concluded (based on an extensive review of the literature) that increased needs for closure lead to "group-centrism," a cluster of related behaviors including in-group favoritism, out-group derogation, praise of conformists, opinion uniformity, intolerance for diversity and norm violations, and general conservatism. The researchers explained that the needs for unambiguous knowledge are well served by homogenous groups because the clear-cut goals, explanations, and realities provided by the group create a strong sense of shared reality, allowing group members to ground their beliefs in group consensus (Kruglanski et al., 2006). Thus, the tendency to cast the ideological out-group as deviant, selfish, or immoral—as exemplified by Buchanan's indictment of the "immoral" liberal culture—may arise from the psychological desire to maintain certainty in one's own belief system.

Individuals who are relatively high on the Need for Cognitive Closure are prone to embrace competitive conflict schemas, apparently because they "seize" on immediately available cues of competition when formulating their own response strategy (De Zavala, Federico, Cislak, & Sigger, 2008). Social dominance orientation is also likely to foster a competitive outlook on politics and ideology, insofar as individuals who are high in social dominance seek to establish their group's dominance over another (typically subordinate) group (Duckitt, 2006; Sidanius & Pratto, 1999). Such competitive stances tend to increase negative intergroup perceptions (Esses, Dovidio, Jackson, & Armstrong, 2001), further exacerbating ideological as well as ethnic and other forms of intergroup polarization and conflict.

Naive Realism and Exaggerated Perceptions of Group Differences

Naive realism refers to the conviction that one's own opinions are based purely on objective rationality and that those who disagree must be either irrational or misinformed (Keltner & Robinson, 1993; Robinson, Keltner, Ward, & Ross, 1995). With regard to the affirmative action debate, for example, Sherman, Nelson, and Ross (2003) noted that:

> [P]eople who support the policy tend to view their support as being based on the continued existence of race and gender differences in employment and opportunity …. They see their support as the product of a careful and objective evaluation of the situation, whereas that same support is characterized by opponents of affirmative action as the product of knee-jerk liberalism or group interests …. In contrast, opponents of affirmative action often see their opposition as reflective of an evaluation of the fairness of the proposal in accordance with basic American values (Sniderman & Piazza, 1993), whereas that same opposition is characterized by affirmative action supporters as reflective of racism … or high levels of prejudice and the desire to maintain hegemonic advantage …. In other words, both opponents and proponents feel that their views are based on evaluations of the evidence, whereas the other side's views are based on ideology or self-interest (p. 276).

Of course, it is possible (and even likely) that the positions taken by one side in a given political debate are more logically and empirically valid than those taken by the other. Nevertheless, several studies suggest that partisans frequently overestimate the magnitude of opinion differences between themselves and their ideological opponents (Chambers, Baron, & Inman, 2006; Robinson et al., 1995; Sherman et al., 2003). As a result, shared goals and areas of potential agreement are often overlooked as the two sides perceive one another in increasingly hostile or unfavorable ways (Keltner & Robinson, 1993).

Zero-sum Thinking   Zero-sum thinking involves the assumption of competition between two or more parties over indivisible resources or outcomes. To the extent that any potentially overlapping interests are overlooked, zero-sum thinking is a form of rigidity in that it exclusively emphasizes an opposition of interests among the involved parties (Bazerman & Neale, 1993). Framing a conflict in zero-sum terms means that whatever is interpreted as favorable to one side of the dispute is also necessarily interpreted as unfavorable to the other side; Ross (1995) refers to this process as "reactive devaluation." Zero-sum thinking is more common under high Need for Cognitive Closure (De Dreu, 2006) and among right-wing authoritarians (Halevy, Sagiv, Roccas, & Bornstein, 2006). It leads disproportionately to "lose–lose" agreements, accelerates conflict escalation, and increases hostility toward members of ideological (as well as racial and ethnic) out-groups (Pruitt & Kim, 2005; Thompson & Hrebec, 1996).

Stereotyping   Political conflict is also exacerbated by reliance on overly simplistic perceptions or stereotypes to characterize "the opposing side," including stereotypes used to characterize liberals and conservatives (Brewer, 2005; Moscovici & Zavalloni, 1969; Tetlock & Mitchell, 1993). Work by Farwell and Weiner (2006) suggests that the use of category-based stereotypes of the left and right leads to exaggerated ascriptions of avarice to conservatives and indiscriminate generosity to liberals. Although liberal and conservative participants in two studies differed in terms of how much assistance they were willing to provide to recipients seen as responsible for their hardship, they did not favor different allocation schemes when it came to needy parties whose plight was clearly due to external circumstances. In other words, liberals and conservatives were not as divided as people assumed when deciding whether to assist nonresponsible victims of hardship; rather, it seems that accessible stereotypes of liberals and conservatives rendered perceivers insensitive to shared values and assumptions.

Consistent with research on political conservatism as a form of motivated social cognition (Jost et al., 2003), conservative participants in the studies by Farwell and Weiner (2006) were more likely to exaggerate popular stereotypes of liberal groups than liberal participants were to exaggerate stereotypes of conservatives. When estimating how much aid a typical liberal would provide to various needy groups, conservatives exhibited a so-called "Limbaugh effect"—they were more likely than liberals (or moderates) to overestimate the extent to which liberals possessed "bleeding hearts" when it came to individuals who were seen as responsible for their own misfortunes. Taken as a whole, these findings imply that liberal–conservative conflict, while rooted in genuine psychological and ideological differences (Jost, 2006), may also reflect cultural stereotypes that exaggerate political disagreement. A deeper understanding of the role of stereotyping and intergroup perceptions in ideological conflict may allow researchers (and perhaps practitioners) to specify domains of perceived conflict that do not actually derive from fundamental differences in beliefs, motives, and values in order to identify areas of compatibility that may make it possible to bridge the ideological divide, which may stand in the way of conflict resolution along racial, ethnic, religious, and other lines.

Intergroup Contact   Research on the consequences of intergroup contact has proliferated since Allport first articulated the prerequisite conditions necessary for the reduction of intergroup conflict through intergroup contact (Allport, 1954; Dovidio, Gaertner, & Kawakami, 2003; Pettigrew & Tropp, 2006). Although the contact hypothesis has enjoyed considerable empirical support in a wide variety of intergroup contexts, the ideological divide appears difficult to bridge through contact between liberals and conservatives because of the competitive and discordant context in which the two groups generally come into contact. In the context of a political discussion, for example, interaction between members of ideologically distinct groups was found to increase ideological consistency within groups, lead neutral participants to shift in the direction of the majority opinion, and encourage ideologically committed members to move further to the extremes (Gastil et al., 2008). This research also suggested that conservatives in particular exhibited a "repulsion" tendency: they shifted further to the right when they interacted with a greater number of liberals in the discussion group. Given the frequently competitive and antagonistic nature of ideological discussion, intergroup contact may actually serve to increase polarization between liberals and conservatives. We consider the countervailing possibility that contact between ideological adversaries (under certain favorable conditions) may reduce conflict when we discuss factors mitigating ideological polarization in the next section.

Social Psychological Factors that Mitigate Ideological Conflict and Polarization

Theory and research in social psychology also afford several potential antidotes to ideological conflict and polarization (see second column of Table 6.1). In general, greater cooperation between the political left and right should be associated with more productive efforts to reduce racial, ethnic, and religious conflict. Factors expected to reduce polarization include superordinate identification, shared goals, and the experience of common fate; processes of decategorization and recategorization; system justification and certain responses to external attack; self-affirmation; self-disclosure and individual-based judgment; ideological log-rolling and integrative bargaining; and intergroup contact under favorable conditions. We consider each of these in turn.

Superordinate Identification, Shared Goals, and Common Fate   The tendency to categorize oneself and others into social groups (Tajfel & Turner, 1986) is highly malleable when it comes to the particular social categories applied to relevant social targets (Turner, 1991). Because of this apparent flexibility, there is a possibility that processes of self-categorization and social identification may be harnessed in the service of reducing polarization. When a superordinate identity is emphasized over smaller, more divisive subgroup identities, social distance between former opponents is reduced (Gaertner, Dovidio, Nier, Ward, & Banker, 1999; Smith & Tyler, 1996). This strategy has been shown to facilitate intergroup cooperation in the context of American politics. In a study conducted by Transue (2007), participants were more likely to support tax increases that would benefit minority out-group members when they focused on attributes they shared with other Americans (superordinate identity salience condition) rather than attributes that were unique to their own racial or ethnic group (subgroup identity salience condition). This suggests that superordinate identification with the nation—and perhaps even with humanity itself—can facilitate pro-social (over competitive or self-interested) behavior.

Kramer and Brewer (1984) provided an empirical demonstration of the unifying effects of "common fate." They found that making a superordinate identity salient increased intergroup cooperation and restraint in the use of common resources. In addition, when group members knew that a collective pool was depleted, having to share outcomes equally (i.e., receiving the same outcome by lottery) reduced individual withdrawals from the pool. In a similar vein, joint effort directed at a shared superordinate goal can facilitate cooperation, liking, and conflict resolution (Sherif, Harvey, White, Hood, & Sherif, 1961). With respect to ideological conflict, then, we would expect that emphasizing social values, objectives, and ideals shared by liberals and conservatives (e.g., freedom of speech and equality of opportunity) and focusing on the long-term implications of social and economic policies for the health of society as a whole should facilitate positive interaction between liberals and conservatives.

Decategorization and Recategorization   Along the same lines, Gaertner and Dovidio proposed a common in-group identity model—a process-oriented account of the conditions for successful intergroup conflict. On this account, conditions of equality, cooperation, and interdependence foster particular modes of processing information about out-group members (Gaertner, Dovidio, Anastasio, Bachman, & Rust, 1993). Specifically, these circumstances encourage people to decategorize members of the out-group, shifting the basis for the mental representation of the target from his or her category membership to the distinctive or interpersonal aspects of the target individual (Fiske & Neuberg, 1990). Once the target is no longer categorized as "one of them," s/he may be recategorized as a member of a more inclusive or "common" in-group (Gaertner, Rust, Dovidio, Bachman, & Anastasio, 1994). By focusing attention on the overarching category of superordinate group membership, social contact makes salient similarities among members of the superordinate group, and differences formerly emphasized between groups tend to fade into the background (Dovidio et al., 2003).

The common in-group identity model has been criticized for its emphasis on assimilation into the larger group at the apparent expense of maintaining a meaningful subgroup identity (Hornsey & Hogg, 2000; Krochik & Tyler, 2009). However, Dovidio, Gaertner, and Saguy (2009) have revised their prescription for reducing intergroup conflict. Because group members often derive substantial value and self-knowledge from their group identities, the researchers recommend that leaders who wish to improve intergroup relations emphasize a "dual identity." Consistent with this perspective, Hornsey and Hogg (2000) argued that subgroup identities be recognized and maintained but also bound together under a single superordinate identity. In the context of liberal–conservative conflict, the common in-group identity model may be applied to situations in which ideological opponents must work together to accomplish a shared goal.

System Justification and Responses to External Threat

Although liberals and conservatives may pose psychological threats to one another when they are conceptualized (by themselves and others) as oppositional groups in society, external threats to the superordinate group or social system (e.g., the nation) can sometimes bring them together. After the September 11, 2001 terrorist attacks on New York and Washington, for example, university students in the United States became more strongly attached to the country as well as to their own university (Moskalenko, McCauley, & Rozin, 2006). The large increase in Presidential and other approval ratings observed after the attacks similarly suggests a major "rally-round-the-flag" effect (Jones, 2003; Jost, Liviatan, van der Toorn, Ledgerwood, Mandisodza, & Nosek, 2009).

It may seem surprising or counterintuitive that system justification—defined as the motivation to defend and bolster the overarching social system—would be associated with decreased polarization. Because people belong to multiple social systems varying in size (e.g., local high school vs. nation) and domain (e.g., cultural, economic, and political systems), most individuals justify one or more systems (Blasi & Jost, 2006; Jost & Kay, 2005). When external threats to the status quo are psychologically salient, liberals tend to become more politically conservative—and thus more ideologically proximal to conservatives (Bonanno & Jost, 2006; Cohen et al., 2005; Landau et al., 2004; Nail et al., 2009; Thorisdottir & Jost, 2009; Ullrich & Cohrs, 2007; Weise et al., 2008). It should be noted that although the motive to protect one's system against external threats may serve to unite liberals and conservatives within a given society, it may exacerbate ethnic and other forms of conflict between societies.

Self-affirmation

Some research suggests that affirming one's own values and self-worth may serve to decrease defensiveness and increase open-mindedness, thereby exerting a salutary effect with respect to ideological conflict (Cohen et al., 2007). Self-affirmation provides an alternative route to the satisfaction of human needs for positive self-regard, which may otherwise be expressed through ideological intransigence and stubborn insistence on the objectivity of one's own beliefs and perceptions. In this way, self-affirmation provides a buffer against the various forms of threat elicited by political opponents, especially when political identity is salient.

Intergroup Contact and Self-Disclosure

Pettigrew and Tropp (2006) conducted a meta-analysis of 515 studies that provided conclusive evidence that intergroup contact effectively reduces intergroup bias and conflict across a wide range of settings and group types, even when some of Allport's conditions for optimal contact are violated. Although the sheer effectiveness of intergroup contact is noteworthy in itself, conditions of equal group status, cooperative interdependence, shared goals, and positive norms for intergroup contact, along with intergroup friendship and personal acquaintance, all facilitate the prejudice-reducing effects of contact (Brewer & Miller, 1984; Dovidio et al., 2003; Eller & Abrams, 2004; Pettigrew, 1998). The competitive context in which ideological disputes often occur stands in the way of productive intergroup contact between liberals and conservatives, but cooperative problem-solving situations are not unheard of in the political arena. Thus, more cooperative or civil norms of political communication and discussion can presumably be nurtured in the service of reducing ideological polarization through intergroup contact.

Building on the longstanding notion that self-disclosure leads to liking (Jourard, 1959), some researchers have suggested that personalized disclosure during negotiation can increase cooperation, concession-making, and the likelihood of reaching agreement (Moore, Kurtzberg, & Thompson, 1999). Similarly, Keltner and Robinson (1993) demonstrated that ideologically dissimilar negotiators who were given an opportunity to disclose, clarify, and discuss their actual views and values before participating in a budget negotiation, reached broader, more integrative agreements and experienced higher levels of cooperation and positive affect toward their negotiation partners, apparently because the discussion reduced reliance on stereotypes and exaggerated perceptions. It appears that self-disclosure facilitates conflict resolution in purely interpersonal or dyadic contexts but not when subgroup (i.e., ideological) differences remain salient, as was the case in several of the studies we described above.

According to Brewer and Miller's (1984) personalization model, mutual self-disclosure allows interaction partners to establish a basis for acquaintance on a personal level. When category-based information and stereotypes are overshadowed (or contradicted) by distinctive, personalized information about the ideological "counterpart," negative expectations should be reduced, paving the way for increased cooperation. In contrast to strategies associated with the development of a superordinate or common in-group identity, which emerge from the human desire for social belongingness, personalization operates on the need for personal distinctiveness (Brewer, 1991; McGuire, 1984).

Ideological Log-rolling and Integrative Bargaining   Many of the social psychological factors for alleviating ideological conflict discussed thus far suggest strategies for overcoming social, cognitive, and motivational biases. This implies that actual differences between leftists and rightists may not be as great as partisans often assume (Cohen, 2003; Fiorina et al., 2006; Sherman et al., 2003). However, we have also suggested that genuine philosophical differences do exist with respect to attitudes concerning social change and equality of outcomes, as do psychological differences in orientations toward uncertainty and threat (Jost, 2006; Jost et al., 2003a, 2003b, 2007, 2008, 2009). Thus, truly bridging the ideological divide is not simply a matter of reducing ego-defensiveness, stereotyping, and other misperceptions. Given that some ideological disagreements are deep and substantive, is it really possible for the left and right to collaborate when it comes to policy-making—setting aside the question of whether it would be desirable for them to do so?

Kerlinger (1967, 1984) proposed that liberalism and conservatism represent orthogonal dimensions rather than opposite poles of a single dimension. Specifically, he suggested that there are some issue positions that are extremely important to liberals but not very important to conservatives, and vice versa. For the most part, empirical evidence indicates that liberalism and conservatism are negatively correlated and thus not truly orthogonal (Jost, Federico, & Napier, 2009), yet they are not so highly intercorrelated as to preclude the possibility of finding issues that are more important to one "side" than the other. In this respect, Kerlinger's approach provides at least some theoretical basis for imagining modes of compromise or mutual concession-making (Carsey et al., 2006; Conover & Feldman, 1981). To the extent that this is possible, it suggests that, from the perspective of bilateral negotiations (Bazerman & Neale, 1993), there is potential to "create value" by engaging in "log-rolling" or strategic "trade-offs." In other words, by conceding issues that are more important to the other party, one may be able to obtain favorable outcomes with respect to issues that are of greater importance to oneself or one's own constituency.

We asked the managers of several dozen political blogs to help us investigate this possibility further. They agreed to post a link to our survey and encouraged their readers to participate in our research, which addressed political priorities on the right and left. Data were collected approximately one month before the 2008 US Presidential election. In Table 6.2 we have listed 24 political issues in order of perceived importance as rated by the obtained sample of politically sophisticated liberal and conservative readers of political blogs. It is clear that there are several differences in the relative importance of specific issues, which means that the potential for log-rolling is substantial. Both groups judged "war and peace," "foreign policy," and "iraq" to be among the top six most important issues. However, conservatives judged "national security" and "taxes" to be the two most important issues, and these were clearly given less weight by liberals. Conservatives also felt that "oil drilling" and "religious values in society" were far more important than liberals did. Liberals, on the other hand, believed that "environment and energy," "health care," "gay rights," and support for "women and minorities" were much more important, in comparison with conservatives.

Thus, despite formidable challenges involved in overcoming ideological conflicts between leftists and rightists (or doves and hawks), such conflicts are probably not as intractable as many of the ethnic or religious conflicts described in other chapters of this book. It appears that the potential, at least, exists for the creation of value through negotiation processes, assuming that each side is willing to compromise on issues that are of comparatively less importance to them. Of course, a certain amount of trust and cooperation is necessary for ideological adversaries to even try to negotiate agreements that could be mutually beneficial (Bazerman & Neale, 1993). If such cooperation can be accomplished, it may also be possible to address racial, ethnic, and religious conflicts that are reinforced by ideological divisions. On the other hand, increased agreement between the left and right may stifle necessary debate over how to deal with ethnic conflict in society.

TABLE 6.2   Means and Standard Deviations of Liberals' and Conservatives' Issue Importance Ratings Listed in Descending Order of Importance

Liberals' Issue Ratings	*M*	SD	Conservatives' Issue Ratings	*M*	SD
Economy	6.68	0.73	National Security	6.90	0.44
War & Peace	6.62	0.75	Taxes	6.67	0.74
Environment & Energy	6.53	0.92	Oil Drilling	6.64	0.82
Health Care	6.51	0.97	War & Peace	6.60	0.82
Foreign Policy	6.50	0.84	Foreign Policy	6.58	0.83
Iraq	6.29	1.07	Iraq	6.49	0.92
Patriot Act	5.89	1.44	Economy	6.47	0.98
Gay Rights	5.74	1.40	Iran	6.43	0.97
Women & Minorities	5.67	1.44	Immigration	6.37	1.12
Government Ethics Reform	5.58	1.44	Government Ethics Reform	6.20	1.38
National Security	5.46	1.33	Abortion	6.20	1.54
Taxes	5.38	1.47	Crime	6.05	1.29
Iran	5.31	1.58	Foreign Trade	5.96	1.25
Abortion	5.29	1.84	Environment & Energy	5.95	1.42
Stem Cell research	5.27	1.54	Patriot Act	5.90	1.59
Foreign Trade	5.09	1.35	Religious Values in society	5.89	1.57
Crime	4.22	1.57	Religion in Schools	5.52	1.72
Religion in Schools	4.21	2.17	Gun Control	5.33	2.12
Immigration	4.16	1.65	Health Care	4.82	1.88
Oil Drilling	3.82	2.02	Stem Cell research	4.32	2.07
Gun Control	3.55	1.83	Women & Minorities	4.22	1.88
Investment in Space Exploration	3.28	1.79	Investment in Space Exploration	3.73	1.89
Religious Values in society	2.54	1.95	Gay Rights	3.42	2.42

Note: Liberals were individuals who self-identified as "very liberal" and placed themselves at the liberal end-point of a 7-point scale of political orientation, whereas conservatives self-identified as "very conservative" and placed themselves at the conservative end-point of the scale. N's for liberals' ratings = 811–825; N's for conservatives' ratings = 236–240. Importance ratings ranged from 1 (not at all important) to 7 (very important).

CONCLUDING REMARKS: IS IDEOLOGICAL CONFLICT DESIRABLE OR UNDESIRABLE?

Although we have identified a number of social psychological factors that are likely to increase or decrease the extent of ideological conflict and polarization in society, we have remained agnostic about whether the existence of ideological conflict is generally desirable or undesirable. That is, we make no a priori assumption that—as researchers of prejudice and other forms of intergroup conflict frequently take for granted—the goal of minimizing ideological polarization is necessarily a good one. In concluding this chapter, we mention a handful of fairly obvious disadvantages and some less obvious advantages of ideological conflict and diversity.

When it comes to political elites, such as members of parliamentary bodies, it seems clear that both partisanship and ideological polarization can produce "legislative gridlock," policy paralysis, and stalemate, so that legislators may find it impossible to pass any new laws, even when some initiative, reform, or reduction in intergroup tensions is desperately needed (Alden & Schurmann, 1990; Binder, 2003; Brady & Volden, 2005; Carsey et al., 2006). It is also potentially damaging to democratic morale when citizens realize how much their elected officials disagree about fundamental questions, such as foreign policy; among other things, this implies that at least some legislators must simply be wrong (Shapiro & Bloch-Elkon, 2006). To the extent that ideological polarization reflects incompatible interests associated with different social groups (McCarty, Poole, & Rosenthal, 2006), its presence among political elites threatens to widen societal rifts along economic and racial/ethnic faultlines. With respect to ordinary citizens, ideological polarization and conflict can seriously damage the civility of political discourse and the tolerance for diversity of opinion that democratic institutions require in order to function (Barker, 2002; Brock, 2004; Dean, 2006). Nearly everyone would agree that these societal consequences of left–right division are lamentable.

Nevertheless, there are some reasons to think that certain consequences of ideological conflict are in fact highly desirable. For one thing, social psychological research reveals that members of ideologically diverse problem-solving groups engage in greater cognitive elaboration and produce solutions that are more creative and otherwise superior to those generated by homogeneous groups (Basadur & Head, 2001; Nemeth, 1986; Schulz-Hardt, Brodbeck, Mojzisch, Kerschreiter, & Frey, 2006). Thus, there is some reason to expect that ideological diversity will engender more innovative public policies and a broader range of strategies aimed at reducing racial, ethnic, or religious conflict in society (Alden & Schurmann, 1990). Furthermore, intense ideological competition during elections is associated with increased civic participation (Jackson & Carsey, 2006; Sinclair, 2006) and more efficient information flow from political elites to ordinary citizens (Blumkin & Grossman, 2004). Finally, some would suggest that left–right conflict comes about because of inherent contradictions in our society and that social justice itself requires bringing these contradictions to the fore. And if, at the end of the day, one side is right and the other is wrong when it comes to an issue as fundamentally important as ethnic and other forms of intergroup conflict in society, it seems hard to justify social psychological or other interventions that are designed not to obtain the best outcome for the parties involved in the conflict (e.g., victims of ethnic violence) and for society as a whole but to reduce conflict simply for the sake of reducing it. Here we come to perhaps the greatest challenge of all, at least when it comes to the subject matter of this chapter: How to distinguish those historical moments in which ideological confrontation is necessary, right, and beneficial from those moments in which it is a genuine hindrance to peace and progress.

REFERENCES

Abramowitz, A. I., & Saunders, K. L. (1998). Ideological realignment in the US electorate. *Journal of Politics*, *60*, 634–652.

Abramowitz, A. I., & Saunders, K. L. (2006). Exploring the bases of partisanship in the American electorate: Social identity vs. ideology. *Political Research Quarterly*, *59*, 175–187.

Abramowitz, A. I., & Saunders, K. L. (2008). Is polarization a myth? *The Journal of Politics*, *70*, 542–555.

Alden, E. H., & Schurmann, F. (1990). *Why we need ideologies in American foreign policy: Democratic politics and world order*. Berkeley: Institute of International Studies, University of California.

Allport, G. W. (1954). *The nature of prejudice*. Cambridge, MA: Addison-Wesley.

Altemeyer, B. (1998). The other "authoritarian personality." In M. Zanna (Ed.), *Advances in experimental social psychology* (Vol. 30, pp. 47–92). San Diego: Academic Press.

Altemeyer, R. A. (1996). *The authoritarian specter*. Cambridge, MA: Harvard University Press.

Baldassari, D., & Gelman, A. (2008). Partisans without constraint: Political polarization and trends in American public opinion. *American Journal of Sociology*, *114*, 408–446.

Barker, D. C. (2002). *Rushed to judgment: Talk radio, persuasion, and American political behavior*. New York: Columbia University.

Bar-Tal, D. (1990). *Group beliefs*. New York: Springer-Verlag.

Bar-Tal, D., Raviv, A., Raviv, A., & Dgani-Hirsh, A. (2009). The influence of the ethos of conflict on Israeli Jews' interpretation of Jewish–Palestinian encounters. *Journal of Conflict Resolution*, *53*, 94–118.

Basadur, M., & Head, M. (2001). Team performance and satisfaction: A link to cognitive style within a process framework. *Journal of Creative Behavior*, *35*, 227–248.

Batson, C. D., & Burris, C. T. (1994). Personal religion: Depressant or stimulant of prejudice and discrimination? In M. P. Zanna (Ed.), *Ontario symposium: The psychology of prejudice* (pp. 149–169). Hillsdale, NJ: Erlbaum.

Bazerman, M. H., & Neale, M. A. (1993). *Negotiating rationally*. New York: Free Press.

Beck, P. A., & Jennings, M. K. (1975). Parents as "middlepersons" in political socialization. *Journal of Politics*, *37*, 83–107.

Biernat, M., Vescio, T. K., & Theno, S. A. (1996). Violating American values: A "value congruence" approach to understanding outgroup attitudes. *Journal of Experimental Social Psychology*, *32*, 387–410.

Binder, S. A. (2003). *Stalemate: Causes and consequences of legislative gridlock*. Washington, DC: Brookings Institution.

Bishop, G. (2005). *The illusion of public opinion*. Lanham, MD: Rowman & Littlefield.

Blasi, G., & Jost, J. T. (2006). System justification theory and research: Implications for law, legal advocacy, and social justice. *California Law Review*, *94*, 1119–1168.

Blumkin, T., & Grossman, V. (2004). *Ideological polarization, sticky information, and policy reforms*. CESinfo Working Paper No. 1274.

Bobbio, N. (1996). *Left and right: The significance of a political distinction*. Cambridge, UK: Polity Press.

Bonanno, G. A., & Jost, J. T. (2006). Conservative shift among high-exposure survivors of the September 11th terrorist attacks. *Basic and Applied Social Psychology*, *28*, 311–323.

Brady, D. W., & Volden, C. (2005). *Revolving gridlock: Politics from Jimmy Carter to George W. Bush*. Boulder, CO: Westview.

Brewer, M. B. (1991). On being the same and different at the same time. *Personality and Social Psychology Bulletin*, *17*, 475–482.

Gaertner, S. L., Rust, M. C., Dovidio, J. F., Bachman, B. A., & Anastasio, P. A. (1994). The contact hypothesis: The role of common ingroup identity on reducing intergroup bias. *Small Group Research*, 25, 224–249.

Gastil, J., Black, L., & Moscovitz, K. (2008). Ideology, attitude change, and deliberation in small face-to-face groups. *Political Communication*, 25, 23–46.

Gastil, J., & Dillard, J. P. (1999). Increasing political sophistication through public deliberation. *Political Communication*, 16, 3–23.

Golec, A. (2001, July). *Need for cognitive closure and political conservatism: Studies on the nature of the relationship.* Paper presented at the annual meeting of the International Society of Political Psychology, Cuernavaca, Mexico.

Graham, J., Haidt, J., & Nosek, B. N. (2009). Liberals and conservatives rely on different sets of moral foundations. *Journal of Personality and Social Psychology*, 96, 1029–1046.

Granberg, D., & Brown, T. A. (1992). The perception of ideological distance. *The Western Political Quarterly*, 45, 727–750.

Green, D., Palmquist, B., & Schickler, E. (2002). *Partisan hearts and minds: Political parties and the social identities of voters.* New Haven, CT: Yale University Press.

Halevy, N., Sagiv, L., Roccas, S., & Bornstein, G. (2006). Perceiving intergroup conflict: From game models to mental templates. *Personality and Social Psychology Bulletin*, 32, 1674–1689.

Hardin, C. D., & Conley, T. D. (2000). A relational approach to cognition: Shared experience and relationship affirmation in social cognition. In G. B. Moskowitz (Ed.), *Future directions in social cognition* (pp. 3–17). Hillsdale, NJ: Erlbaum.

Hardin, C., & Higgins, E. T. (1996). Shared reality: How social verification makes the subjective objective. In R. M. Sorrentino & E. T. Higgins (Eds.), *Handbook of motivation and cognition: Foundations of social behavior* (Vol. 3, pp. 28–84). New York: Guilford Press.

Herrmann, R. K., Tetlock, P. E., & Visser, P. S. (1999). Mass public decisions to go to war: A cognitive-interactionist framework. *American Political Science Review*, 93, 553–573.

Hetherington, M. (2001). Resurgent mass partisanship: The role of elite polarization. *The American Political Science Review*, 95, 619–631.

Hewstone, M., Rubin, M., & Willis, H. (2002). Intergroup bias. *Annual Review of Psychology*, 53, 575–604.

Higgins, E. T. (1996). Knowledge activation: Accessibility, applicability, and salience. In E. T. Higgins & A. W. Kruglanski (Eds.), *Social psychology: Handbook of basic principles* (pp. 133–168). New York: Guilford.

Hogg, M. A. (2001). A social identity theory of leadership. *Personality and Social Psychology Review*, 5, 184–200.

Holsti, O. R., & Rosenau, J. N. (1988). The domestic and foreign policy beliefs of American leaders. *Journal of Conflict Resolution*, 32, 248–294.

Holsti, O. R., & Rosenau, J. N. (1996). Liberals, populists, libertarians, and conservatives: The link between domestic and international affairs. *International Political Science Review*, 17, 29–54.

Hornsey, M. J., & Hogg, M. A. (2000). Assimilation and diversity: An integrative model of subgroup relations. *Personality and Social Psychology Review*, 4, 143–156.

Huckfeldt, H. R., & Kohfeld, C. W. (1989). *Race and the decline of class in American politics.* Urbana, IL: University of Illinois.

Hunter, J. D. (1991). *Culture wars: The struggle to control the family, art, education, law, and politics in America.* New York: Basic Books.

Jackson, R. A., & Carsey, T. M. (2006). Presidential voting across the American states. *American Politics Quarterly*, 27, 379–402.

Jacoby, W. G. (1991). Ideological identification and issue attitudes. *American Journal of Political Science*, 35, 178–205.

Jennings, M. K., & Niemi, R. G. (1981). *Generations and politics*. Princeton: Princeton University Press.

Jones, J. M. (2003, September 9). *September 11 effects, though largely faded, persist*. The Gallup Poll. Retrieved on September 27, 2004 from http://www.gallup.com/poll. content/?ci=9208

Jost, J. T. (2006). The end of the end of ideology. *American Psychologist, 61*, 651–670.

Jost, J. T., Banaji, M. R., & Nosek, B. A. (2004). A decade of system justification theory: Accumulated evidence of the conscious and unconscious bolstering of the status quo. *Political Psychology, 25*, 881–919.

Jost, J. T., Federico, C. M., & Napier, J. L. (2009). Political ideology: Its structure, functions, and elective affinities. *Annual Review of Psychology, 60*, 307–338.

Jost, J. T., Fitzsimons, G., & Kay, A. C. (2004). The ideological animal: A system justification view. In J. Greenberg, S. L. Koole, & T. Pyszczynski (Eds.), *Handbook of experimental existential psychology* (pp. 263–282). New York: Guilford Press.

Jost, J. T., Glaser, J., Kruglanski, A. W., & Sulloway, F. (2003a). Political conservatism as motivated social cognition. *Psychological Bulletin, 129*, 339–375.

Jost, J. T., Glaser, J., Kruglanski, A. W., & Sulloway, F. (2003b). Exceptions that prove the rule: Using a theory of motivated social cognition to account for ideological incongruities and political anomalies. *Psychological Bulletin, 129*, 383–393.

Jost, J. T., & Kay, A. C. (2005). Exposure to benevolent sexism and complementary gender stereotypes: Consequences for specific and diffuse forms of system justification. *Journal of Personality and Social Psychology, 88*, 498–509.

Jost, J. T., Kruglanski, A. W., & Simon, L. (1999). Effects of epistemic motivation on conservatism, intolerance, and other system justifying attitudes. In L. Thompson, D. M. Messick, & J. M. Levine (Eds.), *Shared cognition in organizations: The management of knowledge* (pp. 91–116). Mahwah, NJ: Erlbaum.

Jost, J. T., Ledgerwood, A., & Hardin, C. D. (2008). Shared reality, system justification, and the relational basis of ideological beliefs. *Social and Personality Psychology Compass, 2*, 171–186.

Jost, J. T., Liviatan, I., Van der Toorn, J., Lederwood, A., Mandisodza, A., & Nosek, B. A. (2010). System justification: How do we know it's motivated? In D. R. Bobocel, A. C. Kay, M. P. Zanna, & J. M. Olson (Eds.), *The psychology of justice and legitimacy: The Ontario symposium* (pp. 173–202). Hillsdale, NJ: Erlbaum.

Jost, J. T., Napier, J. L., Thorisdottir, H., Gosling, S. D., Palfai, T. P., & Ostafin, B. (2007). Are needs to manage uncertainty and threat associated with political conservatism or ideological extremity? *Personality and Social Psychology Bulletin, 33*, 989–1007.

Jost, J. T., Nosek, B. A. & Gosling, S. D. (2008). Ideology: Its resurgence in social, personality, and political psychology. *Perspectives on Psychological Science, 3*, 126–136.

Jost, J. T., West, T. V., & Gosling, S. D. (2009). Personality and ideology as determinants of candidate preferences and "Obama conversion" in the 2008 US presidential election. *Dubois Review: Social Science on Race, 6*, 103–124.

Jourard, S. M. (1959). Self-disclosure and other-cathexis. *Journal of Abnormal and Social Psychology, 59*, 428–431.

Kay, A. C., Gaucher, D., Napier, J., Callan, M. J., & Laurin, K. (2008). God and the government: Testing a compensatory control mechanism for the support of external systems. *Journal of Personality and Social Psychology, 95*, 18–35.

Kay, A. C., Jost, J. T., & Young, S. (2005). Victim derogation and victim enhancement as alternate routes to system justification. *Psychological Science, 16*, 240–246.

Kelman, H. C. (1958). Compliance, identification, and internalization: Three processes of attitude change. *Journal of Conflict Resolution, 2*, 51–60.

Keltner, D., & Robinson, R. J. (1993). Imagined ideological differences in conflict escalation and resolution. *International Journal of Conflict Management, 4*, 249–262.

Kemmelmeier, M. (1997). Need for closure and political orientation among German university students. *Journal of Social Psychology, 137,* 787–789.

Kerlinger, F. N. (1967). Social attitudes and their criterial referents: A structural theory. *Psychological Review, 74,* 110–122.

Kerlinger, F. N. (1984). *Liberalism and conservatism: The nature and structure of social attitudes.* Hillsdale, NJ: Erlbaum.

Kinder, D. R., & Sears, D. O. (1985). Public opinion and political action. In G. Lindzey & E. Aronson (Eds.), *Handbook of social psychology* (Vol. 2, pp. 659–741). New York: Random House.

Kosterman, R., & Feshbach, S. (1989). Toward a measure of patriotic and nationalistic attitudes. *Political Psychology, 10,* 257–274.

Kramer, R. M., & Brewer, M. B., (1984). Effects of group identity on resource use in a simulated commons dilemma. *Journal of Personality and Social Psychology, 46,* 1044–1057.

Krochik, M., Jost, J. T., & Nosek, B. (2007). *Ideology informs structure: Social and motivational influences on the attitude strength of liberals and conservatives.* Paper presented at the 30th annual meeting of the International Society for Political Psychology, Portland, OR.

Krochik, M., & Tyler, T. R. (2009). Leading amid pluralism: The benefits and limits of superordinate identification. In T. L. Pittinsky (Ed.), *Crossing the divide: Intergroup leadership in a world of difference.* Boston: Harvard Business School Press.

Kruglanski, A. W. (1989). *Lay epistemics and human knowledge: Cognitive and motivational bases.* New York: Plenum.

Kruglanski, A. W. (1996). Motivated social cognition: Principles of the interface. In E. T. Higgins & A. W. Kruglanski (Eds.), *Social psychology: A handbook of basic principles* (pp. 493–522). New York: Guilford Press.

Kruglanski, A. W., Pierro, A., Mannetti, L., & De Grada, E. (2006). Groups as epistemic providers: Need for closure and the unfolding of group-centrism. *Psychological Review, 113,* 84–100.

Kunda, Z. (1990). The case for motivated reasoning. *Psychological Bulletin, 108,* 480–498.

Landau, M. J., Greenberg, J., & Rothschild, Z. K. (2009). Motivated cultural worldview adherence and culturally loaded test performance. *Personality and Social Psychology Bulletin, 35,* 442–453.

Landau, M. J., Solomon, S., Greenberg, J., Cohen, F., Pyszczynski, T., & Arndt, J. (2004). Deliver us from evil: The effects of mortality salience and reminders of 9/11 on support for President George W. Bush. *Personality and Social Psychology Bulletin, 30,* 1136–1150.

Lavine, H., Polichak, J., & Lodge, M. (1999, September). *Authoritarianism and threat: A response latency analysis.* Paper presented at the annual meeting of the American Political Science Association, Atlanta, GA.

Layman, G. C., & Carsey, T. M. (2002a). Party polarization and "conflict extension" in the American electorate. *American Journal of Political Science, 46,* 786–802.

Layman, G. C., & Carsey, T. M. (2002b). Party polarization and the structuring of policy attitudes: A comparison of three NES Panel studies. *Political Behavior, 24,* 199–236.

Layman, G. C., Carsey, T. M., & Horowitz, J. M. (2006). Party polarization in American politics: Characteristics, causes, and consequences. *Annual Review of Political Science, 9,* 83–110.

Ledgerwood, A., & Chaiken, S. (2007). Priming us and them: Automatic assimilation and contrast in group attitudes. *Journal of Personality and Social Psychology, 93,* 940–956.

Lerner, M. J. (1975). The justice motive of social behavior: Introduction. *Journal of Social Issues, 31*, 1–19.

Lewin, L. (1948). *Resolving social conflicts: Selected papers on group dynamics.* New York: Harper.

Liebes, T., Katz, E., & Ribak, R. (1991). Ideological reproduction. *Political Behavior, 13*, 237–252.

Lipset, S., & Raab, E. (1978). *The politics of unreason: Right-wing extremism in America, 1790–1977.* Chicago: University of Chicago Press.

Lodge, M., & Hamill, R. (1986). A partisan schema for political information processing. *The American Political Science Review, 80*, 505–520.

Luskin, R. C. (1987). Measuring political sophistication. *American Journal of Political Science, 31*, 856–899.

Mackie, D. M. (1986). Social identification effects in group polarization. *Journal of Personality and Social Psychology, 50*, 720–728.

Mackie, D. M., Devos, T., & Smith, E. R. (2000). Intergroup emotions: Explaining offensive action tendencies in an intergroup context. *Journal of Personality and Social Psychology, 79*, 602–616.

McCarty, N., Poole, K. T., & Rosenthal, H. (2006). *Polarized America.* Cambridge, MA: MIT.

McGuire, W. J. (1984). Search for the self: Going beyond self-esteem and the reactive self. In R. A. Zucker, J. Aronoff, & A. I. Rabin (Eds.), *Personality and the prediction of behavior* (pp. 73–120). New York: Academic Press.

McGuire, W. J. (1985). Attitudes and attitude change. In G. Lindzey & E. Aronson (Eds.), *Handbook of social psychology* (pp. 233–346). New York: Random House.

Miller, A. S., & Hoffman, J. P. (1999). The growing divisiveness: Culture wars or a war of words? *Social Forces, 78*, 721–745.

Moore, D. A., Kurtzberg, T. R., & Thompson, L. L. (1999). Long and short routes to success in electronically mediated negotiations: Group affiliations and good vibrations. *Organizational Behavior and Human Decision Processes, 77*, 22–43.

Moskalenko, S., McCauley, C., & Rozin, P. (2006). Group identification under conditions of threat: College students' attachment to country, family, ethnicity, religion, and university before and after September 11, 2001. *Political Psychology, 27*, 77–97.

Moscovici, S. (1976). *Social influence and social change.* London, UK: Academic Press.

Moscovici, S., & Zavalloni, M. (1969). The group as a polarizer of attitudes. *Journal of Personality and Social Psychology, 12*, 125–135.

Moskowitz, A. N., & Jenkins, J. C. (2004). Structuring political opinions: Attitude consistency and democratic competence among the US mass public. *The Sociological Quarterly, 45*, 395–419.

Murray, S. K., Cowden, J. A., & Russett, B. M. (1999). The convergence of American elites' domestic beliefs with their foreign policy beliefs. *International Interactions 25*, 153–180.

Nail, P. R., McGregor, I., Drinkwater, A. E., Steele, G. M., & Thompson, A. W. (2009). Threat causes liberals to think like conservatives. *Journal of Experimental Social Psychology, 45*, 901–907.

Napier, J. L., & Jost, J. T. (2008). The "anti-democratic personality" revisited: A cross-national investigation of working class authoritarianism. *Journal of Social Issues, 64*, 595–617.

Nemeth, C. J. (1986). Differential contributions of majority and minority influence. *Psychological Review, 93*, 23–32.

Nie, N. H., Verba, S., & Petrocik, J. R. (1979). *The changing American voter.* Cambridge: Harvard University.

Nosek, B. A., Banaji, M. R., & Jost, J. T. (2009). The politics of intergroup attitudes. In J. T. Jost, A. C. Kay, & H. Thorisdottir (Eds.), *Social and psychological bases of ideology and system justification* (pp. 480–506). New York: Oxford.

Oxley, D. R., Smith, K. B., Alford, J. R., Hibbing, M. V., Miller, J. L., Scalora, M. et al. (2008). Political attitudes vary with physiological traits. *Science, 321*, 1667–1670.

Pettigrew, T. F. (1998). Intergroup contact theory. *Annual Review of Psychology, 49*, 65–85.

Pettigrew, T. F., & Tropp, L. R. (2006). A meta-analytic test of intergroup contact theory. *Journal of Personality and Social Psychology, 90*, 751–783.

Petty, R. E., & Cacioppo, J. T. (1984). The effects of involvement on responses to argument quantity and quality: Central and peripheral routes to persuasion. *Journal of Personality and Social Psychology, 46*, 69–81.

Prentice, D. A., & Miller, D. T. (Eds.). (1999). *Cultural divides: Understanding and overcoming group conflict*. New York: Russell Sage Foundation.

Pruitt, D. G., & Kim, S. H. (1995). *Social conflict: Escalation, stalemate, and settlement* (3rd ed.). New York: McGraw-Hill.

Putz, D. W. (2002). Partisan conversion in the 1990s: Ideological realignment meets measurement theory. *Journal of Politics, 64*, 1199–1209.

Pyszczynski, T., Solomon, S., & Greenberg, J. (2003). *In the wake of 9/11: The psychology of terror*. Washington, DC: American Psychological Association.

Rathbun, B. (2007). Hierarchy and community at home and abroad: Evidence of a common structure of domestic and foreign policy beliefs in American elites. *Journal of Conflict Resolution, 51*, 379–407.

Robinson, R. J., Keltner, D., Ward, A., & Ross, L. (1995). Actual versus assumed differences in construal: "Naive realism" in intergroup perception and conflict. *Journal of Personality and Social Psychology, 68*, 404–417.

Ross, L. (1995). Reactive devaluation in negotiation and conflict resolution. In K. Arrow, R. Mnookin, L. Ross, A. Tversky, & R. Wilson (Eds.), *Barriers to conflict resolution* (pp. 26–42). New York: Norton.

Ross, L., & Ward, A. (1995). Psychological barriers to dispute resolution. In M. P. Zanna (Ed.), *Advances in experimental social psychology* (Vol. 27, pp. 255–304). San Diego, CA: Academic Press.

Sargent, M. (2004). Less thought, more punishment: Need for cognition predicts support for punitive responses to crime. *Personality and Social Psychology Bulletin, 30*, 1485–1493.

Schulz-Hardt, S., Brodbeck, F. C., Mojzisch, A., Kerschreiter, R., & Frey, D. (2006). Group decision making in hidden profile situations: Dissent as a facilitator for decision quality. *Journal of Personality and Social Psychology, 91*, 1080–1093.

Shakespeare, W. (1909–1914). The tragedy of Hamlet Prince of Denmark (Vol. XLVI, Part 2, Act 1, Scene 3). *The Harvard classics*. New York: P.F. Collier & Son. Bartleby.com, 2001. Retrieved on July 5, 2010 from http://www.bartleby.com/46/2/13.html

Shakespeare, W. (2005). In C. Jordan (Ed.), *Hamlet, prince of Denmark* . New York: Pearson/Longman.

Shapiro, R. Y., & Bloch-Elkon, Y. (2006, May). *Political polarization and the rational public*. Paper presented at the annual meeting of the American Association for Public Opinion Research, Montreal, Quebec, Canada.

Sherif, M., Harvey, O. J., White, B. J., Hood, W. R., & Sherif, C. W. (1961). *The Robbers Cave experiment: Intergroup conflict and cooperation*. Norman, OK: University of Oklahoma Book Exchange.

Sherman, D. K., Nelson, L. D., & Ross, L. D. (2003). Naïve realism and affirmative action: Adversaries are more similar than they think. *Basic and Applied Psychology, 25*, 275–289.

Sidanius, J., & Pratto, F. (1999). *Social dominance: An intergroup theory of social hierarchy and oppression*. New York, NY: Cambridge University.

Sinclair, B. (2006). *Party wars: Polarization and the politics of national policy making*. Norman, OK: University of Oklahoma.

Skitka, L. J., Mullen, E., Griffin, T., Hutchinson, S., & Chamberlin, B. (2002). Dispositions, ideological scripts, or motivated correction? Understanding ideological differences in attributions for special problems. *Journal of Personality and Social Psychology*, *83*, 470–487.

Skitka, L. J., & Tetlock, P. E. (1993). Providing public assistance: Cognitive and motivational processes underlying liberal and conservative policy preferences. *Journal of Personality and Social Psychology*, *65*, 1205–1223.

Smith, H. J., & Tyler, T. R. (1996). Justice and power: When will justice concerns encourage the advantaged to support policies which redistribute economic resources and the disadvantaged to willingly obey the law? *European Journal of Social Psychology*, *26*, 171–200.

Sniderman, P. M., & Piazza, R. (1993). *The scar of race*. Cambridge, MA: Harvard University.

Solomon, S., Greenberg, J., & Pyszczynski, T. (2004). The cultural animal: Twenty years of terror management theory and research. In J. Greenberg, S. L. Koole, & T. Pyszczynski (Eds.), *Handbook of experimental existential psychology* (pp. 13–34). New York: Guilford.

Stephan, W. G., & Stephan, C. W. (1996). *Intergroup relations*. Boulder, CO: Westview.

Stephan, W. G., & Stephan, C. W. (2000). An integrated threat theory of prejudice. In S. Oskamp (Ed.), *Reducing prejudice and discrimination* (pp. 23–46). Hillsdale, NJ: Lawrence Erlbaum.

Stephan, W. G., & Stephan, C. W. (2001). *Improving intergroup relations*. Thousand Oaks, CA: Sage Publications, Inc.

Tajfel, H. (1982). Social psychology of intergroup relations. *Annual Review of Psychology*, *33*, 1–39.

Tajfel, H., & Turner, J. C. (1979). An integrative theory of intergroup conflict. In W. G. Austin & S. Worchel (Eds.), *The social psychology of intergroup relations* (pp. 33–47). Monterey, CA: Brooks-Cole.

Tajfel, H., & Turner, J. C. (1986). The social identity theory of intergroup behavior. In S. Worchel & W. Austin (Eds.), *The psychology of intergroup relations* (pp. 7–24). Chicago: Nelson-Hall.

Tedin, K. L. (1987). Political ideology and the vote. *Research in Micropolitics*, *2*, 63–94.

Tetlock, P. E. (1983). Cognitive style and political ideology. *Journal of Personality and Social Psychology*, *45*, 118–126.

Tetlock, P. E. (1984). Cognitive style and political belief systems in the British House of Commons. *Journal of Personality and Social Psychology*, *46*, 365–375.

Tetlock, P. E., Bernzweig, J., & Gallant, J. L. (1985). Supreme Court decision making: Cognitive style as a predictor of ideological consistency of voting. *Journal of Personality and Social Psychology*, *48*, 1227–1239.

Tetlock, P. E., & Mitchell, P. G. (1993). Liberal and conservative approaches to justice: Conflicting psychological portraits. In B. Mellers & J. Baron (Eds.), *Psychological perspectives on justice* (pp. 234–255). Cambridge, MA: Cambridge University.

Thompson, L., & Hrebec, D. (1996). Lose–lose agreements in interdependent decision making. *Psychological Bulletin*, *120*, 396–409.

Thorisdottir, H., & Jost, J. Y. (in press). Motivated closed-mindedness mediates the effect of threat on political conservatism. *Political Psychology*.

Transue, J. E. (2007). Identity salience, identity acceptance, and racial policy attitudes: American national identity as a uniting force. *American Journal of Political Science*, *51*, 78–91.

Turner, J. C. (1991). *Social influence*. Buckingham, England: Open University Press.

Turner, J. C., Hogg, M. A., Oakes, P. J., Reicher, S. D., & Wetherell, M. S. (1987). *Rediscovering the social group: A self-categorization theory*. Oxford: Basil Blackwell.

Ullrich, J., & Cohrs, J. C. (2007). Terrorism salience increases system justification: Experimental evidence. *Social Justice Research, 20*, 117–139.

Van Knippenberg, D., Lossie, N., & Wilke, H. (1994). In-group prototypicality and persuasion: Determinants of heuristic and systematic message processing. *British Journal of Social Psychology, 33*, 289–300.

Webster, D. M., & Kruglanski, A. W. (1994). Individual differences in need for cognitive closure. *Journal of Personality and Social Psychology, 67*, 1049–1062.

Weise, D. R., Pyszczynski, T., Cox, C. R., Arndt, J., Greenberg, J., Solomon, S. et al. (2008). Interpersonal politics: The role of terror management and attachment processes in shaping political preferences. *Psychological Science, 19*, 448–445.

Wilson, G. D. (Ed.). (1973). *The psychology of conservatism*. London: Academic Press.

Worchel, S. (1999). *Written in blood: Ethnic identity and the struggle for human harmony*. New York: Worth.

Zaller, J. (1992). *The nature and origins of mass opinion*. New York: Cambridge University.

7

Political Violence, Intergroup Conflict, and Ethnic Categories

GUY ELCHEROTH and DARIO SPINI

*I*n this chapter, we aim to highlight how recent research leads to revisit traditional assumptions about the interplay between ethnicity, violence, and conflict. Instead of asking the usual questions about how conflict between ethnic groups would lead to collective violence, it urges us to develop new questions about the way ethnic categories themselves are shaped by political violence grounded in multilayered social conflicts and struggles over power. This challenge will be taken up here in three steps. In the first section, we will confront the increasing prominence of ethnicity as a descriptive and explanatory concept in studies on collective violence, with its lack of definitional and analytical precision. We will critically revisit the notion that ethnic conflict, or even diversity, lead to ethnic violence, and stress the need for specific explanations of the qualitative shift from nonviolent conflict to violent conflict. In the second section, we will review work showing how political violence not only transforms intergroup relations, but also the "ethnic in-group": how it dramatically affects moral climates and the social fabric in the midst of communities that are supposed to be struggling together against a common enemy. In the third section, we will discuss in more detail processes through which complex experiences of violence are transformed into simple in-group narratives by way of directed forgetting, how these narratives provide prescriptive frameworks for actions against declared enemies, but also how and when they can be effectively challenged. This will finally lead to discuss the potential contribution of criminal tribunals to social reconstruction following political violence: how can their work help to clarify boundaries of responsibility, agency, and power, which are typically obfuscated by reifying depictions of "ethnic conflict"?

POLITICAL VIOLENCE AND ETHNIC CONFLICT: CURRENT WISDOM AND NEW PUZZLES

The majority of recent armed conflicts have been described as ethnic clashes. According to the "Major Episodes of Political Violence" database (Marshall, 2002) there was a steady raise in ethnic violence from the end of Second World War until the mid-1990s. A peak of 160 cases of "ethnic warfare" was registered between 1985 and 1994. During that period, ethnic warfare and other forms of "ethnic violence" accounted for 67% of all registered episodes of political violence; whereas they constituted lower proportions—but still the majority—of episodes of political violence registered during the previous decade (55%), as well as the subsequent decade (52%). Contrastingly, the 50 cases of ethnic warfare registered between 1964 and 1975, together with other forms of ethnic violence, only accounted for 36% of all episodes of political violence during these 10 years, and most cases of within-state violence occurring during that period are not classified as ethnic violence. These trends paralleled by shifts in academic interest in the phenomenon, is what led Brubaker and Laitin (1998) to notice that "a pronounced 'ethnic turn' has occurred in the study of political violence" (p. 426). When instances of collective violence can be framed neither as nation-states going to war against each other, nor as revolutionary acts, or (counter-) colonial violence, then belligerents are now commonly identified as "ethnic groups" fighting an "ethnic war." Ethnic identity is also becoming an increasingly prominent explanatory concept in social psychological models of conflict and violence. Following Worchel (1999), ethnicity would even play "a starring role on the historical stage of human identity and conflict" (p. 13). But what does the notion of "ethnic groups" actually stand for?

The first striking feature of ethnicity as an analytic category is its malleability. As a means of categorization, it is used to differentiate groups either by culture (language, religion, habits, or folklore), territory (homeland, geographical topology), or sometimes—still—nature (phenotype, race, or descent). When ethnicity is placed at stake, it has the potential to form a mythical narrative for a community, encompassing the group's (idealized) past and its present, as well as its (promised) future. Ethnicity has not simply become a major analytical category for differentiating groups in conflict; it actually functions as a practical *meta-category*, grouping together a rather diverse set of social dimensions used to make sense out of collective antagonisms and violence. As Brubaker and Laitin (1998) have pointed out, this flexibility in the concept is not to be seen as accidental; it is indeed part of what makes the label of ethnic war so attractive—notably for conflict analysts.

However, ethnicity is not typically a notion invoked by belligerents themselves. Political leaders are generally more eager to speak out for "their nation," or the "people of …," rather than "their ethnic group," especially when they need to address their constituencies in inclusive terms, in order to mobilize the widest possible support. Such mobilization can be labeled as nationalist to the extent that it conveys a claim for statehood. Conversely, in the absence of such a claim, even groups that carry some sort of consciousness of their ethnic distinctiveness do not necessarily conceive themselves as nations. As Billig (1995) puts it: "To be sure, there are ethnic and racial ghettoes within [American] cities; but there is no

African–American of Italian–American state, with its own bordered territory and with its claims for national independence" (p. 146). However, the whole point about nationalism is that nationalists do not wait for an independent and recognized nation-state to exist, before they call the corresponding population a "nation." It would indeed be difficult to imagine, for example, how the Irish Republican Army or the Scottish National Party could articulate a claim for independence had they chosen to label themselves "Army of the Ethnic Irish," or "Scottish Ethnic Party." To be more precise, while the presence of a specific ethnic dimension can sometimes be a resource for national mobilization—it facilitates stressing the distinctiveness and longevity of the national in-group—it can often be an obstacle as well. Reicher and Hopkins (2001) have emphasized this point in the context of a comparison between early Catalonian nationalism, which strongly focused on language, and early Basque nationalism, which did not: "In contrast to Catalan, Euskara had become a minority language. To mobilize on the basis of a linguistically defined category would be to exclude most of the population" (p. 156). This refers to the more general problem that nationalism typically attempts to create a compelling association between a population, a territory, and a destiny, and that most specific categorical criteria for ethnic affiliation are more likely to make salient the mismatch between these three elements, rather than the assumed naturalness of their association. Therefore, ethnic nationalism often either tends to undermine the plausibility of the national project or, in the most tragic cases, to pave the way to extreme strategies for "redressing" the mismatch, such as mass expulsions, ethnic cleansing, or genocide.

As a consequence, whether a collective is labeled as a "nation" or an "ethnic group" might tell relatively little about its intrinsic properties, but much about the legitimacy of the groups' claim to sovereignty in the eyes of those who use the term. More generally, different labels, when used purposely or repeated routinely to characterize collective actors and collective violence, imply different modes of legitimate action. As pointed out by Roberts (1996), "calling the conflict in former Yugoslavia a case of 'ancient ethnic hatred' and 'civil war' has often been code language for recommending a policy of partial or total nonintervention: while calling it a case of 'aggression,' and defence of a multiethnic Bosnia, has been associated with support for a more militant outside response" (p. 177).

Questioning the Radical Argument: Ethnic Diversity Leads to Ethnic Violence

The most straightforward attempts to link ethnicity and violence empirically can be found in a growing body of quantitative studies in the political sciences literature. It has become a routine now to include an indicator of "ethnic fractionalization" or "ethnic polarization" in the analyses of large macrolevel datasets of armed conflict worldwide, with the aim of predicting the likelihood of an outbreak of violence (Collier & Hoeffler, 2004; Montalvo & Reynal-Querol, 2005; Vanhanen, 1999). The general conclusion from these studies is then that more heterogeneity leads to higher risk of violence. A rather extreme example of a deterministic approach to ethnic diversity can be found in the work by Lim, Metzler, and Bar-Yam

(2007). Based on analogies with physical or chemical processes of separation, the authors assume that violence arises "due to the structure of boundaries between groups rather than as a result of inherent conflicts" (p. 1541). Outbreaks of violence simulated on the basis of this model and on historical census reporting the geographical locations of ethnic groups in India and the former Yugoslavia did strongly correlate with the empirical coordinates of reported violence in both contexts. These findings led their authors to the surprising conclusion that "separation may be indicated as a way of preventing violence" (p. 1544) and, in even more concrete terms, that ethnic areas of "width less than 10 km or greater than 100 km may provide sufficient mixing or isolation to reduce the chance of violence" (p. 1544).

Obviously, part of the flaw in the argument stems from what could technically be described as a sampling bias. An appropriate test of the claimed generality of the model would require a larger universe of "multiethnic" countries, including some of the many who did not experience ethnic violence in the recent past. In their current form, the results tell us little more than that in contexts which have been chosen precisely because violence between ethnic groups has occurred, this violence was located in places were these groups previously lived together in "mixed" settings. To take the example of the former Yugoslavia, there is certainly nothing surprising about such evidence; it echoes many descriptive accounts of the war, without adding a genuine element of explanation. Gagnon (2004) and Hartmann (2002), described how the architects of war and ethnic cleansing purposefully targeted multiethnic cities when they sent out their military and paramilitary forces, with the appalling aim to create irreversible new demographic and political–psychological realities among the populations they aspired to rule over.

Had Lim et al. (2007) carried out their analyses on a larger territory over the same period—for instance, the European continent as a whole—then they would have faced great difficulties in demonstrating that patterns of co-location across ethnic groups tend to predict the outbreak of violence. They might have had a hard time defining a spatial model that differentiates patterns of religious coexistence in Bosnia and Northern Ireland, where violence occurred between groups from different religions, from those in Scotland, Switzerland, or Germany, where it did not. But the problem goes further: why would groups of different religious affiliations, for example, be identified as relevant at all for such analyses? When in some contexts it occurs natural to us to differentiate between groups of different faith, and in others among groups of different language, phenotype, or geographical origin, then we should wonder what makes specific markers of "ethnicity" appear meaningful in specific contexts. Without the ethnic violence of the 1990s, would we take it for granted that currently Bosnia is composed of three distinct ethnic communities, even though those whom we now label routinely as "Bosniaks," "Croats," and "Serbs" have shared a territory over centuries, as well as many habits and an idiom which, until the outbreak of violence, was labeled "Serbo-Croatian"? Would we find it relevant to specify that there are African–Americans and European-Americans living in the United States, if there had not been a history of slavery? That there are Roma, Armenian, or Jewish minorities in many countries over the world, had these groups not been the target of genocidal violence in the past? Thus, there is some implicit circularity in the argument, hidden by the flexibility of the concept of "ethnicity": first, violence directs the definition of ethnic subgroups within a larger population, and then violence is explained by the (co)existence of these ethnic subgroups.

Questioning the Moderate Argument: Ethnic Conflict Leads to Ethnic Violence

A more subtle and widespread variant of the argument that interethnic relations cause violence is that armed conflicts are provoked by unresolved issues, grievances, or tensions between ethnic groups. Petersen's (2002) prominent book *Understanding Ethnic Violence* provides a good example. His explicit aim is to explain the occurrence of collective violence by collective emotions shared among members of the same ethnic group, and provoked by structural changes in the relations between ethnic groups. Applying this methodology to the case of the former Yugoslavia, the author concludes that "resentment toward Muslims appears to have helped drive Croatian and Serbian actions in Bosnia....Hatred pervaded Serbian actions in the expulsion of Albanians from Kosovo....Fear and resentment mixed to create the carnage of the Croatian War" (p. 250). As Sekulic, Massey, and Hodson (2006) have pointed out, similar ways of thinking are shared by many experts and nonexperts, obsessed with understanding the psychological motives that supposedly led the masses to engage in furious violence against "ethnic others."

However, empirical studies of the motives of the masses on the eve of the outbreak of violence in Croatia and Bosnia suggest that this might be the wrong starting point. Analyzing representative survey data, Hodson, Sekulic, and Massey (1994) failed to show any correspondence between preexistent ethnic animosities and subsequent violence. Ethnic intolerance was the highest in relatively homogenous Slovenia, where subsequent war was of very low intensity, whereas in Croatia, and especially in Bosnia-Herzegovina, ethnic tolerance was relatively high, but followed by particularly intense violence. In a later study, focusing on the case of Croatia, the authors broadened the temporal scope of their analyses (Sekulic et al., 2006). They analyzed data from four comparable surveys that took place in 1985, 1989 (before the war), 1996 (immediately after the war), and in 2003. Two scales of ethnic intolerance were used. Both led to the same conclusion: intolerance between ethnic groups increased dramatically after the war, followed in the last wave by only a partial return to more tolerant attitudes. These findings suggest that widespread ethnic animosities are insufficient, if not irrelevant, to explain the causes of political violence, but that they are to be taken into account as important consequences of violence. In neighbouring Bosnia, Maček (2009), who experienced and documented the siege of Sarajevo as an anthropologist, reached a similar conclusion: "In Bosnia, the identity of the enemy shifted over time as alliances and antipathies among national groups and military forces changed; the enemy was produced by the war, not the other way round .... Nationalist solidarities and oppositions were generated by the war itself, not *vice versa*; this war was a means of creating new states with exclusive ethnonational claims" (p. 191).

Cross-temporal comparisons carried out in other contexts lead to similar conclusions. Bar-Tal and Labin (2001) showed in a longitudinal study that negative stereotypic perceptions and attitudes toward people from surrounding Muslim countries, increased heavily one day after two terrorist attacks, which occurred during a relatively peaceful period of time. Three months after the events, some measures remained negative, whereas others indicated a return to more positive attitudes. Bar-Tal (2004) and Oren and Bar-Tal (2007) show similar examples related to the interplay between violent conflict and intergroup perceptions in the middle East. Similarly, in the United States and in the United Kingdom, attitudes toward Muslims in general, be it within the country or outside, became more negative in the aftermath of the 9/11 terrorist attacks (Panagopoulos, 2006; Sheridan & Gillet, 2005). Research done in Rwanda (Staub & Pearlman, 2001), Northern Ireland (Hewstone et al., 2004; McLernon, Cairns, Hewstone, & Smith, 2004), and Bosnia-Herzegovina (Cehajic, Brown, & Castano, 2008), has shown that communities exposed to massive violence and subsequent separation tend to have difficulties in developing trust or, more generally, positive attitudes or feelings across ethnic boundaries (Staub, 2006, for a review). Such symbolic changes are often grounded in changes in the material world, which cause younger generations to grow up in a very different world than their forebears did. The Croatian city of Vukovar provides a tragic example: the well-integrated, "multiethnic" city that it was before the outbreak of war in 1991, became a place were communities live in widely segregated settings and where children from different ethnic backgrounds attend separate schools (Ajdukovic & Čorkalo Biruški, 2008). In other cases, social separation has materialized itself throughout divisive walls, as in Belfast or in the West Bank, which are defended as a functional and reassuring solution by those who built them.

Putting Violence into Context

Another problem with the assumption that high levels of conflict between ethnic groups would almost naturally lead to the outbreak of ethnic violence is that it tends to overlook why conflict would turn into violence at specific times, in specific places. Since Tajfel's (1978) seminal work, social psychologists have been interested in periods of social instability. Following Tajfel, subordinate groups are more likely to challenge the status quo when they perceive the intergroup system as illegitimate, unstable, and impermeable. However, group mobilization toward social change might not be driven by the same factors as group radicalization toward violent struggle. As Gurr (1993) showed in his classical analyses on collective action among minority groups within nation-states, the experience of discrimination and changes in group status predicted group organization and the expression of grievances and collective claims. But they failed to predict the outbreak of violent group action. The latter had to do much more with the political organization of the group, its leadership and, particularly, (repressive) state reactions to group protest, than with the status history of the group itself: "objective conditions (poverty, discriminatory treatment, loss of autonomy) determine the issues around which leaders are able to mobilize collective action .... But once a group is committed to a particular strategy, self-sustaining conflict dynamics tend to develop: fighting groups and their opponents get locked in to action–reaction sequences from which it is difficult to escape" (p. 189). The interesting lesson to learn is that we need to be very cautious before transposing theoretical models designed to explain intergroup conflict to the prediction of intergroup violence. Brubaker and Laitin (1998) emphasized this important point, when they urged scholars:

> to ask specific questions about, and seek specific explanations for, the occurrence and nonoccurrence ... of violence in conflictual situations. These questions and explanations should be distinguished from questions and explanations of the existence, and even the intensity, of conflict. We lack strong evidence show- ing that higher levels of conflict (measured independently of violence) lead to higher levels of violence. Even where violence is clearly rooted in preexisting conflict, it should not be treated as a natural, self-explanatory outgrowth of such conflict, something that occurs automatically when the conflict reaches certain intensity, a certain "temperature." Violence is not a quantitative degree of conflict but a qualitative form of conflict, with its own dynamics. (p. 426)

During economic or political crises, there is an increase of insecurity among the masses, as well as fear among elites to lose political power or control over eco- nomic resources. These are also periods in which some groups may see opportuni- ties for political change. In the former Yugoslavia, the death of Tito in May 1980, economic recession, a crisis of federalism, and changes in international geopolitics with the end of the cold war, concurrently created a climate of political instability, which paved the way to extreme forms of ethno-nationalism (Wilmer, 2002). Banton (1997) has similarly drawn our attention to the relationship between a period of societal change in Rwanda and the rise of ethnic divides between Tutsis et Hutus before the beginning of genocide. However, political divergences are normal in any political system. They are even the basis of democratic functioning and most divergences between groups do not result in violence. Unless people perceive no other alternative, the vast majority of individuals—even army officers—will be always reluctant to use violence (Brubaker & Laitin, 1998).

When periods of political instability occur along with the establishment of incon- testable or hegemonic representations of other groups and their intentions (Bar-Tal, 2004), criminal behavior, which in other circumstances would be interpreted as acts of individuals, is then likely to be construed as "intergroup violence," threatening the "ingroup" in its existence. Further, Ajdukovic (2007) described how in times of upheaval, social norms are systematically violated or presented as altered by the media and elites. For example, the first episodes of violence in Croatia were heavily instrumentalized on both sides by the mass media, which were largely controlled by Slobodan Milošević or Franjo Tudjman, and their entourage (Hartmann, 2002). As a consequence, in times of uncertainty and violence, social institutions and relationships appear to no longer function as they used to. People feel existentially confused and neither know whom to trust, nor how to behave rightly. In situations in which violence threatens to spread, turning to "one's group" then seems the most functional thing to do. Groups have a protective function for individuals exposed to political violence (Muldoon, Schmid, & Downes, 2009), and enable individuals to react collectively to perceived threat or disorder (Ajdukovic, 2007).

But this does still not explain why people would turn to their *ethnic* group, rather than to any other type of collective. For sure, people do not seek protection at random among all social categories they are affiliated to. They will give preference to those collectives from which they expect mutual recognition and solidarity. Therefore, entrepreneurs of ethnic identity (Reicher, Hopkins, Levine, & Rath, 2005) need to make it sound credible, first, that people's fates are tied to the fate of their ethnic community and, second, that this type of community is more likely to provide them with protection and purpose than any other type of community. Further, the best way to convince people that a community will act together in solidarity in the future is to show that it has always done so in the past. This leads to clarify the previous argument that collective violence typically brings into being ethnic groups. The important point is that it rarely does so at once. Certainly, entrepreneurs of ethnic identity do not create ethnic categories out of nothing when violence breaks out. Past experiences, and how they are remembered, constrain the versions of group identity that leaders or activists can make plausible in times of crisis.

POLITICAL VIOLENCE AND THE TRANSFORMATION OF THE "ETHNIC IN-GROUP"

If ethnic violence is not only directed against ethnic out-groups, but also—as we have argued in the previous section—a vehicle for promoting and freezing new alignments within ethnic categories, then there is an (often overlooked) "in-group" side to the "intergroup" story. Political violence not only dramatically changes what "they" (i.e., people categorized as enemies) mean to "us," it also insidiously, but not less consequentially, changes the way "we" are. It transmutes the normative and structural context that constrains, directs, and sanctions those social interactions which make a distinctive collective out of people that happen to share a territory, a language, a religion, or a series of customs. In this section, we will therefore aim to scrutinize in more detail how political violence transforms moral climates and social ties among those who fight together "on the same side" in "ethnic war."

Violence and Moral Climates

A first consideration is that political violence tends to increase the exposure of members of society to violence beyond the temporary, territorial, and social boundaries of an explicitly defined armed conflict. Archer and Gartner (1987) conducted a systematic investigation with the aim to clarify how state-organized killing during war relates to killing as an "ordinary crime," committed by individuals without a uniform. They compared prewar and postwar homicide rates for the two world wars and 12 other twentieth century wars—across countries that took part in the fighting and those that did not—and found a consistent pattern. Homicide rates were systematically higher within postwar nations than in the corresponding prewar societies, whereas no similar imbalance was found over the same period among a parallel sample of control nations. Those nations that had the highest number of combat-related fatalities also had the highest increase in postwar homicides. Several counter-intuitive findings further allowed Archer and Gartner to refute a series of existing models. First, homicide rates increased even among noncombatant groups, such as women, or people above 45 years old. This allows ruling out violent veterans as a sufficient explanation. Second, the increase in homicides proved to be as strong in those countries that were in better economic shape after the war than before the war as it was in those countries that did experience a worsening of economic circumstances. Third, they increased even more markedly in victorious than in defeated nations.

According to the authors, the only kind of explanation that cannot be ruled out by their data takes into account a shared state of mind, which is the outcome of legitimate authorities' repeatedly asserting that killing can be a highly virtuous things to do: "war involves homicide legitimated by the highest auspices of the state. During many years, the killing of enemy soldiers has been treated not merely as a regrettable and expedient measure but as praiseworthy and heroic .... This wartime reversal of the customary peacetime prohibition against killing may some-how influence the threshold for using homicide as a means for settling conflict in everyday life" (Archer & Gartner, 1987, p. 94). Exposure to official justification of violence is indeed common in different subgroups in society; it is likely to be more pronounced in the context of large-scale and/or enduring wars causing many fatalities, and more persuasive when the promise of national victory is eventually kept rather than denied.

More recently, Rosler, Bar-Tal, Sharvit, Halperin, and Raviv (2009) developed a similar argument regarding the "moral-social costs" (p. 21) of prolonged occupation by Israeli military forces of the West Bank and Golan Heights for the occupying society. According to these authors, growing accustomed to violence against Palestinian residents, to the arbitrary use of power against them, and to legal double-standards, is likely to backfire on the occupiers. A dysfunctional judicial system and spreading corruption in the administration eventually makes everyone more vulnerable to a lack of protection of basic rights. The diffusion of violent norms eventually results in higher levels of violence in the schools and in the streets. The circulation of a psychological repertoire of coping mechanisms that enable ordinary citizens to reduce dissonance and guilt in the face of violence perpetrated by their own nation (Bandura, 1999), "will likely permeate other domains of life in the occupying society," contribute to the "banality of brutalization," and "eventually endanger manifold categories of citizens, including ethnic minorities and other weakened groups" (Rosler et al., 2009, p. 25).

Violence and Gender Relations

One of these groups that become increasingly vulnerable when the glorification of violence spreads within a society is women. As Nikolic-Ristanovic (1999) noted: "because a weapon in hand (usually men's hands) means power, the militarization of the ethnic conflict in the former Yugoslavia increased the power imbalance between women and men and made women more vulnerable to violence in different ways" (p. 69). Sadly, during these wars, rape has repeatedly become an extension of warfare (Wilmer, 2002). As was the case for other forms of violence, sexual violence against women from other ethnic groups—or women who married across ethnic boundaries—created irrevocable social divides along ethnic lines. But the very fact that violence against women became a means for humiliating their husbands, fathers, or brothers, inevitably transformed gender relations in a sinister way, even within ethnic communities. All too often, raped women further accumulated secondary victimization stemming from different public sources: political leaders who instrumentalized victims of rape in order to demonize the out-group and mobilize the in-group for retaliatory violence, foreign journalists who were looking for sensational personalized testimonies, religious leaders who stigmatized abortion even when pregnancy was a consequence of rape, and police officers who often were blind toward this particular form of crime. Intriguingly, Nikolic-Ristanovic (1999) reports that in the Federal Republic of Yugoslavia, while war was fought in Croatia and Bosnia, rates of women calling SOS lines increased steadily. However, during the same period, official figures on sexual offenders reported to the police, as well as the number of convictions, decreased year by year, which inspired the following appreciation to the author: "these data tell us more about the nonfunctioning of formal social controls, including the police and the courts, than about the crime rate" (p. 76). Altogether, both the reality of systematic rape and the way public voices or institutions have reacted to it have contributed to a climate that is more overtly misogynous than it was before the war, leaving many women with an increased sense of their own vulnerability within their communities.

In Croatia, too, among the high societal prices paid for fighting an eventually victorious "homeland war," a significant burden is carried by women. Egalitarian gender relations, such as they were at least formally encouraged under the previous socialist regime, have been reconsidered. Kunovich and Deitelbaum (2004) showed that, one year after the end of combat, there was an indirect relation between a context of war and traditional gender roles: first, people living in those areas where most of the fighting took place were more prone to express distrust and fear toward members of other nations. Second, those who expressed more distrust and fear toward members of other nations were also more likely to oppose gender equality. These findings further highlight that the regendering of social values is far from being a simple reflection of the division of labor during war. It is better understood as a by-product of the overall reorganization of social relations in terms of exclusive national identities and its virile undertones, which distribute roles among those who threaten the nation (ethnic out-groups), those who defend it (combatants), and those who give birth to its sons (mothers).

Violence and the Social Fabric

War confronts those who experience it with the boundaries of the human capacity to preserve psychological integrity in the face of hardship and trauma. There are two reasons for this: one obvious and the other ill-defined. The obvious reason is that war creates existentially threatening events, which generate traumatic experience, in great number and intensity. The (yet) ill-defined reason has to do with the fact that people who have experienced traumatic events need to rely on their social environments to maintain or restore a sense of psychological closure. Contrary to the trauma created by, say, road accidents or burglary, political violence not only threatens an individual life with disruption, but it does the same to entire communities. As a consequence, in the aftermath of war, individuals are typically confronted with a social environment that is likely to reactivate and reinforce the traumatic experience, rather than to provide support and coping resources. In a specific sense, the postwar environment is even part of the traumatic experience: it confronts the individual with the threat of disappearance of important social dimensions of the self.

This problem is perfectly illustrated in a study conducted by Abramowitz (2005) among five local Guinean communities two or three years after they had been attacked and largely devastated by military incursions from the neighboring Sierra Leonean and Liberian forces in 2000–2001. In this study, the prevalence of PTSD-type symptoms of psychological distress seemed to reflect current efforts to maintain some continuity in the social organization of the community: signs of psychological suffering were the highest in those communities in which social practices—such as market activities or the schooling of children—and collective rituals—such as marriages and funerals—had vanished. These findings invite us to look more closely at the interplay between psychological integrity and social order in postconflict communities, and to consider that the disruption of social practice could be all the more psychologically threatening as it reveals causes beyond the material destruction of infra-structures. People not only cease to interact because of a shortage of opportunities. They also withdraw from social life when the turmoil triggered by political violence leaves them unsure about the relevance of those shared values that provided meaning and purpose to everyday interactions.

POLITICAL VIOLENCE AND THE CONSTRUCTION OF COLLECTIVE MEMORY

In this section, we will engage with a simple, central, but often overlooked question: How are complex experiences of violence transmuted into simple narratives of collective ethnic victimization (Bar-Tal, Chernyak-Hai, Schori, & Gundar, 2009)? At the heart of such transformative processes there appears to be a multi-faceted effort in directed forgetting. First, the emergence of a narrative of ethnic violence presupposes that instances of solidarity across ethnic lines fall into oblivion. As Ramanathapillai (2006) has pointed out, the outbreak of insurgency against the Sri Lankan government by the Liberation Tigers of Tamil Eelam in 1983 was preceded by periodic, state-tolerated (if not instigated) riots targeting Tamil residents in ethnically mixed regions since 1956 and the publicizing of selective accounts of these events by rebel leaders. Typically, atrocities committed by Sinhalese against Tamils were loudly remembered, while no word was said about the "hundreds of cases where Sinhalese and Muslim risked their lives to help Tamils in the midst of riots" (p. 15). Tamil nationalist discourse thus echoed the intentions of the extremist instigators of these riots, creating the impression of an undifferentiated "Sinhala mob," united by pervasive "Sinhala racism." Similarly, Broz (2005) has gathered an impressive number of forgotten testimonies of victims of war in Bosnia and Herzegovina, which were all helped at one crucial point by "ethnic out-groups," in a few cases even at the cost of their own life.

Second, narratives of ethnic victimization imply that interethnic violence is remembered, while intraethnic violence is forgotten. Gagnon (2004) has argued that even though Serbs have attacked other Serbs in the Krajina Republic for political purposes, Croats have killed Croats in Herzeg-Bosnia, and Muslims fought against Muslims in other parts of Bosnia-Herzegovina, these instances of political violence have systematically been overseen by internal and external observers. They did not fit into the simplifying narrative of "ethnic war." The fact that "in-group policing" and "intergroup violence" can be two sides of the same coin does not seem to be a peculiarity of the former Yugoslavian wars. Brubaker and Laitin (1998) quote similar practices of ritualized violence against "in-groups" used in Southern African townships, Northern Ireland, Palestinian territories, and LTTE-controlled zones in Sri Lanka.

A related kind of oblivion concerns "in-group" resistance or desertion. When the war broke out in Croatia in 1991, and young Serbs in Serbia were drafted in order to save Serbs in Croatia from what was then depicted by the state-held mass media as ongoing genocide, about 200,000 of them still preferred to hide or to flee abroad, rather than to serve in Croatia (Gagnon, 2004). Again, this counter-evidence to the representation of violence driven by grass-roots ethnic hatred or resentment was largely ignored, not only by domestic warmongers, but also by foreign journalists and scholars (Petersen, 2002), who kept on wondering which deep-rooted collective emotions could have driven Serbs, conceived as a consistent entity, to fight so passionately against Croats (and *vice versa*).

Fourth, narratives of collective victimization tend to portray the suffering of "in-group" members not only as a common fate, but also as unique or exceptional. In other words, the suffering of "others" is forgotten or downplayed, creating the impression of bounded experiences within the community. Vollhardt (2009) has therefore argued that decreasing perceptions of the exclusiveness of the in-group's suffering might be the first step toward transforming narratives of in-group victimization into more inclusive victim beliefs, which foster empathy and proso-cial behavior beyond group boundaries.

Collective Memory and Collective Agency

There are three important corollaries to this reconceptualization of "in-group victimization" narratives as outcomes of directed forgetting. First, memories are consequential for actions toward declared enemies. Systematic "gaps" in the memory of events facilitate similar "simplifications" in the representation of out-group conduct and intentions. Once the in-group is portrayed as a consistent entity bounded together by collective suffering, explanations for this suffering are needed. As Bar-Tal (1990) argued, delegitimization of out-groups, that is, their categorization into extremely negative entities, enables "parsimonious understanding" (p. 68) of the calamities that hit the in-group and it does even more: "on the one hand, it explains why the other group threatens, and on the other hand, it predicts what the other group will do in the future" (p. 68). Pervasive in-group suffering then becomes the reflection of pervasive out-group evil. These interpretative templates are likely to make even constructive initiatives or genuine concessions from the other side more difficult to be perceived as such. Further, just as collective memories of in-group victimization are institutionalized through official commemorations or history books, the same can be true for out-group delegitimization. Oren and Bar-Tal (2007) found depictions of Jews in Palestinian textbooks asserting that "treachery and disloyalty are character traits of the Jews and therefore one should beware of them" (p. 119), mirroring the depiction of Arabs in Israeli textbooks as "robbers, vandals, primitives, and easily agitated" (p. 117).

Second, far from being spontaneous and inevitable consequences of massive suffering, collective narratives require agents and efforts. Collective memories of victimization are inseparable from the construction of the collectives who remember. The battle over memories is at the same time a battle over the definition of identities. Further, as Reicher et al. (2005) have argued, those who win the symbolic struggle over the definition of a common identity are in a privileged position to guide the behavior of the group, that is, to exert social power and influence. Remembering who has suffered in the past for what reason and identifying the implications for subsequent actions is therefore an inherently political and controversial process.

As a consequence, particular constructions of the in-group, as well as of past suffering or current threat, can be challenged. Across the different territories that the German Nazi state had occupied in the early 1940s, there were contrasting reactions to its appalling policies of persecution and then extermination of the Jewish population. In Bulgaria, effective resistance to the regime's material policies—which made the difference between life and death for so many—went hand-in-hand with a discursive resistance to the underlying construal of Jews as a racial out-group, to be eliminated for the sake of the defence of a threatened civilization: in their public speeches, prominent oppositional figures consistently portrayed, Jews as integral parts of the Bulgarian nation, and the Nazi project as alien to the core values of the national community (Reicher, Cassidy, Wolpert, Hopkins, & Levine, 2006).

The struggle over the definition of group boundaries and group norms is mostly also a struggle over the legitimacy of a plurality of perspectives within the in-group. In a thought-provoking study, Roccas, Klar, and Liviatan (2006) confronted young contemporary Israeli Jews with the historical depiction of a massacre perpetrated by the Israeli army against inhabitants of an Arab village in 1956. Not surprisingly, those participants who strongly glorified the Israeli nation (which means that they affirmed its superiority over other nations and derogated critics of the nation), were the most likely to exonerate actions of the military, and to reject guilt. However, when levels of glorification were controlled for, the more the participants were attached to their nation, the less they exonerated, and the more they accepted guilt. A substantial minority of participants thus seemed to hold a belief that a critical view toward the in-group's past should not be mistaken as a sign of disloyalty but, on the contrary, should be recognized as a moral concern grounded in genuine identification. Their stance appears to be that attachment entitles to criticism.

Third, narratives of victimization evolve, and some periods might be more favourable to critical revision than others. As mentioned before, Maček (2009) described, first, a move toward a temporary suspension of heterogeneity at the onset of the siege of Sarajevo. Interestingly, this trend was then followed by a return to heterogeneity while fighting endured. In a context were protection and solidarity were more and more organized along ethnic lines, people first progressively turned to "their" ethnic community in their struggle for survival, shifting from a "civilian" to a "soldier" mode of action. During that stage, most people were led to embrace, at least in public, exclusive ethno-national identities, and to support the struggle of "their" community. However, as the siege evolved, many inhabitants became increasingly cynical about the purpose of the war, and moved toward a "deserter" mode of distancing themselves from the official justification of this struggle.

Comparative analyses conducted by Spini, Elcheroth, and Fasel (2008) provide further evidence for situations were simple realities break down in the aftermath of prolonged violence: Populations exposed to more long-lasting and devastating armed violence were more prone to condemn violations of basic human rights during combat than populations exposed to shorter periods of violence and/or producing fewer victims. Furthermore, this effect of the magnitude of war on the condemnation of violations of universal rights was entirely mediated by the generalization of risks related to combats across ethnic categories. These findings thus indicate that prolonged violence tends to create new communities of victimization beyond combat lines. Most likely, the subsequent problematization of exclusive group membership then leads people to embrace more inclusive norms more easily.

Collective Memory and Institutional Frameworks: The Role of Criminal Tribunals

After having clarified what it means to remember collective victimization, we are now better prepared to consider the contribution of an emerging social psychological literature on the impact of judicial responses as a particular means of addressing a violent past in order to lay the grounds for a more peaceful future. When narratives of collective suffering are actively constructed and central to the definition of collective identities, then the patient work of precisely documenting who gave the orders and who designed mass atrocities, might indeed stimulate critical revision of over-simplified narratives of collective agency as completely bounded within ethnic categories. Further, if people's propensity to distance themselves from exclusive identification to the "in-group's" struggle evolves over time, then there might be specific windows of opportunity for trials.

First of all, recent findings lead us to problematize the common-sense notion that trials are above all to be held for the sake of the victims. Studying a Mayan community during its participation in a trial over massacres perpetrated during armed conflict and state terror in Guatemala, Lykes, Beristain, and Perez-Arminan (2007) depicted the process as a psychologically difficult experience for direct victims of violence. Compared to other witnesses participating in the trial, they displayed higher levels of emotional pain, concern, and anxiety. They were more likely to prefer to forget events rather than to remember them, or to express their frustration over the trial. Interestingly though, when community members who participated in the trials were compared to those who did not, they more frequently emphasized the positive effects of social bonding created by the shared action. Overall, the study suggests that the trial strengthened the community as a whole in an important way, rather than those who suffered the most individually from violent trauma. In a similar way, Biro et al. (2004) showed, on the one hand, that across three local communities highly exposed to war atrocities during war in Croatia and Bosnia, direct victims of war were highly ambivalent toward the work of the ICTY. On the other hand, however, support for the tribunal was an important predictor of people's readiness to reconciliation across ethnic boundaries.

Individual and collective exposures to armed conflict appear indeed to produce opposite effects on people's support for the prosecution of war crimes. Two comparative studies showed that while those who were directly affected in their personal lives by loss brought on by war were typically more skeptical toward prosecution than other members from the same community, the more such loss became a prevalent experience within a community, the more its members were likely to support prosecution of war crimes. This pattern held when comparing 14 postwar communities worldwide (Elcheroth, 2006), as well as when comparing, in a more fine-grained manner, different contexts within the former Yugoslavia (Elcheroth & Spini, 2009). While these findings altogether lead us to be very suspicious of the common sense notion that trials might have some direct therapeutic value for individuals who have to cope with the memory of war trauma, they clarify at the same time the genuine and important functions that trials can accomplish at the level of entire communities, helping them to strive toward a definition of past narratives, collective identities, and normative frameworks that would allow them to avoid repeating tomorrow the horrors of yesterday.

CONCLUSION

In the context of a debate on current theories of intergroup relations, Reicher (2004) argued that

> psychological theory is not only a commentary on the world and how we behave within it; it is also part of our world and serves to shape our own self-understandings. Those models that serve to reify social categories in theory may also help to reify categories in practice." This led him to turn the question whether our theories are useful into for whom they are useful: "it may well be true that reified accounts of social action are of little use to those who have an interest in understanding or producing change. In contrast, they are all too helpful to those who wish to keep the social world as it is. (p. 942)

Are there social categories that we reify when we write about violence (as well as about reconciliation or forgiveness) between groups defined in ethno-national terms? What dimensions of social reality might we help to forget this way? Why would such oblivion facilitate some modes of social action and hamper others? In the first section of this chapter, we have questioned traditional assumptions about the relationship between political violence, in-group conflict, and ethnic categories. We have developed the argument that "ethnic groups" cannot be conceived independently from the forces that brought them into being as bounded entities of fate. Whenever we take for granted the current existence of separate ethnic groups, looking backwards on a history of violence or oppression that opposes people according a particular dimension of "ethnic" attributes, informs us how these attributes have become structuring principles of social relations. We have then shown how political violence not only materializes intergroup boundaries, but how it transforms also the ethnic in-group. In the last section, we emphasized that complex experiences of violence can lay the grounds for ethnic violence in the future (only) to the extent that they are collectively remembered through simplified narratives, which identify warring parties, victims and perpetrators in ethnic terms, and bracket out other social divides potentially revealed by the fighting.

There are important consequences of these outcomes from our literature review, at both theoretical and practical levels. Above all, they lead to problematize two kinds of related assumptions, which still underlie many studies in the field. The first is to conceive violence (more or less explicitly) as a high level of conflict on a continuous scale: the more social relations are harmonious, the less violence is likely to occur in the future. The second is to conceive group actions as driven by the sum of the motives of the individuals that compose the group: if we want the group to refrain from violent actions, then we have to find ways to channel individual coping strategies in a nonviolent direction.

Basically, the issue comes down to: Do we elude or do we address the problem of power? If we assume that the most effective way to build a peaceful society is to make sure that most people do not carry with them aggressive motives, then we implicitly assume that collective violence reflects the will of the majority. However, neither war nor genocide is a democratic contest. The relevant question for the analyst is therefore not why the majority is driven by destructive motives, but how a minority managed to convince the majority that there was no viable alternative to their particular way of defining the group, its struggle, its enemies, and its means. The relevant question for the activist might less be how to reconcile the majority of ordinary people among themselves, than how to build frameworks for collective action in which the reification of an over-simplified social reality that claims to be incontestable will be more difficult to push forward, and easier to resist.

This points to a potential peril of an "interethnic reconciliation" approach to the prevention of violence, which would be to focus on the materialized outcomes of ethnicized violence and to bracket out the central problem of the processes which led to these outcomes: How has the construction of ethnic categories as homogeneous social entities been achieved? Why did ethnicity become the over-arching principle of collective agency? Neglecting to address these questions might then lead us to overlook the royal road to the reconstruction of a nonviolent society, which is to ask how other types of identities, and hence of agency, can resurface again. We have concluded our review by highlighting the potential of criminal tribunal as one particular means to challenge reifying narratives of "ethnic conflict" and "ethnic violence." However, trials can never be more than a starting point for the reconstruction of peaceful societies: Whenever they reach their goal of effectively clarifying responsibility for past crimes, they provide no more and no less than new raw material, which can be molded in a collective effort to identify communities of fate and potential collective agents other than those promoted by instigators of ethnic violence.

The more general challenge for social psychological scholars and practitioners will be to extend Kelman's famous principle that national identities need to be overtly negotiated between conflicting groups and that social scientists' contribution to peace processes should include "the development of a methodology for negotiating identity" (Kelman, 1997, p. 334). Today, we still lack such a methodology. But insights gained from contemporary research in social psychology and its neighboring fields already allow—and urge—us to clarify its purpose and broaden its scope. We are now in a better position than ever to be aware of the crucial importance of appropriate settings within which identities can not only be negotiated *between* ethno-national groups, as they have been produced by political violence, but also within such groups. It would be theoretically ill-informed to imagine that such settings only exist where they are explicitly designed by third parties to facilitate the negotiation of identities, and it would be politically naive to imagine that power holders would easily lose their grip on much more influential "real-world" settings for these debates, such as provided by mass media, public rallies, or classrooms. It rarely is social psychologists' vocation to be the architects of these settings, but we might aspire to be their critical and—why not—creative commentators. Our conceptual toolbox puts us in a privileged position for remembering the options that are tacitly excluded by a given setting. The critical test we should actively promote is whether a setting is more likely to allow for a plurality of social cleavages underlying collective experiences, aspirations, and commitments to express themselves, than to reify the simplification of social reality brought on by ethno-national violence. Only then can we be certain enough that our theories are more useful for those who strive to prevent violence than to those who capitalize on violence.

ACKNOWLEDGMENTS

Many of our encounters with studies, scholars, ideas, and backgrounds quoted in this chapter have been greatly facilitated by a three-year program grant within the Scientific Co-operation between Switzerland and Eastern Europe (SCOPES Fund No IB-111094) framework, as well as by a one-year research fellowship to the first author (Grant No PBLA1-118289), both financed by the Swiss National Science Foundation (SNF).

REFERENCES

Abramowitz, S. A. (2005). The poor have become rich, and the rich have become poor: Collective trauma in the Guinean Languette. *Social Science and Medicine, 61*, 2106–2118.

Ajdukovic, D. (2007). Social contexts of trauma and healing. *Medicine, Conflict and Survival*, *20*(2), 120–135.

Ajdukovic, D., & Corkalo Biruski, D. (2008). Caught between the ethnic sides: Children growing up in a divided post-war community. *International Journal of Behavioral Development, 32*(4), 337–347.

Archer, D., & Gartner, R. (1984). *Violence and crime in cross-national perspective.* New Haven, CT: Yale University Press.

Bandura, A. (1999). Moral disengagement in the perpetration of inhumanities. *Personality and Social Psychology Review, 3*(3), 193–209.

Banton, M. (1997). *Ethnic and racial consciousness* (2nd ed.). London: Longman.

Bar-Tal, D. (1990). Causes and consequences of delegitimization: Models of conflicts and ethnocentrism. *Journal of Social Issues, 46*(1), 65–81.

Bar-Tal, D. (2004). The necessity of observing real life situations: Palestinian–Israeli violence as a laboratory for learning about social behaviour. *European Journal of Social Psychology, 34*, 677–701.

Bar-Tal, D., Chernyak-Hai, L., Schori, N., & Gundar, A. (2009). A sense of self-collective victimhood in intractable conflict: Nature, antecedents, functions, and consequences. *International Red Cross Review, 229*–258.

Bar-Tal, D., & Labin, D. (2001). The effect of major event on stereotyping: Terrorist attacks in Israel and Israeli adolescent's perceptions of Palestinian, Jordanians and Arabs. *European Journal of Social Psychology, 31*, 265–280.

Billig, M. (1995). *Banal nationalism.* London: Sage.

Biro, M., Ajdukovic, D., Corkalo, D., Djipa, D., Milin, P., & Weinstein, H. M. (2004). Attitudes toward justice and social reconstruction in Bosnia and Herzegovina and Croatia. In E. Stover & H. M. Weinstein (Eds.), *My neighbor, my enemy. Justice and community in the aftermath of mass atrocity* (pp. 183–205). Cambridge: Cambridge University Press.

Broz, S. (2005). *Good people in an evil time: Portraits of complicity and resistance in the Bosnian war.* New York: Other Press.

Brubaker, R., & Laitin, D. D. (1998). Ethnic and nationalist violence. *Annual Review of Sociology, 24*, 423–452.

Cehajic, S., Brown, R., & Castano, E. (2008). Forgive and forget? Antecedents and consequences of intergroup forgiveness in Bosnia and Herzegovina. *European Journal of Social Psychology, 29*(3), 351–367.

Collier, P., & Hoeffler, A. (2004). Greed and grievance in civil war. *Oxford Economic Papers, 56*, 563–595.

Elcheroth, G. (2006). Individual-level and community-level effects of war trauma on social representations related to humanitarian law. *European Journal of Social Psychology, 36*(6), 907–930.

Elcheroth, G., & Spini, D. (2009). Public support for the prosecution of human rights violations in the former Yugoslavia. *Peace and Conflict: Journal of Peace Psychology, 15*(2), 189–214.

Gagnon, V. P. J. (2004). *The myth of ethnic war: Serbia and Croatia in the 1990s.* Ithaca and London: Cornell University Press.

Gurr, T. R. (1993). Why minorities rebel: A global analysis of communal mobilization and conflict since 1945. *International Political Science Review, 14*, 161–201.

Hartmann, F. (2002). *Milosevic, la diagonale du fou.* Paris: Denoël.

Hewstone, M., Cairns, E., Voci, A., McLernon, F., Niens, U., & Noor, M. (2004). Intergroup forgiveness and guilt in Northern Ireland: Social psychological dimensions of "The Troubles". In N. R. Branscombe & B. Doosje (Eds.), *Collective guilt: International perspectives* (pp. 193–215). Cambridge: Cambridge University Press.

Hodson, R., Sekulic, D., & Massey, G. (1994). National tolerance in the former Yugoslavia. *The American Journal of Sociology*, 99(6), 1534–1558.

Kelman, H. C. (1997). Negotiating national identity and self-determination in ethnic conflicts: The choice between pluralism and ethnic cleansing. *Negotiation Journal*, 13(4), 327–339.

Kunovich, R. M., & Deitelbaum, C. (2004). Ethnic conflict, group polarization, and gender attitudes in Croatia. *Journal of Marriage and the Family*, 66(5), 1089–1107.

Lim, M., Metzler, R., & Bar-Yam, M. Y. (2007). Global pattern formation and ethnic/cultural violence. *Science*, 317, 1540–1544.

Lykes, M. B., Beristain, C. M., & Perez-Arminan, M. L. C. (2007). Political violence, impunity, and emotional climate in Maya communities. *Journal of Social Issues*, 63(2), 369–385.

Maček, I. (2009). *Sarajevo Under Siege: Anthropology in Wartime*. Philadelphia: University of Pennsylvania Press.

Marshall, M. G. (2002). Measuring the societal impact of war. In O. Hampson & D. M. Malone (Eds.), *From reaction to prevention*. Boulder: Lynne Rienner.

McLernon, F., Cairns, E., Hewstone, M., & Smith, R. (2004). The development of inter-group forgiveness in Northern Ireland. *Journal of Social Issues*, 60(3), 587–601.

Montalvo, J. G., & Reynal-Querol, M. (2005). Ethnic polarization, potential conflict, and civil wars. *American Economic Review*, 95(3), 796–816.

Muldoon, O. T., Schmid, K., & Downes, C. (2009). Political violence and psychological well-being. *Applied Psychology: An International Review*, 58(1), 129–145.

Nikolic-Ristanovic, V. (1999). Living without democracy and peace. Violence against women in the former Yugoslavia. *Violence Against Women*, 5(1), 63–80.

Oren, N., & Bar-Tal, D. (2007). The detrimental dynamics of delegitimization in intractable conflicts: The Israeli–Palestinian case. *International Journal of Intercultural Relations*, 31, 111–126.

Panagopoulos, C. (2006). Arab and Muslim Americans and Islam in the aftermath of 9/11. *Public Opinion Quarterly*, 70(4), 608–624.

Petersen, R. (2002). *Understanding ethnic violence. Fear, hatred, and resentment in twentieth-century Eastern Europe*. Cambridge: Cambridge University Press.

Ramanathapillai, R. (2006). The politicizing of trauma: A case study of Sri Lanka. *Peace and Conflict: Journal of Peace Psychology*, 12(1), 1–18.

Reicher, S. (2004). The context of social identity: Domination, resistance and change. *Political Psychology*, 25(6), 921–946.

Reicher, S., Cassidy, C., Wolpert, I., Hopkins, N., & Levine, M. (2006). Saving Bulgaria's Jews: An analysis of social identity and the mobilisation of social solidarity. *European Journal of Social Psychology*, 36(1), 49–72.

Reicher, S., & Hopkins, N. (2001). *Self and nation*. London: Sage.

Reicher, S., Hopkins, N., Levine, M., & Rath, R. (2005). Entrepreneurs of hate and entrepreneurs of solidarity: Social identity as a basis for mass communication. *International Review of the Red Cross*, 87(860), 621–637.

Roberts, A. (1996). Communal conflict as a challenge to international organisation. In A. Danchev & T. Halverson (Eds.), *International perspectives on the Yugoslav conflict*. Oxford: MacMillan Press Ltd.

Roccas, S., Klar, Y., & Liviatan, I. (2006). The paradox of group-based guilt: Modes of national identification, conflict vehemence, and reactions to the in-group's moral violations. *Journal of Personality and Social Psychology*, 91(4), 698–711.

Rosler, N., Bar-Tal, D., Sharvit, K., Halperin, E., & Raviv, A. (2009). Moral aspects of prolonged occupation: Implications for an occupying society. In S. Scuzzarello, C. Kinnvall, & K. R. Monroe (Eds.), *On behalf of others: The psychology of care in a global world* (pp. 211–232). New York: Oxford University Press.

Sekulic, D., Massey, G., & Hodson, R. (2006). Ethnic intolerance and ethnic conflict in the dissolution of Yugoslavia. *Ethnic and Racial Studies*, 29(5), 797–827.

Sheridan, L. P., & Gillet, R. (2005). Major world events and discrimination. *Asian Journal of Social Psychology*, 8, 191–197.

Spini, D., Elcheroth, G., & Fasel, R. (2008). The impact of group norms and generalization of risks across groups on judgments of war behavior. *Political Psychology*, 29(6), 919–941.

Staub, E. (2006). Reconciliation after genocide, mass killing and intractable conflict: Understanding the roots of violence, psychological recovery, and steps toward a general theory. *Political Psychology*, 27(6), 867–894.

Staub, E., & Pearlman, L. A. (2001). Healing, reconciliation, and forgiving after genocide and other collective violence. In S. J. Helmick & R. L. Petersen (Eds.), *Forgiveness and reconciliation: Religion, public policy and conflict transformation*. Radnor, PA: Templeton Foundation Press.

Tajfel, H. (1978). *Differentiation between social groups*. London: Academic Press.

Vanhanen, T. (1999). Domestic ethnic conflict and ethnic nepotism: A comparative analysis. *Journal of Peace Research*, 36(1), 55–73.

Vollhardt, J. R. (2009). The role of victim beliefs in the Israeli–Palestinian conflict: Risk or potential for peace? *Peace and Conflict: Journal of Peace Psychology*, 15(2), 135–159.

Wilmer, F. (2002). *The social construction of man, the state and war. Identity, conflict, and violence in former Yugoslavia*. New York: Routledge.

Worchel, S. (1999). *Written in blood: Ethnic identity and the struggle for human harmony*. New York: Worth.

8

Workings of the Terrorist Mind
Its Individual, Group, and Organizational Psychologies

ARIE W. KRUGLANSKI, KEREN SHARVIT, and
SHIRA FISHMAN

*T*errorist attacks are some of the bloodiest manifestations of intense inter-group conflicts observed in recent years. The coordinated attacks on the United States on September 11, 2001, the March 4, 2004 bombing of the Madrid train station, the London transit bombing of July 5, 2005, the frequent ongoing suicide bombings in Iraq, Afghanistan and Israel, the political ascendancy of terrorism using groups, such as Hamas and Hezbollah, and the emergence of the global Salafi jihad inspired by Al Qaeda have made the task of opposing terrorism as difficult as it is pressing. As one author put it, "international terrorism [is] the most serious strategic threat to global peace and safety" (Ganor, 2005, p. 293).

Despite the vast interest that terrorism has generated, scholars have not been able to arrive at a consensual definition of terrorism (Schmid & Jongman, 1988). One reason for the difficulty is that the term "terrorism" has highly negative connotations, and is often used to distinguish between forms of aggression that one wishes to condemn and those that one believes to be legitimate. Hence, the definition of terrorism is often a matter of perspective and motivation (Carr, 2002; Kruglanski & Fishman, 2006). Groups that are involved in intense conflicts are often motivated to delegitimize their opponents (Bar-Tal, 1990), creating situations where one side's terrorist is the other's freedom fighter.

Nevertheless, it is possible to identify several elements that are common to many definitions of terrorism. These include indiscriminate use of force, having a political agenda, and aiming to spread feelings of threat and fear (Schmid & Jongman, 1988). In the present chapter, we argue that terrorism is a means that groups and/or individuals employ in order to achieve certain goals. Intergroup conflicts are often waged over competing goals (Mitchell, 1981; Rubin, Pruitt, & Kim, 1994), and terrorism is one form of violence among many that groups involved in such conflicts may choose to employ in order to promote goal attainment (Wilkinson, 2003).

We consider terrorism as an extreme means of goal promotion, because while instrumental to the goals over which the conflict is waged, it is often highly detrimental to other goals (e.g., preservation of human life and upholding moral values). Therefore, terrorism is typically employed when the goal that it is meant to promote is considered more important than other goals (Kruglanski & Fishman, 2006). Research indicates that commitment to a focal goal leads to the suppression of alternative goals (Shah, Friedman, & Kruglanski, 2002). Hence, high commitment of group members to collective goals increases the likelihood of using terrorism to attain these goals. In addition, the likelihood of terrorism increases when group members believe that alternative means of promoting their goals are not available or are inefficient (Kruglanski & Fishman, 2006). For this reason, terrorism is often observed in the context of ethnic conflict, where it is utilized by minorities or national-separatist groups lacking the political power to advance their goals by alternative means (DeNardo, 1985; Miller, 2007; Pape, 2003; Wilkinson, 2003). In some cases, however, terrorism may be employed by powerful actors such as states, when they believe that the goals served by terrorism are more important than the goals to which it is detrimental (Rummel, 1996).

When terrorism is employed by national-separatist or minority groups, it may be considered a tool of minority influence through which a minority hopes to elicit some desired reaction from the targeted majority (Kruglanski & Chen, 2009). Although the targeted majority often considers terrorism as illegitimate and despicable and attempts to suppress it with force, the provocative nature of terrorist attacks may nevertheless succeed in drawing attention to the terrorists' demands. Moreover, the majority's forceful reactions to the terrorists' provocations may elicit sympathy to the minority's demands among the international community, especially if the response is indiscriminate and hurts members of the minority who are not terrorists (Crenshaw, 1990). If the terrorists are able to persist in their activities, causing extensive loss of lives, disruption of routine functioning and enduring experiences of threat and fear, they may eventually lead the majority to "unfreeze" and reconsider their existing positions. However, if the terrorists fail to seize the opportunity to switch to more legitimate forms of minority action, or if they make demands that the majority considers unacceptable, then the use of terrorism may lead to an escalation in the conflict with consequences that are opposite to what the terrorists intended (Kruglanski & Chen, 2009).

In what follows, we examine the social and psychological processes that lead individuals and groups to opt for terrorism as a means of achieving their goals. We consider three psychological levels of analysis, having to do with the individual, the group and the organization. On the individual level, we consider individuals' motivations for joining a terrorist organization and whether there exists a uniform motivational basis for terrorist missions. On the group level, we discuss processes of shared reality construction and social influence in recruitment, indoctrination and inculcation of ideologies that justify terrorism. On the organizational level we consider issues of training, logistics and cost effectiveness as they apply to the decisions to employ terrorism as a strategic tool. In the concluding section we discuss the implications of our analysis for possible means of countering terrorism.

INDIVIDUAL LEVEL OF ANALYSIS

Approaches to Understanding Individuals' Involvement in Terrorism

The Psychopathology/Personality Hypothesis   The hypothesis that terrorism represents a form of psychopathology comes to mind naturally in light of the atrocities that terrorists have perpetrated (e.g., the seemingly callous perpetration of massive casualties). In the early 1970s, it was widely believed that there would be an exceptionally high number of clinical psychopaths, narcissists, and paranoids among terrorists (Silke, 2003). Nonetheless, the quest for a systematic terrorist psychopathology or a unique terrorist personality has yielded few positive results. Painstaking empirical studies of the German Red Army Faction (the Bader Meinhoff Gang), the Italian Red Army Brigades, the Basque ETA and various Palestinian terror-employing groups, found nothing unique about the psychological makeup of members of terrorist organizations (Horgan, 2003; Victoroff, 2005).

Environmental "Root Causes" of Terrorism   Having failed to identify dispositional or psychopathological factors that might contribute to terrorism, scholars turned their attention to aspects of the social environment that might constitute "root causes" of terrorism. The factors explored included socioeconomic status, poverty, relative deprivation, or foreign occupation. However, this line of research has suffered from conceptual and empirical problems. The conceptual problem was one of specificity (Sageman, 2004). While many people share oppressive environments, only few ever consider joining a terrorist organization. On the empirical side, research failed to discern a relationship between terrorism and poverty or low socioeconomic status (Atran, 2003; Berrebi, 2003; Krueger & Maleckova, 2002; Pape, 2005; Sageman, 2004; Stern, 2003). Experts presently agree that neither poverty nor political oppression constitute necessary and sufficient conditions for terrorism (Kruglanski & Fishman, 2006).

Sageman (2004) describes how Arabs in the European diasporas were alienated, underemployed, and perhaps discriminated against, thus experiencing deprivation relative to the native citizens of their host countries. Such circumstances may have produced a sense of unhappiness and humiliation, which may have been alleviated by embracing radical Islam. It is doubtful, however, that relative deprivation underlies all cases of terrorism. For instance, there is little evidence that the Weathermen underground in the United States, the Bader Meinhoff group in Germany, or the anticolonialist movements in mid-twentieth century were concerned specifically with relative deprivation.

The foregoing arguments hardly imply that personality traits or environmental conditions are irrelevant to terrorism. Instead, they may be considered as contributing factors to terrorism. In contrast to "root causes," assumed to constitute sufficient conditions for terrorism, contributing factors may predict individuals' support for or involvement in terrorism under specific circumstances and may contribute to the motivation for terrorism if the right conditions exist (Silke, 2003). The crucial topic of terrorists' motivation is considered next.

Terrorists' Motivations

Several analyses of terrorist motivations have been put forth in the recent years[*] (Bloom, 2005; Pedahzur, 2005; Sageman, 2004; Stern, 2003). Some authors emphasized a singular motivation as critical to terrorism, whereas others listed a potpourri of motives. Sageman (2004) identified the quest for emotional and social support as a major motivation for creating terrorist cells. Pape (2005) highlighted resistance to foreign occupation as a main motivating force. Spekhard and Akhmedova (2005) assigned this role to personal loss and trauma, and Hassan (2001), who interviewed hundreds of Hamas militants, concluded that their main motivation was religious.

In contrast to an emphasis on a single crucial motivation, Bloom (2005) and Stern (2003) listed diverse motivations for terrorism, including but not limited to honor, dedication to the leader, social status, personal significance, group pressure, humiliation, injustice, vengeance, exposure to violence, lack of alternative prospects, modernization, poverty, moral obligation, simplification of life, and glamour. Ricolfi (2005, p. 106) suggested that "the motivational drive to engage in suicide missions is likely to be found in a *cocktail of feelings*, which include desire for revenge, resentment, and a sense of obligation toward the victims" (emphasis added).

A reasonable step in dealing with such a heterogeneity is to aggregate the diverse motives into more general categories. Several authors have hinted at a distinction between ideological and personal causes (Pedahzur, 2005; Taarnby, 2005). For instance, alienated individuals' quest for social and emotional support (Sageman, 2004) stems from their personal experience, whereas liberation of one's land or carrying out God's will pertain to ideological factors (Atran, 2004, 2006).

A third motivational category pertinent to suicidal attacks involves a sense of duty and obligation, whether internalized or induced by social pressure. This is highlighted in data on the Japanese Kamikaze pilots (Ohnuki-Tierney, 2006) but it is highly relevant to present day terrorism as well (Bloom, 2005; Gambetta, 2005; Merari, 2002; Stern, 2003).

Quest for Significance as an Overarching Motivational Category

We have recently proposed that a central motivation underlying most terrorist attacks is the quest for personal significance (Kruglanski, Chen, Dechesne, Fishman, & Orehek, 2009). Such quest has been hailed by psychologists as a major motivational force, having to do with transcendence of the self and attachment to larger causes. According to Victor Frankl (2000), the ability to transcend immediate

---

[*] In particular reference to the seemingly incomprehensible phenomenon of motivations for suicidal terrorism (Kruglanski, Chen, Dechesne, Fishman, & Orehek, 2009).

survival concerns and to believe that there are persons, ideas or values that are worth fighting for is the essence of human existence. Maslow's (1943) theory of motivation identifies self-esteem and self actualization as top level human strivings of obvious affinity to Frankl's "search for meaning."

Frankl (1963) and others (Antonovsky, 1987; Moos & Schaefer, 1986; Taylor, 1983) have linked the search for meaning and significance to processes of coping with adversities. Commitment to an important societal cause and/or to an ideology that justifies it may facilitate the search for meaning. As noted, intense intergroup conflicts are typically waged over important societal goals (Mitchell, 1981; Rubin et al., 1994), and justifications of these goals are a central in ideological belief systems that characterize the groups involved (Bar-Tal, 1998, 2007). Hence, members of such groups who experience adversities may turn to terrorism as a means of affirming their commitment to the societal goals and thus attaining significance. Indeed, Spekhard and Akhmedova (2005), who studied Chechen suicide terrorists via interviews with their significant others and hostages that they had captured, found that all the interviewees mentioned traumatic events that appeared to have motivated the fallen terrorists to engage in terrorism. Of even greater interest, the authors observed that their subjects sought ideological inspiration in response to their personal trauma.

However, personal trauma is not the only process that may lead to a search for personal significance. A recent analysis of human motivations has linked the quest for physical survival with the desire for personal meaning and significance (Greenberg, Koole, & Pyszczynski, 2004). According to this analysis, awareness of one's mortality and the fear of living an insignificant life motivate people to be "good" members of society. The ultimate "goodness" is the sacrifice of one's self for sake of the group, usually in the case of a severe threat to the group's existence, which is a common experience in intense intergroup conflicts (Jervis, 1985; Kelman, 1997; Worchel, 1999). Hence, groups that are involved in such conflicts place high value on self-sacrifice for the protection of the group (Bar-Tal & Staub, 1997). In such cases, putting the group first brings the promise of immortality, by becoming a hero or martyr engraved forever in the group's collective memory. Ironically then, the willingness to die in an act of suicidal terrorism may be motivated by the desire to live forever.

Our theory of significance quest has a number of testable implications. First, adoption of cultural causes that lend a sense of personal significance should reduce death-anxiety. Furthermore, perceived loss of significance through events other than mortality reminders should fuel efforts at significance restoration. Finally, a threat of potential loss of significance should instigate preventive actions. Empirical findings relevant to these implications are reviewed below.

Commitment to Collectivistic Causes and Fear of Death   In the terror management literature, many empirical studies show that reminders of mortality lead to embracement of the group's culture and its ideology (Castano & Dechesne, 2005; Greenberg, Solomon, & Pyszczynski, 1997). According to Castano and Dechesne (2005), "becoming part of collective entities [allows] individuals to extend their selves in space and time [and hence] to overcome the inherent limitations of their individual identity inextricably linked to a perishable body" (p. 233). Pyszczynski et al. (2006) looked directly at the effect of mortality salience on support for terrorism. When Iranian students answered questions about their own death, they evaluated a fellow student who supported martyrdom attacks more favorably than a student who opposed martyrdom. The opposite was true when they answered questions about an aversive topic unrelated to death. Thus, the fear of death appears to increase commitment to collectivistic causes couched in ideological terms.

There is also data that commitment to collectivistic causes reduces death anxiety. Specifically, Durlak (1972) found a high negative correlation between purpose in life defined in terms of commitment to cultural objectives and fear of death. Arndt, Greenberg, Solomon, Pyszczynski, and Simon (1997) found that accessibility of death thoughts increased after a death reminder and declined after an opportunity to defend the cultural norm.

If commitment to collectivistic causes reduces death anxiety, and if participation in terrorism involves the risk of death, then commitment to collectivistic causes may enhance support for terrorism. A recent study by the National Consortium for the Study of Terrorism and Responses to Terrorism (START) found that among a sample of Internet users in 12 Muslim countries, collectivistic goals were associated with greater support for terrorism against the West (Orehek, Fishman, Kruglanski, Dechesne, & Chen, 2010; see Figure 8.1). Thus, the desire to restore significance to one's life may lead to engagement with a collective and to support for an ideological cause (violence against the West).

Additional Sources of Significance Loss Mortality salience is by no means the only route to significance loss. For instance, feelings of social isolation, disenfranchisement (Sageman, 2004), and ostracism by one's own group can create a loss of significance. There are cases of suicidal terrorism in which the

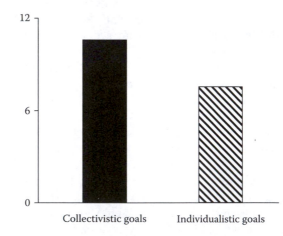

Figure 8.1 Support for attacks against the United States in individuals who endorse collectivistic goals versus individualistic goals.

perpetrators appeared to be motivated by the need to compensate for their deviant status in the community. Women bombers in particular have often been reported to be on a mission to redeem themselves in the eyes of the community for such shame bestowing occurrences as divorce, infertility, extramarital sex, or rape (Bloom, 2005; Pedahzur, 2005). Loss of significance as a consequence of deviating from normative injunctions may well introduce a strong quest for significance restoration believed to be served by sacrificing oneself for a cause.

In summary, the notion of significance-quest affords an integration of seemingly disparate motivational contexts of terrorism involving personal traumas, ideological reasons, and social pressures. All of these factors represent significance loss, motivating the quest for significance restoration, resulting from the constant human yearning for significance (Frankl, 2000) arguably born of awareness of our temporality (Greenberg et al., 2004). When direct restoration of one's sense of significance seems impossible, individuals may seek to do so indirectly through identification with a collective cause that affords a path to renewed significance via militancy and terrorism. Yet significance loss brought about by personal hardships seems neither sufficient nor necessary for motivating terrorism. Terrorism may also arise from a perceived opportunity for significance gain that offers individuals a rare shot at immense "stardom" (Sprinzak, 2001), or from the desire to avert future significance loss, as illustrated by the Kamikaze pilots of World War II who sought to avert the shame and dishonor of mission refusal (Ohnuki-Tierney, 2006).

In more general terms, adoption of ideologically based means (terrorism in this instance) may constitute a vehicle for significance restoration, maintenance or gain (Kruglanski et al., 2002). Ideologies elucidate what constitutes significance gain according to one's group and afford a way of preventing significance loss. A terrorism justifying ideology identifies a culprit (e.g., the West, Israel, and infidels) presumed responsible for a discrepancy from an ideal state and portrays violence against that culprit as an effective means for moving toward the ideal state.

During intense intergroup conflicts, which involve severe danger to one's group, an ideology may call for the ultimate sacrifice from its members, to be repaid by the group's veneration. Promoting one's sense of significance or preventing its loss thus seems to constitute the common motivational denominator in numerous instances of terrorism. Through a kind of "collectivistic shift," individual powerlessness may be overcome by an empowering collectivistic ideology, in the name of which terrorist acts are carried out. This analysis is supported by a variety of data referred to earlier including the prevalence of ideological narratives in suicide bombers' discourse (Hafez, 2007), findings that personal traumas seem to prompt embracement of such narratives (Spekhard & Akhmedova, 2005), and psychological theorizing and research that identified the quest for personal significance as a major motivating force in human behavior (Frankl, 2000; Greenberg et al., 2004).

From a psychological perspective, an ideology that glorifies terrorism need not be of any particular kind or content. It can be religious, ethno-nationalist or socialist as long as it portrays terrorist missions on behalf of the collective as means to the end of significance. According to this analysis, the importance of other contributing factors identified in the literature (e.g., loss, deprivation, and humiliation) lies in facilitating the adoption of the ideological goals.

Thus, rather than explaining terrorism by a "fatal mix" of motives that does not distinguish between the different ingredients of the "cocktail" (Crenshaw, 2007; Ricolfi, 2005), our analysis draws the functional distinction between (1) the crucial motivational nucleus of the phenomenon, ideologically based adoption of terrorism as means of promoting a collective cause, and (2) various motivational and cognitive factors that may drive persons toward adoption of such a cause.

GROUP LEVEL OF ANALYSIS

Violence and particularly the killing of innocents constitute forms of deviant conduct that fall outside the norms of civilized societies. Yet situations of intense intergroup conflict seem to facilitate such violent behavior (Staub, 1989; see also other chapters in this volume). One reason for this may be that groups provide social support for their members' pursuits, including violent acts, and ground such acts in shared realities and ideological justifications that make them appear legitimate rather than deviant (Bar-Tal, 2007; Hardin & Higgins, 1996; Jost & Major, 2001; Staub, 1989). In what follows, we discuss several socio psychological aspects of the relations between individual terrorists and their groups. These include recruitment to the group, construction and maintenance of shared group beliefs (Bar-Tal, 2000), community support, and the mechanism of public commitment.

Recruitment

1. *Networking* The mechanism of introduction is a frequent feature of joining terrorist groups (Horgan, 2005; Reinares, 2001; Sageman, 2004; Weinberg & Eubank, 1987). An individual has a relationship with a person involved in a terrorist organization, a family member, a friend, or a romantic partner, who considers membership in a terrorist group as central to their social identity. It may be difficult to maintain closeness with such persons without sharing their important values and concerns (Heider, 1958). Thus, a motivational process is set in motion to buy into the terrorist justifying ideology and seek membership in the terrorist group. A group socialization process may then ensue (Moreland & Levine, 1982) in which members acquire increasing centrality in the group and in which group membership becomes increasingly central to their social identity.

2. *Terrorism Promoting Institutions* Whereas recruitment through networking can be thought of as a "bottom-up" process, commencing with individuals' social relationships, a more "top-down" form of recruitment may take place at institutions whose climate and/or explicit objectives concern ideological indoctrination.

    In the case of Islamic radicalization, one important institution of recruitment may be the mosque. Post, Sprinzak, and Denny (2003) found that most of the Palestinian terrorists that they interviewed were initially introduced to the Palestinian cause at a mosque. Authority figures from the mosque were prominent in all of the interviews, and most dramatically so for members of the Islamist organizations.

It has also been proposed that madrassas, Muslim religious schools, might play a role in promoting terrorism. However, the evidence regarding the contribution of madrassas to recruitment or embarkation upon terrorism has been inconclusive (Bergen & Pandey, 2005).

3. *Self-recruitment* Done via the Internet, self-recruitment is another important source of "top-down" recruitment, which Coolsaet (2005) characterized as:

the result of an individual track of self-radicalization outside usual meeting places .... It mixes a psychological process of personal *reidentification* ... implying searching ... for others with a similar world view .... In this process groupthink gradually eliminates alternative views [and] simplifies reality. (pp. 6–7)

Experts agree that the Internet is playing an important role in radicalization and self-recruitment into terrorist groups. The head of intelligence at central command responsible for Iraq and Afghanistan recently stated, "without doubt, the Internet is the single most important venue for the radicalization of Islamic youth" (CBS News, 2007). Indeed, Al Qaeda's Web sites urge Muslim Internet professionals to spread and disseminate news and information about the Jihad through e-mail lists, discussion groups, and their own Web sites.

It should be noted that different recruitment processes are inextricably intertwined. Internet messages furnish the ideological arguments, while personal relations provide access to and validation of terrorist worldviews and ideologies as well as social motivation to buy into the ideologies (Taarnby, 2005).

Social Reality

Creation of an Ensconced Culture Typically, terrorist groups exist within larger societies with whom they have varying degrees of world-view overlap. In many cases, the larger society may not support the values and beliefs held by the terrorist groups. Even in situations of intense conflict, the highly violent terrorist activities may appear too extreme to some society members. Hence, exposure to views emanating from the larger society may instill doubt in the terrorists' minds concerning the justness of their ways. To protect their ideological premises from external influences, terrorist groups often reduce their members' contact with outside sources and create a unique culture wherein the terrorism justifying ideology is repeatedly highlighted.

Indoctrination A number of social psychological processes are set in motion once an individual has joined a militant organization and has declared (or intimated) willingness to carry out a suicide attack. First, she or he is cast into a social reality that forcefully affirms his "newborn" identity of a future "martyr." Hafez (2006) stressed the role of culture in establishing the social reality of "martyrdom." In his words "[violence] must also be legitimated as fulfilling a duty to one's own values, family, friends, community, or religion. Failure to act, consequently, is perceived as a betrayal" (p. 169). In this sense, the terrorist acts become "obligatory altruistic suicides" (as opposed to egoistic or anomic ones in Durkheim's terminology, see Jones, 1986).

"Living martyrs" are subjects to indoctrination containing elements of glorification of their own group, religion, their special saintly status, and extensive antienemy propaganda (Moghadam, 2003). Themes of in-group glorification, delegitimization of the opponents and justifications of one's collective goals are frequently found in the societal belief systems of groups that are engaged in intense conflicts, and dominate the socialization process of all society members (Bar-Tal, 1998). The unique aspect of terrorist indoctrination is that the would-be terrorists are led to believe that they have the unique privilege to act in order to promote the collective cause.

An important element in creating this "social reality" involves the use of language. The would-be suicide bomber is not described as such, nor as a terrorist or even a freedom fighter. Instead, he is depicted as a "living martyr" (al Shahid al hai) even before he carries out the attack. The attack is depicted as a tremendous act of self-sacrifice, to be rewarded in the afterlife. After the attack, advertisements of the martyr's afterlife fate in the local press signify his ascendance to the exalted status of a cultural hero.

The enemy, in turn, is portrayed in highly negative terms, such as "sons of dogs and monkeys," "devils," or "demons." Religious terrorist organizations often refer to the adversaries as "enemies of God" or "evil infidels" (Iannaccone, 2005). According to Pape (2005, p. 90), "Religious difference can enable extreme demonization—the belief that the enemy is morally inferior as well as militarily dangerous, and so must be dealt with harshly." Bin Laden had the following to say during one of his sermons:

> The Jews have lied about the Creator, and even more so about His creations. The Jews are the murderers of the prophets, the violators of agreements. These are the Jews: usurers and whoremongers. They will leave you nothing, neither this world nor religion. (MEMRI, March 5, 2003)

Such language portrays the opponents as inhuman and evil, and consequently removes the moral impediments on causing them severe harm. It aims to derogate and diminish the targets of one's aggression, and depict them as undeserving of basic consideration accorded to other human beings (Bandura, 1990; Bar-Tal, 1990; Pape, 2005).

To be sure, strategies of delegitimization and dehumanization are not unique to terrorists. They are quite common among groups that are involved in intense conflicts (Bar-Tal, 2007) and may be often part and parcel of any aggressive behavior toward fellow humans. In the instance of suicide terrorism, however, involving an act as extreme as sacrificing one's own life, the derogation of the victims may be particularly extreme and vituperative.

Public Commitment

Defection from the terrorist group may be demoralizing as well as dangerous to the group. Hence, terrorist organizations induce public commitment and apply social pressure to create "reliable" martyrs who will not change their minds (Berman & Laitin, 2008). An important element of the group process brought to bear on the suicidal terrorist in training is the creation of a psychological "point of no return" that few can overcome (Merari, 2002). The candidate is made to prepare his will and write last letters to family and friends. He/she is then videotaped bidding everybody farewell and encouraging others to follow his example.

Epistemic Authority

Not every terrorist has broad expertise and deep understanding of ideological arguments. More likely, the "rank and file" bombers put their trust in "epistemic authorities" (Kruglanski et al., 2005) who tell them what the ideology requires. One type of "epistemic authority," namely expert authority, has received particular attention in the social psychological literature (Chaiken, Lieberman, & Eagly, 1989; Petty & Cacioppo, 1986).

The role of expert authority in terrorism is illustrated by the contribution of Sayid Muhammad Husayn Fadlalla, the supreme spiritual leader of Hezbollah, to the suicide bombings first employed by this organization in 1983. Early in 1983, Fadlalla voiced his moral reservations about suicidal tactics, but subsequently gave them his fullest possible endorsement short of an explicit *fatwa*. This provided the needed spiritual "seal of approval" for unleashing a wave of suicide attacks that have been widely emulated since. Similarly, religious authorities inside and outside Palestine have depicted "martyrdom operations" (i.e., suicide attacks) as "the highest and noblest form of resistance and one that is most effective" (Hafez, 2006, p. 179).

According to Friedkin (2005) it is in the vital interest of terrorist organizations that their members do not have "minds of their own," and hence would be susceptible to the influence of authority figures. Accordingly, terrorist organizations may purposely aim at diminishing the self-ascribed authority of their members. They cut off sources of external support and diminish members' individuality and personal needs, allowing the ideological goals to dominate their awareness. In short, as far as the terrorist "foot soldiers" are concerned, "theirs is not to reason why." They rely on authorities for instructions and interpretations, even when it comes to such critical decisions as taking their own lives.

Community Support

The group or community may also represent a trusted "epistemic authority" whose consensus determines whether terrorist acts are legitimate and desirable. In addition, community support may provide the terrorists with material assistance (McCauly, 2004). Hence, community support allows the terrorists to persist in their actions and increases the likelihood of successful minority influence.

Revolutionary terrorist groups, such as the Red Army Faction in Germany and the Weatherman in the United States, typically advocate dramatic societal change and therefore do not receive broad support in their respective communities (Miller, 2007). Therefore, the existence of such groups is often fraught with considerable hardship and they are ultimately apprehended and/or defeated. In contrast, national-separatist terrorist groups often enjoy considerable support from the minority communities that they pertain to represent, which allows them to persist in their activities despite attempts of suppression by the ruling majority. For instance, the Palestinian public support for suicide bombing amounted to only 20% in March, 1996, and rose to 70–80% in June, 2002. Correspondingly, between September 1993 and September 2000 there was an average of four suicide attacks per year, whereas between October 2000 and December 2003 the rate amounted to more than 36 per year. The breadth of community support to national-separatist terrorism may partially explain why this type of terrorism often contributes to the escalation of ethnic conflicts, whereas revolutionary terrorism is less likely to lead to violent escalations.

THE ORGANIZATIONAL LEVEL

Terrorist groups vary immensely in degree and type of organization. Some organizations are organized around a single leader, for instance, the PKK around Abdullah Ocalan and the Peruvian Shining Path around Abimail Guzman. Indeed, the arrests of these two leaders considerably limited the operations of their respective organizations for many years. Other organizations are less leader-centered in their structure (e.g., the Palestinian Islamic Jihad or Hamas).

Decision Making and the Rationality of Terrorism

As noted above, terrorism may be thought of as a means to the attainment of goals (Kruglanski & Fishman, 2006). Psychological analyses of goal pursuit suggest that terrorist organizations may have different goals that may be activated at different times and appropriately affect decisions concerning the use of terror (Kruglanski et al., 2002). Specifically, terrorist organizations can decide whether or not to launch attacks according to their assessment of what best serves their goals under given political, social, and economic conditions (Berman & Laitin, 2008; Hafez, 2006; Krueger & Laitin, 2008). For instance, terrorism using organizations like Hamas or Hezbollah may have goals related to internal politics, which at times could be inconsistent with launching terrorist attacks. Hezbollah markedly reduced their rocket attacks against Israel following the Israeli withdrawal from Lebanon in 2000, possibly because their main base of political support, the Shia population of Southern Lebanon, did not want to risk reoccupation. Nonetheless, Hezbollah's goal of struggle against Israel was not relinquished, and was reactivated in 2006 by events in the area. Similarly, Hamas refrained from carrying out suicide attacks early in the Oslo peace process (between the Palestinians and the Israelis), presumably because of their concern that the Palestinian public would not support it (Merari, 2002).

The decision whether or not to launch terrorist attacks may also be affected by their perceived effectiveness. Several authors have commented on the cost effectiveness of terrorist attacks as a tactic in the context of asymmetric warfare (Atran, 2006; Berman & Laitin, 2008; Bloom, 2005; Hafez, 2006; Jasso & Meyersson-Milgrom, 2005; Kruglanski, 2006; Moghadam, 2003; Pape, 2005). According to the database on global suicide terrorist attacks, such attacks "amount to just 3% of all terrorist incidents from 1980 through 2003, but account for 48% of all fatalities" (Pape, 2005, p. 6). Suicide terrorism is especially cheap—the 9/11 attacks, for example, cost less than a $100,000 and inflicted damage in billions of dollars. There is also no concern that the operatives will divulge information when caught, and no need for complex and costly escape plans. At the same time, terrorism gives its perpetrators considerable power, because it instills in its targets a feeling of pervasive danger. Thibaut and Kelley (1959) defined social power as the ability of one party to move another party over a range of outcomes between "good" and "bad" as subjectively defined. According to this notion, the terrorists wield substantial power, because the worst outcome that they can potentially effectuate is the horrific prospect of mass annihilation.

Due to its effectiveness and relatively low cost, terrorism may be particularly appealing to minority and national-separatist groups, who believe that they lack the power to promote their goals by alternative means. Precisely such logic is articulated in the words of LTTE leader, Prabhakaran, "In terms of manpower, firepower and resources, the enemy was strong and the balance of military power was in his favor. Yet we had an extraordinary weapon. ... The courage and commitment of our fighters was our most powerful weapon in the battle."[°] However, even such groups may relinquish or suspend the use of terrorism when alternative effective means to their goal become apparent. For instance, in 2002 the LTTE reached a ceasefire agreement with the Sri Lankan government, when it appeared that negotiations may lead to progress toward a mutually acceptable solution to the conflict.

Implications for Deterrence   The rationality of terrorist organizations has implications for the concept of deterrence, which denotes a threat of aggression against an actor contingent on the latter carrying out some undesirable activity (Schelling, 1960/2007). The feasibility of deterrence as a counterterrorist strategy is a positive function of the size of the organization. The larger the organization, the greater are its needs in terms of territorial niche, infrastructures, and sponsorship by organized states. These can be threatened and targeted, making continued terrorist activities potentially costly for the organization. However, deterrence is less likely to be effective in regards to smaller terrorist organizations with less material vulnerabilities, and is even less applicable to individual suicide bombers who are willing to sacrifice their lives for the cause.

[°] "LTTE leader on Sri Lanka's Military Campaign," speech released by International Secretariat of LTTE, London, United Kingdom, May 13, 1998. Available at http://www.eelamweb.com

exist alternative, more effective means to the organization's ends; and (c) that terrorism hinders the attainment of other important objectives. These different avenues are not necessarily independent. Thus, if terrorism appears to constitute the sole means to the organization's end it may be difficult to convince the organization to relinquish it, even if were contrary to other (less important) goals.

Nonetheless, occasionally alternative avenues may appear feasible, and these could be highlighted. For instance, following the election of Mahmud Abbas to the presidency of the Palestinian authority in 2005, representing an alternative means to ending the Israeli occupation through revival of the peace process, support for suicide attacks among the Palestinians dipped to an all time low in seven years (Shikaki, 2005), and attacks against Israel on part of the Fatah organization had all but ceased.

Multifinality Beside its presumed advancement of the organization's ideological objectives, terrorism affords the emotional satisfaction of watching the enemy suffer. In that sense, terrorism is a "multifinal" means, compounding its appeal (Kruglanski et al., 2002). Hence, policies such as "ethnic profiling" or the inadvertent "collateral damage" inflicted during antiterrorist campaigns might backfire by amplifying the goal of vengeance (Atran, 2003). A recent study suggests that "targeted assassinations" by Israeli forces boosted recruitment to the "terrorist stock," presumably due to the increased appeal of terrorism. In contrast, the less inflammatory means of arresting terrorism suspects tended to reduce the "terrorist stock" and the incidence of terrorism (Kaplan, Mintz, Mishal, & Samban, 2005).

Alternative Objectives Dissuading organizations from using terrorism may involve rekindling alternative objectives incompatible with terrorism. Many terrorist-using organizations have political objectives of gaining power and influence within their respective communities beyond their goal of fighting an external adversary. For instance, increased political involvement of the Sinn Fein and other paramilitary factions in Northern Ireland led to a reduction in their violent activities (Fitzduff, 2002). More generally, activating alternative goals and stressing their incompatibility with terrorism may constitute an important way of reducing organizations' tendency to employ terrorism.

A Means-Ends Classification of Terrorism Users The "tool" view of terrorism affords a classification of terrorism using organizations according to their commitment to the terrorism means as well as to the ends believed to be served by terrorism. Users can be strongly committed to terrorism because of its intrinsic properties, such as the sense of power it bestows or the appeal of violence, as in the cases of Utopian and Apocalyptic Islamist groups (Gunaratna, 2002). It is unlikely that anything short of a total defeat will convince such groups to relinquish terrorism.

The situation is rather different for groups for whom terrorism represents one among several available instruments. As noted earlier, organizations like Hamas, Hezbollah, or Sinn Fein, though hardly shy of using terrorism, have other means at their disposal (diplomacy, media campaigns) as well as other goals of political or social variety. Therefore, they may desist from the use of terrorism when it appears that their goals would be best served by doing so.

In sum, different organizations may differ in their potential for relinquishing terrorism. Whereas negotiations attempting to effect shifts to alternative goals or means are unlikely to succeed with perpetrators whose commitment to terrorism is total and unconditional, it might work with terrorist groups who value alternative goals.

CONCLUDING COMMENTS

Psychological factors play an essential role in terrorism at all its relevant levels of analysis: the individual, group and organizational levels. Though in this chapter we have treated these categories of factors separately, in reality they are all inextricably intertwined. Individual belief and attitude formation processes determine populations' degree of support for a terrorist cause, affecting the organization's political base and ultimately its potency. Recursively, an organization's potency may increase its status as a trusted "epistemic authority," and hence its ability to attract new recruits to its ranks.

The psychological essence of terrorism affords suggestions for effective counterterrorist strategies. Considerable caution is advised, however, because counterterrorist activities that may appear desirable at a given analytic level may prove to be detrimental at another level. For instance, the use of military force against vulnerable organizational targets may cripple an organization's ability to function, but at the same time fuel the outrage of the affected community and increase individuals' motivation to support the terrorists and buy into their ideology. Negotiating with terrorist organizations may communicate that there exist alternative means to their goals, hence presumably reducing the tendency to launch attacks. Yet negotiations also convey that terrorism is an efficient tactic, encouraging its future use. In deploying psychology in aid of counterterrorism, it is important to be aware of these tradeoffs and paradoxes.

It is also important to note that terrorism often takes place against the backdrop of an intense intergroup conflict. Hence, peaceful resolution of conflicts, though not always explicitly intended as a counterterrorist strategy, may lead to a reduction in terrorism. Although during negotiations terrorist organizations may continue to operate and act as "spoilers" (Kydd & Walter, 2006; Stedman, 1997), the eventual settlement would presumably address the grievances of both parties in a mutually acceptable manner, thus undermining a central element of terrorism-justifying ideologies. Furthermore, if maintaining peace becomes a central societal goal, to which terrorism is detrimental, then terrorism should no longer constitute a means of attaining significance through self-sacrifice for the collective cause. In sum, the psychological processes underlying intergroup conflicts and terrorism are interrelated. Therefore, psychologically based counterterrorism attempts should take into consideration the various psychological processes at play in intergroup conflicts, as outlined in this volume.

REFERENCES

Antonovsky, A. (1987). *Unraveling the mystery of health: How people manage stress and stay well*. San Francisco: Jossey-Bass.

Arndt, J., Greenberg, J., Solomon, S., Pyszczynski, T., & Simon, L. (1997). Suppression, accessibility of death-related thoughts, and cultural worldview defense: Exploring the psychodynamics of terror management. *Journal of Personality and Social Psychology, 73*, 5–18.

Atran, S. (2003). Genesis of suicide terrorism. *Science, 299*, 1534–1539.

Atran, S. (2004). Mishandling suicide terrorism. *Washington Quarterly, 27*, 67–90.

Atran, S. (2006). The moral logic and growth of suicide terrorism. *The Washington Quarterly, 29*, 127–147.

Bandura, A. (1990). Mechanisms of moral disengagement. In W. Reich (Ed.), *Origins of terrorism: Psychologies, ideologies, theologies, states of mind* (pp. 161–191). Cambridge: Cambridge University Press.

Bar-Tal, D. (1990). Causes and consequences of delegitimization: Models of conflict and ethnocentrism. *Journal of Social Issues, 46*, 65–81.

Bar-Tal, D. (1998). Societal beliefs in times of intractable conflict: The Israeli case. *International Journal of Conflict Management, 9*, 22–50.

Bar-Tal, D. (2000). *Shared beliefs in a society: Social psychological analysis*. Thousand Oaks, CA: Sage.

Bar-Tal, D. (2007). Sociopsychological foundations of intractable conflicts. *American Behavioral Scientist, 50*, 1430–1453.

Bar-Tal, D., & Staub, E. (Eds.). (1997). *Patriotism in the life of individuals and nations*. Chicago: Nelson-Hall.

CBS News (2007). http://www.cbsnews.com/stories/2007/03/02/60minutes/main2531546.shtml

Bergen, P., & Pandey, S. (2005, June 14). The madrassa myth. *The New York Times*, p. A23.

Berman, E., & Laitin, D. D. (2008). Religion, terrorism and public goods: Testing the club model. *Journal of Public Economics, 92*, 1942–1967.

Berrebi, C. (2003). *Evidence about the link between education, poverty, and terrorism among Palestinians*. Princeton University Industrial Relations Section Working Paper #477.

Bloom, M. (2005). *Dying to kill: The allure of suicide terrorism*. New York: Columbia University Press.

Brophy-Baerman, B., & Conybeare, J. A. C. (1994). Retaliating against terrorism: Rational expectations and the optimality of rules versus discretion. *American Journal of Political Science, 38*, 196–210.

Carr, C. (2002). *The lessons of terror: A history of warfare against civilians*. New York: Random House.

Castano, E., & Dechesne, M. (2005). On defeating death: Group reification and social identification as strategies for transcendence. *European Review of Social Psychology, 16*, 221–255.

Chaiken, S., Lieberman, A., & Eagly, A. (1989). Heuristic and systematic information processing within and beyond the persuasion context. In J. S. Uleman & J. A. Bargh (Eds.), *Unintended thought* (pp. 212–252). New York: Guilford Press.

Coolsaet, R. (2005). *Between al-Andalus and a failing integration: Europe's pursuit of a long-term counterterrorism strategy in the post-al Qaeda era*. Egmont Paper 5. Brussels: Royal Institute for International Relations (IRRI-KIB).

Cordesman, A. H. (2006). *Preliminary "lessons" of the Israeli-Hezbollah war*. Center for Strategic and International Studies.

Crenshaw, M. (1990). Questions to be answered, research to be done, knowledge to be applied. In W. Reich (Ed.), *Origins of terrorism: Psychologies, ideologies, theologies, states of mind* (pp. 247–260). Washington, DC: Woodrow Wilson Center Press.

Crenshaw, M. (2007). Explaining suicide terrorism: A review essay. *Security Studies, 16,* 133–162.

DeNardo, J. (1985). *The amateur strategist: Intuitive deterrence theories and the politics of the nuclear arms race.* Cambridge, England: Cambridge University Press.

Durlak, J. A. (1972). Relationship between individual attitudes toward life and death. *Journal of Consulting and Clinical Psychology, 38,* 460–473.

Fitzduff, M. (2002). *Beyond violence: Conflict resolution process in Northern Ireland.* Tokyo, Japan: United Nations University Press.

Frankl, V. E. (1963). *Man's search for meaning.* New York: Washington Square Press.

Frankl, V. E. (2000). *Man's search for ultimate meaning.* New York: Basic Books.

Friedkin, N. E. (2005). The interpersonal influence systems and organized suicides of death cults. In E. M. Meyersson-Milgrom (Chair), Workshop on *Suicide Missions and the Market for Martyrs, A Multidisciplinary Approach.* Stanford University.

Gambetta, D. (2005). *Making sense of suicide missions.* Oxford: Oxford University Press.

Ganor, B. (2005). *The counter-terrorism puzzle: A guide for decision makers.* Herzlia, Israel: The Interdisciplinary Center for Herzliya Projects.

Greenberg, J., Koole, S. L., & Pyszczynski, T. (Eds.). (2004). *Handbook of experimental existential psychology.* New York: Guilford Press.

Greenberg, J., Solomon, S., & Pyszczynski, T. (1997). Terror management theory of self-esteem and cultural worldviews: Empirical assessment and conceptual refinements. In M. Zanna (Ed.), *Advances in experimental social psychology* (Vol. 30, pp. 61–139). San Diego: Academic Press.

Gunaratna, R. (2002). *Inside Al Qaeda: Global network of terror.* New York: Columbia University Press.

Gunaratna, R. (2007). Ideology in terrorism and counter terrorism: Lessons from Al Qaeda. In A. Aldis & G. P. Herd (Eds.), *The ideological war on terror: Worldwide strategies for counter-terrorism.* New York: Routledge.

Hafez, M. M. (2006). Rationality, culture, and structure in the making of suicide bombers: A preliminary theoretical synthesis and illustrative vase study. *Studies in Conflict and Terrorism, 29,* 165–185.

Hafez, M. M. (2007). *Manufacturing human bombs: The making of Palestinian suicide bombers.* Washington, DC: United States Institute of Peace Press.

Hardin, C. D., & Higgins, E. T. (1996). Shared reality: How social verification makes the subjective objective. In R. M. Sorrentino & E. T. Higgins (Eds.), *Handbook of motivation and cognition* (Vol. 3, pp. 28–84). New York: The Guilford Press.

Hassan, N. (2001). An arsenal of believers: Talking to the "human bombs." *The New Yorker,* Retrieved from: http://www.newyorker.com/archive/2001/11/19/011119fa_FACT1 (Accessed on November 19, 2001).

Heider, F. (1958). *The psychology of interpersonal relations.* New York: Wiley.

Horgan, J. (2003). The search for the terrorist personality. In A. Silke (Ed.), *Terrorists, victims and society: Psychological perspectives on terrorism and its consequences.* Chichester, UK: John Wiley & Sons.

Horgan, J. (2005). *The psychology of terrorism.* London: Routledge.

Iannaccone, L. R. (2005). The market for martyrs. In E. M. Meyerson-Milgrom (Chair), *Workshop on suicide missions and the market for martyrs: A multidisciplinary approach.* Stanford University.

Jasso, G., & Meyersson-Milgrom, E. M. (2005). Identity, social distance and Palestinian support for the road map. In E. M. Meyersson-Milgrom (Chair). Workshop on *suicide missions and the market for martyrs: A multidisciplinary approach.* Stanford University.

Jervis, R. C. (1985). Perceiving and coping with threat. In R. Jervis, R. N. Lebow, & J. G. Stein (Eds.), *Psychology and deterrence* (pp. 13–33). Baltimore: Johns Hopkins University Press.

Jones, A. (1986). *Emile Durkheim: An introduction to four major works.* Beverly Hills, CA: Sage Publications, Inc.

Jost, J. T., & Major, B. (Eds.). (2001). *The psychology of legitimacy: Emerging perspectives on ideology, justice, and intergroup relations.* New York: Cambridge University Press.

Kaplan, E., Mintz, A., Mishal, S., & Samban, C. (2005). What happened to suicide bombings in Israel? Insights from a terror stock model. *Studies in Conflict and Terrorism, 28,* 225–235.

Katz, E. (1973). The two-step flow of communication: an up-to-date report of a hypothesis. In B. M. Enis & K. K. Cox (Eds.), *Marketing classics* (pp. 175–193). Columbus, OH: Allyn & Bacon.

Katz, E., & Lazarsfeld, P. (1955). *Personal influence.* New York: The Free Press.

Kelman, H. C. (1997). Social-psychological dimensions of international conflict. In I. W. Zartman & J. L. Rasmussen (Eds.), *Peacemaking in international conflict: Methods and techniques* (pp. 191–237). Washington, DC: United States Institute of Peace Press.

Kepel, G. (2004). *The war for Muslim minds: Islam and the West.* Boston: Harvard University Press.

Krueger, A. B., & Laitin, D. D. (2008). Kto kogo?: A cross-country study of the origins and targets of terrorism. In P. Keefer & N. Loayza (Eds.), *Terrorism, economic development, and political openness* (pp. 148–173). Cambridge: Cambridge University Press.

Krueger, A. B., & Maleckova, J. (2002). Does poverty cause terrorism? *The New Republic, 226,* 27–33.

Kruglanski, A. W. (2006). Inside the terrorist mind: The relevance of ideology. *Estudios de Psicología, 27*(3), 1–16.

Kruglanski, A. W., & Chen, X. (2009). Terrorism as a tactic of minority influence. In F. Butera & J. Levine (Eds.), *Coping with minority status: Responses to exclusion and inclusion* (pp. 202–221). Cambridge: Cambridge University Press.

Kruglanski, A. W., Chen, X., Dechesne, M., Fishman, S., & Orehek, E. (2009). Fully committed: Suicide bombers' motivation and the quest for personal significance. *Political Psychology, 30,* 331–357.

Kruglanski, A. W., & Fishman, S. (2006). The psychology of terrorism: "Syndrome" versus "tool" perspectives. *Terrorism and Political Violence, 18,* 193–215.

Kruglanski, A. W., Raviv, A., Bar-Tal, D., Raviv, A., Sharvit, K., Ellis, S. et al. (2005). Says who? Epistemic authority effects in social judgment. In M. P. Zanna (Ed.), *Advances in experimental social psychology* (Vol. 37, pp. 346–392). New York: Academic Press.

Kruglanski, A. W., Shah, J. Y., Fishbach, A., Friedman, R., Chun, W., & Sleeth-Keppler, D. (2002). A theory of goals systems. In M. P. Zanna (Ed.), *Advances in experimental social psychology* (Vol. 34, pp. 331–378). New York: Academic Press.

Kydd, A. H., & Walter, B. F. (2006). The strategies of terrorism. *International Security, 31,* 49–80.

Lazarsfeld, P. F., Berelson, B., & Gaudet, H. (1944). *The people's choice: How the voter makes up his mind in a presidential campaign.* New York: Columbia University Press.

Lewin, K. (1958). Group decision and social change. In E. E. Maccoby, T. M. Newcomb, & E. L. Hartley (Eds.), *Readings in social psychology* (pp. 197–211). New York: Holt, Reinhart & Winston.

Maslow, A. H. (1943). A theory of human motivation. *Psychological Review, 50,* 370–396.

McCauley, C. (2004). Psychological issues in understanding terrorism and the response to terrorism. In C. Stout (Ed.), *Psychology of terrorism: Coping with the continuing threat* (pp. 33–66). Westport, CT: Greenwood Publishing.

McGuire, W. J. (1961). The effectiveness of supportive and refutational defenses in immunizing and restoring beliefs against persuasion. *Sociometry*, 24, 184–197.

McGuire, W. J. (1964). Inducing resistance to persuasion: Some contemporary approaches. In L. Berkowitz (Ed.), *Advances in experimental social psychology* (Vol. 1, pp. 191–229). New York: Academic Press.

MEMRI (2003, March 5). Special Dispatch Series—No. 476.

Merari, A. (2002). Personal communication, January 13.

Miller, G. D. (2007). Confronting terrorisms: Group motivation and successful state policies. *Terrorism and Political Violence*, 19, 331–350.

Mitchell, C. R. (1981). *The structure of international conflict*. London: Macmillan.

Moghadam, A. (2003). Palestinian suicide terrorism in the Second Intifada: Motivations and organizational aspects. *Studies in Conflict and Terrorism*, 26, 65–92.

Moos, R. H., & Schaefer, J. A. (1986). Life transitions and crises: A conceptual overview. In R. H. Moos (Ed.), *Coping with life crises: An integrated approach* (pp. 3–28). New York: Plenum Press.

Moreland, R. L., & Levine, J. M. (1982). Socialization in small groups: Temporal changes in individual–group relations. In L. Berkowitz (Ed.), *Advances in experimental social psychology* (Vol. 15, pp. 137–193). New York: Academic Press.

Ohnuki-Tierney, E. (2006). *Kamikaze diaries: Reflections of Japanese student soldiers*. Chicago: University of Chicago Press.

Orehek, E., Fishman, S., Kruglanski, A. W., Dechesne, M. & Chen, X. (2010). *The role of individualistic and collectivistic goals in support for terrorist attacks*. Unpublished Manuscript, University of Maryland.

Pape, R. A. (2003). The strategic logic of suicide terrorism. *American Political Science Review*, 97, 343–361.

Pape, R. A. (2005). *Dying to win: The strategic logic of suicide terrorism*. New York: Random House.

Pedahzur, A. (2005). *Suicide terrorism*. England: Polity Press.

Petty, R. E., & Cacioppo, J. T. (1986). The Elaboration Likelihood Model of persuasion. In L. Berkowitz (Ed.), *Advances in experimental social psychology* (Vol. 19, pp. 123–205). New York: Academic Press.

Post, J. (2006). *The mind of the terrorist: The psychology of terrorism from the IRA to Al Qaeda*. New York: Palgrave Macmillan.

Post, J. M., Sprinzak, E., & Denny, L. M. (2003). The terrorists in their own words: Interviews with 35 incarcerated Middle Eastern terrorists. *Terrorism and Political Violence*, 15, 171–184.

Pyszczynski, T., Abdollahi, A., Solomon, S., Greenberg, J., Cohen, F., & Weise, D. (2006). Mortality salience, martyrdom, and military might: The great Satan versus the axis of evil. *Personality and Social Psychology Bulletin*, 32, 525–537.

Reinares, F. (2001). *Patriotas de la muerte. Quines militan en ETA y por que. (Patriots of death: Who fights in the ETA and why?)*. Madrid: Taurus.

Ricolfi, L. (2005). Palestinians, 1981–2003. In D. Gambetta (Ed.), *Making sense of suicide missions* (pp. 77–129). New York: Oxford University Press.

Riedel, B. (2007). Al Qaeda strikes back. *Foreign Affairs*, 86(3), 24–70.

Rubin, J. Z., Pruitt, D. G., & Kim, S. (1994). *Social conflict: Escalation, stalemate, and settlement*. New York: McGraw-Hill

Rummel, R. J. (1996). *Death by government*. New Brunswick, NJ: Transaction Publishers.

Sageman, M. (2004). *Understanding terror networks*. Philadelphia: University of Pennsylvania Press.

Schelling, T. C. (1960/2007). *The strategy of conflict*. Cambridge, MA: Harvard University Press.

Schmid, A. P., & Jongman, A. J. (1988). *Political terrorism*. Amsterdam: North Holland Publishing.

Shah, J. Y., Friedman, R., & Kruglanski, A. W. (2002). Forgetting all else: On the antecedents and consequences of goal shielding. *Journal of Personality and Social Psychology*, 83, 1261–1280.

Shikaki, K. (2005). *Palestinian center for policy and survey research*. Retrieved from http://www.pcpsr.org/index.html

Silke, A. (2003). Becoming a terrorist. In A. Silke (Ed.), *Terrorists, victims and society: Psychological perspectives on terrorism and its consequences* (pp. 29–54). Chichester, UK: John Wiley & Sons.

Spekhard, A., & Akhmedova, K. (2005). Talking to terrorists. *Journal of Psychohistory*, 33, 125–156.

Sprinzak, E. (2001). The lone gunmen: The global war on terrorism faces a new brand of enemy. *Foreign Policy*, 127, 72–73.

Staub, E. (1989). *The roots of evil: The origins of genocide and other group violence*. New York: Cambridge University Press.

Stedman, S. (1997). Spoiler problems in peace processes. *International Security*, 22, 7–16.

Stern, J. (2003) *Terror in the name of God: Why religious militants kill*. New York: Harper Collins.

Taarnby, M. (2005, January 14). Research report funded by the Danish Ministry of Justice.

Taylor, S. E. (1983). Adjustment to threatening events: A theory of cognitive adaptation. *American Psychologist*, 38, 1161–1173.

Thibaut, J. W., & Kelley, H. (1959). *The social psychology of groups*. New York: Wiley.

Victoroff, J. (2005). The mind of the terrorist: A review and critique of psychological approaches. *Journal of Conflict Resolution*, 49, 3–42.

Victoroff, J. (in press). I have a dream: Terrorism as terrible group relations. *Terrorism and Political Violence*.

Weinberg, L., & Eubank, W. L. (1987). Italian women terrorists. *Terrorism: An International Journal*, 9, 241–262.

Wilkinson, P. (2003). Why modern terrorism? Differentiating types and distinguishing ideological motivations. In C. W. Kegley, Jr. (Ed.), *The new global terrorism: Characteristics, causes, controls* (pp. 106–138). Upper Saddle River, NJ: Prentice-Hall.

Worchel, S. (1999). *Written in blood: Ethnic identity and the struggle for human harmony*. New York: Worth.

9

Socio-Psychological Barriers to Conflict Resolution

DANIEL BAR-TAL and ERAN HALPERIN

*T*he intergroup conflicts that rage in different parts of the world over territories, natural resources, power, economic wealth, self-determination, and/or basic values are real. They center over disagreements which focus on contradictory goals and interests in different domains and there is no doubt that these real issues have to be addressed in conflict resolution. But it is well known that the disagreements could potentially be resolved if not the various powerful forces which fuel and maintain the conflicts. These forces, which underlie the mere disagreements, are the barriers that inhibit and impede progress toward peaceful settlement of the conflict. They stand as major obstacles to begin the negotiation, to carry the negotiation, to achieve an agreement and later to engage in a process of reconciliation. These barriers are found among the leaders, as well as among society members that are involved in intergroup conflict.

The present chapter will focus on the socio-psychological barriers that are of special importance as they have dominant detrimental power in preventing peace making (Arrow, Mnookin, Ross, Tversky, & Wilson, 1999; Bar-Siman-Tov, 1995; Ross & Ward, 1995). Specifically, the chapter in its first part will review the various approaches to socio-psychological barriers. In the second part, a general model of socio-psychological barriers, that integrates different views and perspectives, will be introduced. This part will also elaborate specifically on the content-based socio-psychological barriers. It will discuss the causes for freezing, focusing mainly on the structural, motivational, emotional, and contextual factors. In the third part we will describe the functioning of the socio-psychological barriers in their selective, biased and distorting information processing in the context of conflict. Finally, we will draw several conclusions.

SOCIO-PSYCHOLOGICAL BARRIERS TO CONFLICT RESOLUTION: PAST APPROACHES

Review of the literature about the socio-psychological barriers identifies at least four different but complementary directions. The first one focused on the contents of societal beliefs* that fuel the continuation of the conflict. Kelman (1987) suggested that perceptions of the relations in zero-sum terms, the denial of the other group's identity and the extremely negative and monolithic view of the adversary (also defined as delegitimization) delay any progress toward successful negotiation. In fact the content approach can be found almost in every major study about serious and prolonged conflict. Nevertheless, the lists of beliefs that serve as barriers can be a long one. Thus, in addition to the beliefs already noted, the different lists include beliefs that pertain to self-moral glorification, overconfidence in own strength, sense of being a victim, strong feeling of patriotism, being vulnerable, being helpless, and so on (Bar-Tal, 1998, 2007a; Coleman, 2003; Eidelson & Eidelson, 2003 for recent work; Kelman, 1965; White, 1970 for early work; also see Chapter 2).

Another important psychological phenomenon, frequently presented as the most important barrier for conflict resolution, is intergroup mistrust (Kelman, 2005; Kramer & Carnevale, 2001; Kydd, 2005). The importance of (mis)trust in delaying possible solution stems from its negative affect on levels of expectations about future behavior of the rival (Yamagishi & Yamagishi, 1994), which leads almost directly to refusal to take risks in negotiations and to support of conflict continuation (Larsen, 1997; Lewicki, 2006). This stems, mainly from the fear of being betrayed by the adversary, given the confrontational history of the mutual relations. Hence, despite some affective aspects of trust, it should be classified into the long list of content-based barriers, concentrating mainly on the view of the adversary and his expected actions.

A totally different view of socio-psychological barriers was presented in the important line of works of Ross and his colleagues in the Stanford Center on International Conflict and Negotiation (Maoz, Ward, Katz, & Ross, 2002; Mnookin & Ross, 1995; Ross & Ward, 1995). These scholars focused on the cognitive and motivational processes as pivotal barriers in times of negotiation. According to their view, socio-psychological barriers are "cognitive and motivational processes that impede mutually beneficial exchanges of concessions and render seemingly tractable conflicts refractory to negotiated resolution" (Ross & Ward, 1995, p. 254). These barriers "governing the way that human beings interpret information, evaluate risks, set priorities, and experience feelings of gain and loss" (p. 263). As few examples of the processes we will mention optimistic overconfidence (i.e., overestimation of the capability to achieve beneficial results in the absence of successful negotiation, Kahneman & Tversky, 1995) and *divergent construal* (i.e., each party in the conflict goes beyond the given information and differently interpret

---

* *Societal beliefs* are defined as the society's members shared cognitions on topics and issues that are of special concern to society and contribute to its unique characteristics. They are organized around themes and consist of such contents as collective memories, ideologies, goals, myths, and so on (Bar-Tal, 2000). They may be shared by the great majority of society members or only part of them.

the events, Ross & Ward, 1995).* It is worth noting that while the content-based barriers reflect long-standing, enduring psychological phenomenon, the perspective of Ross and his colleagues focus on "on-line" processes that rise in response to specific new events or information. Interestingly, empirical work that tries to integrate these two perspectives is rare.

Another notable example of socio-psychological barriers that leads to selective biased and distorting information is found in the perspective focusing on the affective and emotional factors that underlie many of the conflicts (refer to Chapter 3 for an elaborated general discussion; for more specific level contributions about fear, refer to Bar-Tal, 2001; Lake & Rothchild, 1998; or about hatred, refer to Baumeister & Butz, 2005; Halperin, 2008a, 2008b; White, 1984). This direction is a result of a shift in social psychology from pure cognitive research to a more integrated perspective that is also observed in the study of conflict resolution (de Rivera & Paez, 2007; Lerner, Gonzalez, Small, & Fischhoff, 2003). Most importantly, this developing line of research enables to point at the unique contribution of discrete emotions in biasing information processing and hindering support for peaceful resolutions (Brown, González, Zagefka, & Cehajic, 2008; Cheung-Blunden & Blunden, 2008; Halperin, 2008b).

An examination of the above review suggests a tendency among students of conflict to examine single aspects of the barriers, while neglecting the attempts to integrate the different parts of the puzzle. Therefore, in the present chapter we would like to propose an integrative approach, which combines different perspectives into an interactive model that outlines the functioning of the socio-psychological barriers.

INTEGRATIVE APPROACH

The proposed approach integrates a number of socio-psychological elements that have interactive mutual influence and it can be described as a conceptual process model (see Figure 9.1). This conceptual model applies to individual as well as to collective level of analysis because group members share beliefs, values, attitudes and emotions (Bar-Tal, 2000; see also Chapter 3). Moreover, identification with the group in the context of serious conflict increases the similarity of society members in their use of the barriers (Chapter 5).

Our lengthy description will focus mainly on these parts that are relatively original and only present briefly these parts which have been discussed widely in the socio-psychological literature elsewhere.

In this presentation we focus on the socio-psychological barriers in the context of intractable conflict, which represents the most difficult, prolonged and violent intergroup confrontation over major disagreements between the two (or more) parties about existential goals and interests (Bar-Tal, 1998; Coleman, 2006).†

---

* A longer list of this type of barriers will be presented in the last part of this chapter.
† Intractable conflicts are characterized as lasting at least 25 years, over goals that are perceived as existential, being violent, perceived as unsolvable and of zero sum nature, preoccupying greatly society members, with parties involved investing much in their continuation (Bar-Tal, 1998, 2007a; Kriesberg, 1993).

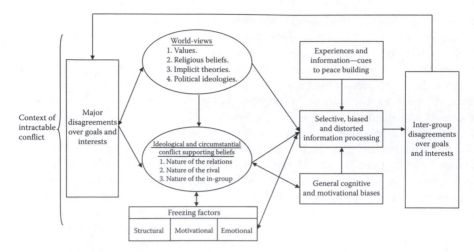

Figure 9.1   Socio-psychological barriers to peaceful conflict resolution.

Recently Bar-Tal, Halperin, and Oren (in press) used the integrative model in an analysis of the functioning of the social–psychological barriers in the Jewish Israeli society in the present stalemate of the negotiations between the state of Israel and the Palestinian Authority.

The major disagreements are the explicit causes of the conflict, but the long-term preservation of the conflict stems also from the enduring inability to overcome them because of the crystallization and functioning of various barriers including the socio-psychological ones. Socio-psychological barriers pertain to an integrated operation of cognitive, emotional and motivational processes, combined with preexisting repertoire of rigid supporting beliefs, world views and emotions that result in selective, biased and distorting information processing. This processing obstructs and inhibits a penetration of new information that can contribute to the facilitation of the development of the peace process. We will now describe the conceptual framework, beginning with ideological and circumstantial conflict supporting beliefs.

Ideological and Circumstantial Conflict Supporting Beliefs

The cores of the socio-psychological barriers that underlie the disagreements, preserve, and feed them are societal beliefs that are directly related to the confrontation and therefore are called as conflict supporting beliefs. There are two categories of these beliefs: ideological and circumstantial societal beliefs. Ideological conflict supporting beliefs provide a stable conceptual framework that allows society members involved in intractable conflict to organize and comprehend the world in which they live, and to act toward its preservation or alteration in accordance with its standpoint (Bar-Tal, Raviv, Raviv, & Dgani-Hirsch, 2009; see Chapter 6). They do not refer to specific issues or disagreements that are raised in particular conditions but are general ideological system of societal beliefs that serve as a prism to view the conflict. They pertain to at least three important themes that greatly feed the continuations of the conflict: first, they draw the conflict as a "zero sum game," justify the outbreak of the conflict, its development and insistence on its continuation (i.e., the nature of the conflict), mobilizing society members to actively participate in it. Second, they put all the blame for the outbreak of the conflict and its continuation on the rival and delegitimize him (i.e., nature of the rival). Third, they present a positive image of the in-group with self-glorification and present the in-group as being the sole victim of the conflict (i.e., nature of the in-group). More specifically these beliefs reflect systems of societal beliefs of collective memories° and ethos of conflict† that evolve under the harsh, violent and stressful conditions of intractable conflict in order to facilitate adaptation to these conditions (Bar-Tal, 2007a). Thus, the themes of the ideological conflict supporting beliefs that derive from collective memory and ethos of conflict are one sided, simplistic and provide black–white picture of the situation. They evolve through the years of the conflict to meet the challenges that it poses, and by being functional they facilitate adaptation to the harsh conditions of the conflict and allow satisfaction of the social needs on the individual and collective level (Bar-Tal, 2007a; Sharvit, 2008).

But we also recognize that additional beliefs may be added to the repertoire of the supporting beliefs as a result of particular conditions that develop in a conflict. We call these beliefs circumstantial conflict supporting beliefs as they appear in a specific context and later disappear (e.g., the leader of the rival group is weak and therefore is perceived as unable to implement the potential peace agreement). Nevertheless, all the supporting beliefs create mistrust, hostility and sense of threat. They serve as explicit barriers to the peace process by providing an epistemic basis for the continuation of the conflict.

General World Views

In addition, we suggest that the described conflict supporting beliefs are often fed by beliefs that are not directly related to the conflict but reflect general world

---

° Societal beliefs of collective memory evolve to present to society members the history of the intractable conflict in accordance to the needs of the society (Cairns & Roe, 2003).

† Ethos of conflict, defined as configuration of central societal beliefs that provide particular dominant orientation to a society experiencing prolonged intractable conflict (Bar-Tal, 2000). It has been proposed that in the context of intractable conflict evolves ethos with eight themes (Bar-Tal, 1998, 2007a). They include: societal beliefs about the justness of one's own goals, which first of all outline the goals in conflict, indicate their crucial importance, and provide their explanations and rationales. Societal beliefs about security stress the importance of personal safety and national survival, and outline the conditions for their achievement. Societal beliefs of positive collective self-image concern the ethnocentric tendency to attribute positive traits, values and behavior to own society. Societal beliefs of own victimization concern self-presentation as a victim, especially in the context of the intractable conflict. Societal beliefs of delegitimizing the opponent concern beliefs which deny the adversary's humanity. Societal beliefs of patriotism generate attachment to the country and society, by propagating loyalty, love, care, and sacrifice. Societal beliefs of unity refer to the importance of ignoring internal conflicts and disagreements during intractable conflict in order to unite the forces in the face of the external threat. Finally, societal beliefs of peace refer to peace as the ultimate desire of the society.

views. General world views are systems of beliefs not related to the particular conflict but provide orientations which contribute to the continuation of the conflicts because of the perspectives, norms, and values that they propagate. The list of these general views is long, but among the more distinctive ones it is possible to note as examples, political ideology (such as authoritarianism or conservatism) that is not directly related to the conflict (Adorno, Frenkel-Brunswick, Levinson, & Sanford, 1950; Altemeyer, 1981; Jost, 2006; Sidanius & Pratto, 1999) specific values such as related to power or conservatism (Schwartz, 1992), religious beliefs (Kimball, 2002) and entity theory about the nature of human qualities (Dweck, 1999). All these world views have influence on how society members perceive the conflict disagreements and form their other beliefs about the nature of the conflict, the rival, and the own group (Beit-Hallahmi & Argyle, 1997; Dweck & Ehrlinger, 2006; Golec & Federico, 2004; Jost, Glaser, Kruglanski, & Sulloway, 2003; Maoz & Eidelson, 2007; Sibley & Duckitt, 2008). Eventually, the two content-related clusters of beliefs (i.e., the two types of conflict supporting beliefs and the general world-view beliefs) that were just described provide a prism through which individuals perceive and interpret the reality of the conflict.

Freezing Factors

The contents themselves of the conflict supporting beliefs are only minor part of the problem. Theoretically they could be easily changed, but the essence of their functioning as barriers is their freezing (Kruglanski, 2004; Kruglanski & Webster, 1996). This freezing process is fed by structural, motivational, emotional factors that turn the conflict supporting beliefs to be rigid. Rigidity implies that the societal beliefs are resistant to change, being organized in a coherent manner with little complexity and great differentiation from alternative beliefs (Rokeach, 1960; Tetlock, 1989). It constitutes an important foundation of the barriers because it is responsible for the fact that the contents of the societal beliefs supporting the conflict do not change easily but are maintained even when the most convincing alternative arguments that suggest peaceful resolution of the conflict are presented. Now each of the factors will be presented.

Structural Factor   The first factor that contributes to the freezing is structural, as it pertains to the rigid structure of the rigid conflict supporting beliefs. There are a number of causes for this rigid structure and they will be elaborated now.

Functionality   The first reason refers to the functionality of the described societal beliefs. That is, they fulfill important functions on the individual and collective levels for societies involved in severe conflicts, especially during their intractable phase. Among them needs for identity, security, recognition, autonomy, self-esteem, differentiation, justice, and so on (Bar-Tal, 2007a; Burton, 1990; Kelman & Fisher, 2003; Staub & Bar-Tal, 2003). This functionality plays a role in the rigidity because it is well established that it is very difficult to change attitudes, beliefs or emotions when they satisfy human needs (Eagly & Chaiken, 1993, 1998).

Kruglanski (2004) proposed that society members tend "to freeze on their prior knowledge if such knowledge was congruent with their needs" (pp. 17–18). In our case, the evolved repertoire helps to meet the challenges that intractable conflict poses: it helps to satisfy the deprived needs, facilitates coping with stress and is functional to withstanding the enemy through many years of conflict (Bar-Tal, 2007a). Specifically, among various needs it fulfills the epistemic function of illuminating the conflict situation; provides moral function of justifying immoral acts of the in-group toward the enemy, including violence and destruction; allows maintenance of positive identity, sense of differentiation and superiority; satisfies the needs of security by elaborating the nature of threats and the conditions that can overcome them; and motivates for solidarity, mobilization and action for the causes of the conflict. These major functions are crucial for the society members and therefore the repertoire that serves them is inoculated against attempts to change it.

Structural Interrelationship Another reason for the rigidly of the conflict supporting beliefs is their coherent interrelated structure which can be considered as a type of conflict ideology (Bar-Tal et al., 2009; Tetlock, 1989; see Chapter 6). Ideology is considered as a closed system of systematically formulated beliefs which guide reality perception and behavior (van Dijk, 1998). Hence, it reduces openness to information and its processing. Eagly & Chaiken (1993, 1998) similarly proposed that embeddedness of beliefs and attitudes in an interrelated system creates resistance to change because coherent structure creates dependency and support among the beliefs and attitudes in this system (Rokeach, 1960). Changing one belief and/or attitude requires a change of other beliefs and attitudes as well. Accordingly, it may be assumed that the mode of thinking of those who hold an ideology is characterized (relatively to those who do not hold it) by an inclination to adhere to that which is familiar, to be selective in information search, and to think in a biased, simplistic and stereotypical way (Feldman, 2003; Jost, 2006; Jost et al., 2003).

Characteristics of the Repertoire   In addition, the rigidity of the conflict supporting beliefs lies in their characteristics: They are central, held with great confidence and highly involve the society members (Eagly & Chaiken, 1993). Central (or important) beliefs and attitudes are easily accessible and are relevant to various taken decisions (Bar-Tal, Raviv, & Freund, 1994; Krosnick, 1989). A number of studies demonstrated that when beliefs and attitudes are central, they resist change (Fazio, 1995). Also, beliefs that are considered valid and truthful are less prone to change than beliefs considered as hypothesis or possibilities (Kruglanski, 1989). A number of studies found that the greater the confidence or certainty with which beliefs or attitudes are held, the more likely they are to resist change and remain stable over time (Bassili, 1996; Petrocelli, Tormala, & Rucker, 2007). In addition, ego-involvement with beliefs or attitudes indicates motivational tendency to adhere to them because of their implications for important values and/or needs (Lavine, Borgida, & Sullivan, 2000). We would like to propose that in most of the serious conflict cases, beliefs, attitudes, and emotions of the socio-psychological repertoire that evolve during harsh and prolonged conflict are central, considered as truthful and are of ego involving. The recent thorough analysis of the Jewish Israeli society engaged in the intractable conflict demonstrates this premise very clearly (Bar-Tal, 2007b).

Motivational Factor We suggest in line with the lay epistemic theory the freezing stems also from the fact that the held knowledge is underlined by a motivational factor-specific closure needs (Kruglanski, 1989, 2004), that is, society members are motivated to view the held knowledge as being truthful and valid because it fulfills for them various needs (Burton, 1990). Therefore, society members use various cognitive strategies to increase the likelihood of reaching particular conclusions that is line with this knowledge (Kunda, 1990).

Emotional Factor Third factor that affects the level of freezing is emotional. Emotions function to freeze the repertoire and stabilize the rigidity of the conflict supporting beliefs, but they also may act directly on the information processing. It is well established that inter-group negative emotional sentiments play also a pivotal role in preventing progress toward peaceful conflict resolution (Baumeister & Butz, 2005; Corradi, Fagen, & Garreton, 1992; Halperin, 2008a, 2008b; Scheff & Retzinger, 1991; Staub, 2005; White, 1984; see also Chapter 3). These emotions are shared by society members. Averill (1994) argued more than a decade ago that "emotional feelings are stories we tell ourselves in order to guide and account for our own behavior" (p. 385). We suggest that these emotional stories, which are characterized by high stability and resistance to change (Abelson & Prentice, 1989), serve as glue, holding the conflict supporting beliefs together.

The enduring emotional states that contribute to the stabilization of the supporting content are different in their nature from the well-known classic concept of emotions, that is, psychological states that occur as short-term reactions to specific events (Frijda, 1986). These emotional sentiments consist of all features of the classical emotions, yet they endure for a much longer period of time and therefore frequently defined as chronic (Arnold, 1960; Lazarus, 1994). They differ from general moods in that they are object or event directed (Frijda, 1986). Different scholars of emotions differently defined enduring or long-term emotions. Notable examples for such conceptualizations are "emotional climate" (de Rivera, 1992) or "collective emotional orientation" (Bar-Tal, Halperin, & de Rivera, 2007). Despite the differences between these two concepts (and others), in both of them the negative emotional states turn out to be part of the conflict's culture (de Rivera & Paez, 2007), and continuously interact with the long-term societal beliefs about the conflict.

The link that connects between the emotional sentiments and the conflict supporting societal beliefs is the appraisal component of the emotions. Each and every emotion is related to unique configuration of comprehensive (conscious or unconscious) evaluations of the emotional stimulus (Roseman, 1984). Hence, emotions and beliefs are closely related and reinforce each other steadily. A decade ago, Lerner and Keltner (2000) argued that each emotion activates a cognitive predisposition to appraise future events in line with the central-appraisal dimensions that triggered the emotion (Lerner et al., 2003). This appraisal tendency approach is of great importance in our context, mainly because a seemingly positive action or statement of the adversary can be appraised negatively, due to the long-term negative emotional sentiments, and strengthens the already extremely negative ethos of conflict. Therefore, for example, emotional sentiment of fear that is related to the appraisal of the situation as threatening and to the appraisal of low control capabilities (Lazarus, 1991), will bring about a tendency to appraise each statement or actions in the same pattern (Jarymowicz & Bar-Tal, 2006). In turn, this appraisal will reinforce existing content of victimhood, siege mentality and mistrust. Emotional sentiment of hatred, that involve appraisals about the intentionality of the harms caused by the rival as well as appraisals regarding stable, evil character of this group and its members (Halperin, 2008b), will amplify extreme delegitimization, and will enable initiation of extreme aggressive actions without eroding the positive self-collective group image.

Threatening Context   Finally, the freezing of the socio-psychological repertoire can be attributed to the stressful and threatening context of conflict in which society members live. This stressful and threatening context leads to closure and limiting information processing (Driskell & Salas, 1996; Staal, 2004). Indeed numerous studies provide empirical evidence about the effect of threat and stress on cognitive functioning (see the extensive review of Staal, 2004). For example, the effect can be reflected in premature closure of decision alternatives (Keinan, 1987), restricted consideration of the number and quality of alternatives (Janis, Defares, & Grossman, 1983), sole reliance on previously stored knowledge (Bar-Tal, Raviv, & Spitzer, 1999; Pally, 1955), persistence in use of previous methods to solve problems even after they ceased to be useful and helpful (Staw, Sandelands, & Dutton, 1981) and increased use of schematic or stereotyped judgments (Hamilton, 1982).

In the context of conflict, studies found that threat is causing to closure of the societal beliefs of the conflict which means support for continuation of the conflict, use of violence and opposition to compromises (Arian, 1995; Gordon & Arian, 2001; Halperin, Bar-Tal, Nets-Zehngut, & Drori, 2008; Maoz & McCauley, 2008). Various explanations were offered for this detrimental effect of threat and stress and they range from the proposal that emotional arousal as a result of stress acts consistently reduces the range of information that individuals use (Easterbrook, 1959) to the proposal that coping with stress requires cognitive capacities and this leads to their reduced allocation for other cognitive tasks and therefore individuals in these situations use simplified and superficial cognitive strategies (Chajut & Algom, 2003).

According to Mitzen (2006), situation of conflict, which is full of threats leads to ontological security seeking which is defined as the need to create certainty and stability as part of identity fulfillment. This need is achieved by the establishment of routines that are familiar, trusted and well practiced. These routines sustain identity but at the same time perpetuate and eternalize the conflict because they prevent movement toward a different situation–situation of peace making, which requires risk taking and uncertainty. Thus, society members involved in conflict have difficulty to imagine peaceful situation after living through years in a conflict, in which the patterns of thoughts and behavior became well established and continuously used, and thus continue dogmatically to pursue the familiar line of conflict societal beliefs and behaviors, without examining alternatives.

In sum, freezing resulting from rigidity of the conflict supporting beliefs serves as the dominant cause for their functioning as socio-psychological barriers because of their major influence on information processing. The barriers lead to selective collection of information, which means that society members involved in intractable conflict tend to search and absorb information that validates the societal beliefs of the repertoire while ignoring and omitting contradictory information (Kelman, 2007; Kruglanski, 2004; Kruglanski & Webster, 1996; Kunda, 1990). But even when ambiguous or contradictory information is absorbed, it is encoded and cognitively processed in accordance with the held repertoire through bias, addition and distortion.

Moreover, since the repertoire is indoctrinated in the early years of the childhood via societal institutions and channels of communications, it is possible to assume that almost all the young generation absorbs the contents of the conflict supporting beliefs (i.e., collective memory and ethos of conflict). Moreover during the childhood probably most of this generation holds the conflict supporting beliefs as valid and truthful. It is possible that when the peace process begins and progresses at least some of them acquire alternative beliefs which promote the peace process. But recent dramatic findings reveal that even when society members acquire through the years alternative beliefs and attitudes that support peace making, the learned repertoire at the early age continues to be stored in mind as implicit beliefs and attitudes and has influence on human functioning (Sharvit, 2008).

Before turning to the description of the consequences we would like only to note that the strength of the socio-psychological barriers does not lie only in the rigid structure of the conflict supporting societal beliefs and the fueling emotions, but also in the societal mechanisms, which are set to maintain the socio-psychological repertoire of conflict. Societies involved in intractable conflict exert great efforts to assure that society members would adhere to the dominant narrative and ignore alternative information. In other words, the society constructs mechanisms to assure that the themes of collective memory and the ethos of conflict, as well as collective emotions, will be maintained and alternative knowledge about possibilities of peace making will no penetrate into the social sphere and even when penetrates would be rejected (Bar-Tal, 2007b; Horowitz, 2000; Kelman, 2007). We will briefly note the most notable mechanisms below (for detailed descriptions of the mechanisms and examples from various conflicts, refer to Burns-Bisogno, 1997; Miller, 1994; Morris, 2000; Wolfsfeld, 2004).

Control of the mass media is practiced when the media is controlled by the governmental sources and relies mostly on information provided by them. In the situation of control the governmental sources provide information that is in line with the dominant narrative and avoid providing information that may challenge this narrative.

Censorship on information functions when the governmental authorities practice censorship on the information. This mechanism assures that contradicted information does not appear in the media and other channels.

Delegitimization of alternative information and its sources attempts to close a likelihood of appearance of alternative information about possibilities of peace. Therefore the authorities delegitimize either the alternative information and/or its sources in order to influence the public to reject the information.

Punishment is carried through formal and informal sanctions of social and/or physical nature for providers of alternative information in an attempt to silence these sources that may contradict the dominant narrative.

Closure of archives is done either completely or for a long period of time by the authorities with the aim of preventing information that may contradict the dominant repertoire.

Encouragement and rewarding mechanism uses a "carrot" for those sources, channels, agents, and products that support the psychological repertoire of conflict. Authorities may reward and encourage various sources that provide information, knowledge, art, and other products which transmit and disseminate the repertoire of conflict.

THE CONSEQUENCES OF THE CONTENT-BASED BARRIERS

During the years of the conflict, the well established conflict supporting beliefs held with rigidity by many of society members, together with the general worldviews, become a prism through which society members construe their reality, collect new information, interpret their experiences and then make decisions about their course of action. This process is crystallized and accelerated by the previously described cognitive-structural, motivational, and emotional factors. Subsequently, these supporting beliefs have important cognitive, affective, and behavioral influences on society members as individuals and on the society as a whole. On the general level it is possible to describe the selective, biased and distorting information processing that inhibits the exposure, consideration and acquisition of the alternative new information with the following characteristics.[*]

1. The conflict supporting beliefs tend to be automatically activated when cues about the conflict become salient (Bargh, Chen, & Burrows, 1996; Devine, 1989).
2. Information that is consistent with the conflict supporting beliefs tends to be more attended and remembered, whereas inconsistent information is often neglected (Macrae, Milne, & Bodenhausen, 1994; Stangor & Mc Millan, 1992).

---

[*] The list of the characteristics is compiled on the basis of empirical research which shows the effect of held beliefs (including stereotypes), ideologies, values or affect on information processing (Iyengar & Ottati, 1994; Ottati & Wyer, 1993; Smith, 1998; Taber, 2003). In fact few studies were carried with conflict situation. We nevertheless assume that there is not reason to assume that society members in conflict context function with their held societal beliefs, fueled by emotions, in a different manner.

3. Ambiguous information tends to be construed in line with the conflict supporting beliefs (von Hippel, Sekaquaptewa, & Vergas, 1995).
4. Society members are more sensitive to information, which confirms their conflict supporting beliefs, in other words, they are selectively attentive and absorb confirmatory information more easily (Sweeney & Gruber, 1984; Vallone, Ross, & Lepper, 1985).
5. Society members actively search for information that confirms their conflict supporting beliefs (Schultz-Hardt, Frey, Luthgens, & Moscovici, 2000).
6. Society members less critically examine information that confirms their conflict supporting beliefs (Ditto & Lopez, 1992; Edwards & Smith, 1996).
7. Society members tend to interpret acquired information in line with the stored conflict supporting beliefs (Pfeifer & Ogloff, 1991; Rosenberg & Wolfsfeld, 1977; Shamir & Shikaki, 2002; Sommers & Ellsworth, 2000).
8. Society members tend to use their conflict supporting beliefs as a framework when organizing new information (Feldman, 1988).
9. Society members tend to use their conflict supporting beliefs in making attributions, evaluations, judgments, or decisions about the conflict (Bartels, 2002; Sibley, Liu, Duckitt, & Khan, 2008; Skitka, Mullen, Griffin, Hutchinson, & Chamberlin, 2002).
10. Based on their conflict supporting beliefs, society members tend to expect particular events, behaviors of the rival and other groups, and experiences all associated with the conflict (Darley & Gross, 1983; Hamilton, Sherman, & Ruvolo, 1990).
11. Society members tend to be guided by the conflict supporting beliefs in their behavior (Jost, 2006).

The above description of the psychological functioning suggests that the handling of the information in conflict situations is characterized by top-down processing because of the barriers. This process is affected more by what fits the contents of the conflict supporting beliefs and less by details of incongruent information. That is to say, in harsh conflict evolve socio-psychological barriers that tend to "close minds" and facilitate tunnel vision, precluding the contemplation of incongruent information and alternative approaches to the conflict. They often prevent even entertainment of ideas that may initiate peace making process.

In this vein it is important to note that the processing of new information and experiences is also amplified by universal cognitive and motivational biases that characterize all human beings as they are, in every context. Social psychology has contributed greatly to their elucidation as well as description of their functioning: Among them can be found the cognitive heuristics, automatic cognitive processing, and various motivations such as ego-enhancement (Bargh, 2007; Jarymowicz, 2008; Kunda, 1990; Nisbett & Ross, 1980). It can be assumed that the conflictive intergroup context, accompanied by the conflict supporting beliefs, provides an ultimate platform for the development of these biases (Ross & Ward, 1995). Interestingly, these biases, in turn, reinforce the rigidity and the stability of societal beliefs with contents that support the continuation of the conflict.

At present very few studies illustrated the functioning of the content-based barriers showing the effect of the conflict supporting beliefs on information processing by society members involved in a conflict (Bar-Tal et al., 2009). One notable exception is a very recent study that attempted to validate the described process model, using a correlative large-scale design with the Israeli Jewish national sample (Halperin & Bar-Tal, 2010). The survey included scales that captured representation of the potential socio-psychological barriers presented in the model, that is, (a) general world views (values, implicit theories about groups, authoritarianism, and political orientation); (b) conflict supporting societal beliefs, including specific long-term beliefs (self-perception of collective victimhood of the in-group and delegitimization of the rival group) and circumstantial beliefs about the current situation of the conflict; and (c) negative lasting emotions. As dependent variables (i.e., the result of the barriers), openness to information about the conflict and support for compromises for peace were assessed. Analysis of the results confirmed the basic patterns proposed in the presented theoretical model. The general world views influenced levels of openness to conflict-related information as well as support for compromises mainly through the mediation of the conflict supporting societal beliefs and the negative lasting emotions.

In contrast most studies demonstrated the mere selective, biased and distorting effects of the information processing in the context of conflict, with no actual reference to the group's held psychological repertoire of the conflict. This line of studies either applied previously presented biases to the area of conflict or elucidated new ones. These biases were presented as specific consequences of conflict or as barriers themselves. In some of the studies, the individual's political position was integrated into the equation, mostly used as a moderator of the effect of the bias on current attitudes. Hence, it seems that though not explicitly spelled out or empirically examined, in most of these studies the existence of content-based barriers was implicitly assumed. Among the most notable effects of information processing, the consequences mentioned below can also be found.

Double Standard   Double standard indicates that a judgment or an evaluation of similar acts by the in-group and by the rival is done with two different standards favoring the in-group. This bias is well demonstrated in the study by Sande, Geothals, Ferrari, and Worth (1989) done in 1985, which found that American high school and college students gave opposing explanations of similar acts performed either by the Soviet Union or the United States (a positive act of smashing ice fields to allow whales to reach an open sea and a negative act of building a new fleet of nuclear-powered submarines). Thus while the actions of the United States were attributed to the positive moral characteristics of the Americans, the same acts of the Soviet Union were attributed to the self-serving and negative motives of the Russians in line with their enemy image. Similar results were found in other studies as well (Ashmore, Bird, Del-Boca, & Vanderet, 1979; Burn & Oskamp, 1989; Oskamp, 1965; Oskamp & Levenson, 1968). Highly relevant to our general model are results of a study conducted in the mid-1960s that found differences between doves and hawks in the implementation of that bias (Oskamp & Levenson, 1968).

Fundamental Attributional Error   Another example of a bias is found in cases in which the negative behavior of the rival group is attributed to innate characteristics, while situational factors are disregarded (Pettigrew, 1979, who labeled this tendency as the "ultimate attribution error"). A study by Hunter, Stringer, and Watson (1991) demonstrates this error in a study in which Catholic and Protestant students in Northern Ireland were presented with newsreel footage showing scenes of violence performed by Protestants and Catholics and were asked to explain why the involved people behaved in the depicted way. The results showed very clearly that the violence of the in-group was attributed to external causes such as "retaliation" or "fear of being attacked," while the violence of the out-group was attributed to internal dispositions such as being "psychopath" or "blood lust." In a recent study, Bar-Tal et al. (2009) found that the fundamental attribution error was much more prevalent among Jews who adhere the supporting beliefs of the conflict, in comparison to those that do not (Taylor & Jaggi, 1974).

Reactive Devaluation   Another consequence of the way society members involved in conflict process information is called reactive devaluation. Reactive devaluation suggests that an evaluation of a specific package deal or compromise offer is evaluated in accordance to what side proposed it. When the offer is proposed by own side it is accepted but when the same offer is proposed by the rival it is rejected (Maoz, 2006; Ross, 1995). Maoz et al. (2002) showed that Israeli Jews evaluated an actual Israeli-authored peace plan less favorably when it was presented as being a Palestinian plan than when it was attributed to their own government. Moreover, they also showed that the evaluation of the proposal was much more negative among extremists Jews and Arabs (Hawks), than among Doves from the same sides, implying for interaction between enduring political positions and the process of reactive devaluation.

False Polarization   This is another notable example of cognitive bias which is based upon some preliminary beliefs about the in-group, the out-group and the nature of the relations between them (Robinson, Keltner, Ward, & Ross, 1995). It gives expression to exaggeration of the disparity in the basic values, beliefs, and positions and therefore it stabilizes the disagreements. According to previous studies, society members engaged in conflict tend to exaggerate the extent of the disagreements that stand at the core of the conflict (Robinson et al., 1995; Rouhana, O'Dwyer, & Morrison Vaso, 1997). This tendency is especially pronounced for beliefs that were related to own ideology than to the ideology of the rival (Chambers, Baron, & Inman, 2006). Corresponding with our assumption about the interaction between previous beliefs and on-line psychological mechanisms, in a study conducted among Jews and Arabs in the Middle-East, Rouhana et al. (1997) found that this tendency was much more common among supporters of less conciliatory political parties (i.e., hawks) than among supporters of more conciliatory political parties (i.e., doves).

Bias Perception   This is one important aspect of a wider set of biases originally defined by Lee Ross and his collogues as *Naïve Realism* (Ross & Ward, 1995, 1996), which is the tendency for people to assume that their perceptions and judgments are more objective and attuned to reality than the differing perceptions and judgments of their peers. It is assumed that this tendency amplifies in conflict situations in which people tend to perceive their opponents as biased and this perception causes them to act in violent way which escalates the confrontations (Pronin, Gilovich, & Ross, 2004). In three studies by Kennedy and Pronin (2008) it has been demonstrated that people perceive those who disagree with then as biased, take toward them conflict-escalating approaches, and eventually act toward then in a conflictive way.

Biased Assimilation plays an important role in the conflict situation as it leads society members to evaluate beliefs-consistent information more positively than beliefs-inconsistent information (Greitemayer, Fischer, Frey, & Schulz-Hardt, 2009). This bias prevents the unfreezing of the held beliefs that support the continuation of the conflict.

The presented list of biases is not exhaustible and probably additional biases that are related to conflicts can be added (e.g., fixation on particular information, denial of wrong doing, self-focus on own needs and goals, disregard of empathetic information about rival, or perception of in-group uniqueness). As noted, there is lack of systematic empirical research that examines comprehensively various societal beliefs of the repertoire of conflict, their rigidity and its functioning in real life context. Most importantly, there is lack of studies that integrate the different aspects of the socio-psychological barriers, as presented in our model. But there are numerous references to beliefs and emotions, as well as to the deficient information processing, in various analyses of different conflicts that fuel continuation of the conflict and prevent its peaceful resolution (Chirot & Seligman, 2001; Frank, 1967; Heradstveit, 1981; Jervis, 1976; Kriesberg, 2007; Lake & Rothchild, 1998; Petersen, 2002; Sandole, 1999; Vertzberger, 1991; Volkan, 1997; White, 1970, 1984). Social psychology should extend its scope to include in its agenda research on the intractable conflicts and especially the socio-psychological barriers which contribute to their continuation and prevent peace making.

CONCLUSIONS

In this chapter we attempted to describe the nature and the functioning of the socio-psychological barriers that prevent peaceful resolution of intractable conflicts. An integrated operation of cognitive, emotional, and motivational processes, combined with preexisting repertoire of rigid conflict supporting beliefs, world views and emotions leads to selective, biased and distorting information processing. In essence, we suggest that the set of the conflict supporting societal beliefs constitute a well entrenched ideology supported by conservative world views and emotions. These two sets of beliefs constitute a coherent system that has a consistent structure with teleological basis that inhibits peace making.

Thus, the presented model outlines the process through which various socio-psychological views, beliefs and processes, join together to obstruct any penetration of new, positive information or proposals that can potentially advance peace making into the individual and societal cognitive sphere. Thus, for example, peaceful gestures initiated by the adversary, new proposals raised by third parties or by the other side and/or new information about the other side's willingness to compromise, may not get a proper attention and consideration. The consequence of this functioning is preservation and even reinforcement of the basic disagreements, as well as of the supporting beliefs. Under these circumstances overcoming the basic disagreements is a very difficult challenge.

The described ensemble of socio-psychological barriers and specially its orchestrated effect on information processing serve as a catalyst for continuation of the conflict and in fact it operates as part of the vicious cycle in the intractable conflict. Considering that this process is mirror imaged by the two parties in the conflict, it can be well understood how the vicious cycle of violence operates. As the conflict evolves, each of the opponents develops a negative and rigid socio-psychological repertoire that is based upon the conflict supporting beliefs. This repertoire fulfills important roles, on the individual and collective levels. With time, however, this repertoire comes to be one of the factors determining the courses of policy and action taken by each side in the conflict, by serving as the major motivating, justifying, and rationalizing factor. The taken negative actions then serve as validating information to the existing negative psychological repertoire and in turn magnify the motivation and readiness to engage in conflict. The behaviors of each side confirm the held negative socio-psychological repertoire and justify harming the rival.

These vicious cycles of intractable conflict are detrimental to the well being of both the individuals and societies involved, as well as posing a danger to the world. The negative socio-psychological repertoire with its rigidity plays an important role in these cycles. It is, therefore, of vital necessity to change this repertoire, in order to establish new relations between the rival groups. But this change is not easy because of the other socio-psychological barriers that play a powerful role in preventing a transformation that may lead to the emergence of a repertoire that facilitates peace making. Nevertheless, changing the developed socio-psychological repertoire that is maintained by societies involved in intractable conflict is a necessary condition for advancing peace process and stopping the violence. This is a crucial challenge in view of the behavioral consequences that this rigid repertoire has in situations of intractable conflict, leading to violence, including losses of human life, ethnic cleansing and even genocide. Thus, studying how it is possible to overcome the barriers including the socio-psychological ones should be a mission placed with high priority on the agenda of social sciences and especially of social psychology.

REFERENCES

Abelson, R. B., & Prentice, D. A. (1989). Beliers as possessions: A functional perspective. In A. R. Pratkanis, S. J. Breckler, & A. G. Greenwald (Eds.), *Attitude structure and function* (pp. 361–381). Hillsdale, NJ: Erlbaum.

Adorno, T. W., Frenkel-Brunswik, E., Levinson, D. J., & Sanford, R. N. (1950). *The authoritarian personality*. New York: Harper.

Altemeyer, B. (1981). *Right-wing authoritarianism*. Winnipeg, Canada: University of Manitoba Press.

Arian, A. (1995). *Security threatened: Surveying Israeli opinion on peace and war*. Cambridge: Cambridge University Press.

Arnold, M. B. (1960). *Emotion and personality* (Vols. 1 and 2). New York: Columbia University Press.

Ashmore, D. R., Bird, D., Del-Boca, F. K., & Vanderet, R. C. (1979). An experimental investigation of the double standard in the perception of international affairs. *Political Behavior, 1*, 123–135.

Averill, J. R. (1994). In the eyes of the beholder. In P. Ekman & R. J. Davidson (Eds.), *The nature of emotion: Fundamental question* (pp. 7–15). New York: Oxford University Press.

Bargh, J. A. (2007). *Social psychology and the unconsciousness: The automaticity of higher mental processes*. New York: Psychology Press.

Bargh, J. A., Chen, M., & Burrows, L. (1996). Automaticity of social behavior: Direct effects of trait construct and stereotype activation on action. *Journal of Personality and Social Psychology, 71*, 230–244.

Bar-Siman-Tov, Y. (1995). Value-complexity in shifting form war to peace: The Israeli peace-making experience with Egypt. *Political Psychology, 16*, 545–565.

Bar-Tal, D. (1998). Societal beliefs in times of intractable conflict: The Israeli case. *International Journal of Conflict Management, 9*, 22–50.

Bar-Tal, D. (2000). *Shared beliefs in a society: Social psychological analysis*. Thousand Oaks, CA: Sage.

Bar-Tal, D. (2001). Why does fear override hope in societies engulfed by intractable conflict, as it does in the Israeli society? *Political Psychology, 22*, 601–627.

Bar-Tal, D. (2007a). Sociopsychological foundations of intractable conflicts. *American Behavioral Scientist, 50*, 1430–1453.

Bar-Tal, D. (2007b). *Living with the conflict: Socio-psychological analysis of the Israeli–Jewish society*. Jerusalem: Carmel (in Hebrew).

Bar-Tal, D., Halperin, E., & de Rivera, J. (2007). Collective emotions in conflict situations: Societal implications. *Journal of Social Issues, 63*, 441–460.

Bar-Tal, D., Halperin, E., & Oren, N. (in press). Socio-psychological barriers to peace making: The case of the Israeli Jewish society. *Social Issues and Policy Review*.

Bar-Tal, D., Raviv, A., & Freund, T. (1994). An anatomy of political beliefs: A study of their centrality, confidence, contents, and epistemic authority. *Journal of Applied Social Psychology, 24*, 849–872.

Bar-Tal, D., Raviv, A., Raviv, A., & Dgani-Hirsch, A. (2009). The influence of the ethos of conflict on the Israeli Jews' interpretation of Jewish-Palestinian encounters. *Journal of Conflict Resolution, 53*, 94–118.

Bar-Tal, Y., Raviv, A., & Spitzer, A. (1999). Individual differences that moderate the effect of stress on information processing. *Journal of Personality and Social Psychology, 77*, 33–51.

Bartels, L. M. (2002). Beyond the running tally: Partisan bias in political perceptions. *Political Behavior, 24*, 117–150.

Bassili, J. N. (1996). Meta-judgmental versus operative indexes of psychological attributes: The case of measures of attitude strength. *Journal of Personality and Social Psychology, 71*, 637–653.

Baumeister, R. F., & Butz, J. (2005). Roots of hate, violence and evil. In R. J. Sternberg (Ed.), *The psychology of hate* (pp. 87–102). Washington, DC: American Psychological Association.

Brown, R., González, R., Zagefka, H., & Cehajic, M. J. (2008). Nuestra Culpa: Collective guilt and shame as predictors of reparation for historical wrongdoing. *Journal of Personality and Social Psychology, 94*, 75–90.

Burn, S. M., & Oskamp, S. (1989). Ingroup biases and the US–Soviet conflict. *Journal of Social Issues, 45*(2), 73–990.

Burns-Bisogno, L. (1997). *Censoring Irish nationalism: The British, Irish and American suppression of Republican images in film and television, 1909–1995*. Jefferson, NC: McFarland.

Burton, J. W. (Ed.). (1990). *Conflict: Human needs theory*. New York: St. Martin's Press.

Cairns, E., & Roe, M. D. (Eds.). (2003). *The role of memory in ethnic conflict*. New York: Palgrave Macmillan.

Chajut, E., & Algom, D. (2003). Selective attention under stress: Implications for theories of social cognition. *Journal of Personality and Social Psychology, 85*, 231–248.

Chambers, J. R., Baron, R. S., & Inman, M. (2006). Misperception in intergroup conflict: Disagreeing about what we disagree about. *Psychological Science, 17*, 38–45.

Cheung-Blunden, V., & Blunden, B. (2008). The emotional construal of war: Anger, fear and other negative emotions. *Peace and Conflict—Journal of Peace Psychology, 14*, 123–150.

Chirot, D., & Seligman, M. (Eds.). (2001). *Ethnopolitical warfare: Causes, consequences and possible solutions*. Washington, DC: American Psychological Association.

Coleman, P. T. (2003). Characteristics of protracted, intractable conflict: Towards the development of a metaframework—I. *Peace and Conflict: Journal of Peace Psychology, 9*(1), 1–37.

Coleman, P. T. (2006). Intractable conflict. In M. Deutsch, P. T. Coleman, & E. C. Marcus (Eds.), *The handbook of conflict resolution: Theory and practice* (2nd ed., pp. 533–559). San Francisco: Jossey-Bass Publishers.

Corradi, J. E., Fagen, P. W., & Garreton, M. A. (Eds.). (1992). *Fear at the edge: State terror and resistance in Latin America*. Berkeley, CA: University of California Press.

Darley, J. M., & Gross, P. H. (1983). A hypothesis-confirming bias in labeling effects. *Journal of Personality and Social Psychology, 44*, 20–33.

de Rivera, J. (1992). Emotional climate: Social structure and emotional dynamics. In K. T. Strongman (Ed.), *International review of studies on emotion* (Vol. 2, pp. 199–218). New York: John Wiley.

de Rivera, J., & Paez, D. (Eds.). (2007). Emotional climate, human security, and culture of peace. *Journal of Social Issues, 63*(2), Whole issue.

Devine, P. G. (1989). Stereotype and prejudice: Their automatic and controlled components. *Journal of Personality and Social Psychology, 56*, 680–690.

Ditto, P. H., & Lopez, D. F. (1992). Motivated skepticism: Use of differential criteria for preferred and nonpreferred conclusions. *Journal of Personality and Social Psychology, 63*, 568–684.

Driskell, J. E., & Salas, E. M. (Eds.). (1996). *Stress and human performance*. Hillsdale, NJ: Erlbaum.

Dweck, C. S. (1999). *Self-theories: Their role in motivation, personality and development*. Philadelphia: Taylor & Francis/Psychology Press.

Dweck, C. S., & Ehrlinger, J. (2006). Implicit theories and conflict resolution. In M. Deutsch, P. T. Coleman, & E. C. Marcus (Eds.), *The handbook of conflict resolution: Theory and practice* (2nd ed., pp. 317–330). San Francisco: Jossey-Bass Publishers.

Eagley, A. H., & Chaiken, S. (1993). *The psychology of attitudes*. Fort Worth: Harcourt Brace College Publishers.

Eagley, A. H., & Chaiken, S. (1998). Attitude structure and function. *The handbook of social psychology* (Vol. 1, 4th ed., pp. 269–322). New York: McGraw-Hill.

Easterbrook, J. A. (1959). The effect of emotion on cue utilization and the organization of behavior. *Psychological Review, 66*, 183–201.

Edwards, K., & Smith, E. E. (1996). A disconfirmation bias in the evaluation of arguments. *Journal of Personality and Social Psychology, 71*, 5–24.

Eidelson, R. J., & Eidelson, J. I. (2003). Dangerous ideas: Five beliefs that propel groups toward conflict. *American Psychologist, 58*, 182–192.

Fazio, R. H. (1995). Attitudes as object-evaluation associations. Determinants, consequences, and correlates of attitude accessibility. In R. E. Petty & J. A. Krosnick (Eds.), *Attitude strength: Antecedents and consequences* (pp. 247–283). Mahwah, NJ: Erlbaum.

Feldman, S. (1988). Structure and consistency in public opinion: The role of core beliefs and values. *American Journal of Political Science*, 32, 416–440.

Feldman, S. (2003). Values, ideology, and the structure of political attitudes. In D. O. Sears, L. Huddy, & R. Jervis (Eds.), *Oxford handbook of political psychology* (pp. 477–508). New York: Oxford University Press.

Frank, J. D. (1967). *Sanity and survival: Psychological aspects of war and peace*. New York: Vintage.

Frijda, N. H. (1986). *The emotions*. Cambridge: Cambridge University Press.

Golec, A., & Federico, C. M. (2004). Understanding responses to political conflict: Interactive effects of the need for closure and salient conflict schema. *Journal of Personality and Social Psychology*, 87, 750–762.

Gordon, C., & Arian, A. (2001). Threat and decision making. *Journal of Conflict Resolution*, 45, 196–215.

Greitemayer, T., Fischer, P., Frey, D., & Schulz-Hardt, S. (2009). Biased assimilation. The role of source position. *European Journal of Social Psychology*, 39, 22–39.

Halperin, E. (2008a). Emotional barriers to peace: Negative emotions and public opinion about the peace process in the Middle East. *Paper presented at the Annual Meeting of ISPP*, July, 2008, Paris, France.

Halperin, E. (2008b). Group-based hatred in intractable conflict in Israel. *Journal of Conflict Resolution*, 52, 713–736.

Halperin, E., & Bar-Tal, D. (2010). *Socio-psychological barriers to peace making: An empirical examination within the Israeli Jewish society*. Manuscript submitted for publication.

Halperin, E., Bar-Tal, D., Nets-Zehngut, R., & Drori, E. (2008). Emotions in conflict: Correlates of fear and hope in the Israeli–Jewish society. *Peace and Conflict: Journal of Peace Psychology*, 14, 1–26.

Hamilton, D. L., Sherman, S. J., & Ruvolo, C. M. (1990). Stereotype-based expectancies: Effects on information processing and social behavior. *Journal of Social Issues*, 46(2), 35–60.

Hamilton, V. (1982). Cognition and stress: An information processing model. In L. L. Goldberg & S. Breznitz (Eds.), *Handbook of stress: Theoretical and clinical aspects* (pp. 105–120). New York: The Free Press.

Horowitz, D. L. (2000). *Ethnic groups in conflict*. Berkeley: University of California Press.

Heradstveit, D. (1981). *The Arab–Israeli conflict: Psychological obstacles to peace*. Oslo: Universitetsforlaget.

Hunter, J. A., Stringer, M., & Watson, R. P. (1991). Intergroup violence and intergroup attributions. *British Journal of Social Psychology*, 30, 261–266.

Iyengar, S., & Ottai, V. (1994). Cognitive perspective in political psychology. In R. S. Wyer Jr. & T. K. Srull (Eds.), *Handbook of social cognition* (2nd ed., Vol. 2, pp. 143–188). Hillsdale, NJ: Erlbaum.

Janis, I., Defares, P., & Grossman, P. (1983). Hypervigilant reactions to threat. In H. Selye (Ed.), *Selye's guide to stress research* (Vol. 3, pp. 1–42). New York: Van Nostrand Reinhold.

Jarymowicz, M. (2008). *Psychologiczne podstawy podmiotowości (The Self as a subject: Psychological bases)*. Warszawa: Wydawnictwo Naukowe PWN (in Polish).

Jarymowicz, M., & Bar-Tal, D. (2006). The dominance of fear over hope in the life of individuals and collectives. *European Journal of Social Psychology*, 36, 367–392.

Jervis, R. (1976). *Perception and misperception in international politics*. Princeton: Princeton University Press.

Jost, J. T. (2006). The end of the end of ideology. *American Psychologist*, *61*, 651–670.

Jost, T. J., Glaser, J., Kruglanski, A. W., & Sulloway, F. J. (2003). Political conservatism as motivated social cognition. *Psychological Bulletin*, *129*, 339–375.

Kahneman, D., & Tversky, A. (1995). Conflict resolution: A cognitive perspective. In K. Arrow, R. Mnookin, L. Ross, A. Tversky, & R. Wilson (Eds.), *Barriers to conflict resolution* (pp. 44–61). New York: Norton.

Keinan, G. (1987). Decision making under stress: Scanning of alternatives under controllable and uncontrollable threats. *Journal of Personality and Social Psychology*, *52*, 629–644.

Kelman, H. C. (Ed.). (1965). *International behavior: A social psychological analysis*. New York: Holt, Rinehart and Winston.

Kelman, H. C. (1987). The political psychology of the Israeli–Palestinian conflict: How can we overcome the barriers to a negotiated solution? *Political Psychology*, *8*, 347–363.

Kelman, H. C. (2005). Building trust among enemies: The central challenge for peace-making efforts. *International Journal of Intercultural Relations*, *29*, 639–650.

Kelman, H. C. (2007). Social-psychological dimensions of international conflict. In I. W. Zartman (Ed.), *Peacemaking in international conflict: Methods and techniques* (rev. ed., pp. 61–107). Washington, DC: United States Institute of Peace Press.

Kelman, H. C., & Fisher, R. J. (2003). Conflict analysis and resolution. In D. O. Sears, L. Huddy, & R. Jervis (Eds.), *Oxford handbook of political psychology* (pp. 315–353). New York: Oxford University Press.

Kennedy, K. A., & Pronin, E. (2008). When disagreement gets ugly: Perception of bias and the escalation of conflict. *Personality and Social Psychology Bulletin*, *34*, 833–848.

Kimball, C. (2002). *When religion becomes evil*. San Francisco: Harper Collins Publishers.

Kramer, R. M., & Carnevale, P. J. (2001). Trust and intergroup negotiation. In R. Brown & S. Gaertner (Eds.), *Blackwell handbook of social psychology: Intergroup processes* (pp. 431–450). Malden, MA: Blackwell Publishing.

Kriesberg, L. (1993). Intractable conflict. *Peace Review*, *5*, 417–421.

Kriesberg, L. (2007). *Constructive conflicts: From escalation to resolution* (3rd ed.). Lanham, MD: Rowman & Littlefield.

Krosnick, J. A. (1989). Attitude importance and attitude accessibility. *Personality and Social Psychology Bulletin*, *15*, 297–308.

Kruglanski, A. W. (1989). *Lay epistemics and human knowledge: Cognitive and motivational bases*. New York: Plenum.

Kruglanski, A. W. (2004). *The psychology of closed mindedness*. New York: Psychology Press.

Kruglanski, A. W., & Webster, D. M. (1996). Motivated closing of the mind: 'seizing' and 'freezing'. *Psychological Review*, *103*, 263–283.

Kunda, Z. (1990). The case for motivated reasoning. *Psychological Bulletin*, *108*, 480–498.

Kydd, A. H. (2005). *Trust and mistrust in international relations*. Princeton: Princeton University Press.

Lake, D. A., & Rothchild, D. (Eds.). (1998). *The international spread of ethnic conflict: Fear, diffusion, and escalation*. Princeton: Princeton University Press.

Larsen, D. (1997). *Anatomy of mistrust: US–Soviet relations during the cold war*. Ithaca: Cornell University Press.

Lavine, H., Borgida, E., & Sullivan, J. L. (2000). On the relationship between involvement and attitude accessibility: Toward a cognitive-motivational model of political information processing. *Political Psychology*, *21*, 81–106.

Lazarus, R. S. (1991). *Emotion and adaptation*. New York: Oxford University Press.

Lazarus, R. S. (1994). Universal antecedents of the emotions. In P. Ekman & R. J. Davidson (Eds.), *The nature of emotion: Fundamental question* (pp. 163–171). New York: Oxford University Press.

Lerner, J. S., Gonzalez, R. M., Small, D. A., & Fischhoff, B. (2003). Effects of fear and anger on perceived risks of terrorism: A national field experiment. *Psychological Science, 14*, 144–150.

Lerner, J. S., & Keltner, D. (2000). Beyond valence: Toward a model of emotion-specific influences on judgment and choice. *Cognition and Emotion, 14*, 473–493.

Lewicki, R. J. (2006). Trust, trust development, and trust repair. In M. Deutsch, P. T. Coleman, & E. C. Marcus (Eds.), *The handbook of conflict resolution: Theory and practice* (2nd ed., pp. 92–119). San Francisco: Jossey-Bass Publishers.

Macrae, C. N., Milne, A. B., & Bodenhausen, G. V. (1994). Stereotypes as energy-saving devices: A peek inside the cognitive toolbox. *Journal of Personality and Social Psychology, 66*, 37–47.

Maoz, I. (2006). The effect of news coverage concerning the opponents' reaction to a concession on its evaluation in the Israeli–Palestinian conflict. *The International Journal of Press/Politics, 11*, 70–88.

Maoz, I., & Eidelson, R. (2007). Psychological bases of extreme policy preferences: How the personal beliefs of Israeli–Jews predict their support for population transfer in the Israeli–Palestinian conflict. *American Behavioral Scientists, 50*, 1476–1497.

Maoz, I., & McCauley, C. (2005). Psychological correlates of support for compromise: A polling study of Jewish–Israeli attitudes toward solutions to the Israeli–Palestinian conflict. *Political Psychology, 26*, 791–808.

Maoz, I., Ward, A., Katz, M., & Ross, L. (2002). Reactive devaluation of an Israeli and a Palestinian peace proposal. *Journal of Conflict Resolution, 46*, 515–546.

Miller, D. (1994). *Don't mention the war: Northern Ireland, propaganda, and the media.* London: Pluto.

Mitzen, J. (2006). Ontological security in world politics: State identity and the security dilemma. *European Journal of International Relations, 12*, 341–370.

Mnookin, R. H., & Ross, L. (1995). Introduction. In K. Arrow, R. Mnookin, L. Ross, A. Tversky, & R. Wilson (Eds.), *Barriers to conflict resolution*. New York: Norton.

Morris, B. (2000). Israeli journalism in the "Kiviya" affair. In B. Morris (Ed.), *Jews and Arabs in Palestine/Israel 1936–1956* (pp. 175–198). Tel-Aviv: Am-Oved (in Hebrew).

Nisbett, R., & Ross, L. (1980). *Human inferences: Strategies and shortcomings of social judgment*. Englewood Cliffs, NJ: Prentice-Hall.

Oskamp, S. (1965). Attitudes toward US and Russian actions: A double standard. *Psychological Reports, 16*, 6–43.

Oskamp, S., & Levenson, H. (1968). *The double standard in international attitudes: differences between doves and hawks*. Proceedings of the 76th Annual Convention of the American Psychological Association, pp. 379–380.

Ottati, V. C., & Wyer, R. S. Jr. (1993). Affect and political judgment. In S. Iyengar & W. McGuire (Eds.), *Explorations in political psychology* (pp. 296–315). Durham, NC: Duke University Press.

Pally, S. (1955). Cognitive rigidity as a function of threat. *Journal of Personality, 23*, 346–355.

Petersen, R.G. (2002). *Understanding ethnic violence: Fear, hatred, and resentment in twentieth-century Eastern Europe*. Cambridge: Cambridge University Press.

Petrocelli, J. V., Tormala, Z. L., & Rucker, D. D. (2007). Unpacking attitude certainty: Attitude clarity and attitude correctness. *Journal of Personality and Social Psychology, 92*, 30–41.

Pettigrew, T. F. (1979). The ultimate attribution error: Extending Allport's cognitive analysis of prejudice. *Personality and Social Psychology Bulletin, 5*, 461–467.

Pfeifer, J. E., & Ogloff, J. R. P. (1991). Ambiguity and guilt determinations: A modern racism perspective. *Journal of Applied Social Psychology, 21*, 1713–1725.

Pronin, E., Gilovich, T., & Ross, L. (2004). Objectivity in the eye of the beholder: Divergent perceptions of bias in self versus others. *Psychological Review, 111*, 781–799.

Robinson, R. J., Keltner, D., Ward, A., & Ross, L. (1995). Actual versus assumed differences in construal: "Naïve realism" in intergroup perception and conflict. *Journal of Personality and Social Psychology, 68*, 404–417.

Rokeach, M. (1960). *The open and closed mind*. New York: Basic Books.

Roseman, I. J. (1984). Cognitive determinants of emotions: A structural theory. In P. Shaver (Ed.), *Review of personality and social psychology* (Vol. 5, pp. 11–36). Beverly Hills, CA: Sage Publications.

Rosenberg, W., S., & Wolfsfeld, G. (1977). International conflict and the problem of attribution. *Journal of Conflict Resolution, 21*, 73–103.

Ross, L. (1995). Reactive devaluation in negotiation and conflict resolution. In K. Arrow, R. Mnookin, L. Ross, A. Tversky, & R. Wilson (Eds.), *Barriers to conflict resolution*. New York: Norton.

Ross, L., & Ward, A. (1995). Psychological barriers to dispute resolution. In M. Zanna (Ed.), *Advances in experimental social psychology* (Vol. 27, pp. 255–304). San Diego: Academic Press.

Ross, L., & Ward, A. (1996). Naive realism: Implications for social conflict and misunderstanding. In T. Brown, E. Reed, & E. Turiel (Eds.), *Values and knowledge* (pp. 103–135). Hillsdale, NJ: Erlbaum.

Rouhana, N. N., O'Dwyer, A., & Morrison Vaso, S. K. (1997). Cognitive biases and political party affiliation in intergroup conflict. *Journal of Applied Social Psychology, 27*, 37–57.

Sande, G. M., Geothals, G. R., Ferrari, L., & Worth, L. T. (1989). Value-Guided attributions: Maintaining the moral self-image and the diabolical enemy-image. *Journal of Social Issues, 45*, 91–118.

Sandole, D. (1999). *Capturing the complexity of conflict: Dealing with violent ethnic conflicts of the Post-Cold War era*. London: Pinter/Continuum.

Scheff, T. J., & Retzinger, S. (1991). *Emotion and violence: Shame/rage spirals in intermiable conflicts*. Lexington: Lexington Books.

Schultz-Hardt, S., Frey, D., Luthgens, C., & Moscovici, S. (2000). Biases information search in group decision making. *Journal of Personality and Social Psychology, 78*, 655–669.

Schwartz, S. H. (1992). Universals in the content and structure of values: Theory and empirical tests in 20 countries. In M. Zanna (Ed.), *Advances in experimental social psychology* (Vol. 25, pp. 1–65). New York: Academic Press.

Shamir, J., & Shikaki, K. (2002). Self serving perceptions of terrorism among Israelis and Palestinians. *Political Psychology, 23*, 537–557.

Sharvit, K. (2008). Activation of the ethos of conflict while coping with stress resulting from intractable conflict. Unpublished doctoral dissertation, Tel Aviv University, Tel Aviv.

Sibley, C. G., & Duckitt, J. (2008). Personality and prejudice: A meta-analysis and theoretical review. *Personality and Social Psychology Review, 12*, 248–279.

Sibley, C. G., Liu, J. H., Duckitt, J., & Khan, S. S. (2008). Social representations of history and the legitimation of social inequality: The form and function of historical negation. *European Journal of Social Psychology, 38*, 542–565.

Sidanius, J., & Pratto, F. (1999). *Social dominance*. New York: Cambridge University Press.

Skitka, L. J., Mullen, E., Griffin, T., Hutchinson, S., & Chamberlin, B. (2002). Dispositions, scripts, or motivated corrections? Understanding ideological differences in explanations for social problems. *Journal of Personality and Social Psychology, 83*, 470–487.

Smith, E. R. (1998). Mental representation and memory. In D. T. Gilbert, S. T. Fiske, & G. Lindzey (Eds.), *The handbook of social psychology* (4th ed., Vol. 1, pp. 391–445). Boston: McGraw-Hill.

Sommers, S. R., & Ellsworth, P. C. (2000). Race in the courtroom: Perceptions of guilt and dispositional attributions. *Personality and Social Psychology Bulletin, 26*, 1367–1379.

Staal, M. A. (2004). *Stress, cognition and human performance: A literature review and conceptual framework.* Hanover, MD: NASA, Center for Aerospace Information.

Stangor, C., & McMillan, D. (1992). Memory for expectancy-congruent and expectancy-incongruent information: A review of the social and developmental literatures. *Psychological Bulletin, 111*, 42–61.

Staub, E. (2005). The origins and evolution of hate, with notes on prevention. In R. J. Sternberg (Ed.), *The psychology of hate* (pp. 51–66). Washington, DC: American Psychological Association.

Staub, E., & Bar-Tal, D. (2003). Genocide, mass killing and intractable conflict: Roots, evolution, prevention and reconciliation. In D. O. Sears, L. Huddy, & R. Jervis (Eds.), *Oxford handbook of political psychology* (pp. 710–751). New York: Oxford University Press.

Staw, R. M., Sandelands, L. E., & Dutton, J. E. (1981). Threat-rigidity effects in organizational behavior: A multi-level analysis. *Administrative Science Quarterly, 26*, 501–524.

Sweeney, P. D., & Gruber, K. L. (1984). Subjective exposure: Voter information preferences and the Watergate affair. *Journal of Personality and Social Psychology, 46*, 1208–1221.

Taber, C. S. (2003). Information processing and public opinion. In D. O. Sears, L. Huddy, & R. Jervis (Eds.), *Oxford handbook of political psychology* (pp. 433–476). Oxford: Oxford University Press.

Taylor, D. M., & Jaggi, V. (1974). Ethnocentrism and causal attribution in a South Indian context. *Journal of Cross-Cultural Psychology, 5*, 162–171.

Tetlock, P. E. (1989). Structure and function in political belief system. In A. R. Pratkanis, S. J. Breckler, & A. G. Greenwald (Eds.), *Attitude structure and function* (pp. 126–151). Hillsdale, NJ: Erlbaum.

Vallone, R. P., Ross, L., & Lepper, M. R. (1985). The hostile media phenomenon: Biased perceptions of media bias in coverage of the Beirut massacre. *Journal of Personality and Social Psychology, 49*, 577–585.

Van Dijk, T. A. (1998). *Ideology: A multidisciplinary study.* London: Sage

Vertzberger, Y. (1991). *The world in their minds.* Palo Alto, CA: Stanford University Press.

Volkan, V. (1997). *Blood lines: From ethnic pride to ethnic terrorism.* New York: Farrar, Straus and Giroux.

von Hippel, W., Sekaquaptewa, D., & Vergas, P. (1995). On the role of encoding processes in stereotype maintenance. In M. P. Zanna (Ed.), *Advances in experimental social psychology* (Vol. 27, pp. 177–253). San Diego, CA: Academic Press.

White, R. K. (1970). *Nobody wanted war: Misperception in Vietnam and other wars.* Garden City, NY: Anchor Books.

White, R. K. (1984). *Fearful warriors: A psychological profile of US-Soviet relations.* New York: Free Press.

Wolfsfeld, G. (2004). *Media and the path to peace.* Cambridge: Cambridge University Press.

Yamagishi, T., & Yamagishi, M. (1994). Trust and commitment in the United States and Japan. *Motivation and Emotion, 18*, 129–166.

10

Socio-Psychological Approaches to Conflict Resolution[*]

JANUSZ REYKOWSKI and ALEKSANDRA CISŁAK[†]

CONFLICT RESOLUTION: THE MEANING OF THE CONCEPT

Ronald Fisher, one of the leading researchers on interpersonal and group conflicts, has defined the term conflict resolution as "a transformation of the relationship and situation such that solutions developed by parties are sustainable and self-correcting in the long term. It also requires that an adequate degree of reconciliation occurs between the parties, in that harmony has been restored through processes such as acknowledgment of transgressions, forgiveness by the victims, and assurance of future peace" (Fisher, 2006, p. 189). This definition seems to describe the ideal model of conflict resolution. In the real life situations more limited version of conflict resolution would be acceptable. Namely, we may say that the conflict is resolved, if all or most of its major causes are eliminated or reduced, and the parties have learned how to live and work together avoiding violent encounters and hostile actions.

Conflict resolution should not be looked upon as an achievement of a final state of equilibrium of a social system. Such equilibrium can never last for extended period of time. Conflicts between individuals or groups tend to appear and evolve as part of an everyday life. Elimination of all the conflicts is neither possible, nor desirable, as conflicts are powerful means of individual and social change and development (Coleman & Deutsch, 2006; Marcus, 2006). Thus, conflict resolution is rather an ongoing task that comprises prevention of the conflict escalation,

[*] The present chapter focuses primarily on the recent research published between 1995 and 2010, assuming that earlier research were covered in the major volume published in 1998 (Gilbert, Fiske, & Lindzey, 1998).

[†] The contribution of the second author was financed by the START scholarship awarded to Aleksandra Cisłak by the Foundation for Polish Science.

elimination of its violent and destructive components, and facilitation of constructive change in people and in their social relations.

Fisher (2006) indicates that the concept of conflict resolution refers not only to the outcome, but also to the process "by which differences are handled" (p. 189). Groups and societies develop various "devices" for conflict resolution. According to Dunlop (1983), in many societies there are two approved arrangements for resolving conflicting interests among groups, organizations and their constituent members: market place and governmental regulatory mechanisms. In fact, in almost every society—on a group, state or international level—some mechanisms of conflict resolution have been developed. But the effectiveness of these mechanisms is limited. First of all, because people who are engaged in protracted conflicts tend to ignore or violate the existing regulations, and quite often try to achieve their goals by coercion or various forms of clandestine actions. Moreover, the changing conditions of life create new conflict situations that are difficult to handle by means of the available norms, procedures, and institutions. Finding solutions to such conflicts may require a direct interaction between members of the groups or their representatives to elaborate adequate solutions.

Depending on its origin, such interactions aimed at conflict resolution may take different forms. The conflict that originates as a consequence of divergent perspectives, that is, divergent opinions, beliefs, narratives, and so on can be handled by means of a debate while divergent interests, that is, competition over resources (such as space, money, property, food, power, etc.) by means of bargaining, trade off, concessions, or compromises. Such solutions seem possible, when the divergent interests are not perceived as a zero-sum situation, in which only one party could win.

Debate, bargaining, and trade off are not likely to solve conflicts that are initiated by the direct threat for basic (existential) needs, sacred values (such as freedom, justice, legitimacy or holy places and symbols), or values related to the self (involving identity, prestige, dignity, positive self-image). The resolution of such conflicts requires from the protagonists mutual recognitions of their needs and values (Atran & Axelrod, 2008)—they have to make the necessary accommodations within the same relational dimension (Fiske & Tetlock, 1997). One example of such solution is "parity of esteem"—the approach applied in Northern Ireland conflict (though not very successfully; see Mac Ginty & du Toit, 2007). It consisted in arrangements that were supposed to guarantee equal status for both sides. Similar solutions are needed in conflicts over justice. Such conflicts require a resolution that would guarantee justice for both sides; in many societies and groups, justice could not be compensated by monetary or other material reward (taboo trade-off; Tetlock et al., 2000).

The conflicts instigated by harm or wrongdoings would not be negotiable, at least in many or most societies. Rather, the resolution would have to be based on mutual forgiveness and reconciliation. As it is a very difficult process that usually requires a long time, some authors argue that before the reconciliation could be achieved, parties should work on recovery of social relations, that is on a social reconstruction (Biruski & Ajducovic, 2009).

Many long lasting group and social conflicts are very complex. They involve disagreements concerning the beliefs about the past, present, and future relationship between groups (opposed narratives), conflict of interests, threat to basic needs and values and to identity and self-esteem, as well as involving serious mutual violence that causes harm. Such conflicts may turn out to be intractable, when threats to major values and basic needs become their salient feature and when solutions that are considered while eliminating threat for one side, would cause even greater harm or threat to another one (as is the case with the Jewish settlements on West Bank).[*] It is the situation when the vital interests and basic values of two sides are perceived, using Deutsch's term, as contriently interdependent (Deutsch, 1973, p. 20). Such conflicts are maintained by a system of psychological and social mechanisms—the "socio-psychological infrastructure" of the conflict (Bar-Tal, 2007; also see Chapter 9).

Resolution of conflicts, especially the more complex ones, depends primarily on intention of the participants; whether their primary goal is to defeat the other side perceived as an enemy and impose its own will (competitive approach) or to find a solution that can be accepted by both sides (cooperative approach). The competitive approach is combative and hostile. It implies a strategy of fight by using superior power and/or manipulation, and by seeking means of defeating or punishing the other side. As a result of such an approach the conflict is likely to escalate and take a destructive course. The cooperative approach is focused on looking for constructive solutions, seeking agreement, and choosing actions that may reduce tension as well as eliminate its causes. In many real-life conflicts the both approaches may appear in the same conflict, and participants may oscillate between those two.

The choice of the given approach depends primarily on the cognitive construal of conflict situation that is on definition of the nature of the conflict and its participants. The conflict that is defined as divergence of opinions or interests (especially if it is perceived as a mixed-motive conflict) is more likely to activate the cooperative problem solving approach than situations that are defined as threats or harm. The threat and harm tend to engender intense affective reactions, first of all fear, anger, and hostility. These reactions may instigate strong aggressive responses toward the opponent perceived as an enemy. But even in situations that involve threats and harm people may preserve a hope for a constructive solution of the conflict, if they believe that the other side is not a mortal enemy but adversary or an opponent (Reykowski, 1993).

Thus, the main psychological preconditions of resolution of the long lasting, destructive intergroup conflicts are changes in cognitive construal of the conflict situation and in affective reactions.

COGNITIVE CONSTRUAL OF THE CONFLICT SITUATION

Salient Conflict Schemas

The way in which the conflict is interpreted may depend on the salient conflict schema, which comprises individual beliefs about the nature of the conflict and appropriate behavior in conflict (Bar-Tal, Kruglanski, & Klar, 1989). Confrontational

---

[*] There are various definitions of intractable conflicts as given by Bar-Tal (2007) and Coleman (2006b). These authors provide extensive characteristics of this phenomenon.

conflict schema represents parties as enemies and the solution as a zero-sum game, when only one party may win; therefore coercion is regarded as an appropriate behavior in the conflict. The cooperative conflict schema represents parties rather as partners and a prospective solution as potentially satisfying for both sides, therefore constructive discussion and cooperative problem solving seems a more suitable strategy (Golec & Federico, 2004). Once activated, confrontational schema triggers negative emotions and leads to more hostile and aggressive behavior toward partner, both verbal and nonverbal (Golec de Zavala, Federico, Cislak, & Sigger, 2008; Zuroff & Duncan, 1999). Activation of the confrontational versus cooperative conflict schemas depends on various factors such as epistemic abilities, personal beliefs, political ideologies and situational cues that frame the conflict (Golec & Federico, 2004; Golec de Zavala, Cislak, & Wesolowska, in press; Zuroff & Duncan, 1999).

Epistemic Abilities

It has been theorized and empirically confirmed that the level of complexity in conflict interpretation has a great impact on the preferred strategies of conflict resolution, and specifically that limited cognitive abilities and simplistic perspective result in competitive and aggressive tendencies toward out-groups (Golec de Zavala, 2006; Pruitt & Carnevale, 1982; Suedfeld & Tetlock, 1977; Winter, 2007).

One of the important factors that affect the complexity of information processing is the need for cognitive closure (NFC), a motivation to possess clear, unambiguous, and stable knowledge as opposed to discomforting ambiguity and uncertainty (Webster & Kruglanski, 1994). In order to reduce this discomfort, individuals with high need for closure tend to seize on easily available or more prominent information and to rely on ideological cues and group norms in intergroup behavior (Fu et al., 2007). In consequence, they tend to perceive intergroup situations in a less complex and nuanced way and they favor in-groups even more strongly (De Dreu, Koole, & Steinel, 2000; Shah, Kruglanski, & Thompson, 1998) that in turn brings about the preference for coercion and hostility.

Although it might suggest that high NFC should facilitate confrontational response to conflict, it is not always the case. The recently activated conflict schema might be used by high need for closure individuals as an easily accessible cue framing the conflict. Therefore, on the one hand it leads to more hostile and coercive response to conflict, when confrontational conflict schema has been activated. On the other hand, activation of cooperative conflict schema attenuates the relationship between high need for closure and coercion (Golec et al., 2008).

Beliefs and Ideology

Some political ideologies or systems of beliefs might predispose people to respond with aggression toward out-groups (see Chapter 6). Specifically, political or group ideologies that highlight the in-group superiority over out-groups like nationalism (but not patriotism—Golec, Federico, Cislak, & Dial, 2004) and sharp us–them categorizations, have been demonstrated to intensify the effect of need for closure on hostility and aggressiveness in conflict. Conservative ideology that may serve psychological needs of personal and social security, system justification, epistemic certainty, and ambiguity avoidance (Jost, Glaser, Kruglanski, & Sulloway, 2003; see Chapter 6) has also been proved to amplify tendency to use coercion and aggression, especially under threat (Bonanno & Jost, 2006; McCann, 2008) and again to intensify the association of the need for closure and aggressiveness (Golec, Cislak, & Wesolowska, in press).

Beliefs about the cause of the conflict, the opponents, and the necessary actions that must be undertaken (for conflict ethos see Bar-Tal, 1998) influence the choice of strategy in conflict situation. If societal beliefs comprise elevated positive self-image, intense patriotism, strong conviction in justness of one's goals and at the same time delegitimization of the enemy and its goals, they motivate contentious approach to the conflict situation (see Chapter 9). Such an approach can also be facilitated by beliefs about the nature of social world as a fixed-pie (Thompson, Nadler, & Lount, 2006) or belief in life as zero-sum game (Wojciszke, Różycka, & Baryła, 2009).

It should be noted, however, that beliefs hold by many individuals are not highly consistent and stable. According to Feldman and Zaller (1992), majority of people have opposing views on most issues—views that may lead them to decide on the issues either way. The actual decisions may depend on accessibility of the given consideration (Kinder, 1998) and accessibility can be influenced by contextual factors. It has been shown that presenting the same controversial issue in the context of different values may strongly affect political choices (Chong & Druckman, 2007). It means that the same people might take cooperative or competitive approach to the same conflict situation depending on a particular cognitive frame of the conflict issues or on socio-political context. This is why in a relatively short period of time large proportion of the population may shift between two opposite kinds of orientations—for example, in Israeli society over period of two years high proportion of the population (almost 30%) changed their attitudes from doves to hawks, that is, from the cooperative to confrontational schemas (Halperin & Bar-Tal, 2007).

Implications

Conflict situation can be construed by means of cooperative or confrontational schema. The likelihood of activation of the given schema depends on some structural characteristics of the cognitive system (complexity and epistemic needs) and on the belief system (ideology). However, contextual factors may affect both the effects of epistemic motivation on responses to conflict, and the cognitive availability of a particular set of beliefs.

EMOTIONS AND COGNITIVE CONSTRUAL OF THE CONFLICT SITUATION*

Emotions shape our interpretation and responses to stimuli, sometimes in an uncontrolled, fast, and unintentional fashion (Bargh, 1994). Both individual and

---

* See Chapter 5.

collective emotions are fundamental when considering conflict resolution dynamics such as the positive or negative cycles, negotiating the settlement, motivation to reconcile and compensate (Bar-Tal & Sharvit, 2008; Brown, Gonzáles, Zagefka, Manzi, & Čehajić, 2008; Jarymowicz & Bar-Tal, 2006).

Fear, Hope, and Conflict Dynamics

Contemporary conflict resolution research coincides with the advances in neuroscience, and the recent findings demonstrate the role of affective processes in shaping the responses to conflict and opponents on an individual level. For instance, in their recent work, Wheeler and Fiske (2005) probed the effect of amygdale activation in reaction to perceiving different ethnic groups' members. They found that in social categorization tasks the participants' amygdale reaction resembled threat response pattern. These findings imply that negative affective reaction toward members of different ethnic groups might be an automatic one, making interethnic conflicts especially easily aroused.

According to recent theorizing by Jarymowicz and Bar-Tal (2006) fear tends to override more positive emotions in conflict as it is primary and automatically activated in threat situations. Consequently, in many conflicts it may lead to preemptive aggression and hostility. Collective orientation of fear enhanced by ethos of conflict becomes a considerable hindrance to conflict resolution (Bar-Tal, 2000b; Bar-Tal & Sharvit, 2008). Overcoming fear and instigation of hope seems to be an important prerequisite of successful conflict resolution and reconciliation (see Chapter 3).

Fear and hope orientation may be associated with respectively confrontational and cooperative conflict schema. Applying more common in political studies distinction of hawks and doves, Zafran and Bar-Tal (2002) demonstrated in the context of Israeli–Palestinian conflict that fear orientation was associated with hawkish approach to conflict resolution and preference for rather coercive strategies, while hope orientation was more typical for doves, who preferred conciliatory strategies. Therefore, the efforts aimed at reducing fear may facilitate activation the cooperative conflict schemas. It should be taken into consideration, however, that the effects of hope on conflict resolution process may depend on the specific direction of this emotion. If people have a strong hope that they might overcome their enemies they would rather fight than think about the conflict resolution.

Anger and Hate

Anger has been proved to have both detrimental and beneficial effects on conflict resolution. Friedman et al. (2004) showed that anger exerts disruptive influence on conflict resolution. Moreover, experiencing anger seems to hinder reasoning and decision-making. For example, angry individuals are more willing to irrationally reject offers and accept losses when negotiating with others, just to punish the opponents (Nowak, Page, & Sigmund, 2000; Pillutla & Murnighan, 1996). Anger more commonly occurs when individuals actually hold power in a given situation or have higher status, whereas individuals with lower status tend to experience guilt or shame (Fischer & Roseman, 2007; Tiedens, 2001). In consequence, those with higher status or power tend to use coercion rather than more constructive strategies of conflict resolution like cooperation or compromise (Callister & Wall, 2001). Negative effects of experiencing anger can be prevented by inducing cognitive reappraisal of the anger-evoking stimuli, for example by exercising recategorization of opponents' behavior as challenge rather than as hostile action (Fabiansson & Denson, in press).

There is an important difference between short-term anger and less intense but long-term contempt or hate. Anger may serve as an emotional trigger to alter the irritating situation, and therefore it may have long-term positive effects leading to conflict resolution and reconciliation. Contempt, at the other side, implies more negative evaluation of the opponents, their derogation and exclusion. Halperin, Russell, Dweck, and Gross (2009) found a relationship between anger, hate and Israeli support for compromise: Israelis revealing high level of anger and low level of hate for Palestinians expressed much stronger support for compromise than people revealing the opposite pattern of emotions (low anger—high hate). In other words, the same emotion of anger can have different effects depending on other emotions, in this case, on hatred. Interestingly, the authors also found that hatred was related to people's conception of the opposite group (Palestinians), namely to their belief that the opposite group has fixed nature, in other words, to their so called implicit entity theory of the group. If people were led to believe that the group can change the level of hate decreased, they also reacted in more constructive ways to reminders of anger-evoking events (see also Chapter 3).

Self-critical Emotions Following Harms in Inter group Reconciliation

Anger in conflict situation might also be evoked by in-group misdeeds and directed toward in-group (or rather toward in-group decision-makers). It may result in enhanced willingness to compensate those harmed and to confront those responsible for the harm (Iyer, Schmader, & Lickel, 2007; Leach, Iyer, & Pedersen, 2007). Group-based self-criticism may also result in feelings of guilt and shame, with shame originating to the higher extent from social reputation concerns (Brown et al., 2008; Brown & Čehajić, 2008).

Emotional Reciprocity

Initial responses to conflict might have crucial impact on conflict resolution, triggering potentially vicious cycle of negative reciprocity that by means of vicarious retribution might affect individuals not involved in the original conflict (Lickel, Miller, Stenstrom, Denson, & Schmader, 2006). But they also may lead to constructive cycle of positive reciprocity (Friedman et al., 2004). These recent findings are in line with the classical crude law of social relations by Deutsch (1973), showing that initial reactions may shape the conflict resolution dynamics and affect final settlement. However, positive cycles are less frequently observed (Weingart & Olekalns, 2004), probably because of automatic negative emotional responses generated by conflict that once started tend to continue via negative reciprocity,

addition to all the negative consequences of victimhood, experience menacing lack of power and threat to their self-image while perpetrators experience threat to their moral image of respected human beings. Removal of those symbolic threats to opponents' identity seems to be an important prerequisite of intergroup reconciliation (Shnabel & Nadler, 2008). As demonstrated in the context of Jewish–Arab and German–Jewish relations (Shnabel, Nadler, Ulrich, Dovidio, & Carmi, 2009), satisfying different social needs mutually by victims and former perpetrators enhances their willingness to reconcile. A message of social acceptance sent to the perpetrators (Jews or Germans, respectively) and empowerment (or putting it in different words: social face affirmation) to the victimized group (Arabs or Jews) is a social exchange that can satisfy those identity threat concerns.

These findings suggest that in case of intractable conflicts with a long history of aggression, social face concerns and need for respect seem to be especially important both for the victimized group and for the group of former perpetrators, as well.

Implications

Protracted conflicts engage individual and collective identity and self esteem. Self-protection or self-enhancement—both for individuals and social self—become important motives in conflict and these motives tend to foster competitive conflict schemas. Conflict resolution process therefore requires recognition of the need for positive self-image. The research findings suggest that in case of large (intractable) conflicts with a long history of aggression, social face concerns and need for respect seem to be especially important. Those social needs have to be satisfied mutually, what might be especially hard to attain in real-life context.

CONFLICT RESOLUTION AND PERSONALITY

There are good reasons to expect that personality dispositions may play an important role in forming an approach to conflict situation.

Agreeableness and Unconditional Respect for Others

In terms of the Big Five model, agreeableness seems to be the personality trait commonly associated with social functioning in conflict situations. Agreeableness refers to the individual difference in the desire for social harmony and cooperation (Graziano & Eisenberg, 1997). Individuals high in agreeableness seem to be more emotionally responsive toward others, and more prone to help others, even in the absence of typical factors enhancing helping like kinship or empathy (Graziano, Habashi, Sheese, & Tobin, 2007). High-agreeable individuals perceive coercion and power assertion as less acceptable and appropriate than those low in agreeableness. Individuals low in agreeableness perceive conflicts as more protracted than those high in agreeableness, and they derogate their opponents to the higher extent (Graziano, Jensen-Campbell, & Hair, 1996). As suggested by developmental psychologists, the emergence of agreeableness may origin from attempts at controlling frustration and anger in social situations (Ahadi & Rothbart, 1994). Agreeableness (together with extraversion) has been found to affect success in distributive negotiations, that is, in negotiations which aim at deciding how to distribute a fixed resource that cannot be expanded (Barry & Friedman, 1998). Individuals high in agreeableness thanks to their higher negotiating abilities may also be more successful in integrative negotiations, aimed at finding a "win–win" solution (Amanatullah, Morris, & Curhan, 2008).

Another personality characteristic, which may play an important role in conflict situations is unconditional respect for persons regardless of their status, power, group membership or personal achievements. The unconditional respect is a general orientation toward others as morally equal human beings that holds across different social interactions. In the context of intergroup conflict, unconditional respect as an individual-level variable attenuates negative behavioral tendencies toward conflicted out-groups (Lallje, Tam, Hewstone, Laham, & Lee, 2009). Those, who tend to respect others regardless of their position, are also less prone to prefer avoidance and aggressive actions against out-group in conflict, even if out-group is perceived as threatening (as in the case of Protestants and Catholics in Northern Ireland).

Unmitigated Communion

Unmitigated communion is a more extreme form of agreeableness and refers to "a focus on others to the exclusion of the self" (Fritz & Helgeson, 1998, p. 121). Individuals focusing on others to the point of self-neglect were shown to view themselves in a negative way and to have external standards of self-evaluation (Helgeson & Fritz, 1998). Unmitigated communion as a personality construct captures therefore ego-defensiveness and anxiety concerning social image and one's own worth in the eyes of partners of social interactions. In the context of conflict resolution, unmitigated communion results in conceding, when reciprocity would be a more appropriate response. These unnecessary concessions hinder integrative negotiations, as they stop negotiators from creating added economic value, although may still keep opponents satisfied about the interaction itself. Interestingly, these effects were observed even among business executives (Amanatullah et al., 2008).

Social Value Orientation

Social values defined as individuals' preferences for a particular social outcome (McClintock, 1972) have been traditionally in the center of conflict resolution research since the publication of Deutsch's classical work in 1973. Social value orientation theory is based on the assumption that individuals differ in their preferences concerning the well-being of both sides of the conflict (Messick & McClintock, 1968). Research has focused on three distinct social orientations: competitive orientation, that is a tendency to maximize one's advantage over others, prosocial orientation, a tendency to maximize joint gains, and individualistic orientation, a tendency to care for one's own gains, with little regard for others. It has been found that prosocial orientation encourages cooperation in social dilemmas to a higher extent than individualistic or competitive orientation with the last encouraging most defection and least cooperation.

Presumably, the effect of social values on behavior is driven by certain cognitive "transformations" of dilemmas made by individuals with different social orientations (Kelley & Thibaut, 1978). The persons with different social orientations tend to develop different construal of the conflict situations (Simpson, 2004). For example, the prisoner dilemma, a game commonly used in social value orientation research, tends to be perceived by individualists in the competitive terms. Consequently, they are significantly less likely to cooperate. Persons with prosocial orientation, on the other hand, were demonstrated to interpret the same standard prisoner dilemma as the assurance dilemma and responded with cooperation rather than defection. Importantly, according to recent integrative model of social value orientation (Van Lange, 1999), prosocial orientation enhances not only interest in joint outcomes, but also in equality of those outcomes. This interest in equality of outcomes prevents prosocials from making unnecessarily high concessions and from being exploited by others, as they actually reciprocate cooperation to the extent of perceived cooperation of the other side. This idea seems to be in line with the theorizing on different effects of prosocial or caring relational orientation and unmitigated communion on social functioning in conflicts.

More importantly, a number of studies suggest that social orientations can be modified by situational cues (Grzelak, 1994). Framing the conflict as competitive or cooperative, even on the implicit level, shapes the responses toward competition or cooperation respectively. For example, individuals playing the prisoners dilemma game choose different strategies depending on the name of the game (used as cognitive priming). When playing Wall Street Game (competitive prime) they choose the defection over cooperation much more often than in situations when the same game was called the Community Game (cooperative prime) (Kay & Ross, 2003). The effects of situational cues on social behavior are qualified by self-concept salience (Smeesters, Yzerbyt, Corneille, & Warlop, 2009). High chronic accessibility or recent activation of self-concept regarding social value orientation (either prosocial or proself) mitigates the effects of situational cues framing the conflict. Low consistency on the other hand enhances the impact of situational cues on social behavior.

Difficult Personalities

Sometimes the conflict participants have a special combination of personality traits that interfere strongly with the process of conflict resolution. Hostility, unmitigated overt aggression, passive–aggressive orientation, strong tendency for blaming others, and so on are just the examples of the traits that may ruin negotiations (Sandy, Boardman, & Deutsch, 2006), especially if they characterize the group leaders. But these attributes, like other personality traits, may have different intensity in different situations.

Implications

Personality characteristics such as agreeableness and social value orientation play an important role in cognitive construal of the conflict situations. However, their influence can be modified by situational cues. The degree of the modification depends on stability (internal consistency) of the given trait, and those with high consistency may be relatively resistant to such cues.[*]

GROUP PROCESSES

Conflict dynamics and conflict resolution processes depend on various psychological mechanisms—perceptual, cognitive, emotional, personality, and so on. Group forces affect important characteristics of these mechanisms.

Group Forces

According to Abelson the group forces are different in in-group and intergroup contexts: in the in-group context they foster homogenization, in intergroup polarization (Huckfeldt, Johnson, & Sprague, 2004). The in-group–out-group distinction is a consequence of categorization processes and formation of social identity (Hogg, 2003; Tajfel et al., 1971; Turner, Hogg, Oakes, Reicher, & Wetherell, 1987). In-group homogeneity manifests itself in various ways such as convergence of beliefs (Siegel & Siegel, 1957), shared cognitions (Bar-Tal, 2000a; Tindale, 2003), enhancing similarity in lifestyles, tastes, and so on, formation of common group norms (Sherif, 1936; Turner & Kilian, 1987), liking, solidarity, and in-group favoritism (Tajfel et al., 1973). These group forces may be described as synergic tendencies (ST). On the other hand, negative processes like enhancing differences, disliking, and propensity to negative reactions are likely to appear in the in-group–out-group relations (Turner & Reynolds, 2003) and can be described as antagonistic tendencies (AT). In fact, the negative reactions can be evoked by mere differences between in- and out-group perceived as in-group–out-group contrast (opposite characteristic). Especially, the differences in life styles and values are likely to be interpreted as a symbolic threat for the in-group (Brewer, 2007) engendering prejudice.

One important effect of the in-group–out-group distinction is infrahumanization, a belief that human essence is restricted to the in-group, whereas out-group members possess humanity to a lesser degree (Cortes, Demoulin, Rodrigues, Rodrigues, & Leyens, 2005; Leyens et al., 2001). This distinction is associated also with a sense of moral superiority and distrust. Such attitudes may be exacerbated through deliberate political manipulation of group leaders, but can also appear as a consequence of a harm done to the out-group (Castano & Giner-Sorolla, 2006). The strength of these effects depends on the degree of in-group identification; the differences between in-group and out-group are perceived as bigger by those who more strongly identify with their in-group and perceive intergroup

---

[*] For extensive review of the role of personality in conflict dynamics and conflict resolution see Sandy, Boardman, and Deutsch (2006).

conflict as more intense (Riketta, 2005). It means that factors that reinforce group identity and make it more salient contribute to the increase of the Antagonistic Tendencies.

The Antagonistic Tendencies are likely to facilitate competitive conflict schema while Synergic Tendencies the cooperative one. Conflicts and disagreements in the in-group context generate dissonance and movement toward group consensus by persuasion and changes own position as well as by other means (Matz & Wood, 2005). But the in-group conflicts that are not solved satisfactorily may lead to break up of the group.

Group Norms

The reactions in conflict situations are modified by group norms. For example, in organizations where norms of procedural justice are respected conflicts are more likely to be solved peacefully (Aquino, Tripp, & Bies, 2006). Some group norms may be developed as a result of interaction between groups in conflict: A good illustration of this process was provided by Reicher (1996) who described the formation of the group norms during conflict between a crowd and police, showing that the behavior of each side contributed to the formation of the confrontational norms of the other side. Groups can also espouse norms that foster cooperative approach do conflict situations, like for example the norms of deliberative debate (Gutmann & Thompson, 1996; Reykowski, 2006).

The behavior in conflict situations depends not only on the norms that have been developed in particular groups or environments but also on more general norms functioning in the given culture and subculture. Cultures differ with respect to the norms concerning conflict resolution especially collectivist and individualist cultures (Jetten, McAuliffe, Horsney, & Hogg, 2006; Tinsley, 2001). In collectivist cultures various norms support harmony-enhancing strategies in in-group conflicts, but competition is the appropriate reaction in the relations with an out-group. In individualist cultures the difference between norms for the in-group and out-group relations is less pronounced (Triandis & Trafimow, 2003). It might be related to the fact that individualists are less likely to develop highly cohesive groups. Nevertheless, in-group–out-group categorization is a universal phenomenon and its effects are universal. There are also important cultural differences in norms inhibiting conflicts (like politeness) or regulating expression of anger and hostility (Cohen, Vandello, Puente, & Rantilla, 1999). In the cultures of honor, the norm of retaliation shapes behavior of those in conflict (Nisbett & Cohen, 1996).

Group Forces and Conflict Resolution

All that we know about the role of group forces seem to indicate that social category differentiation provides the fault lines in any social system (Brewer, 2007). There are good reasons to assume therefore that elimination and modification of this "fault line" could be one of the main factors in conflict prevention and conflict resolution. There are various theoretical propositions concerning the preconditions of such modification. One such proposition is the theory of intergroup contact originally formulated by Allport (1954) and recently reformulated by Pettigrew (Brown, Eller, Leeds, & Stace, 2006; Eller & Abrams, 2004; Pettigrew & Tropp, 2008). Although, the intergroup contact may, under certain conditions, help in reduction of prejudice, it is less likely that it might seriously contribute to the resolution of the more advanced conflicts. In the advanced or acute conflicts, especially in the intractable ones, the contact between hostile groups is likely to become an occasion for exchange of hostilities. It may actually intensify the conflict instead of reducing it.

Another theoretical proposition stresses the role of modification the dominant social categorization. According to the common in-group identity model (CIIM) recategorization that leads to application a common in-group category for groups that perceive themselves as separate units reduces out-group bias and increases willingness to engage in intergroup contact. There is a number of experimental research demonstrating this effect (Dovidio, Gaertner, & Saguy, 2007; Gomez, Dovidio, Huici, Gaertner, & Cuadrado, 2008).

The basic implications of the model concern the changes in mutual attitudes between members of opposite group while they become the members of the common group. It should have important bearings on conflict resolution processes. Especially, creating a basis for some kind of superordinate identity may reduce intensity of the negative emotions and facilitate Synergic Tendencies helping in search for the means of the conflict resolution.

In many situations, however, the formation of the common, superordinate identities may be difficult because people do not want to replace the existing identify with a new one, especially if there is a strong social support for the given identity. To deal with this problem, Dovidio et al. (2007) suggest creating the "dual identity": "If people continue to regard themselves as members of different groups but at the same time part of the same superordinate entity, intergroup relations between these subgroups will be more positive ..." (p. 301). While the authors provide some empirical support for this contention there are also various data indicating that the dual identity may engender some problems. Especially, the common identity tends to be rejected when people believe that it may interfere with their ability to live by their particular social identity. The illustration of such rejection is provided in the study of Sindic and Reicher (2008) who found that the Scottish subjects who felt that British identity undermines their ability to enact their norms, values and priorities, manifested rather strong separatist attitudes, that is the rejection of the superordinate identity.

Another limitation of the dual identity approach is pointed out by Wenzel, Mummendey, and Waldzus (2007). On the basis of their in-group projection model (Mummendey & Wendzel, 1999), they claim that formation of dual identity implies a development a common standard of comparison and tends to initiate competition over entitlements of each of the group: which group is more prototypical and therefore more important, and deserves more privileges. Hence, unlike the common in-group identity model, the in-group projection model argues that mere sharing of superordinate identity is not sufficient for the development of positive intergroup relations. For positive relations, it is necessary to develop the common understanding of the superordinate identity that might legitimize is the basis for cognitive construal of conflict situation in cooperative terms, that is, activation of the cooperative conflict schema (Sherif, 1958).

Attitudes and Norms

Cooperative conflict schema can support attitudes and norms that foster partnership relations with the other side. One such attitude is mutual respect. The attitude of respect inhibits the behavior that might be perceived as offending to the other side or as disregard for partners' interests and values. Due to the fact that in many or most conflicts the protection of self-identity and self-regard is the major goal, the attitude of respect may reduce serious obstacles to getting agreements. The significance of such an approach is not obvious for people involved in conflicts. Many of them assume that the "natural" behavior in conflicts is demonstration of own strength and superiority *vis-à-vis* the opponent. For conflict resolution such behavior may be dysfunctional.

The norm of partnership requires also some degree of perspective taking—an effort at looking at the conflict situation also from the perspective of the other side. Perspective taking is a precondition of effective communication. But it should not be equated with unmitigated communion, that is, with devaluation of own goals. It is rather an orientation on coordination of the values and interests of both sides.[*]

Importance of Rational Analysis of the Conflict Situation

Coordination of divergent interests and priorities, especially in deep sited conflicts, is a very difficult task requiring rational analysis based on extensive knowledge and advanced cognitive competences, that is, it requires a high level of cognitive functioning. The level of cognitive functioning is related to people's approach to conflict situation: competitive orientation, unlike the cooperative one, tends to reduce problem solving abilities, evokes close-mindedness, and egocentric bias (Carnevale & Probst, 1998).

The impairment of the cognitive functioning may also result from arousal of strong emotions such as fear, anger, and hate. Such emotions are likely to be evoked by salient memories of the past injustices, harms, and cruelties. The events that contribute to arousal of the strong negative emotions (such as for example, reminding the adversaries about their past negative actions) may inhibit process of conflict resolutions. But past injuries are a very important part of the group's experience and suppressing them is both morally wrong and harmful for the group identity. In fact, satisfactory solutions of conflicts can not be achieved if the past injustices are ignored. It does not mean however, that the memories of the past should be dealt with at the same time as the current problems. It seems more feasible to treat the conflict resolution as the two-stage process: the first stage focused on problem solving, dealing primarily with the current problems and with the future, and the

---

[*] In psychological literature various procedures aimed at the change of attitudes and norms of conflict participants have been described. One of the best known, the Interactive Problem-Solving Workshops, was developed by H. Kelman (Kelman & Fisher, 2003).

second stage when painful experience and reconciliation is the main issue.[*] As they may interfere with each other, separating these two stages may be crucial for successful conflict resolution. Moreover, successful solution of the major current problems may actually help in future reconciliation.

The Final Remark

In most of the conflict situations conflict resolution is a desirable and legitimate goal. But it should not be confused with an appeasement. In some conflicts, when the basic humane and moral values are at stake, the necessity of using superior force can be unavoidable as it was during World War II.

REFERENCES

Ahadi, S. A., & Rothbart, M. K. (1994). Temperament, development, and the Big Five. In W. C. F. Halverson, G. A. Kohnstamm, & R. P. Martin (Eds.), *The developing structure of temperament and personality from infancy to adulthood* (pp. 189–208). Hillsdale, NJ: Erlbaum.

Allport, G. W. (1954). *The nature of prejudice.* Garden City, NY: Doubleday Anchor.

Amanatullah, E. T., Morris, M., & Curhan, J. R. (2008). Negotiators who give too much: unmitigated communion, relational anxieties, and economic costs in distributive and integrative bargaining. *Journal of Personality and Social Psychology*, 95, 723–738.

Aquino, K., Tripp, T. M., & Bies, R. J. (2006). Getting even or moving on? Power, procedural justice, and types of offense as predictors of revenge, forgiveness, reconciliation, and avoidance in organizations. *Journal of Applied Psychology*, 91, 653–668.

Atran, S., & Axelrod, R. (2008). Reframing sacred values. *Negotiation Journal*, 24, 221–246.

Bargh, J. A. (1994). The four horsemen of automaticity: Awareness, efficiency, intention, and control in social cognition. In R. S. Wyer, Jr. & T. K. Srull (Eds.), *Handbook of social cognition* (2nd ed., pp. 1–40). Hillsdale, NJ: Erlbaum.

Barry, B., & Friedman, R. (1998). Bargainer characteristics in distributive and integrative negotiation. *Journal of Personality and Social Psychology*, 74, 345–359.

Bar-Tal, D. (1998). Societal beliefs in times of intractable conflict: The Israeli case. *International Journal of Conflict Management*, 9, 22–50.

Bar-Tal, D. (2000a). *Shared beliefs in a society.* Thousand Oaks, CA: Sage.

Bar-Tal, D. (2000b). From intractable conflict through conflict resolution to reconciliation: Psychological analysis. *Political Psychology*, 21, 351–365.

Bar-Tal, D. (2007). Socio-psychological foundations of intractable conflicts. *American Behavioral Scientist*, 50, 1430–1453.

Bar-Tal, D., & Halperin, E. (2009). Overcoming psychological barriers to peace process: The influence of beliefs about losses. In M. Mikulincer & P. R. Shaver (Eds.), *Prosocial motives, emotions and behaviors: The better angels of our nature* (pp. 431–448). Washington, DC: American Psychological Association Press.

Bar-Tal, D., Kruglanski, A. W., & Klar, Y. (1989). Conflict termination: An epistemological analysis of international cases. *Political Psychology*, 10, 233–255.

Bar-Tal, D., & Sharvit, K. (2008). Psychological foundations of Israeli Jews' reactions to Al Aqsa Intifada: The role of the threatening transitional context. In V. M. Esses & R. Vernon (Eds.), *Explaining the breakdown of ethnic relations: Why neighbors kill* (pp. 147–170). Oxford: Blackwell.

---

[*] The problems of reconciliation are discussed in Chapter 12.

Biruski, D. C., & Ajducovic, D. (2009). Intergroup reconciliation or social reconstruction: A scale for measuring social recovery after the war. *Paper presented at Small Group Meeting of European Association of Social Psychology*, September 7–10, 2009, Herzliya.

Brewer, M. B. (2007). The social psychology of intergroup relations: Social categorization, ingroup bias, and outgroup prejudice. In A. W. Kruglanski & E. T. Higgins (Eds.), *Social psychology* (pp. 695–715). New York: Guilford Press.

Brown, R., & Čehajić, S. (2008). Dealing with the past and facing the future: Mediators of the effects of collective guilt and shame in Bosnia and Herzegovina. *European Journal of Social Psychology*, 38, 669–684.

Brown, R., Eller, A., Leeds, S., & Stace, K. (2006). Intergroup contact and intergroup attitudes: A longitudinal study. *European Journal of Social Psychology*, 37, 692–703.

Brown, R., Gonzalez, R., Zagefka, H., Manzi, J., & Čehajić, S. (2008). Nuestra Culpa: Collective guilt and shame as predictors of reparation for historical wrongdoing. *Journal of Personality and Social Psychology*, 94, 75–90.

Callister, R. R., & Wall, J. A. Jr., (2001). Conflict across organizational boundaries: Managed care organizations versus health care providers. *Journal of Applied Psychology*, 86, 754–763.

Carnevale, P. J., & Probst, T. M. (1998). Social values and social conflicts in creative problem solving and categorization. *Journal of Personality and Social Psychology*, 74, 1300–1309.

Castano, E., & Giner-Sorolla, R. (2006). Not quite human: Infrahumanization in response to responsibility for intergroup killing. *Journal of Personality and Social Psychology*, 90, 804–818.

Chong, D., & Druckman, J. N. (2007). Framing public opinions in competitive democracies. *American Political Science Review*, 101, 637–655.

Cohen, D., Nisbett, R. E., Bowdle, B. F., & Schwarz, N. (1996). Insult, aggression, and the southern culture of honor: an "experimental ethnography". *Journal of Personality and Social Psychology*, 70, 945–960.

Cohen, D., Vandello, J., Puente, S., & Rantilla, A. (1999). "When you call me that, smile!" how norms for politeness, interaction styles, and aggression work together in southern culture. *Social Psychology Quarterly*, 62, 257–275.

Coleman, P. T. (2006a). Power and conflict. In M. Deutsch, P. T. Coleman, & E. C. Marcus (Eds.), *The handbook of conflict resolution* (pp. 120–143). San Francisco: Jossey-Bass.

Coleman, P. T. (2006b). Intractable conflict. In M. Deutsch, P. T. Coleman, & E. C. Marcus (Eds.), *The handbook of conflict resolution* (pp. 533–559). San Francisco: Jossey-Bass.

Coleman, P. T., & Deutsch, M. (2006). Some guidelines for developing a creative approach to conflict. In M. Deutsch, P. T. Coleman, & E. C. Marcus (Eds.), *The handbook of conflict resolution* (pp. 402–413). San Francisco: Jossey-Bass.

Cortes, B. P., Demoulin, S., Rodrigues, R. T., Rodrigues, A. P., & Leyens, J. P. (2005). Infrahumanization or familiarity? Attribution of uniquely human emotions to the self, the ingroup, and the outgroup. *Personality and Social Psychology Bulletin*, 31, 243–253.

De Dreu, C. K. W., Koole, S., & Steinel, W. (2000). Unfixing the fixed pie: A motivated information-processing approach to integrative negotiation. *Journal of Personality and Social Psychology*, 79, 975–987.

De Dreu, C. K. W., Nijstad, B. A., & van Knippenberg, D. (2008). Motivated information processing in group judgment and decision making. *Personality and Social Psychology Review*, 12, 22–49.

De Dreu, C. K. W., & van Knippenberg, D. (2005). The possessive self as a barrier to conflict resolution: Effects of mere ownership, process accountability, and self-concept clarity on competitive cognitions and behavior. *Journal of Personality and Social Psychology*, 89, 345–357.

De Dreu, C. K. W., & Weingart, L. R. (2003). Task versus relationship conflict, team performance and team member satisfaction: A meta-analysis. *Journal of Applied Psychology*,
88, 741–749.

Deutsch, M. (1962). Cooperation and trust: Some theoretical notes. In M. Jones (Ed.),
Nebraska symposium on motivation (pp. 275–319). Lincoln, NE: University of
Nebraska Press.

Deutsch, M. (1973). *The resolution of conflict: Constructive and destructive processes*.
New Haven, CT: Yale University Press.

Dovidio, J. F., Gaertner, S. L., & Saguy, T. (2007). Another view of "we": Majority and
minority group perspectives on a common ingroup identity. *European Review of
Social Psychology*, *18*, 296–330.

Dunlop, J. T. (1983). The negotiation alternative in dispute resolution. *Villanova Law
Review*, *29*, 1421–1448.

Eller, A., & Abrams, D. (2004). Come together: Longitudinal comparisons of Pettigrew's
reformulated intergroup contact model and the common ingroup identity model
in Anglo-French and Mexican-American context. *European Journal of Social
Psychology*, *34*, 229–256.

Fabiansson, E. C., & Denson, T. F. (in press). Anger regulation in negotiations. In C. Quin
& S. Tawse (Eds.), *Handbook of aggressive behavior research*. Hauppauge, NY: Nova
Science Publishers.

Feldman, S., & Zaller, J. (1992). The political culture of ambivalence: Ideological responses
to the welfare state. *American Journal of Political Science*, *36*, 268–307.

Fischer, A. H., & Roseman, I. J. (2007). Beat them or ban them: The characteristics and
social functions of anger and contempt. *Journal of Personality and Social Psychology*,
93, 103–115.

Fisher, R. J. (2006). Intergroup conflict. In M. Deutsch, P. T. Coleman, & E. C. Marcus
(Eds.), *The handbook of conflict resolution* (pp. 176–196). San Francisco: Jossey-Bass.

Fiske, A. P., & Tetlock, P. E. (1997). Taboo trade-offs: Reactions to transactions that transgress the spheres of justice. *Political Psychology*, *18*(2), 255–298.

Friedman, R., Anderson, C., Brett, J., Olekalns, M., Goates, N., & Lisco, C. C. (2004). The
positive and negative effects of anger on dispute resolution: Evidence from electronically mediated disputes. *Journal of Applied Psychology*, *89*, 368–376.

Fritz, H. L., & Helgeson, V. S. (1998). Distinctions of unmitigated communion from
communion: Self-neglect and over involvement with others. *Journal of Personality
and Social Psychology*, *75*, 121–140.

Fu, H. J., Morris, M., Sau-lai, L., Chao, M., Chi-yue, C., & Ying-yi, H. (2007). Epistemic
motives and cultural conformity: Need for closure, culture, and context as determinants
of conflict judgments. *Journal of Personality and Social Psychology*, *92*, 191–207.

Gilbert, D. T., Fiske, S. T., & Lindzey, G. (Eds.). (1998). *The handbook of social psychology*.
Boston: McGraw-Hill.

Goffman, E. (1967). *Interaction ritual: Essays in face-to-face behavior*. Hawthorne, NY:
Aldine de Gruyter.

Golec, A., & Federico, C. (2004). Understanding responses to political conflict: Interactive
effects of the need for closure and salient conflict schemas. *Journal of Personality
and Social Psychology*, *87*, 750–762.

Golec, A., Federico, C., Cislak, A., & Dial, J. (2004). Need for closure, national attachment,
and attitudes toward international conflict: Distinguishing the roles of patriotism and
nationalism. *Advances in Psychology Research*, *33*, 231–251.

Golec de Zavala, A. (2006). Cognitive and motivational factors underlying individual
responses to political conflicts. In A. Golec de Zavala & K. Skarzynska (Eds.),
Understanding social change: political psychology in Poland (pp. 13–32). Hauppauge,
NY: Nova Science Publishers.

Golec de Zavala, A., Cislak, A., & Wesolowska, E. (2010). Political conservatism, need for cognitive closure and inter-group hostility. *Political Psychology*, *31*, 521–541.

Golec de Zavala, A., Federico, C., Cislak, A., & Sigger, J. (2008). Need for closure and coercion in inter-group conflicts: Experimental evidence for the mitigating effect of accessible conflict schemas. *European Journal of Social Psychology*, *38*, 84–105.

Gomez, A., Dovidio, J. F., Huici, C., Gaertner, S. L., & Cuadrado, I. (2008). The other side of we: When outgroup members express common identity. *Personality and Social Psychology Bulletin*, *34*(12), 1613–1626.

Graziano, W. G., & Eisenberg, N. (1997). Agreeableness: A dimension of personality. In R. Hogan, J. Johnson, & S. Briggs (Eds.), *Handbook of personality psychology* (pp. 767–793). San Diego: Academic Press.

Graziano, W. G., Habashi, M. M., Sheese, B. E., & Tobin, R. M. (2007). Agreeableness, empathy, and helping: A person X situation perspective. *Journal of Personality and Social Psychology*, *93*, 583–599.

Graziano, W. G., Jensen-Campbell, L. A., & Hair, E. C. (1996). Perceiving interpersonal conflict and reacting to it: The case for agreeableness. *Journal of Personality and Social Psychology*, *70*, 820–835.

Grzelak, J. (1994). Conflict and cooperation. Motivational basis. In P. Bertelson, P. Eelen, & G. d'Ydewalle (Eds.), *International perspectives on psychological science, II: The state of the art* (Vol. 2, pp. 249–264). New York: Erlbaum.

Gutmann, A., & Thompson, D. (1996). *Democracy and disagreement*. Cambridge, MA: The Belknap Press of Harvard University Press.

Halperin, E., & Bar-Tal, D. (2007). The influence of Prime Minister Ehud Barak on Israeli public opinion: July 2000–February 2001. *Conflict & Communication Online*, *6*, 1–18.

Halperin, E., Russell, G. A., Dweck, C., & Gross, J. J. (2009). Anger, hatred, and the quest for peace: Prospective emotion regulation in the Israeli-Palestinian conflict. *Paper presented at the annual meeting of ISPP*, July 14–17, 2009, Dublin.

Helgeson, V. S., & Fritz, H. L. (1998). A theory of unmitigated communion. *Personality and Social Psychology Review*, *2*, 173–183.

Hogg, M. A. (2003). Social categorization, depersonalization, and group behavior. In M. A. Hogg, & R. S. Tindale (Eds.), *Group processes* (pp. 56–85). Malden, MA: Blackwell.

Huckfeldt, R., Johnson, P. E., & Sprague, J. (2004). *Political disagreement*. Cambridge, UK: Cambridge University Press.

Iyer, A., Schmader, T., & Lickel, B. (2007). Why individuals protest the perceived transgressions of their country: The role of anger, shame, and guilt. *Personality and Social Psychology Bulletin*, *33*, 572–587.

Jarymowicz, M., & Bar-Tal, D. (2006). The dominance of fear over hope in the life of individuals and collectives. *European Journal of Social Psychology*, *36*, 367–392.

Jetten, J., McAuliffe, B. J., Horsney, M. J., & Hogg, M. A. (2006). Differentiation between and within groups: The influence of individualist and collectivist group norms. *European Journal of Social Psychology*, *36*, 825–844.

Jost, J. T., Glaser, J., Kruglanski, A. W., & Sulloway, F. (2003). Political conservatism as motivated social cognition. *Psychological Bulletin*, *129*, 339–375.

Kay, A. C., & Ross, L. (2003). The perceptual push: The interplay of implicit cues and explicit situational construal in the Prisoner's Dilemma. *Journal of Experimental Social Psychology*, *39*, 634–643.

Kelley, H. H., & Thibaut, J. W. (1978). *Interpersonal relations: A theory of interdependence*. New York: Wiley.

Kelman, H. C., & Fisher, R. J. (2003). Conflict analysis and resolution. In D. O. Sears, L. Huddy, & R. Jervis (Eds.), *Oxford handbook of political psychology* (pp. 315–356). Oxford: Oxford University Press.

Kinder, D. R. (1998). Opinion and action in the realm of politics. In D. T. Gibert, S. T. Fiske, & G. Lindzey (Eds.), *The handbook of social psychology* (pp. 778–867). Boston: McGraw-Hill.

Krämer, U. M., Jansma, H., Tempelmann, C., & Münte, T. F. (2007). Tit-for-tat: The neural basis of reactive aggression. *Neuroimage, 38,* 203–211.

Lallje, M., Tam, T., Hewstone, M., Laham, S., & Lee, J. (2009). Unconditional respect for persons and the prediction of intergroup action tendencies. *European Journal of Social Psychology, 39,* 666–683.

Leach, C. W., Iyer, A., & Pedersen, A. (2007). Angry opposition to government redress: When the structurally advantaged perceive themselves as relatively deprived. *British Journal of Social Psychology, 46,* 191–204.

Leyens, J. P., Rodrigues-Perez, A., Rodrigues-Torres, R., Gaunt, R., Paladino, M. P., Vaes, J. et al. (2001). Psychological essentialism and the differential attribution of uniquely human emotions to ingroup and outgroup. *European Journal of Social Psychology, 31,* 395–411.

Lickel, B., Miller, N., Stenstrom, D. M., Denson, T. F., & Schmader, T. (2006). Vicarious retribution: The role of collective blame in intergroup aggression. *Personality and Social Psychology Review, 10,* 372–390.

Mac Ginty, R., & du Toit, P. (2007). A disparity of esteem: Relative group status in Northern Ireland after the Belfast agreement. *Political Psychology, 28,* 13–32.

Marcus, E. C. (2006). Change and conflict: Motivation, resistance and commitment. In M. Deutsch, P. T. Coleman, & E. C. Marcus (Eds.), *The handbook of conflict resolution* (pp. 436–454). San Francisco: Jossey-Bass.

Matz, D., & Wood, W. (2005). Cognitive dissonance in groups. The consequences of disagreement. *Journal of Personality and Social Psychology, 88,* 22–37.

McCann, S. (2008). Societal threat, authoritarianism, conservatism, and US state death penalty sentencing (1977–2004). *Journal of Personality and Social Psychology, 94,* 913–923.

McClintock, C. G. (1972). Social motivation—A set of propositions. *Behavioral Science, 17,* 438–454.

Messick, D. M., & McClintock, C. G. (1968). Motivational bases of choice in experimental games. *Journal of Experimental Social Psychology, 4,* 1–25.

Mummendey, A., & Wenzel, M. (1999). Social discrimination and tolerance in intergroup relations: Reactions to intergroup difference. *Personality and Social Psychology Review, 3,* 158–174.

Nisbett, R. E. & Cohen, D. (1996). *Culture of honor: The psychology of violence in the South.* New York: Perseus Publishing.

Nowak, M. A., Page, K. M., & Sigmund, K. (2000). Fairness versus reason in the ultimatum game. *Science, 289,* 1773–1775.

Pettigrew, T. F., & Tropp, L. R. (2008). How does intergroup contact reduce prejudice? Meta-analytic test of three mediators. *European Journal of Social Psychology, 38,* 922–934.

Pillutla, M. M., & Murnighan, J. K. (1996). Unfairness, anger, and spite: Emotional rejections of ultimatum offers. *Organizational Behavior & Human Decision Processes, 68,* 208–224.

Pruitt, D. G., & Carnevale, P. J. (1982). The development of integrative agreements. In P. Derlega & J. Grzelak (Eds.), *Cooperative and helping behavior: Theories and research* (pp. 151–181). New York: Academic Press.

Pyszczynski, T., Rothschild, Z., & Abdollahi, A. (2008). Terror, violence, and hope for peace: A terror management perspective. *Current Directions in Psychological Science, 17,* 318–322.

Reicher, S. D. (1996). The Battle of Westminster: Developing the social identity model of crowd behavior in order to explain the initiation and development of collective conflict. *European Journal of Social Psychology, 26,* 115–134.

Reykowski, J. (1993). Resolving large-scale political conflict: The case of Round Table negotiations in Poland. In S. Worchel, & J. A. Simpson (Eds.), *Conflict between people and groups* (pp. 214–232). Chicago: Nelson-Hall.

Reykowski, J. (2006). Deliberative democracy and "human nature": An empirical approach. *Political Psychology, 27,* 323–346.

Riketta, M. (2005). Cognitive differentiation between self, ingroup, and outgroup: The roles of identification and perceived intergroup conflict. *European Journal of Social Psychology, 35,* 97–106.

Rosenberg, S. (2003). Restructuring the concept of deliberation. *Paper presented at the annual meeting of the American Political Science Association*, September 6, 2003, Philadelphia.

Sandy, S. V., Boardman, S. K., & Deutsch, M. (2006). Personality and conflict. In M. Deutsch, P. T. Coleman, & E. C. Marcus (Eds.), *The handbook of conflict resolution* (pp. 331–366). San Francisco: Jossey-Bass.

Sedikides, C., Herbst, K. C., Hardin, D. P., & Dardis, G. J. (2002). Accountability as a deterrent to self-enhancement: The search for mechanisms. *Journal of Personality and Social Psychology, 83,* 592–605.

Shah, J., Kruglanski, A. W., & Thompson, E. (1998). Membership has its (epistemic) rewards: Need for closure effects on ingroup bias. *Journal of Personality and Social Psychology, 75,* 383–393.

Sherif, M. (1936). *The psychology of social norms.* New York: Harper.

Sherif, M. (1958). Superordinate goal in the reduction of intergroup conflicts. *American Journal of Sociology, 63,* 349–356.

Shnabel, N., & Nadler, A. (2008). A needs-based model of reconciliation: Satisfying the differential emotional needs of victim and perpetrator as a key to promoting reconciliation. *Journal of Personality and Social Psychology, 94,* 116–132.

Shnabel, N., Nadler, A., Ulrich, J., Dovidio, J. F., & Carmi, D. (2009). Promoting reconciliation through the satisfaction of the emotional needs of victimized and perpetrating group members: The needs-based model of reconciliation. *Personality and Social Psychology Bulletin, 35,* 1021–1030.

Siegel, E., & Siegel, S. (1957). Reference groups, membership groups, and attitude change. *Journal of Abnormal and Social Psychology, 55,* 360–364.

Simon, B., & Stuermer, S. E. (2003). Respect for group members: Intragroup determinants of collective identification and group-serving behaviour. *Personality and Social Psychology Bulletin, 29,* 183–193.

Simpson, B. (2004). Social values, subjective transformations, and cooperation in social dilemmas. *Social Psychology Quarterly, 67,* 385–395.

Sindic, D., & Reicher, S. (2008). "Our way of life is worth defending": Testing a model of attitudes towards superordinate group membership through study of Scots' attitudes toward Britain. *European Journal of Social Psychology, 39,* 114–129.

Smeesters, D., Yzerbyt, V. Y., Corneille, O., & Warlop, L. (2009). When do primes prime? The moderating role of the self-concept in individuals' susceptibility to priming effects on social behavior. *Journal of Experimental Social Psychology, 45,* 211–216.

Suedfeld, P., & Tetlock, P. (1977). Integrative complexity of communications in international crises. *Journal of Conflict Resolution, 21,* 169–184.

Tajfel, H., Billig, M. G., Bundy, R., & Flament, C. (1971). Social categorization and intergroup behavior. *European Journal of Social Psychology, 1*, 149–178.

Tetlock, P. E., Kristerl, O. V., Elson, S. B., Green, M. C., & Lerner, J. S. (2000). The psychology of unthinkable: Taboo trade-offs, forbidden base rates, and heretical counterfactuals. *Journal of Personality and Social Psychology, 78*, 853–870.

Thompson, L., Nadler, J., & Lount, Jr., R. B. (2006). Judgmental biases in conflict resolution and how to overcome them. In M. Deutsch, P. T. Coleman, & E. Marcus (Eds.), *Handbook of Conflict Resolution: Theory and Practice* (2nd ed., pp. 243–267). San Francisco, CA: Jossey-Bass.

Tiedens, L. Z. (2001). Anger and advancement versus sadness and subjugation: The effect of negative emotion expressions on social status conferral. *Journal of Personality and Social Psychology, 80*, 86 –94.

Tindale, R. S., Meisenhelder, H. M., Dykema-Engblade, A. A., & Hogg, M. A. (2003). Shared cognition in small groups. In M. A. Hogg & R. S. Tindale (Eds.), *Group processes* (pp. 1–30). Malden, MA: Blackwell.

Tinsley, C. (2001). How negotiators get to yes: Predicting the constellation of strategies used across cultures to negotiate conflict. *Journal of Applied Psychology, 86*, 583–593.

Tjosvold, D. (1998). The cooperative and competitive goal approach to conflict: Accomplishments and challenges. *Applied Psychology: An International Review, 47*, 285–313.

Tjosvold, D., & Sun, H. (2000). Social face in conflict: Effects of affronts to person and position in China. *Group Dynamics: Theory, Research, and Practice, 4*, 259–271.

Triandis, H. C., & Trafimow, D. (2003). Culture and its implications for intergroup behavior. In R. Brown & S. Gaertner (Eds.), *Intergroup processes* (pp. 367–385). Malden, MA: Blackwell.

Turner, J. C., Hogg, M. A., Oakes, P. J., Reicher, S. D., & Wetherell, M. S. (1987). *Rediscovering the social group.* Oxford: Blackwell.

Turner, J. C., & Reynolds, K. J. (2003). The social identity perspective in intergroup relations: Theories, themes, and controversies. In R. Brown & S. Gaertner (Eds.), *Intergroup processes* (pp. 133–152). Malden, MA: Blackwell.

Turner, R. H., & Kilian, L. M. (1987). *Collective behavior.* Englewood Cliffs, NJ: Prentice-Hall.

Van Lange, P. A. M. (1999). The pursuit of joint outcomes and equality in outcomes: An integrative model of social value orientation. *Journal of Personality and Social Psychology, 77*, 337–349.

Webster, D., & Kruglanski, A. W. (1994). Individual differences in need for cognitive closure. *Journal of Personality and Social Psychology, 67*, 1049–1062.

Weingart, L. R., & Olekalns, M. (2004). Communication processes in negotiation: frequencies, sequences, and phases. In M. Gelfand & J. Brett (Eds.), *The handbook of negotiation and culture* (pp. 143–157). Palo Alto, CA: Stanford University Press.

Wenzel, M., Mummendey, A., & Waldzus, S. (2007). Superordinate identities and intergroup conflict: The ingroup projection model. *European Review of Social Psychology, 18*, 331–372.

Wheeler, M. E., & Fiske, S. T. (2005). Controlling racial prejudice: Social-cognitive goals affect amygdala and stereotype activation. *Psychological Science, 16*, 56–63.

Winter, D. G. (2007). The role of motivation, responsibility, and integrative complexity in crisis escalation: Comparative studies of war and peace crises. *Journal of Personality and Social Psychology, 92*, 920–937.

Wojciszke, B., Różycka, J., & Baryła, W. (2009). Belief in life as a zero-sum game: A conviction of losers. Unpublished manuscript, The Warsaw School of Social Sciences and Humanities, Warsaw.

Zafran, A., & Bar-Tal, D. (2002). The dominance of fear over hope in situations of intractable conflict: The Israeli case. *Paper presented at the annual meeting of the International Society of Political Psychology*, July 16–19, 2002, Berlin.

Zuroff, D. C., & Duncan, N. (1999). Self-criticism and conflict resolution in romantic couples. *Canadian Journal of Behavioural Science, 31*, 137–149.

11

Negotiation and Mediation in Intergroup Conflict

DEAN G. PRUITT

*T*he main topic of this chapter is intergroup negotiation or mediation is an essential part of most peace-making. *Negotiation* is communication between two or more parties aimed at reaching an agreement that will ameliorate or settle a conflict between them. *Mediation* is an extension of negotiation in which outsiders assist parties to reach agreement about a conflict they are having. Three other topics closely related to negotiation and mediation will also be discussed: intermediation, back-channel communication, and alternatives to diplomacy.

The analysis mainly applies to macrolevel intergroup conflicts—especially international conflicts and conflicts between governments and insurgents. However, much of the analysis can be extended to groups of any size and importance, including conflicts between ethnic groups, interdepartmental feuds, and even fighting between gangs on a playground. Groups at all levels will be referred to as "parties."

There is much theory and research about negotiation and mediation,[*] but this chapter will only present material that applies to intergroup conflict or has been developed in intergroup settings. The first section of the chapter will be based on experiments in the social psychological tradition. Later sections will mainly draw on theory and case material from the field of international relations.

---

[*] For theory and research on negotiation in general, see: Bazerman, Curhan, Moore, and Valley (2000); Druckman (1994); Fisher and Ury (1991); Gelfand and Brett (2004); Kremenyuk (2002); Lewicki, Saunders, and Barry (2006); Pruitt (1981); Pruitt and Carnevale (1993); and Thompson (2005, 2006). For theory and research on mediation in general, see: Bercovitch (1984); Herrman (2006); Kolb (1983); Kressel (2006); Kressel and Pruitt (1989); Menkel-Meadow, Love, and Schneider (2006); Moore (2003); and Wall and Lynn (1993).

NEGOTIATION BY GROUPS VERSUS INDIVIDUALS

There is a vigorous tradition of laboratory research comparing negotiation between groups with negotiation between individuals. To understand this research, it is first necessary to define three strategies that are often used by negotiators (Pruitt & Carnevale, 1993; Pruitt & Kim, 2004). These are identified separately but often occur in combination: (1) *Contending*, which is aimed at winning the conflict. Contentious tactics include starting with high demands, conceding slowly, threats, and positional commitments. Contending reduces the likelihood of agreement but, if agreement is reached, increases the outcome of the party most employing it; (2) *Yielding*, also called concession making. The purpose of yielding may be to reach an early agreement, keep the other party from leaving the negotiation, repay the other party's past concessions, or gain credit with the other party. Yielding increases the likelihood of agreement but decreases the outcome of the party most employing it; and (3) *Problem solving*, which is aimed at satisfying both parties' needs. Tactics include soliciting and providing information about goals and values and seeking win–win options. Problem solving increases the likelihood of reaching agreement and the joint value of any agreement reached. Furthermore, it is often the best way to provide benefit to one's own side.

Groups tend to be more contentious than individuals, favoring larger demands (Robert & Carnevale, 1977) and harsher tactics (McGillicuddy, Welton, & Pruitt, 1987). Furthermore, identifying the other party as an out-group member leads individuals to be more contentious than they otherwise would be (Troetschel & Hueffmeier, 2007). A possible explanation for these effects is that there is greater social distance between groups than between individuals, encouraging greater greed and distrust (Schopler & Insko, 1992).

Negotiation by Representatives

Groups usually negotiate through representatives, who tend to be more contentious than people negotiating on their own behalf (Druckman, 1994). The latter is probably because representatives are trying to please their constituents and assume that their constituents favor contentious behavior, as is usually the case (Pruitt & Carnevale, 1993). Occasionally, representatives make the opposite assumption, that their constituents favor cooperation, and the effect is reversed with individuals becoming more contentious than groups (Benton & Druckman, 1974).

Research also shows that representatives are more contentious when they: (a) are more accountable to their group, in the sense of having to report back to a group that has power over their outcomes (Druckman, 1994); (b) are more distrusted by their group (Wall, 1975); (c) have lower status in their group (Kogan, Lamm, & Trommsdorff, 1972); and (d) are under group surveillance while they are negotiating (Carnevale, Pruitt, & Britton, 1979). All of these conditions encourage representatives to try harder to please their constituents.

Interestingly, the usual findings on accountability are reversed for collectivists: higher accountability leads to greater cooperation in negotiation (Gelfand & Realo,

1999). This probably reflects collectivists' beliefs that their constituents favor cooperation.

Negotiation by Teams

When groups consist of teams confronting each other across the negotiation table, the research findings are more complicated than those just described. Teams engage in more problem solving than do individuals, exchanging more information about priorities and underlying values, and achieving higher joint benefit (Thompson, Peterson, & Brodt, 1996); yet, at the same time, they appear to retain their contentious orientation (Morgan & Tindale, 2002). This may reflect the diversity of viewpoints usually found in groups, as diversity has been shown to improve group decision making (Behfar, Friedman, & Brett, 2008). Alternatively, it may stem from a division of labor, with some members holding firm to their initial demands while others engage in uninhibited problem solving.

INTERMEDIARIES

Representatives in intergroup negotiation usually act as intermediaries between their constituents and the other side's representatives. They carry messages and present, explain, and often advocate each side's position to the other. Furthermore, as intermediaries, they frequently engage in problem solving, seeking a way to reconcile the interests of both parties so that an agreement can be reached.[*]

Many other roles in the drama of negotiation can be similarly construed. When mediators shuttle between the negotiators on either side, they are acting as intermediaries. So also are the individuals back home to whom negotiators report— their backups. Backups have the dual function of translating the group's wishes into instructions for their negotiator and transmitting messages and advice from their negotiator to the group. In larger organizations, backups may be communicating with further intermediaries who represent departments or offices, who may be communicating with still further intermediaries. Legislators can also be thought of as intermediaries as can ombudsmen, public relations officers, and problem solving workshop attendees.

The various kinds of intermediaries just mentioned differ in many ways. But they have enough in common that a general theory of intermediation is possible. Preliminary ideas for such a theory are presented below.

Why Intermediaries?

Why do intermediaries exist? Why don't the people on both sides simply talk to each other and work out their differences? There are many answers to this question, including the following four.

---

[*] Putnam (1988) calls this a "two-level game": representatives are negotiating with the adversary and also with their constituents. Crump (2006) points out that the party in the middle may instead be negotiating with the other two parties for its own gain. He argues that if the other parties begin to cooperate with each other, the middle party will suffer.

Understanding and Trust   Successful intermediaries get to know the parties on either side of them and develop a trusting working relationship with them. Knowledge means that they can explain each side's complaints, demands, and seemingly hostile actions to the other side in an informed and sympathetic way. That decreases the likelihood of escalation and encourages the concessions and problem solving needed to reach agreement. Trust means that the parties can tell intermediaries about the needs and values underlying their position without fear that the other side will acquire this information and exploit it. Having such information allows intermediaries to develop possible agreements that elude the adversaries. Trust also means that intermediaries can sometimes push the parties to make concessions they would otherwise avoid.

Distance from the Conflict   When two parties come into severe conflict, they often lose perspective. They only see the arguments for their own side and develop distorted, negative views of the other side. Intermediaries usually have more distance from the conflict, allowing them to challenge these views or develop bridging proposals that elude the biased partisans.

Access to Both Sides   When conflict becomes severe, the parties often refuse to meet each other and intermediaries are the only means to an agreement. Disputants may also lack access to each other because of organizational or custom-based barriers, because they do not speak the same language, or because they do not feel safe in the other's presence. Again intermediaries are the answer.

Extraneous Policy Considerations   In organizations of any complexity, communication must go through intermediaries because they are the repositories of policies that may be impacted by the matter under consideration. For example, in diplomacy between the United States and France, the State Department desk officer for France will often be the negotiator or backup (Pruitt, 1964). One of his duties is to ensure that agreements reached in current negotiations do not contradict prior agreements or other US policy regarding France.

The first three answers just given suggest two hypotheses about intermediaries:

Hypothesis 1: The more severe the conflict between two parties, the greater is the need for an intermediary.

Hypothesis 2: The fuller an intermediary's knowledge of and rapport with those parties, the more likely is the conflict to be resolved.

Chains of Intermediaries

Chain theory (Pruitt, 1994, 2003) is useful for understanding intermediation. Intermediaries can be viewed as the center of a three-part communication chain, stretching from a party on one side to a party on the other, as shown by the solid lines in Figure 11.1a. When intermediaries are dealing with other intermediaries, the chains are extended, as shown by the dashed lines in Figure 11.1a. And when organizations or states are negotiating with each other, the configuration is usually one of a branching chain, with a straight chain in the middle and several branches on either end, as shown in Figure 11.1b.

The larger circles in Figure 11.1b represent two organizations that are negotiating with each other. The points in Figure 11.1b represent individuals; those inside the circles are officers of the organizations and those outside (except for point 7) are clients. Points 1 and 2 are the negotiators and 3 and 4 are their backups. The points at the end of the branches are stakeholders whose interests are being represented in the negotiation. For example, assuming that the organizations are governments, point 5 might be a commercial officer who is trying to establish an oil-procurement agreement with another country and 6 might be the lobbyist for a shipping consortium that hopes to transport the oil.° An outside mediator, if used in this negotiation, would be represented by point 7.

Note that in longer chains, there are two or more intermediaries between the stakeholders. The number of intermediaries in a chain is partly a function of the social distance between the stakeholders and partly a function of the polarization in their broader community. If two stakeholders occupy very different worlds, there may be so few people who understand both of them that no single intermediary can be found. Furthermore, if their enmity is so great that the broader community consists of two warring camps, it will be hard to find an intermediary who is trusted by both sides. The solution in both cases is to have a chain of two or more intermediaries. Perhaps two will be enough, with one intermediary talking with each side and the intermediaries talking with each other.

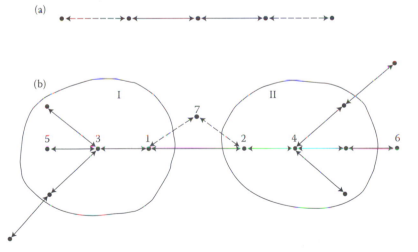

Figure 11.1   Examples of intermediary chains. (a) Three-part (solid lines) and five-part (solid and dashed lines) communication chain. (b) Branching chain involving two organizations (I and II). Points with two arrows are intermediaries. Points with one arrow are stakeholders.

° The people at points 5 and 6 may well be intermediaries for still others not shown in Figure 11.1b. But they are depicted as stakeholders so as to limit the size of Figure 11.1b.

A mutually hurting stalemate can be seen in the period before the opening of the 1993 Oslo talks between Israel and the Palestinian Liberation Organization (PLO) (Pruitt, 1997). The conflict was at a stalemate in that both parties realized that they could not defeat the other. This stalemate was hurting in that Israel became acutely aware of the costs and risks of continuing the conflict with the Palestinians (Rabin was elected president in 1992 on the promise of stopping this conflict) and the PLO had suffered a severe loss of Arab support as a result of backing Iraq in the First Gulf War, and it faced an impending catastrophe of being replaced by Hamas as leader of the Palestinian insurgent movement (Lieberfeld, 2008). At the beginning of 1993, neither side saw a way out of the conflict; but this perception was quickly reversed as a result of progress in the first five (out of 12) sessions of the Oslo talks. These sessions were not actual negotiation since Israel was represented by an unofficial delegation of university professors, but actual negotiation began in the sixth session when Israel sent a delegation of official diplomats.

Pruitt (2005, 2007) has proposed an amendment to ripeness theory, called readiness theory, which looks separately at each party and employs the language of variables rather than necessary conditions. Readiness is a state of mind in a party's leaders. The greater their readiness, the harder they will work to move the situation toward negotiation and the more vigilant they will be for signs of readiness on the other side. Two variables are assumed to combine multiplicatively to produce a state of readiness:

1. Motivation to end the conflict, which can result from pressure by a powerful third party or from any combination of perceived inability to win, perceived cost, or perceived risk associated with the conflict.
2. Optimism about finding a mutually acceptable agreement through negotiation.

Some readiness on both sides is needed for negotiation to begin; the greater the readiness, the more likely negotiation. Rising optimism on both sides is needed to keep a negotiation going.

Motivation to end a conflict sometimes develops out of a shock (Goertz & Diehl, 1997), a sudden reversal of fortunes, such as the PLO's loss of Arab support during the First Gulf War. It can also be fostered by a change in leadership which brings new eyes to bear on the conflict (Mitchell, 2000). An example is the accession of F. W. de Klerk to the presidency of South Africa, which accelerated the movement toward negotiation between the Whites and the Blacks (Lieberfeld, 1999). Third parties can be useful in encouraging the motivation to end a conflict, but their main contribution is to induce optimism.

Optimism is partly based on working trust,° a perception that the other side is motivated to end the conflict and is ready to match our concessions. It is also partly based on a perception that the other negotiator is a valid spokesperson who can commit his or her side. If the other side lacks unity, optimism may fail because there

---

° Kelman (1997) is the originator of this concept.

can be no valid spokesperson. In addition, it is partly based on substantive progress. In severe conflicts, entry into formal negotiation may await development of part or all of a formula°—an agreement in principle that can be fleshed out in the negotiation. In milder conflicts, formula development can await the onset of negotiation.

Ripeness and readiness theory share the belief that negotiation is motivated by the perception that a conflict has become counterproductive. But what about the possibility of mutual gain, for example, building a stronger South Africa through cooperation between whites and blacks? Can that also motivate escape from a conflict? Must motivation always be based on a hurting stalemate? Zartman (2000) maintains that such a "mutually enticing opportunity" can help build momentum once negotiation starts but is seldom if ever the prime mover. An argument for his position is that in severely escalated conflicts, winning becomes such an obsession that little else matters. Hence, rethinking only occurs if winning comes to be seen as impossible or the conflict produces unacceptable costs or risks.

The notion of conflict as obsession can also help explain why a shock or new leadership may be needed to get a peace process going. Only an unexpected catastrophe or the accession of an uncommitted new leader can break through the blinders that maintain such an obsession.

Ripeness and readiness theory are mainly supported by case studies ... not the soundest foundation but a good beginning. Measurement has been a problem in testing these theories, since they concern the thinking of decision makers in conflict. Nevertheless, there are two statistical studies that favor a derivation from these theories, that increased cost of war encourages negotiation. One is a time-series study of the Nagorno–Karabakh War which showed that a cease-fire was negotiated immediately after a sudden dramatic spurt in battlefield fatalities (Mooradian & Druckman, 1999). The other is a role-playing experiment in which participants who saw an internal war as more costly to their country were more likely to opt for negotiation (Ford, 2008).

Ripeness and readiness theory are not designed to predict the outcome of negotiation. But if pushed in that direction, they imply the development of minimal agreements that speak only to the motives that got the parties into negotiation (Druckman & Lyons, 2005). For example, if negotiation is motivated by a perceived stalemate or excessive costs, a simple cease-fire should suffice to solve these problems, as was the case at the end of the Nagorno–Karabakh War. If motivated by the perceived risk that the conflict will escalate to mutual destruction, conflict management should suffice, as it did in the US–USSR negotiations that followed the Cuban Missile Crisis.

Nevertheless, many negotiations end in a deeper resolution of the issues that produced the conflict, for example, changes in the political structure that reduce intergroup inequity. Perhaps in such cases, one or both sides make it clear that they are motivated to end the conflict *but only if* deep changes come about. Insurgents sent such messages loud and clear in the 1993 South African negotiations and the 1998 Northern Ireland negotiations, which produced fundamental political change.

° Zartman (1977) is the originator of this concept.

A valid criticism of ripeness theory and readiness theory is that they say little about the inner workings of groups as they move toward negotiation.

PRENEGOTIATION AND POSTNEGOTIATION

The negotiation process can be divided into three phases: Prenegotiation, negotiation, and postnegotiation. The negotiation phase has already been discussed, but the other two need attention. What we know about them comes mainly from the field of international relations.

Prenegotiation

A number of tasks must be completed before negotiation can get started (Stein, 1989; Zartman, 1996), which include:

1. Building bridges between the parties so that they can communicate.
2. Agreeing on preconditions for entering the negotiation. A ceasefire is common, because most parties refuse to negotiate "with a gun at their head."
3. Identifying the problem—gaining clarity about each side's goals and requirements.
4. Setting the agenda—which issues are to be discussed in what order.
5. Choosing and recruiting participants who can speak for the parties or help in other ways.
6. Deciding whether there will be a mediator and, if so, who it will be.
7. Setting dates and a location.
8. Planning logistics.

In addition, as mentioned earlier, it may be necessary for the parties to develop part or all of a formula—an agreement in principle. Alternatively, formula development can be delayed until the actual negotiation.

The prenegotiation period is sometimes quite extensive and, in cases where there are many complex issues and much distrust, may last a good deal longer than the negotiations themselves. Thus it persisted nine years in Northern Ireland and six years in South Africa. Furthermore, in difficult cases, prenegotiation and negotiation may alternate, as parties who have entered negotiation discover that their plans are inadequate (Stein, 1989).

Postnegotiation

Under what circumstances will an agreement persist and renewed conflict be avoided?

One answer is that an agreement is more likely to persist if it is endorsed by a broad range of subgroups on both sides of the conflict. Otherwise, subgroups that do not support the agreement may become spoilers* and undermine it. One way to

---

* Stedman (2000) is the originator of spoiler theory.

gain broad support is for leaders to negotiate the agreement openly and defend it vigorously in public statements. Another is to hold a referendum in which the agreement is endorsed by a substantial majority of the public, as happened in Northern Ireland.

A second, and probably the most important answer is that the negotiation should include as many as possible of the political and military groups on both sides of the conflict—as broad as possible a "central coalition" (Pruitt, 2005, 2007). It is never feasible to involve all factions ... there are always some holdouts who feel that their side should fight on and not negotiate. But if there are few holdouts or they weakly armed, the participants in the negotiation may be able to isolate them and prevent them from becoming significant spoilers.

In a comparative case study involving 22 peace settlements, Wanis-St. John and Kew (2006) have shown that success also depends on whether representatives of civil society are included in the peace negotiations. A possible explanation is that the groups they represent can then actively promote the settlement in the broader society.

The success of an agreement also depends on whether it satisfies the underlying needs of the parties, especially what Burton (1990) calls their "basic needs." Research on "fraternalistic deprivation" (Brown, 2000) suggests that it is more important to satisfy *group* needs than *individual* needs. Basic group needs include the need for security (the members of our group are safe), identity (our group is able to maintain its self-definition), respect (other groups hold our group in high esteem), equality (our group is treated as well as other groups), and justice (our group receives what is due). Most basic needs can be achieved in several ways, but they cannot easily be compromised or traded for other benefits, because they are likely to reassert themselves at a later time (Avruch, 1998).

In the case of internal wars, agreements are more likely to persist and post-agreement violence to be avoided if a stable and prosperous community develops. This will happen if insurgent groups become legitimate political parties, former fighters are demobilized and integrated into the work force, neighboring states are supportive of the agreement, the economy is sound, political and judicial systems are vigorous and fair, and the previously warring parties are reconciled (Jeong, 2005). To insure such developments, it is often necessary for outside peace keepers and peace builders to enter the country for a time and work with local people (Stedman, 2002).

BACK-CHANNEL COMMUNICATION

Back-channel communication is official, secret communication that is designed to foster successful negotiation (Pruitt, 2008). It contrasts with front-channel communication, which though usually not witnessed by the public, is publicly known to occur. Back-channel communication can be used in three ways: as a prenegotiation device, as an adjunct to front-channel negotiation, or as a substitute for front-channel negotiation. It has been reported in such diverse settings as international conflict (Iklé, 1964), ethno-political conflict (Bartoli, 1999; Wanis-St. John, 2006), labor-management conflict (Walton & McKersie, 1965), and government procurement (Pruitt, 1971).

Back-channel communication takes two forms: direct and indirect. Direct communication involves leaders or other officials conversing informally in out-of-the-way places, such as a private office. Third-party facilitators are sometimes involved (Nan, 2005), but this is not common. Indirect back-channel communication involves intermediaries who shuttle back and forth between officials on both sides. An example of the latter is the communication chain shown in Figure 11.2, which was employed in the prenegotiation period that led up to the negotiations that settled the Northern Ireland conflict. In a chain such as that one, the public may be aware of meetings that are taking place at points in the chain but be unaware that messages and proposals are being passed across the chain.

Communication chains need not be as long as the one shown in Figure 11.2. Indeed they often involve only a single intermediary, who is either an unofficial representative of one side talking to leaders on the other side or a neutral party shuttling between two sets of leaders.

Advantages of Back-channel Communication

Back-channel communication has a number of advantages over front-channel communication.

Flexibility and Future Orientation   One of the big problems with front-channel communication during conflict is its lack of flexibility. Participants have a tendency to make prepared statements and to reiterate demands and arguments, which often leads to deadlock. By contrast, back-channel communication encourages informality and frank discussion of motives and concerns. Needs, goals, values, and fears about the other's proposals can be revealed more readily, along with information about priorities. Hence, the parties are more likely to discover common ground, identify basic needs that must be met in any solution, and develop win–win solutions.

Another problem with front-channel communication is that participants often spend a lot of time rehashing the past and accusing each other of misconduct. This is much less common in back-channels, where participants are more likely to face the future and discuss ways to resolve the conflict. There are four explanations for the improved flexibility and future orientation in back-channel communication: Reduced audience effects, reduced numbers of people interacting, emotional bonding between the participants, and the nonbinding nature of what is said.

The benefits of flexibility and future orientation can sometimes be achieved without full secrecy. For example, publicly known talks can be located at a distance from inquiring constituents, and their time and place can be concealed so that reporters cannot immediately debrief the participants. That is what happened in the 1990 Rome talks that ended the Zimbabwe civil war (Bartoli, 1999).

Political Cover   In intense conflict, when the parties are fighting each other militarily or otherwise, leaders may get into trouble with their constituents or allies if they openly contact the other side and engage in front-channel talks. Political pressure may force cancellation of such talks (Lieberfeld, 2008), and the leaders may risk losing their reputations, their positions, or their lives. Even if talks with the adversary are politically acceptable, a leader may get into trouble if the talks fail (Lieberfeld, 2008). By contrast, back-channel communication provides political cover to leaders who wish to explore the possibility of a negotiated settlement without politically jeopardy. Historical leaders who have moved well ahead of their constituents through back-channel contact with the adversary include Nelson Mandela of the ANC (Mandela, 1994), Gerry Adams of the IRA (Moloney, 2002), Anwar Sadat of Egypt (Stein, 1989), and Yitzhak Rabin of Israel (Lieberfeld, 1999).

Because they are secret, back-channel talks are usually *disavowable* if an outsider finds out about them. The leaders can argue that reports about these talks are faulty or a misinterpretation of innocent events, or that the participants in these talks were not authorized intermediaries. Indirect contacts are easier to keep secret and to disavow than are direct contacts, especially when a chain of several intermediaries is employed.

Cover is also provided when leaders who authorize or engage in back-channel communication continue to make angry public statements and take hostile actions against the adversary. Thus during the time that Gerry Adams was secretly communicating with Britain,° his public statements and those of his colleagues continued to be fiery, and the IRA (on whose Army Council he probably sat) continued its violent campaign (Moloney, 2002).

Lack of Preconditions

Parties in conflict often set preconditions that must be satisfied by the other side before front-channel negotiation can begin, the most common being a cease-fire. However, back-channel communication can occur without satisfying such preconditions. Thus Mandela (1994) reports that front-channel talks between the ANC and the government were scheduled for April 1990, shortly after his release from prison and the legalization of the ANC. But in March, police opened fire on some ANC demonstrators, causing the ANC to cancel these talks. Mandela told President F. W. de Klerk that "he [de Klerk] could not 'talk about negotiations on the one hand and murder our people on the other'" (p. 577). Nevertheless, he "met privately with Mr. de Klerk in Cape Town in order to keep up the momentum for negotiations" (p. 557).

No Acknowledgment of the Other Side's Legitimacy

Front-channel negotiation is sometimes avoided because of fear that it will send the wrong signal—according legitimacy to the adversary or seeming to endorse the adversary's complaints and demands (Spector, 2003). This is especially a problem in internal war, when rebels and the government compete for legitimacy in the eyes of the public and the world. Back-channel talks do not pose this problem, because they are unpublicized.

° The most important segment of the communication chain shown in Figure 11.2 linked Sinn Fein with the British government.

Risks of Back-channel Communication and Their Solution

There are risks associated with back-channel, as opposed to front-channel, communication. One is that leaders are less able to prepare the public for acceptance of the final agreement (Lieberfeld, 2008). Another is that there is a temptation to exclude some crucial players and to fail to address some critical issues, both of which can produce agreements that will fail (Wanis-St. John, 2006). These risks are particularly large when the talks do not end with front-channel negotiations and final agreements are reached without public knowledge, as in the Oslo talks of 1993 that produced the Palestinian Authority. The danger is not in the use of back-channels *per se* but in their exclusive use, which allows an unrepresentative set of parties—a narrow central coalition—to create a controversial and hence fragile agreement (Pruitt, 2008). If this danger can be kept in mind, back-channels can be used to test out the possibility of front-channel negotiation and to assemble negotiating teams that represent a broad enough segment of the political landscape to isolate potential spoilers. The Northern Ireland peace process illustrates this point (Pruitt, 2007).

Stages in Back-channel Communication

In intense conflict, if the parties have developed strongly negative beliefs and feelings about each other and yet are motivated to escape the conflict, initial contacts are usually hesitant and exploratory. They may start with a minimal signal of interest in escaping the conflict, sent through an obscure channel or voiced subtly in an otherwise fiery speech. If the other side is similarly motivated, it is likely to notice this signal and reciprocate subtly. The initial signal may then be strengthened and a more direct approach be adopted. The result is a benevolent circle—a ping–pong-like series of conciliatory messages and actions. Somewhere in this pre-negotiation sequence, back-channel communication begins—often through indirect channels followed by direct channels—moving the process ever closer to negotiation and settlement.

What is happening in such a progression is a steady increase in optimism about the outcome of negotiation. With little optimism, only subtle approaches are feasible. As optimism grows, back-channel communication becomes possible. Finally both sides become sufficiently optimistic to enter negotiation. Without the possibility of subtle signals and back-channel communication, many severe conflicts would not move to negotiation and would not be settled.

ALTERNATIVES TO OFFICIAL DIPLOMACY: TRACK 2, TRACK 1½, AND OTHER INNOVATIONS

Track 2 and Track 1½ diplomacy are close cousins to back-channel communication. In Track 2, elite private citizens from each side meet informally with each other as unofficial intermediaries.* In Track 1½, elite private citizens from one side meet

---

* The elite private citizens may include government officials or legislators who are unauthorized and acting on their own.

informally with officials from the other side.[*] The meetings are seldom secret but always private. Like back-channel communication, such talks allow flexibility and future orientation, avoid preconditions, and imply no official recognition of the other party. They allow people on both sides to discover that there are normal human beings on the other side who are interested in resolving the conflict, and they promote an understanding of the other side's "central concerns … (their) basic needs and fundamental fears that any agreement would have to address" (Fisher, 1997, p. 60). Joint projects and possible solutions to the conflict may also be developed.

An example of Track 2 diplomacy is the problem-solving workshops pioneered by Burton (1969) and Kelman (2002). In these workshops, influential people from both sides meet for a few days under the leadership of trained academics to discuss their conflict. Sometimes the meetings are repeated several times with the same participants (Rouhana & Kelman, 1994). Problem-solving workshops are best viewed as an adjunct to formal negotiation. They are most often found in the prenegotiation period, where they can help structure a climate of optimism about the other party's readiness for meaningful negotiation; provide substantive knowledge about the other party's motives, priorities, and assumptions; and produce knowledgeable personnel who can swing into action once higher officials develop a motivation to escape the conflict. In addition, problem solving workshops are occasionally held during formal negotiation, to provide an informal setting for the development of new insights and possible solutions.

Track 2 diplomacy may also entail local community meetings and action-groups involving members of both parties. Such gatherings contribute to the peace process by encouraging leaders to move toward peace and providing public support for negotiated settlements. Fitzduff (2002) describes an extensive program of this kind that contributed to the Northern Ireland peace process.

Examples of Track 1½ diplomacy are two informal meetings that took place between white South Africans and exiled leaders of the African National Congress (ANC), the black insurgency. The first, a 6-hour meeting that was held in Zambia in 1985, involved four English-speaking businessmen and three reporters, who came away with very positive impressions of the ANC leaders, "that they were patriots, as deeply and passionately committed to South Africa as any of their white visitors (and) that they were human beings—and moderate ones at that" (Waldmeir, 1998, p. 74). This meeting set the stage for a 3-day 1987 meeting in Senegal involving a much larger group of elite Afrikaaners, who reached similar conclusions about the ANC leaders.

These conclusions were widely publicized by the white attendees and appear to have "built a reservoir of latent readiness to accept the ANC as a legitimate participant in a negotiated settlement" (Lieberfeld, 2002, p. 368). The meetings also helped to shape a conciliatory ANC policy statement. Soon after the Senegal

---

[*] The term "Track 1½" is employed by two other authors in a somewhat different way: Lieberfeld (2005) adds the stipulation that the elite private citizens are authorized by, and report back to, officials on their side. This is similar to what was described earlier as back-channel communication by a single intermediary who is authorized by his or her side to meet leaders on the other side. Nan (2005) uses the term to refer to facilitated "informal off-the-record workshops on conflict resolution" involving "senior official representatives of the conflict parties" (p. 161).

meeting, a series of indirect back-channel meetings between intermediaries from the South African government and the ANC leadership was initiated, followed by direct back-channel talks and eventually by publicized negotiations that produced a representative government (Lieberfeld, 2002). Thus Track 1½ contacts began a benevolent circle of optimism building and substantive progress that culminated in productive negotiation.

Another innovation is for high-level, cross-community delegations to be briefed by participants in a previously successful peace process. For example in 1997, Arthur (1999) took representatives of a wide spectrum of Northern Ireland political groups to South Africa to talk with people who had been involved in the events leading up to negotiation there. Arthur reports that besides listening to their hosts, the delegation members talked with each other and developed a better understanding of their own conflict.

MEDIATION

Since mediation is third-party assisted negotiation, much of what was said earlier about negotiation also applies to mediation. Mediation may occur at the behest of the parties or on the initiative of the mediator or the group to which he or she belongs. In less severe conflicts, mediators often enter when negotiation has failed and the parties ask for assistance. But in more severe, intractable conflicts, mediators often take the lead—shuttling between the parties until they are ready to talk directly to each other.

Nature of the Mediator

Mediators may be individuals acting on their own, like Former US President Jimmy Carter, or representatives of a group. In international mediation, they may represent another state, an international organization such as the United Nations, or a private organization such as the Community of Sant'Egidio which mediated the Mozambique internal war (Bartoli, 1999).

Regardless of how recruited, mediators become intermediaries between the disputants, as shown by point 7 in Figure 11.1b, and hence are part of a chain reaching into the organizations on both sides. Often there are multiple mediators, who may be organized as a chain like that shown in Figure 11.2, may operate as a team, or may be sequenced one after the other.

Mediation teams serve at least two functions. One is to impress the disputants by the number and status of the team members. The other is to combine efforts by people who can reach out to different key players—to officials and civil society within the disputing groups or to neighboring countries that might otherwise support spoilers and thus sabotage the agreement (Crocker, Hampson, & Aall, 1999b).

Sequences of mediators are found under two circumstances: (a) when mediators fail and others step into the breach, as occurred before the negotiated peace settlement of the Nagorno–Karabackh War (Mooradian & Druckman, 1999); and (b) when a negotiation cycle requires different talents at different points (Crocker et al., 1999b), as in the Northern Ireland peace process, where prenegotiation was mainly mediated by the intermediary chain shown in Figure 11.2 but the actual negotiation was mediated by former US Senate Majority Leader George Mitchell.

Why do mediators serve? What is their motivation? A number of answers can be given. Individuals may serve for professional reasons—mediation is part of their job—or they may have patriotic or humanitarian concerns. Representatives of international organizations may serve because it is part of the charter of their organization or they have been asked to do so by their board of directors. Representatives of states may serve because the conflict threatens their state's interests or they wish to ingratiate their state with the disputants or other concerned parties (Touval & Zartman, 1985).

What Mediators Do

Mediators have many kinds of tactics for counteracting the forces that are blocking agreement (Wall & Lynn, 1993). In intergroup conflict, they may organize meetings of flexible, highly motivated members of both disputant teams to do problem solving or work with the negotiators' constituents to garner support for the negotiation process or outcome. The latter, though often resented, may be necessary to break a deadlock.

Touval and Zartman (1985), international relations specialists, distinguish the following three types of mediator tactic:

Mediator as communicator: Making contact with the parties and passing messages, proposals, and concessions between them. (To these might be added the other low-pressure activities such as scheduling meetings, arranging facilities, and encouraging optimism and camaraderie.)

Mediator as formulator: Sharpening the issues, proposing agendas, questioning the parties' positions or assumptions, and encouraging them to think up new ideas.

Mediator as manipulator: Pressing the parties to adopt certain formulas, often by using threats and promises. This third category is sometimes also called "mediation with muscle."

Bercovitch and Wells (1993) have done a statistical study, using a large sample of international mediations, to examine the circumstances under which mediators employ the categories of tactics just listed. They found, not surprisingly, that manipulative tactics were more often used by mediators with higher rank and power. They also found that mediators who had previous relations with both parties made less use of manipulative strategies than those at a greater social distance.

Another possible classification of mediator tactics is based on similarities with other types of professionals who work with people. The following three broad categories can be postulated:

Mediator as intermediary, shuttling between parties, passing and interpreting messages and proposals, urging them to develop new ideas, and the like. Theoretical ideas about intermediation were presented earlier in this chapter.

Mediator as group leader, meeting face-to-face with the disputants and encouraging productive discussion.

Mediator as therapist, seeking issues underlying the presenting dispute. Kressel and Gadlin (2009) have described the types of underlying issues often located by the ombudsmen at the US National Institutes of Health.

A different kind of tactical issue concerns optimal timing of mediator intervention. Building on ripeness theory, Crocker, Hampson, and Aall (1999a) suggest that severe, protracted conflicts go through a cycle. At first the parties are engaged in the dispute but have not embarked on major hostilities. Then they move to major hostilities (e.g., war). Finally, if neither side wins, they enter a period of hurting stalemate. These authors argue that disputants will be more receptive to mediation in the first and third stages than the second, when they have become committed to winning by force. However, mediation with muscle can sometimes be imposed in the second stage to move the parties into the third stage.

In partial contradiction to this theory, research has shown that severe international conflicts are seldom mediated in the first stage, before hostilities begin (Bercovitch & Diehl, 1997). Perhaps the international community does not have good early warning systems for anticipating severe conflict, or the first stage is not sufficiently alarming to justify disputant acceptance of outside intervention.

Mediator Effectiveness

What determines whether a mediator will be successful in helping the parties reach agreement? What was said just above implies that success depends in part on mediator power, the capacity to deliver successful threats or promises. Low-power mediators are unlikely to be successful in the second stage, when the disputants are committed to hostile action, whereas high power mediators may be successful at any stage (Pruitt, 2000). Mediator bias or perceived bias toward one of the parties can also interfere with success. One source of bias may lie in the mediator's own constituents if they favor one party over the other (Crocker, Hampson, & Aall, 2009). A solution to the bias problem involves adding to the chain or team a mediator whose biases favor the other party.

Much of what is known about mediator effectiveness derives from a set of statistical studies done by Bercovitch and his colleagues on a data set based on over 300 cases of international mediation after 1945 (Bercovitch & Houston, 1996). Mediator success was defined as the extent to which the mediator had "a discernable ... impact on the dispute or the parties' behavior" (p. 19). Mediation was found to be more successful when: it took place on neutral ground rather than in the territory of one of the parties, both parties were friendly before their conflict, the parties were roughly equal in power, there were few fatalities before the mediation took place, both disputants initiated the mediation rather than only one of them or the mediator, the mediator shared political alignment with both the parties rather than only one, or the mediator used manipulative tactics.

Another measure of effectiveness is whether an agreement persists and severe conflict is subsequently averted. In a continuation of the research just described, mediated agreements proved more likely to persist when the prior conflict involved fewer fatalities, when mediators acted as formulators or manipulators rather than as communicators, when more time was spent on mediation, and when issues were settled rather than a simple cease-fire established (Gartner & Bercovitch, 2006).

CONCLUSIONS

Intergroup conflicts can end in a number of ways: One side may defeat the other, the issues may disappear, or a settlement may be reached through negotiation or its close cousin, mediation. The latter two procedures are becoming increasingly popular in severe international conflicts and internal wars. In intractable conflicts, entry into negotiation or mediation usually results from a ripening process in which mutual motivation to end the conflict is combined with growing optimism about finding an acceptable agreement. In the prenegotiation period, optimism often grows as a result of conciliatory signals, informal meetings involving nonofficial elites, and/or back-channel communication. Reaching a negotiated or mediated agreement is by no means a guarantee of successful conflict resolution. Success is more likely if the agreement is broadly endorsed on both sides, satisfies the parties' basic needs, and—in the case of internal wars—leads to the development of a stable and prosperous community.

There are only two small traditions of statistical research on intergroup negotiation and mediation: One involving experiments done in the small group laboratory and the other involving aggregate data about past international mediations. The rest of the theory in this area is based on individual and comparative case studies. This state of affairs implies a large challenge for the future, as case-based theories must eventually be tested with sample statistics.

REFERENCES

Adams, J. S. (1976). The structure and dynamics of behavior in organizational boundary roles. In M. Dunnette (Ed.), *Handbook of industrial and organizational psychology* (pp. 1175–1199). Chicago: Rand-McNally.

Arthur, P. (1999). Multiparty mediation in Northern Ireland. In C. A. Crocker, F. O. Hampson, & P. Aall (Eds.), *Herding cats: Multiparty mediation in a complex world* (pp. 469–501). Washington: United States Institute of Peace.

Avruch, K. (1988). *Culture and conflict resolution.* Washington, DC: United States Institute of Peace Press.

Bartoli, A. (1999). Mediating peace in Mozambique: The role of the community of Sant'Egidio. In C. A. Crocker, F. O. Hampson, & P. Aall (Eds.), *Herding cats: Multiparty mediation in a complex world* (pp. 247–273). Washington: United States Institute of Peace.

Bazerman, M., Curhan, J. R., Moore, D. A., & Valley, K. L. (2000). Negotiation. *Annual Review of Psychology, 51,* 279–314.

Behfar, K., Friedman, R., & Brett, J. (2008). *The team negotiation challenge: Defining and managing the internal challenges of negotiating teams*. Paper presented at the annual meeting of the International Association of Conflict Management, Chicago.

Benton, A. A., & Druckman, D. (1974). Constituent's bargaining orientation and intergroup negotiations. *Journal of Applied Social Psychology, 4*, 141–150.

Bercovitch, J. (1984). *Social conflicts and third parties: Strategies of conflict resolution*. Boulder, CO: Westview.

Bercovitch, J., & Diehl, P. F. (1997). Conflict management of enduring rivalries: The frequency, timing, and short-term impact of mediation. *International Interactions, 22*, 299–320.

Bercovitch, J., & Houston, A. (1996). The study of international mediation: Theoretical issues and empirical evidence. In J. Bercovitch (Ed.), *Resolving international conflicts: The theory and practice of mediation* (pp. 11–35). Boulder, CO: Lynne Rienner.

Bercovitch, J., & Wells, R. (1993). Evaluating mediation strategies: A theoretical and empirical analysis. *Peace and Change, 18*, 3–25.

Brown, R. (2000). *Group processes: Dynamics within and between groups* (2nd ed.). Oxford, England: Blackwell.

Burton, J. (1969). *Conflict and communication*. London: Macmillan.

Burton, J. (1990). *Conflict: Human needs theory*. New York: St. Martin's Press.

Carnevale, P. J., Pruitt, D. G., & Britton, S. (1979). Looking tough: The negotiator under constituent surveillance. *Personality and Social Psychology Bulletin, 5*, 118–121.

Crocker, C. A., Hampson, F. O., & Aall, P. (Ed.) (1999a). Multiparty mediation and the conflict cycle. In *Herding cats: Multiparty mediation in a complex world* (pp. 19–45). Washington: United States Institute of Peace.

Crocker, C. A., Hampson, F. O., & Aall, P. (Ed.) (1999b). Rising to the challenge of multi-party mediation. In *Herding cats: Multiparty mediation in a complex world* (pp. 665–699). Washington: United States Institute of Peace.

Crocker, C. A., Hampson, F. O., & Aall, P. (2009). Why mediation matters: Ending intractable conflicts. In J. Bercovitch, V. Kremenyuk, & I. W. Zartman (Eds.), *Handbook on conflict resolution*. (pp. 492–505). London: Sage.

Crump, L. (2006). Competitively-linked and non-competitively-linked negotiations: Bilateral trade policy negotiations in Australia, Singapore and the United States. *International Negotiation, 11*, 431–466.

Druckman, D. (1994). Determinants of compromising behavior in negotiation: A meta-analysis. *Journal of Conflict Resolution, 38*, 507–556.

Druckman, D., & Lyons, T. (2005). Negotiation processes and post-settlement relationships: Comparing Nagorno-Karabakh with Mozambique. In I. W. Zartman & V. Kremenyuk (Eds.), *Peace versus justice: Negotiating forward- and backward-looking outcomes (pp. 265–285)*. Lanham, MD: Rowman & Littlefield.

Fisher, R., & Ury, W. (1991). *Getting to yes: Negotiating agreement without giving in* (2nd ed.). New York: Penguin.

Fisher, R. J. (1997). *Interactive conflict resolution*. Syracuse, NY: Syracuse University Press.

Fitzduff, M. (2002). *Beyond violence: Conflict resolution process in Northern Ireland*. New York: United Nations University Press.

Ford, S. E. (2008). *An experimental investigation of ripeness in internal war*. Dissertation accepted by the Institute for Conflict Analysis and Resolution, George Mason University.

Gartner, S. S., & Bercovitch, J. (2006). Overcoming obstacles to peace: The contribution of mediation to short- lived conflict settlements. *International Studies Quarterly, 50*, 819–840.

Gelfand, M. J., & Brett, J. M. (Eds.). (2004). *The handbook of negotiation and culture*. Stanford, CA: Stanford Business Books.

Gelfand, M. J., & Cai, D. A. (2004). Cultural structuring of the social context of negotiation. In M. J. Gelfand & J. M. Brett (Eds.), *The handbook of negotiation and culture* (pp. 238–257). Stanford, CA: Stanford Business Books.

Gelfand, M. J., & Realo, A. (1999). Individualism-collectivism and accountability in organizations: Variations in forms of social control across cultures. *Journal of Applied Psychology*, *84*, 721–736.

Goertz, G., & Diehl, P. F. (1997). The initiation and termination of enduring rivalries: The impact of political shocks. *American Journal of Political Science*, *39*, 30–52.

Herrman, M. S. (Ed.). (2006). *The Blackwell handbook of mediation: Bridging theory, research, and practice.* Oxford, England: Blackwell.

Iklé, F. C. (1964). *How nations negotiate.* New York: Harper & Row.

Jeong, H-W. (2005). *Peacebuilding in postconflict societies: Strategy and process.* Boulder, CO: Lynne Rienner.

Kelman, H. C. (1997). Some determinants of the Oslo breakthrough. *International Negotiation*, *2*, 183–194.

Kelman, H. C. (2002). Interactive problem-solving: Informal mediation by the scholar-practitioner. In J. Bercovitch (Ed.), *Studies in international mediation* (pp. 167–193). Houndmills, England: Palgrave Macmillan.

Kogan, N., Lamm, H., & Trommsdorff, G. (1972). Negotiation constraints in the risk-taking domain: Effects of being observed by partners of higher and lower status. *Journal of Personality and Social Psychology*, *23*, 143–156.

Kolb, D. M. (1983). *The mediators.* Cambridge, MA: MIT Press.

Kremenyuk, V. A. (Ed.). (2002). *International negotiation: Analysis, approaches, issues* (2nd ed.). San Francisco, CA: Jossey-Bass.

Kressel, K. (2006). Mediation revisited. In M. Deutsch, P. T. Coleman, & E. C. Marcus (Eds.), *The handbook of conflict resolution* (2nd ed., pp. 726–756). San Francisco, CA: Wiley.

Kressel, K., & Gadlin, H. (2009). Mediating among scientists: A mental model of expert practice. *Negotiation & Conflict Management Research*, *2*, 308–343.

Kressel, K., Pruitt, D. G., & Associates (1989). *Mediation research: The process and effectiveness of third-party intervention.* San Francisco: Jossey-Bass.

Kriesberg, L. (1998). *Constructive conflicts: From escalation to resolution.* Lanham, MD: Rowman & Littlefield.

Lewicki, R. J., Saunders, D. M., & Barry, B. (2006). *Negotiation* (5th ed.). New York: McGraw/Hill/Irwin.

Lieberfeld, D. (1999). *Talking with the enemy: Negotiation and threat perception in South Africa and Israel/Palestine.* Westport, CT: Praeger.

Lieberfeld, D. (2002). Evaluating the contributions of track-two diplomacy to conflict termination in South Africa, 1984–90. *Journal of Peace Research*, *39*, 355–372.

Lieberfeld, D. (2005). Contributions of a semi-official prenegotiation initiative in South Africa: Afrikaner-ANC meetings in England, 1987–1990. In R. J. Fisher (Ed.), *Paving the way* (pp. 103–125). Lanham, MD: Lexington.

Lieberfeld, D. (2008). Secrecy and "two-level games" in the Oslo accord: What the primary sources tell us. *International Negotiation*, *13*, 133–146.

Mandela, N. (1994). *Long walk to freedom.* New York: Little Brown.

McGillicuddy, N. B., Welton, G. L., & Pruitt, D. G. (1987). Third-party intervention: A field experiment comparing three different models. *Journal of Personality and Social Psychology*, *53*, 104–112.

Menkel-Meadow, C., Love, L. P., & Schneider, A. K. (2006). *Mediation: Practice, policy, and ethics.* New York: Aspen.

Merry, S. E., & Silbey, S. S. (1984). What do plaintiffs want? Reexamining the concept of dispute. *Justice System Journal*, *9*, 151–178.

Mitchell, C. (2000). *Gestures of conciliation.* London: Macmillan.

Moloney, E. (2002). *A secret history of the IRA*. New York: Norton.

Mooradian, M., & Druckman, D. (1999). Hurting stalemate or mediation? The conflict over Nagorno-Karabakh, 1990–95. *Journal of Peace Research, 36*, 709–727.

Moore, C. W. (2003). *The mediation process: Practical strategies for resolving conflict* (3rd ed.). San Francisco, CA: Jossey-Bass.

Morgan, P. M., & Tindale, R. S. (2002). Group vs. individual performance in mixed-motive situations: Exploring an inconsistency. *Organizational Behavior and Human Decision Processes, 87*, 44–65.

Nan, S. A. (2005). Track one-and-a-half diplomacy: Contributions to Georgian-South Ossetian peacemaking. In R. J. Fisher (Ed.), *Paving the way* (pp. 161–173). Lanham, MD: Lexington.

Pruitt, D. G. (1964). *Problem solving in the Department of State* (Social Science Foundation and Department of International Relations Monograph Series in World Affairs, University of Denver), Denver, CO: University of Denver.

Pruitt, D. G. (1971). Indirect communication and the search for agreement in negotiation. *Journal of Applied Social Psychology, 1*, 205–239.

Pruitt, D. G. (1981). *Negotiation behavior*. New York: Academic Press.

Pruitt, D. G. (1994). Negotiation between organizations: A branching chain model. *Negotiation Journal, 10*, 217–230.

Pruitt, D. G. (1997). Ripeness theory and the Oslo talks. *International Negotiation, 2*, 237–250.

Pruitt, D. G. (2000). The tactics of third-party intervention. *Orbis: A Journal of World Affairs, 44*, 245–254.

Pruitt, D. G. (2003). *Communication chains in negotiation between organizations*. Occasional Paper #3, Program on International Conflict Resolution, Sabanci University, Istanbul, Turkey. http://conf.sabanciuniv.edu/sites/conf.sabanciuniv.edu/files/finding_integrative_agreements.pdf

Pruitt, D. G. (2005). *Whither ripeness theory?* Working Paper #25, Institute for Conflict Analysis and Resolution, George Mason University, Fairfax, VA. http://www.gmu.edu/departments/ICAR/wp_25_pruitt.pdf

Pruitt, D. G. (2007). Readiness theory and the Northern Ireland conflict. *American Behavioral Scientist, 50*, 1520–1541.

Pruitt, D. G. (2008). Back-channel communication in the settlement of conflict. *International Negotiation, 13*, 37–54.

Pruitt, D. G., & Carnevale, P. J. (1993). *Negotiation in social conflict*. Buckingham, England: Open University Press and Pacific Grove, CA: Brooks/Cole.

Pruitt, D. G., & Kim, S. H. (2004). *Social conflict: Escalation, stalemate and settlement* (3rd ed.). New York: McGraw-Hill.

Putnam, R. D. (1988). Diplomacy and domestic politics: The logic of two-level games. *International Organization, 42*, 427–460.

Robert, C., & Carnevale, P. J. (1977). Group choice in ultimatum bargaining. *Organizational Behavior and Human Decision Processes, 72*, 256–279.

Rouhana, N. N., & Kelman, H. C. (1994). Promoting joint thinking in international conflicts: An Israeli-Palestinian continuing workshop. *Journal of Social Issues, 50*, 157–178.

Schopler, J., & Insko, C. A. (1992). The discontinuity effect in interpersonal and intergroup relations: Generality and mediation. In W. Stroebe & M. Hewstone (Eds.), *European review of social psychology* (Vol. 3, pp. 121–151). Chichester, England: Wiley.

Spector, B. I. (2003). Negotiating with villains revisited: Research note. *International Negotiation, 8*, 613–621.

Stedman, S. J. (2000). Spoiler problems in peace processes. In P. C. Stern & D. Druckman (Eds.), *International conflict resolution after the cold war* (pp. 174–228). Washington: National Academy Press.

Stedman, S. J. (2002). Policy implications. In S. J. Stedman, D. Rothchild, & E. M. Cousens (Eds.), *Ending civil wars: The implementation of peace agreements* (pp. 663–671). Boulder, CO: Lynne Rienner.

Stein, J. G. (1989). *Getting to the table: The processes of international prenegotiation.* Baltimore, MD: Johns Hopkins University Press.

Thompson, L. L. (2005). *The mind and heart of the negotiator* (3rd ed.). Upper Saddle River, NJ: Prentice-Hall.

Thompson, L. L. (2006). *Negotiation theory and research.* New York: Psychology Press.

Thompson, L., Peterson, E., & Brodt, S. E. (1996). Team negotiation: An examination of integrative and distributive bargaining. *Journal of Personality and Social Psychology, 70,* 66–78.

Touval, S., & Zartman, I. W. (1985). *International mediation in theory and practice.* Boulder, CO: Westview.

Troetschel, R., & Hueffmeier, J. (2007). *Creating and claiming value in intergroup and interpersonal negotiation.* Paper presented at the annual meeting of the International Association of Conflict Management, Budapest.

Waldmeir, P. (1998). *Anatomy of a miracle: the end of Apartheid and the birth of the new South Africa.* New Brunswick, NJ: Rutgers University Press.

Wall, J. A. (1975). Effects of constituent trust and representative bargaining orientation on intergroup bargaining. *Journal of Personality and Social Psychology, 31,* 1004–1012.

Wall, J. A., & Lynn, A. (1993). Mediation: A current review. *Journal of Conflict Resolution, 37,* 160–194.

Walton, R. E., & McKersie, R. B. (1965). *A behavioral theory of labor negotiations.* New York: McGraw-Hill.

Wanis-St. John, A. (2006). Back-channel negotiation: International bargaining in the shadows. *Negotiation Journal, 22,* 119–144.

Wanis-St. John, A., & Kew, D. (2006). *The missing link? Civil society and peace negotiations: Contributions to sustained peace.* Paper presented at the annual convention of the International Studies Association, San Diego.

Zartman, I. W. (1977). Negotiation as a joint decision-making process. *Journal of Conflict Resolution, 21,* 619–638.

Zartman, I. W. (1989). *Ripe for resolution: Conflict resolution in Africa* (2nd ed.). New York: Oxford.

Zartman, I. W. (1996). Bargaining and conflict reduction. In E. A. Kolodziej & R. E. Kanet (Eds.), *Coping with conflict after the cold war* (pp. 271–290). Baltimore: Johns Hopkins Press.

Zartman, I. W. (2000). Ripeness: The hurting stalemate and beyond. In P. C. Stern & D. Druckman (Eds.), *International conflict resolution after the cold war* (pp. 225–250). Washington: National Academy Press.

12

Key Issues in Reconciliation
Challenging Traditional Assumptions on Conflict Resolution and Power Dynamics

INTRODUCTION

Since the term "reconciliation" was introduced to the academic discourse of conflict studies by political developments, scholars from various fields have attempted to define the term, examine its nature, distinguish the reconciliation process from other processes such as conflict resolution or conflict settlement, and determine the requirements for such a process to take place between parties in conflict. One such field was social psychology—in particular, the social psychology of conflict and conflict resolution— but not solely. In this chapter, I will focus on the theoretical and empirical contributions of social psychological approaches, but I will also refer to related fields that have contributed to conflict studies in an effort to demonstrate the strengths and the limitations of such contributions to our understanding of reconciliation, both as a process and as a postconflict outcome.

It is important to notice that initially, most theories on the reconciliation process emerged outside the field of social psychology and that, until recently, the literature on conflict settlement and conflict resolution avoided addressing the fundamental requirements of reconciliation, such as truth, taking historical responsibility and defining a political framework based on justice. In this chapter, I will try to explain why that was the case. Reconciliation, in a way, was imposed on conflict resolution, and I argue that social psychological approaches are still searching for ways to contribute to the understanding and to practically facilitate the reconciliation process.

291

A major difficulty in discussing reconciliation is that the term is cloaked with imprecision in the social psychological literature despite the relative clarity with which it was introduced in other fields, such as transitional justice (although there, too, some discussions have been held, but their focus was on the term's moral perspectives and overtones (VanAntwerpen, 2008). With the proliferation of the language of reconciliation in the aftermath of the Truth and Reconciliation Commission in South Africa, the term "reconciliation" is used to mean different things not only across disciplines but also within social psychology and in the conflict resolution literature.

Across disciplines and spheres of discourses, the term is loosely used. In the political discourse and international media, it could be used to refer to groups in conflict reaching any kind of agreement. It is even not uncommon to hear the term used in reference to approaching a ceasefire or getting parties to start negotiation. Hermann (2004) maintains, after some examination of the literature, that "the lack of a widely accepted definition of reconciliation and its components … makes reconciliation little more than a buzzword, an amenable but loose framework for different contents, depending on the user's disciplinary affiliation, cultural back-ground, or the particularities of the case at hand" (pp. 40–41). Also in social psychology the term is used loosely to refer to a range of conditions and processes including coexistence between adversaries, reaching a workable agreement, and peaceful relations founded on transformation of societal relationships. Malloy (2008) defines reconciliation as the "transition from conflict to peaceful coexis-tence, or possibly cooperation" (p. 347). Harris and Fiske (2008) discuss barriers to intergroup reconciliation without defining the term, but seem to refer to it in terms of the resolution of intergroup conflict. It is therefore of utmost import to have some clarity, at least within the social psychological literature, about the term "rec-onciliation" and how it differs from other processes, such as conflict settlement and conflict resolution. For this distinction to become clear, it is important to recognize the origins of the term.

Two intersecting political and intellectual movements contributed to placing the issue of reconciliation on the academic agenda from a particular perspective (Bashir & Kymlicka, 2008). The first is the emergence of the politics of transitional justice—the transformation of authoritarian regimes and regimes involved in mass human rights violations into democracies that overcome such histories and seek social reconciliation and restorative justice (Crocker, 1999; Dwyer, 1999; Van Zyl, 1999). The second movement derives from the "politics of difference," in which minorities in Western democracies argued that although majoritarian democracies largely eliminate explicit forms of discrimination, they also result in political, cul-tural, and economic inequalities and hierarchies. These movements have nourished the debates on how to introduce past injustices and historical accountability into the definition of democracy and equality, the questioning of democratic processes and theories that fail to do so, and the search for such democratic processes (Bashir, 2008; Bashir & Kymlicka, 2008; Rouhana, 2008).

It is my basic claim in this chapter that social psychology has not been sufficiently responsive to these movements and the intellectual challenges they present. While there is an increasing awareness that formal conflict settlements fall far short of establishing genuine peaceful relations between former adversaries and therefore there is need in reconciliation, social psychological research and the literature that deals with conflict resolution fell short of recognizing the asymmetric nature of many conflicts and in many cases imposed symmetrical analysis on asymmetric conflicts. It is the interaction between the two described movements that left in my view its signature on how the concept of reconciliation should be defined. As such, reconciliation should be considered a process that has its own characteristics, including social and political prerequisites necessary for it to occur; it also has its social consequences and psychological underpinnings. Therefore, it would be important to use the term, at least in the social psychological and associated conflict resolution spheres, to denote a particular process distinct from other processes of bringing conflicting groups to overcome their differences.

Unlike the various processes developed within conflict resolution, which were influenced and fashioned to a great extent by theoretical contributions of academics, freelancers, and organizations with disparate disciplines, motivations, and agendas, reconciliation was placed on the conflict resolution agenda by monumental historical developments transitions of many authoritarian regimes and regimes with massive human rights violations into democracies. The processes, therefore, caught most of the conflict resolution field unprepared for the daring ideas it presented—ideas such as facing past injustice and implementing various forms of justice, principally restorative justice. This is so, because the working assumptions of the conflict resolution methodologies, by and large, did not engage these ideas. I argue that for reconciliation to be achieved between parties in conflict, one has to go much beyond the traditional working assumptions that have been established as the cornerstones of conflict resolution and that social psychology and conflict resolution should consider the political nature of the process and take heed against reducing it to a mere psychological process.

THREE PROCESSES OF DEALING WITH CONFLICT: CONFLICT SETTLEMENT, CONFLICT RESOLUTION, AND RECONCILIATION

In order to help delineate the concept of reconciliation and define its characteristics, I have elsewhere distinguished among three qualitatively different processes in the conflict studies literature: conflict settlement, conflict resolution, and reconciliation (Rouhana, 2004a, 2004b). The three processes differ in terms of goals of agreement, parties to the agreement, nature of the desired political relationship, importance of mutual acceptance, social and political prerequisites, and psychological dynamics. The distinction between the first two processes, which had frequently been used in the literature, was not new to conflict studies. It was introduced mainly by Burton (1990) and adherents of human needs theory (Richmond, 2001). In what follows, I will briefly recap the definitions of the first two and then elaborate on what makes reconciliation a different process and describe some of its political and social dynamics.

CONFLICT SETTLEMENT

According to this distinction (Rouhana, 2004b), conflict settlement seeks a formal termination of open violent conflict based on mutual interests. It is represented by an agreement between the conflicting parties that reflects the power relations that existed on the ground at the time the settlement was reached. Consequently, a settlement does not necessarily reflect equitably the broader collective needs of the parties and often does not represent the weaker party's long-term interests. A settlement is not typically intended to effect a deeper transformation of relations between societies or reach genuine mutual recognition between the parties. It seeks and achieves a cessation of open hostilities, some form of coexistence, and perhaps even cooperation—between governments. As such, conflict settlement includes any strategy—such as negotiations, withdrawal, or coercion—that seeks to bring a public episode of conflict to an end (Ramsbotham, Woodhouse, & Miall, 2005). Thus Worchel and Coutant (2008) prefer to use the term "peaceful coexistence," a condition that allows groups to exist with each other and to interact peacefully. This involves reducing fear of the out-group, which can be achieved by "emphasizing group and personal security and demystifying cultural practices of the out-group" (p. 436); becoming aware of the out-group's heterogeneity; legitimizing differences between the groups; and promoting behaviors associated with peaceful coexistence such as jointly cooperating in some spheres. In protracted social conflicts, as well as in conflicts with massive human rights violations, conflict settlement leaves many issues unresolved that may erupt again later. Actually many argue that such issues will inevitably reemerge (Azar, 1990; Burton, 1990).

CONFLICT RESOLUTION ACTIVITIES

Conflict resolution activities seek to address the underlying causes of conflict and accordingly to reach an agreement designed to address the basic human needs of both sides regardless of the power relations between them. Here, the political needs of both parties are equally addressed, not in accordance with the existing power relations between them but rather in the framework of a new relationship that promotes equality and reciprocity. The agreement, although reached by elites, aims to achieve peaceful relations between societies and is supposed to signal mutual acceptance between the parties. It seeks not only coexistence, but also cooperation that reflects a warm and sustainable peace in which the parties should not make any further claims against each other. The tangible grievances of the two parties are addressed to their satisfaction. This process which was influenced heavily by Burton's Basic Human Needs theory (Burton, 1990; Kelman, 1996; Mitchell, 1990) will be most appropriate for addressing social conflict that, by the nature of conflict involves mutual violence and deep grievances related to identity and recognition. The methodologies used here include facilitation, consultation, and mainly the interactive problem-solving workshops introduced by Burton and enhanced by others (Fisher, 1997).

I argue that these methodologies, at least as presently formulated, are not appropriate for conflicts that involve massive asymmetric human rights violations such as mass killings, military occupation and systematic human rights violations, colonization, ethnic cleansing, crimes against humanity, and war crimes. This is so, because this methodology, particularly the problem-solving workshop, is defined as an inherently symmetrical framework that consistently attempts to impose "balance" by treating all parties to a conflict in parallel fashion. Consequently, in the service of the symmetrical analysis of conflict that is one of their fundamental tenets, such methods purposely and willfully avoid core issues such as historical responsibility, justice, truth, and other transitional justice-related issues.

Some have maintained that the goal of successful conflict resolution is reconciliation. For example, Ramsbotham et al. (2005) argue that "[It] is the long-term process of reconciliation that constitutes the essence of the last transformation that conflict resolution seeks" (p. 231). Similarly, Kelman (2004) argues that reconciliation is "a consequence of successful conflict resolution" (p. 112). But as I have argued above and will elaborate below, the above social psychological methodologies of conflict resolution never sought to achieve reconciliation as a process in which the political transformation is guided by restorative justice, historical truth, and facing history and responsibility, and in which conflicts do have perpetrators and victims and are not all symmetrical. If it were to be claimed that these conflict resolution methodologies sought to achieve social political transformation, I would argue that they have utterly failed, precisely because they ignored the very issues that reconciliation brought to the fore.

RECONCILIATION

By contrast with the first two processes described above, reconciliation is a process that seeks a genuine, just, and enduring end to the conflict between the parties and transformation of the nature of the relationship between the societies through a course of action involving intertwined political and social changes and which addresses both politically tangible issues such as distribution of power and constitutional arrangements as well as intangible issues such as historical truth and historical responsibility; as such, this process has psychological correlates that emerge concurrently with the course of action (Rouhana, 2004a, 2004b). This process is in essence social and political—it involves reaching agreements not only based on restructuring of the power distribution, democratic arrangements, constitutional guarantees for equality and human rights within a framework of restorative justice, but also on reaching inter-subjective agreements on historical truths and addressing the issue of historical responsibilities for the mass violations of human rights that have occurred in whatever forms. As a result, this process becomes founded on mutual legitimacy that is gained within a new moral and political framework.

The open, public, and socially based granting of legitimacy—the culmination of the process—becomes the defining feature of the relationship and the cornerstone of mutual recognition and genuine security. But mutual recognition should be based not on a symmetrical process, but on asymmetrical processes in which the historical truths about the injustice not negotiated by the parties but are revealed, for example in truth commissions, and in which political arrangements are based on principles of justice as defined by international law and international norms. Mutual

parties within a framework that guarantees constitutional rights, democracy, and equality of groups and individuals—as the case may be. First, the frame of reference for reconciliation is justice, not the existing power relations between the parties, the basic human needs as defined by the parties, or the parties' existing ideologies. Second, reconciliation places special importance on historic truth, particularly truth about wrongdoing. I maintain that truth is central and has to be commonly acknowledged by the two parties for the process to proceed (Crocker, 1999; Dwyer, 1999; Little, 1999; Minow, 1999; Peled & Rouhana, 2004; Popkin & Bhuta, 1999; Tutu, 1999). Third, it is essential for reconciliation to have the parties agree on the historical responsibility for human rights abuses. The parties involved in mass physical and cultural violence such as colonization, occupation, genocide, ethnic cleansing, and state-sanctioned oppression or discrimination are expected to face their historical responsibility and their role in human rights' violations. Fourth, reconciliation entails political and structural transformation guided by some sort of justice. The structural changes can be dramatic and are determined by universal standards of equality and human dignity, international law, and international human rights agreements regardless of the implications for the acquired privileges and dominant identity of the perpetrators, who will inevitably have to lose some of the privileges they unjustly gained at the expense of the victims.

Many scholars believe that all or some of the four key requirements mentioned above are essential for a reconciliation process. Thus Bar-Tal and Bennink (2008), while focusing on the psychological prerequisites of reconciliation, seem to agree that justice, truth, and facing responsibility are required, albeit it in a largely symmetrical frame of analysis. Similarly, Kriesberg (2004) includes truth and justice among four required components, and his approach is not incompatible with introducing historical responsibility.[°] Kelman (2004) too incorporates facing history and acknowledging responsibility with his definition of reconciliation, although he waters down their power by forcing them into his symmetrical approach, particularly when it comes to the Israeli–Palestinian conflict; but he sees justice and reconciliation as standing in tension. Ross (2004) emphasizes truth telling and acknowledgment of past injustice. Acknowledgment, he argues might facilitate achieving partial reconciliation. Bar-Siman-Tov (2004), in a perfectly symmetrical manner, argues that a party should include recognition of "one's responsibility for misdeeds" (p. 74), and should "present the past in a balanced and objective way" (p. 74). As to justice and fairness, he argues that these are terms that can cause conflict between parties and hinder reaching agreements, because parties might not agree on what is fair and just.[†]

Reconciliation as a Holistic Social Process

If reconciliation is to be conceived as a process applicable in cases of transitional justice and cases with massive human rights violations as described above, and if it

---

[°] Thus he discusses the possibility of apologizing for past conduct within the larger concept of "regard."

[†] This of course is true. But this is why negotiation theorists such as Fisher (1991) and Rubin and Salacuse (1990) recommend that low-power parties demand external criteria to be used for determining fairness. These criteria can include international law.

entails transformation of power distribution in society, then it becomes clear that it is a holistic process that involves multifaceted courses of action that are designed to create a new relationship based on restoring dignity, equality, and human rights, eliminating the conditions that made it possible for societies to harm one another, and establishing genuinely democratic institutions that ensure the opportunity for all to participate on an equal basis. To succeed, this social transformation requires wrenching and deep social psychological changes that powerfully transform the dynamics that enabled an entire society to violate the rights of another and often to treat them as subhuman or inferior. Thus, while the process of reconciliation is politically driven, if it is to succeed, reconciliation must extend far beyond just the political level and reach deeply into the social, legal, moral, and collective psychological levels.

Thus it is appropriate to consider reconciliation as being composed of multi-faceted, far-reaching processes that touch, in some respect, everyone in a society. The discussion of the social psychological dimension of reconciliation will gain from considering the processes in their entirety. Below, I present what I see as the four components of a reconciliation process that have been examined by different disciplines.

1. *The moral framework—transitional justice:* Reconciliation transforms the power relationship between conflicting parties who have endured asymmetrical injustice and massive human rights violations. The shared moral foundation is a framework defined by social justice, truth, facing historic responsibilities, and establishing institutions that reflect this framework. It makes use of tools of transitional justice as appropriate to the particular conflict including truth commissions, measures for restorative justice and reparations, facing historic responsibility and using apology or acknowledgment, and in some cases deal with individual violators of human rights. These tools cannot be applied mechanically. They will probably be negotiated within the new moral framework. The dilemma of transitional justice usually takes center place: how to advance transitional justice without threatening a new democratic arrangement founded on the shared moral framework? This question occupied transitional justice for a while and social psychological research, as described below, examined some of these issues.

2. *The political:* Reconciliation is a process in which new democratic institutions are created and constitutional transformations are introduced in order to guarantee a future based on equality and democracy and protect against violations of human rights. The constitutional form that guarantees such a future—whether it is integration, federation, bi-nationalism, autonomy, or something else—will depend on the particular history and characteristics of the case but in all cases will be founded on restorative and distributive justice and fair distribution of power.

3. *The social psychological:* The reconciliation process entails cognitive, emotional, and behavioral changes that support the transformation. These changes become possible within the framework presented above.

These are mainly consequences of such a framework, although once instigated they promote its continuation. Similarly, psychological healing can be facilitated and easier to achieve within such moral and political frameworks.

4. *The involvement of public and elites:* These processes are public and involve new political behavior on the parts of the public and elites of both societies. Within such frameworks, state institutions can be legitimately employed to generate public and open support that translates into mutual legitimacy for these frameworks and the transformation they guided.

As we will see below, social psychological research has started looking at many of the issues relevant to the moral framework, including at the transformation in social psychological attitudes that accompanies a genuine reconciliation. Before addressing these studies, I will discuss the social psychological approaches to reconciliation.

Social Psychological (and Related Approaches) to Reconciliation

Even if it is a politically driven process, intergroup reconciliation is characterized by widespread cognitive and affective transformations that parallel the political transformation of all parties involved. Social psychologists, naturally, focus on the psychological dimension of the process. But it is important to keep in mind that these changes are intertwined with political changes and with the power relations between the parties and that, therefore, discussing psychological processes without relating them to the existing power relations might undermine the possibility of understanding the conflict itself.

As it happens, much of the social psychological work on this subject, while presenting their discussions in general theoretical frameworks, often took the Israeli–Palestinian conflict as a case study (Baron, 2008; Kelman, 1998; Nadler & Liviatan, 2006; Shnabel & Nadler, 2008). Other social psychological works referred to different areas where the issue of reconciliation was a matter of public policy or academic interest, such as in Australia and Northern Ireland. I will draw on a broader range of cases when I discuss contributions from the transitional justice literature.

I will group the psychological approaches to reconciliation into two broad clusters in order to highlight the differences in the literature. Future work will need to present more nuanced differentiation.

The first approach sees reconciliation as basically a psychological process. Much of the social psychological literature, but not all, seems to focus on the cognitive and emotional processes in reconciliation. This, of course, is to be expected. However, the risk here is to over-psychologize the reconciliation process by assuming that its essence is psychological instead of treating the psychological manifestations, requirements, and consequences in the context of a broader social and political multifaceted process. This might also result in treating reconciliation mainly as a psychological issue.

Thus, Maoz (2004) refers to reconciliation as "a cluster of cognitive and emotional processes" (p. 225). Noor, Brown, and Prentice (2008) suggest that "at the heart of reconciliation lies the psychological process effecting shifts of one's 'mind and heart' concerning the conflict and the opponent group" (p. 99), which has to address lack of trust and empathy. Kelman (2004) defines reconciliation in terms of identity change in each party, with specific reference to the Israeli–Palestinian case; in this case it is identity change that constitutes reconciliation by "the removal of the negation of the other as a central component of one's own identity" because the centrality of mutual denial of identity in this case (p. 119). I will return to this definition and the perils of the symmetrical framework it sets up for the Israeli–Palestinian conflict in a later section. Bar-Siman-Tov (2004), following Bar-Tal and Bennink, argues that reconciliation requires cognitive changes in societal beliefs focusing on three issues: justness of one's goals, positive self-image, and acceptability of delegitimizing the opponent. Similarly Bar-Tal (2009) claims that "the essence of reconciliation involves socio-psychological processes consisting of changes of motivations, goals, beliefs, attitudes, and emotions by the majority of society members" (p. 365). Staub, Pearlman, Gubin, and Hagengimana (2005), in their work in post genocide Rwanda, define reconciliation in terms of psychological processes such as mutual acceptance and positive attitudes. They mention the need for structures and institutions that promote reconciliation but the essence of the reconciliation process for them is the change in psychological orientations.

Furthermore, according to many social psychological treatments it is the psychological change that is required for reconciliation to take place. Bar-Tal (2009) argues that "the first condition for reconciliation is legitimization and humanization of the rival" (p. 366). He maintains that there are psychological conditions for reconciliation, and accordingly, he tries to outline "the type of cognitive and affective changes that seem necessary for reconciliation" (p. 368). Then he claims that "reconciliation *requires* changes in the following societal beliefs that were formed during the conflict" (p. 368; italics added); or that "reconciliation *requires* a change in the collective emotional orientations of fear, anger and hatred, which often dominate societies in intractable conflict" (p. 369).

Baron (2008) provides, perhaps, the most striking example of seeing reconciliation as a psychological process detached from realities of power distribution, truth, and social justice and indeed from political realities. While most other approaches described above refer to these issues or believe that they follow from or associated with the psychological process, he dwells on the power of contact, even if such contact is disconnected from the political realities on ground. By engaging his approach here, I do not wish to imply in any way that I include him with the first approach, but rather to give an example of how the discussion of psychological requirements for reconciliation without relating this discussion to political realities and moral frameworks undermines the potential value of the contribution.

Baron refers to reconciliation as healing through getting together. The psychological essence of the definition is revealed through the illustration he provides: This is an ongoing process of change "much as the alcoholic who successfully attends AA and stops drinking must continuously monitor his [sic] drinking behavior" (p. 283). Thus using examples from the conflict in the Middle East where this healing can be achieved he endorses shifting the focus of intervention to the small group level, taking place away from the spotlight along the lines of "Kelman's workshops." He refers to these workshops too credulously and uncritically, attributes to them achievements, success, and effectiveness that has not been demonstrated (of the sort that 1990–1995 was the period during which Kelman's workshops were most effective), and makes the dubious claim that "such workshops established conditions where power differentials were eliminated" (p. 283).

According to this approach, reconciliation as healing can work in the Middle East in two ways: (a) Bottom-up, such as by establishing a regional soccer team— "imagine if there was a team consisting of Israelis and Syrians," he writes (p. 289). One cannot appreciate how detached from reality such a recommendation is without reference to basic realities of the conflict. (b) Bottom-down, through activities, in which Palestinian leaders "must model in every clear and consistent term that success cannot be defined by how many Israeli citizens are killed by terrorists" and by which Palestinians can build an identity "that does not rest on the destruction of Israel" (p. 293).

In this analysis, addressing issues such as past wrongs, distribution of power, colonialism, occupation, ethnic cleansing, massive violations of human rights, and so on are to be avoided, and accordingly the South African model "will not be applied to the Middle East" (p. 296).

It is true that this extreme example of an analysis that is detached from political realities on the ground and that lacks a moral and political framework for reconciliation cannot be attributed only to the author's emphasis on the psychological sphere, because the author brings to his analysis prejudiced views anchored in outmoded national character theories and in possible basic bigotry. Yet it is an example of how inappropriate applying social psychological analysis, if it is detached from historical grounding.

The second approach sees the process and its prerequisites in unmistakable societal and political terms. It is in this context that these authors analyze the complexity of the social psychological variables involved in reconciliation. Spears (2008), for example, writing from within the tradition of social identity theory, defines reconciliation as "the stage after group conflict in which real group differences have been made clear, and resolved through struggle, and where groups come to term with the shift in power and status" (p. 338). According to this conception of reconciliation, groups in a postconflict situation grant legitimacy to their new equal status and power relations, recognize the illegitimacy of the past, and seek to achieve, and reward achieving (social) justice. Spears is aware that this process might be easier for the low-power group to seek than the high-power group.

Stephan (2008) defines societal reconciliation as the renewal of a lapsed social contract. This requires "repairing the fundamental institutions of a functioning society" (p. 370), with greater emphasis on inclusiveness, and equality enacting new laws to prevent discrimination and exclusionary policies, establishing "truth and reconciliation commissions" (p. 370), prosecution of crimes against humanity, and employing the media and the arts in such activities. Thus the psychological changes are concomitant to political changes. Stephan directs psychologists who would like to help with promoting reconciliation to study the programs implemented in various countries such South Africa, Peru, and Chile. Psychologists, he argues, have the means to focus on *individual* reconciliation. It is not clear what is the temporal relationship between the societal and the individual, but at least the social context of reconciliation is defined.

Bretherton and Mellor (2006), after reviewing official reports of the Australian Human Rights and Equal Opportunity Commission and examining the effects of colonialism on the Indigenous population in Australia, argue that for the term reconciliation to be meaningful, it requires that nonIndigenous Australians become aware of their colonial past, its effect on the Indigenous population, and its effect on their own identity.

In summary, there are at least two social psychological approaches to understanding reconciliation: One seems to see the essence of the process as psychological changes, to attribute to them the standing of prerequisites for the political process to take place, or to relegate the political transformation to a lower importance process that will need to follow anyway; the other emphasizes the societal and political changes needed to effect a redistribution of power creating a new legitimate order within which psychological processes occur.

In my view, the psychological process is a correlate of a political process grounded in a clear moral framework as outlined above. I use the term "correlate" in order to avoid the implications of a strong causal direction in the relationship between the social–political process and the social–psychological dynamics associated with it. Obviously, the relationship is interactive, and some psychological changes will need to precede the political process. But the watershed of social psychological changes are not *required* for the process to launch but rather *the outcome* of a political transformation, an integral part of which is setting in place mechanisms for dealing with the hard issues of truth, responsibility, collective human rights violations, and restorative justice.

Social Psychology and Reconciliation's Key Issues

The politics of reconciliation and the truth and reconciliation commissions with their emphasis on truth, justice, and historical responsibility, and with their asymmetric context, brought into the academic discourse on conflict resolution issues that—for complex reasons related to how the field emerged—has been ignored, sidestepped, or underemphasized. In those conflicts in which such commissions were established, the historical developments themselves brought these issues to the fore. Scholars, in turn, were then forced to engage with these issues; in other words, it subsequently became impossible to continue the discourse of conflict resolution without, in one way or another, addressing them.

In a way, then, the conflict resolution field was compelled to deal with these new issues that were introduced by groups who, through their political persistence and disciplined struggle, insisted on justice, democracy, facing past injustice, and historical truths. In this case, the field was responding to political changes introduced by the groups who struggled against oppression, exclusion, injustice, colonization, and discrimination from a low-power position. This includes peoples in Africa, Latin America, and Europe who rebelled against tyrannies and authoritarian regimes and in one case, South Africa, against a racist regime. This also includes the persistence of minorities—indigenous and immigrant, who seek to have their histories recognized and the past injustice addressed.

It is precisely because the conflict resolution field and its theorists and practitioners had explicitly avoided these issues—which are associated with the low-power groups—that the field is looked upon with great suspicion across what is known as the Third World where many such protracted conflicts are waged. At this juncture, the conflict resolution field is challenged to develop appropriate methodologies that incorporate these issues and perhaps some of the burgeoning empirical and theoretical insights that engagement with them has produced. On the other hand, it would be a grave mistake to simply incorporate these issues on the surface of the existing traditional conflict resolution methodologies by simply focusing on the psychological processes that reconciliation entails. In one sense, it is correct to assert that conflict resolution methodologies sought to achieve reconciliation. But this is precisely where the problem lies, for it is important to recognize that the main failure of the conflict resolution methodologies in this regard was in trying to achieve reconciliation the easy way; that is without paying the dues that genuine societal reconciliation requires, and thus failing to examine how to transform conflict-ridden societies from systems that by design endorsed inequality, discrimination, and humiliation into systems in which principles of dignity, equality, and justice are the foundation, ensuring that such abuses can never again be collectively inflicted in a way that could be accepted as legitimate. Existing conflict resolution methodologies, by employing, by and large, a symmetrical framework of analysis and avoiding the difficult issues that are associated with the reconciliation process, have fallen far short of what is required to contribute to reconciliation.

On the empirical level, an increasing number of studies in social psychology, including experimental studies, have started catching up with the international political changes, interacting with some transitional justice discourses, and offering some important insights into the dynamics of reconciliation. Thus, some studies have examined the role of apology in promoting forgiveness (Philpot & Hornsey, 2008), the relationship between political empowerment and forgiveness in a postconflict situation (David & Choi, 2006), the importance of collective guilt in the reconciliation process (Halloran, 2007), and the way power relations influence dominant identities and attitudes toward reconciliation (Green & Sonn, 2006). New studies examine the importance of expressions of responsibility on intergroup reconciliation (Nadler & Liviatan, 2006) and the role of forgiveness on enhancing reconciliation (Noor, Brown, Gonzalez, Manzi, & Alan, 2008). Similarly, some studies have examined the effect of victim suffering and the nonvictimized community's support for reparation (Starzyk & Ross, 2008); the relationship between various modes of identification—such as attachment and group glorification—on group-based guilt (Branscombe, 2004; Roccas, Klar, & Liviatan, 2006). Many of these studies were conducted with special attention to power-relations and its possible influence, as I will show below.

What lags behind are the methodologies of conflict resolution that remain stuck in paradigms of symmetrical analysis and avoidance of the core issues and trying to force them into the symmetrical paradigms. In what follows, I will review how some of the recent work in social psychology and its conflict resolution methodologies dealt with key reconciliation issues. In the remainder of this chapter, and for space limitations, I will focus the discussion on the issues of power asymmetry and responsibility and only briefly discuss the issues of justice and truth.

POWER ASYMMETRY AND RECONCILIATION

By and large, the reconciliation literature as introduced by transitional justice makes its point of departure the asymmetric relationships between parties: those who inflicted injustice, and those who were the recipients of injustice. The context is that of colonization and the struggle against it, occupation and its resistance, authoritarianism and its defiance and the transition to democratic regimes, all in asymmetrical frameworks.

It is interesting to see that some empirical work on reconciliation is being conducted with explicit reference to the political power asymmetry or awareness of the fact that attribution of responsibility need not be symmetrical and in fact, is often more appropriately assigned in an asymmetric fashion. For example, Green and Sonn (2006) examined how the unacknowledged power of the dominant group affects their discourse of reconciliation and their political action. Their study, which was conducted among White Australians who were involved in reconciliation activity in the Australian context, revealed four different discourses that describe the power of whiteness, each with different implications for reconciliation "and actions toward justice and equity" (p. 391). In the same context, Halloran (2007) defined reconciliation as "the general desire to acknowledge the past injustices inflicted on indigenous people as result of European colonization" (p. 2) and to address the asymmetric relationship between the communities. Using regression analysis, the study found that the support for the value of egalitarianism among non-Indigenous Australians was a significant predictor of positive attitudes toward reconciliation. In a related study, Halloran (2007) reported that respondents with higher levels of collective guilt over how Indigenous Australians have been treated showed stronger support for reconciliation. Similarly, Bretherton and Mellor (2006) argue that nonIndigenous Australians should face the history of colonialism, and even its impact on their own identity, in order for reconciliation to be meaningful. The psychological attitude needed in this case is not a closure about history but rather taking the pain of facing the past and its pain and becoming self-reflective about collective guilt and shame. According to them, the challenge of psychology is to deal with such issues in order to mitigate structural violence within the context of restorative justice. Thus the political and moral frameworks are stated openly by the authors. Clearly, a rigid insistence on adhering to a symmetrical analysis would have obscured these frameworks and made it impossible to surface these nuanced findings. In contrast, a number of experimental studies (e.g., Nadler & Liviatan, 2006; Roccas et al., 2006; Shnabel & Nadler, 2008; Shnabel, Nadler, Ullrich, Dovidio, & Carmi, 2009) have taken power asymmetry as their point of departure in interpreting their findings, and advanced some insights into the psychology of intergroup reconciliation (see below).

Yet on the part of conflict resolution methodologies, we find a persistent symmetrical frame of analysis. This frame of analysis, I argue, hinders our understanding of the issues and masks a nuanced political framework for reconciliation.

A prominent exception in the conflict resolution field is the "conflict transformation" paradigm, which was introduced to refer to processes that are similar to what this chapter defined as reconciliation (Lederach, 1997). This approach was originally conceived with clear emphasis on justice in asymmetric contexts. But, if one considers the problem-solving workshop and related activities such as multitrack diplomacy and dialogue as the main applied unofficial methodology of the conflict resolution field, the symmetrical framework prevails almost across the board.

If practitioners seeking to define reconciliation continue to insist on symmetricizing the process, they will ensure that it suffers the same failings as the conflict resolution activities. Kelman (2004) who was one who consistently tried to impose symmetry or parallelism on the Israeli–Palestinian conflict, has argued that for reconciliation to take place, there should be "mutual acknowledgment of the other's nationhood and humanity …. [including] political recognition and acknowledgment of the other's legitimacy" (p. 122); or "acknowledging the legitimacy of the other's narrative without necessarily fully agreeing with that narrative" (p. 119). According to him one of the fundamental sources of conflict is that mutual denial of the other's identity characterizes the Israeli–Palestinian conflict. I would like to argue that this formula might indeed be a conflict-perpetuating formula rather than a conflict-resolving one.

What does mutual recognition mean in this case? For Israelis, it means that they should overcome their denial and recognize the reality that before the Zionist project started, Palestine was inhabited by its own people—the Palestinians. This is not an ideological position. It is a simple historic reality. What are Palestinians asked to recognize in return in order to fulfill the symmetrical requirement of this framework? An examination of Kelman's emphasis on mutual recognition (Kelman, 1982, 1986) reveals that Palestinians are required not to recognize the reality that Israel exists or that Israelis are a nation but rather the ideological position that Zionism is legitimate and that its narrative is valid and legitimate. Presenting such a demand in terms of mutual recognition obfuscates its profound conflictive nature, to say the least. Palestinians will be required to recognize the legitimacy of a movement that recognized Palestine with the explicit goal of establishing an exclusive Jewish state in its place. Although Kelman does not approve of the method or the outcome, Zionism effectively dismantled Palestinian society, dispersing the Palestinian nation and taking over their homeland; and refused to allow those who had been expelled or dislocated to return to their homeland and property because such a return is incompatible with Zionism, which they are required to recognize.

One can make a strong argument that within the vast power asymmetry between Israelis and Palestinians, their conflict is not ready for reconciliation mainly because the high power party has no incentive to examine any of the various key issues of reconciliation (Rouhana, 2005). Conflict settlement, might be easier to achieve. But negotiations for arriving at a settlement will need to avoid this issue of requesting Palestinians to recognize Zionism because a settlement, in principle, can be reached without discussing historical truth and responsibility, which the question of Zionism brings to the fore. Insisting on this demand as the current Israeli government does (also presenting it in symmetrical manner) will most likely jeopardize even the chances of reaching a settlement, leave alone genuine reconciliation.

HISTORIC RESPONSIBILITY

Conflict is a process in which all involved sides usually get harmed regardless of the power asymmetry. In many cases of protracted social conflict, as well as in conflicts with past injustice, all parties to the conflict commit violence. Even in the most extreme cases, perpetrators and victims use violence and both get hurt. Thus, while Black South Africans used violence during apartheid, theirs was not equated to the structural, political, and military violence inflicted upon their entire population by the apartheid regime. In fact, the South African Truth and Reconciliation Commission concluded that all sides committed gross human rights violations. But these findings were not sufficient for academics or politicians to analyze the conflict or approach historic responsibility within a symmetric framework. The same commission concluded that apartheid was a crime against humanity (Gibson, 2004, 2006). The point here is that mutually inflicted violence is not a sufficient justification for symmetrical analysis of responsibility.

Facing responsibility for past injustice is a particularly difficult issue in post-conflict reconciliation. If one considers one of the most atrocious and glaringly clear crimes committed against humanity in the last century, that is, the Holocaust that Nazi Germany committed against Jews, one would think that it is only natural and straightforward for the Germans to have taken responsibility and apologized for their crimes. But Lustick (2005) demonstrates that the negotiations between the World Jewish Congress and the Federal Republic of Germany in 1951 that involved both reparations and a statement by German Chancellor failed to produce an admission of guilt and responsibility. The statement describes the opposition of the "overwhelming majority" of Germans to Nazi policies, and does not include reference to contrition, repentance, innocence of the victims, or the role of the German army. The Chancellor states in the Parliament that "unspeakable crimes have been committed in the name of the German people, calling for moral and material indemnity" (Lustick, 2005, p. 111), thus distancing the German people from direct association with the crimes.

Even though the Germans were defeated in war, a new democratic regime was installed, and Germany sought to normalize relations with Europe and the world, and even though the statement was negotiated with the representative of the victims of a crime against humanity with deep symbolic implications for possible future reconciliation, it was still unacceptable for them to take responsibility and admit guilt. This is even more remarkable if one considers that this was one-sided crime and not a conflict in which both sides inflicted violence upon each other. It is true that since then the German state and society have gone a long way, culturally, symbolically, politically, and socially to fully own their role in these crimes.*

---

* Compare Adenauer's statement from 1951 with Shroder's statement in 2005 on the 60th anniversary of the liberation of the Nazi death camp at Auschwitz, in which he owns what Adenauer tried to disown. He states: "The evil manifested in the Nazi ideology was not without its precursors. There was a tradition behind the rise of this brutal ideology and the accompanying loss of moral inhibition. Above all, it needs to be said that the Nazi ideology was something that people supported at the time and that they took part in putting into effect" (http://www.historyplace.com/speeches/schroeder.htm).

Yet this is a powerful example of the difficulty of dealing with the issue of responsibility in a transitional period.

This example might explain why some scholars refrain from dealing with the question of responsibility or of identifying victims and perpetrators. As mentioned earlier, many scholars accept the notion that taking responsibility facilitates the process of reconciliation (Bar-Siman-Tov, 2004; Bar-Tal & Bennink, 2008; Kelman, 2004; Kriesberg, 2004). However, unlike scholars in the transitional justice literature, these scholars employ a framework in which both sides have to take responsibility in a symmetrical manner. Some claim that taking responsibility is not helpful. Worchel and Coutant (2008), for example, argue against a perception that involves perpetrators and victims because their observations of groups involved in social conflict reveal that "both sides are firmly convicted that their group is the victim" (p. 434). Taking the parties perceptions as the bases of our analysis and action without asking questions about them will not help us understand the nature of conflict. To the contrary. The perceptions themselves emerge in the context of the power relations between the groups. Thus the fears of Serbs, Israelis, Afrikaners, and Protestants in Northern Ireland should be problematized. Their deeper examination can provide insights into the fear sources of both the dominant and the dominated groups, how the nature of these fears differs, and how to deal with each.

The lesson from the German–Jewish example should not be to dismiss the question of responsibility or address it in a symmetrical manner, but rather to deal with it carefully. Ross (2004) argues that when parties emphasize their victimhood, apology become impossible to achieve both psychologically and politically. Yet he recommends the use of symbolic action, rituals, and cultural expressions as tools of acknowledgment and mechanisms of redefining the relationships between conflicting parties and as ways of achieving partial reconciliation.

In fact, an increasing number of studies on responsibility, guilt, empathy, and related matters frame the theoretical work as well as the interpretation of findings within an asymmetrical framework. Miron and Branscombe (2008) argue that, "two conditions must be met in order for people to experience collective guilt. First, they must categorize themselves as members of the advantaged group; second, they must perceive that the in-group is responsible for a moral violation against another group" (p. 80), Collective guilt is essential to the reconciliation process, because it motivates the perpetrators to seek reparation and to support a just relationship with their victims. Thus members of the perpetrator group must conclude that their group committed an injustice to the members of the victim group. Miron and Branscombe describe some mechanisms that group members use to avoid guilt feeling. The insights of such discussions would have been lost in a symmetrical framework.

The little experimental research conducted on the importance of taking responsibility seems to point to the value of taking responsibility and expressing empathy for the other's actions, but, in asymmetrical context. In a thoughtfully designed experimental study conducted among Israeli undergraduates, Nadler and Liviatan (2006) examined the effect of a Palestinian leader's (hypothetical) expression of empathy and/or assuming responsibility for the other side's conflict-related suffering on openness to reconciliation. Two studies were conducted, one in 2000, before the start of the second Palestinian *Intifada* against Israeli occupation of Palestinian lands, and the second (basically a replication) in 2001, within the context of violence that was occurring at the time. Trust of Palestinians was also measured as a continuous variable.

The two studies showed that for Israeli Jewish participants with relatively high trust of Palestinians, expression of empathy had a significant positive effect on their willingness for reconciliation. By contrast, participants whose trust of Palestinians was low tended to express less willingness for reconciliation, perhaps because they perceived the hypothetical statement as manipulative. Furthermore, no similar effect for taking responsibility was reported. It is the power asymmetry context that gives these results heightened significance: For the high-power group, the Israelis, what they need most is the empathy of their victims so that their past unjust actions can be "understood." For the low-power group, it would be hypothesized, it is the expressions of responsibility by the perpetrators that is most important because it speaks to their sense of justice and validates their narrative of injustice.

Shnabel and Nadler (2008) present an experimentally supported needs-based model of interpersonal and intergroup reconciliation. According to this model, reconciliation is an act of social exchange between a victim and a perpetrator with asymmetrical needs: the victim's need is to rectify the impaired status, and the perpetrator's need is for understanding and empathy. In a study this model is generally validated in an intergroup context (Shnabel et al., 2009). The perpetrators (Jews in a massacre conducted against Arab citizens of Israel in 1956) offer a sense of empowerment—"the right to live in respect and with their heads up and to feel strong and proud in their homeland," while Arabs offer "understanding and acceptance" for the perpetrators' dealings "with emotions following the killings" (p. 1024).

When it comes to applying reconciliation to the Israeli–Palestinian conflict outside the experimental laboratory, the dilemmas presented at the start of this section become evident. Thus, Nadler and Saguy (2004) argue that reconciliation does not apply at this point to the Israeli–Palestinian conflict for two main reasons: The first is that when mistrust is high, reconciliation (which they call socio-emotional reconciliation) will not be effective and may harm the relationship; the second is that there is no agreement on who is the perpetrator and who is a victim, as each side sees itself as the only victim and the other as the perpetrator. Thus each side expects an apology from the other. In this case, in their view, a gradual and prolonged process of cooperation should precede reconciliation, in which the focus is on the present, the change is gradual, and the ultimate goal is separation between the parties.

But despite the appeal of this approach it has its own internal paradox. Given the power asymmetry between Israelis and Palestinians and the Israelis motivation, as the higher power party to maintain the *status quo* (as the authors mention), why should the "prolonged and gradual cooperation" process change the motivation of the high power group to upset the *status quo*? The argument will be "things are working out fine, as evidenced by the cooperation." So, while the authors seem to want to alley the fears of the parties before starting the reconciliation process, in fact, they manage to do so for the high-power party only. Similarly, the authors do not seem willing to extend the asymmetry they perceive between the parties to the questions of victimhood and responsibility. Instead they emphasize the "perception" of victimhood without problematizing it, as suggested above.

OTHER KEY ISSUES IN RECONCILIATION

In this chapter, I focused on power asymmetry and historical responsibility as two key issues in reconciliation. Because of space limitations, I did not cover truth and justice, both of which I also consider to be central for the reconciliation process (Rouhana, 2004a). The literature on reconciliation, both within transitional justice and social psychology, also examines the issue of intergroup forgiveness and its possible relationship to reconciliation, although I do not consider this issue to be central to political reconciliation.

By and large, the views within the social psychologically related conflict resolution literature treat justice with either dismissal, considering it as non-conducive to reconciliation or as a matter of "perception" within a symmetrical framework. For example, Miron and Branscombe (2008) argue that "reconciliation maybe more easily achieved to the extent that both parties engaged in the intergroup conflict agree upon 'what constitutes justice' and thereby arrive at similar conclusions about the past" (p. 90). Such arguments are most needed and an intersubjective framework can be most useful. Yet, defining justice cannot be left to the power relations between the groups to determine. Parties should benefit from a whole body of international norms, international law, and universal values on human rights, as well as outside experts who can take part in such discussions in general terms in order to determine the framework of justice. It is in a way remarkable that the existing conflict resolution methodologies do not seek any frames of reference for justice, such as international law.

As to the issue of truth, there is a great body of research in the transitional justice literature with strong views that the truths about past human rights violations can contribute to the process of reconciliation (Gibson, 2006; Hayner, 2001; Minow, 1999). The treatment of this issue within the social psychological literature is rudimentary, although some started referring to the importance of historical truth. Bar-Tal (2009) writes that reconciliation necessitates changing societal beliefs about the past. Thus "through the process of negotiation about collective memories, in which one's past is critically revised and synchronized with that of the other group, a new narratives emerges" (p. 367). This has not been the case in many transitional situations in which a truth commission was entrusted with these issues rather than a "negotiation process" between the parties.

SUMMARY

It is important to expand the definition of reconciliation beyond the psychological process and to engage with other fields of research that examine the broader process of reconciliation. There are important key issues in reconciliation that the social psychological research has started to examine. The literature review undertaken in this chapter suggests that while important insights have been advanced by some empirical studies, these insights have not been extended to the applied work, particularly conflict resolution methodologies. If social psychology becomes more attentive to concerns expressed by low power groups, its theoretical base will be enriched and conflict resolution methodologies will become more readily acceptable to wider audiences, not only those represented by powerful groups. In addition, it is time to move beyond the constrictions of a symmetrical framework of analysis, which have for so long dominated conflict resolution methodology and research. The study of social and political reconciliation should be seen as an appropriate opportunity to do so, because power asymmetry is an inherent feature to most situations for which reconciliation is needed.

REFERENCES

Azar, E. E. (1990). *The management of protracted conflict*. Hampshire, England: Dartmouth Publishing Company.

Bar-Siman-Tov, Y. (2008). Dialectics between stable peace and reconciliation. In Y. Bar-Siman-Tov (Ed.), *From conflict resolution to reconciliation* (pp. 61–80). Oxford, NY: Oxford University Press.

Bar-Tal, D. (2009). Reconciliation as a foundation of culture of peace. In J. Rivera (Ed.), *Handbook on building cultures of peace* (pp. 363–375). New York: Springer Science.

Bar-Tal, D., & Bennink, G. H. (2004). The nature of reconciliation as an outcome and as a process. In Y. Bar-Siman-Tov (Ed.), *From conflict resolution to reconciliation* (pp. 11–38). Oxford, NY: Oxford University Press.

Baron, R. M. (2008). Reconciliation, trust, and cooperation: Using bottom-up and top-down strategies to achieve peace in the Israeli-Palestinian conflict. In A. Nadler, T. Malloy, & J. Fisher (Eds.), *The social psychology of intergroup reconciliation* (pp. 275–300). Oxford, NY: Oxford University Press.

Bashir, B. (2008). Accommodating historically oppressed social groups: Deliberative democracy and the politics of reconciliation. In B. Bashir & W. Kymlicka (Eds.), *The politics of reconciliation in multicultural societies* (pp. 48–69). Oxford, NY: Oxford University Press.

Bashir, B., & Kymlicka, W. (Eds.). (2008). Introduction: Struggles for inclusion and reconciliation in modern democracies. *The politics of reconciliation in multicultural societies* (pp. 1–24). Oxford, NY: Oxford University Press.

Branscombe, N. R. (2004). A social psychological process perspective on collective guilt. In N. R. Branscombe & B. Doosje (Eds.), *Collective guilt: International perspectives* (pp. 320–334). New York: Cambridge University Press.

Bretherton, D., & Mellor, D. (2006). Reconciliation between aboriginal and other Australians: The "Stolen Generations". *Journal of Social Issues, 62*(1), 81–98.

Burton, J. W. (1990). *Conflict: Resolution and prevention*. New York: St. Martin's Press.

Crocker, D. A. (1999). Reckoning with past wrongs: A normative framework. *Ethics & International Affairs, 13,* 43–64.

Curle, A. (1971). *Making peace*. London: Tavistock Press.

Dwyer, S. (1999). Reconciliation for realists. *Ethics & International Affairs, 13,* 81–98.

Fisher, R. (1991). Negotiating power: Getting and using influence. In J. W. Breslin & J. Z. Rubin (Eds.), *Negotiation theory and practice* (pp. 127–140). Cambridge: PON Books.

Fisher, R. J. (Ed.). (1997). *Interactive conflict resolution*. Syracuse, New York: Syracuse University Press.

Galtung, J. (1969). Violence, peace, and peace research. *Journal of Peace Research*, 6(3), 167–191.

Galtung, J. (1990). Cultural violence. *Journal of Peace Research*, 27(3), 291–305.

Gibson, J. L. (2004). Does truth lead to reconciliation? Testing the causal assumptions of the South African truth and reconciliation process. *American Journal of Political Science*, 48(2), 201–217.

Gibson, J. L. (2006). The contributions of truth to reconciliation: Lessons from South Africa. *Journal of Conflict Resolution*, 50(3), 409–432.

Gutmann, A., & Thompson, D. (1996). *Democracy and disagreement*. Cambridge, MA: Harvard University Press.

Halloran, M. J. (2007). Indigenous reconciliation in Australia: Do values, identity and collective guilt matter? *Journal of Community and Applied Social Psychology*, 17(1), 1–18.

Harris, L. T., & Fiske, S. T. (2008). Diminishing vertical distance: Power and social status as barriers to intergroup reconciliation. In A. Nadler, T. Malloy, & J. Fisher (Eds.), *The social psychology of intergroup reconciliation* (pp. 301–318). Oxford, NY: Oxford University Press.

Hayner, P. B. (2001). *Unspeakable truths: Confronting state terror and atrocities*. New York: Routledge.

Hermann, T. (2004). Reconciliation: Reflections on the theoretical and practical utility of the term. In Y. Bar-Siman-Tov (Ed.), *From conflict resolution to reconciliation* (pp. 39–60). Oxford, NY: Oxford University Press.

Kelman, H. C. (1982). Creating the conditions for Israeli-Palestinian negotiations. *Journal of Conflict Resolution*, 26, 39–75.

Kelman, H. C. (1986). Overcoming the barriers to negotiation of the Israeli-Palestinian conflict. *Journal of Palestine Studies*, 16(1), 13–28.

Kelman, H. C. (1996). Negotiation as interactive problem-solving. *International Negotiation: A Journal of Theory and Practice*, 1, 99–123.

Kelman, H. C. (1998). Building a sustainable peace: The limits of pragmatism in the Israeli-Palestinian negotiation. *Journal of Palestine Studies*, 28, 36–50.

Kelman, H. C. (2004). Reconciliation as identity change: A social psychological perspective. In Y. Bar-Siman-Tov (Ed.), *From conflict resolution to reconciliation* (pp. 111–124). Oxford, NY: Oxford University Press.

Kriesberg, L. (2004). Comparing reconciliation actions within and between countries. In Y. Bar-Siman-Tov (Ed.), *From conflict resolution to reconciliation* (pp. 81–110). Oxford, NY: Oxford University Press.

Laue, J., & Cormick, G. (1978). The ethics of intervention in community disputes. In G. Bermant, H. C. Kelman, & D. P. Warwick (Eds.), *The ethics of social intervention* (pp. 205–232). Washington, DC: Halsted Press.

Lederach, J. P. (1997). *Building peace: Sustainable reconciliation in divided societies*. Washington, DC: United States Institute of Peace Press.

Little, D. (1999). A different kind of justice: Dealing with human rights violations in transitional societies. *Ethics & International Affairs*, 13, 65–80.

Lustick, I. S. (2005). Negotiating truth: The Holocaust, Lehavdil, and al-Nakba. In A. Lesch & I. Lustick (Eds.), *Exile and return: Predicaments of Palestinians and Jews* (pp. 106–127). Philadelphia, PA: University of Pennsylvania Press.

Malloy, T. E. (2008). Intergroup relations and reconciliation: Theoretical analysis and methodological implications. In A. Nadler, T. Malloy, & J. Fisher (Eds.), *The social psychology of intergroup reconciliation* (pp. 345–368). Oxford, NY: Oxford University Press.

Maoz, I. (2004). Social-cognitive mechanisms in reconciliation. In Y. Bar-Siman-Tov (Ed.), *From conflict resolution to reconciliation* (pp. 197–224). Oxford, NY: Oxford University Press.

Minow, M. (1999). *Between vengeance and forgiveness: Facing history after genocide and mass violence*. Boston: Beacon Press.

Miron, A. M., & Branscombe, N. R. (2008). Social categorization, standard of justice, and collective guilt. In A. Nadler, T. Malloy, & J. Fisher (Eds.), *The social psychology of intergroup reconciliation* (pp. 77–96). Oxford, NY: Oxford University Press.

Mitchell, C. (1990). Necessitous man and conflict resolution: More basic questions about basic human needs theory. In J. Burton (Ed.), *Conflict: Human needs theory* (pp. 149–176). New York: St. Martin's Press.

Nadler, A., & Liviatan, I. (2006). Intergroup reconciliation: Effects of adversary's expressions of empathy, responsibility, and recipients' trust. *Personality and Psychology Bulletin, 32*(4), 459–470.

Nadler, A., & Saguy, T. (2004). Reconciliation between nations: Overcoming emotional deterrents to ending conflicts between groups. In H. Langholtz & C.E. Stout (Eds.), *The Psychology of Diplomacy* (pp. 29–46). Westport, CT: Praeger.

Nadler, A., Malloy, T. E., & Fisher, J. D. (Eds.). (2008). *The social psychology of intergroup reconciliation*. Oxford, NY: Oxford University Press.

Noor, M., Brown, R., & Prentice, G. (2008). Prospects for intergroup reconciliation: Social-psychological predictors of intergroup forgiveness and reparation in northern Ireland and Chile. In A. Nadler, T. Malloy, & J. Fisher (Eds.), *The social psychology of intergroup reconciliation* (pp. 97–116). Oxford, NY: Oxford University Press.

Noor, M., Brown, R., Gonzalez, R., Manzi, J., & Lewis, C.A. (2008). On positive psychological outcomes: What helps groups with a history of conflict to forgive and reconcile with each other? *Personality and Social Psychology Bulletin, 34*(6), 819–832.

Peled, Y., & Rounaha, N. N. (2004). Transitional justice and the right of return of the Palestinian refugees. *Theoretical Inquiries in Law. 5*, 317–332.

Philpot, C. R., & Hornsey, M. J. (2008). What happens when groups say sorry: The effect of intergroup apologies on their recipients. *Personality and Social Psychology Bulletin, 34*(4), 474–486.

Popkin, M., & Bhuta, N. (1999). Latin America amnesties in comparative perspective: Can the past be buried? *Ethics & International Affairs, 13*, 99–122.

Ramsbotham, O., Woodhouse, T., & Miall, H. (2005). *Contemporary conflict resolution*. Cambridge, UK: Polity Press.

Richmond, O. P. (2001). Towards a genealogy of peacemaking: The creation and recreation of order. *Alternatives: Global, Local, Political, 26*(3), 317–343.

Roccas, S., Klar, Y., & Liviatan, I. (2006). The paradox of group-based guilt: Modes of national identification, conflict vehemence, and reactions to the in-group's moral violations. *Journal of Personality and Social Psychology, 91*(4), 698–711.

Ross, M. H. (2004). Ritual and the politics of reconciliation. In Y. Bar-Siman-Tov (Ed.), *From conflict resolution to reconciliation* (pp. 197–224). Oxford, NY: Oxford University Press.

Rouhana, N. N. (2004a). Group identity and power asymmetry in reconciliation processes: The Israeli-Palestinian case. *Peace and Conflict, 10*(1), 33–52.

Rouhana, N. N. (2004b). Identity and power in the reconciliation of national conflict. In A. Eagly, R. Baron, & V. Hamilton (Eds.), *The social psychology of group identity and social conflict: Theory, application, and practice* (pp. 173–187). Washington, DC: American Psychological Association.

Rouhana, N. N. (2005). Truth and reconciliation: The right of return in the context of past injustice. In A. Lesch & I. Lustick (Eds.), *Exile and return: Predicaments of Palestinians and Jews* (pp. 261–278). Philadelphia, PA: University of Pennsylvania Press.

Rouhana, N. N. (2008). Reconciling history and equal citizenship in Israel: Democracy and the politics of historical denial. In B. Bashir & W. Kymlicka (Eds.), *The politics of reconciliation in multicultural societies* (pp. 70–93). Oxford, NY: Oxford University Press.

Rubin, J. Z., & Salacuse, J. W. (1990). The problem of power in negotiation. *International Affairs, 1*, 24–34.

Shnabel, N., & Nadler, A. (2008). A needs-based model of reconciliation: Satisfying the differential emotional needs of victim and perpetrator as a key to promoting reconciliation. *Journal of Personality and Social Psychology, 94*(1), 116–132.

Shnabel, N., Nadler, A., Ullrich, J., Dovidio, J. F., & Carmi, D. (2009). Promoting reconciliation through the satisfaction of the emotional needs of victimized and perpetrating group members: The needs-based model of reconciliation. *Personality and Social Psychology Bulletin, 35*(8), 1021–1030.

Spears, R. M. (2008). Social identity, legitimacy, and intergroup conflict: The rocky road to reconciliation. In A. Nadler, T. Malloy, & J. Fisher (Eds.), *The social psychology of intergroup reconciliation* (pp. 319–344). Oxford, NY: Oxford University Press.

Starzyk, K. B., & Ross, M. (2008). A tarnished silver lining: Victim suffering and support for reparations. *Personality and Social Psychology Bulletin, 34*(3), 366–380.

Staub, E., Pearlman, L. A., Gubin, A., & Hagengimana, A. (2005). Healing, reconciliation, forgiving and the prevention of violence after genocide or mass killing: An intervention and its experimental evaluation in Rwanda. *Journal of Social and Clinical Psychology, 24*(3).

Stephan, W. G. (2008). The road to reconciliation. In A. Nadler, T. Malloy, & J. Fisher (Eds.), *The social psychology of intergroup reconciliation* (pp. 369–394). Oxford, NY: Oxford University Press.

Tutu, D. (1999). *No future without forgiveness*. New York: Doubleday.

VanAntwerpen, J. (2008). Reconciliation reconceived: Religion, secularism, and the language of transition. In B. Bashir & W. Kymlicka (Eds.), *The politics of reconciliation in multicultural societies* (pp. 25–47). Oxford, NY: Oxford University Press.

Van Zyl, P. (1999). Dilemmas of transitional justice: The case of South Africa's truth and reconciliation commission. *Journal of International Affairs, 52*, 647–667.

Worchel, S., & Coutant, D. K. (2008). Between conflict and reconciliation: toward a theory of peaceful coexistence. In A. Nadler, T. Malloy, & J. Fisher (Eds.), *The social psychology of intergroup reconciliation* (pp. 423–446). Oxford, NY: Oxford University Press.

13

Peace-Making
*Socio-Psychological Approaches**

KLAUS BOEHNKE, HENNING SCHMIDTKE,
and MAOR SHANI

INTRODUCTION

*T*he research field "conflict management"[†] is best understood as thoroughly multidisciplinary, encompassing disciplines, such as international law, psychology, socio-biology, political science, economics, and social anthropology. Focusing on questions of the source and nature of conflict as well as on third-party interventions and their characteristics, the research community of conflict management has done little to provide comprehensive state-of-the-art reviews (Reimann, 2004). In light of this diagnosis the present chapter sets out to review one particular subsection of the field.

Following Galtung (1969), peace research can deal with (1) negative peace, concerned with strategies for discontinuing direct violence, and defined as a state of affairs requiring a set of social structures that provide security and protection from acts of direct violence committed by individuals, groups or nations (Woolman, 1985), or with (2) positive peace, aiming at truly overcoming violence by creating a pattern of cooperation and integration in society, which can resolve the underlying

---

° The chapter was written in large parts while the first author was a Visiting Professor at the Department of Psychology of the National University of Singapore. The second author was affiliated to Universität Bremen, Germany, during most of the preparation of the chapter.

† Conflict management is used as an umbrella term encompassing settlement, resolution, and transformation of conflict. It, thus, refers to peace-making activities ranging from military interventions and the implementation and supervision of ceasefires as pure outcome-oriented forms of third-party interventions to more process-oriented and less official approaches such as facilitation of and consultation with largely process- and structure-based activities, such as capacity building, development and human rights work (Reimann, 2004). In general terms, conflict management can be defined as third-party propeace interventions that aim in one way or the other at facilitating the process of ending such conflicts.

causes of conflict that produce violence (O'Kane, 1992). While research on the former often builds upon a game-theoretical and rational choice-based understanding of conflict as a problem of *political* order and puts emphasis on control of direct violence, the latter approaches understand conflict as characterized by "indirect and threatening communication, a lack of trust and respect, with good versus evil images predominating, frustration of basic needs, and win–lose defensive competition between the parties" (Fisher, 2005, p. 221), so that the main focus in this realm is on associative strategies characterized by a high level social interaction. Peace research of the latter kind builds mainly upon theories of human needs (Burton, 1990), or on classic nonviolence concepts (Gandhi, 1950; King, 1963), and is concerned with the social–psychological backdrop of conflict. We will center our attention on this kind of peace research.

Furthermore, a distinction can be made in that research can focus on (a) obstacles to peace, and on (b) catalysts of peace (Cohrs & Boehnke, 2008). The present chapter focuses on catalysts of positive peace as Chapter 9 in this book will focus on the former theme. It will review recent work on socio-psychological aspects of conflict management. Both short- and long-term aspects of catalysts of peace will be discussed.

In general, initiatives to create catalysts for positive peace assume that in intractable conflict each society is characterized by a culture of conflict, resulting from common societal beliefs that form collective memories and emotional orientation. The culture of conflict is widely shared by society members and encompasses many domains of social life (Bar-Tal, 2007; Baumeister & Hastings, 1997), constituting a major obstacle to the transformation of the conflict. Conflict management efforts at both the level of political and social elites and at the grassroots level aim, thus, at gradually converting a culture of conflict into a culture of peace (de Rivera, 2004; Montiel & Wessells, 2001). In a resolution of the United Nations General Assembly (1998) proclaiming the year 2000 as the "International Year for the Culture of Peace," the term was characterized by a set of values, attitudes and behaviors, which are based on principles of freedom, democracy, justice tolerance, nonviolence and dialogue and are shared by society members. The movement toward a culture of peace requires the full engagement of society and its institutes. Herein, psychology can have an important role in facilitating cognitive and emotional processes conducive to culture of peace (Brenes & Wessells, 2001). According to Bar-Tal (2004, 2009) a new culture of peace must include the ethos of peace, encompassing among others societal beliefs about peace and conflict resolution, equalization of the past opponent, and a critical perception of the in-group. In an attempt to transform this rather political proposal into a coherent and fruitful concept in the realm of social sciences Fernández-Dols, Hurtado-de-Mendoza, and Jiménez-de-Lucas (2004) propose to understand it as a changeable script. They identify three sets of values that are related to the main definitional activities of war whose lower levels of endorsement indicate the presence of a culture of peaceful interaction in a society: strategic disposal of individuals, logics that subordinate wealth to ethics, and rhetoric of injustice as intelligence.

There are many aspects of conflict resolution, for which the individual represents the appropriate unit of analysis. Hence, the review alludes to stages of conflict management in which processes central to conflict resolution—such as the cultivation of empathy and insight, creative problem-solving and learning can be facilitated by third-party interventions for a positive peace. The chapter discusses two distinct approaches toward catalysts of positive peace. First, the strand of literature related to a top-down notion of peacebuilding which refers to the creation of a political environment conducive to negotiations is reviewed. In particular, approaches such as "track-two" and "track-one-and-a-half" diplomacy and training are core issues here. Second, an overview will be provided of the grassroots societal process that ought to accompany the structural socio-political facilitators of peace-building (reconciliation) and a discussion of interventions in intergroup relations aiming at eliminating negative socio-psychological dynamics—often referred to as peace education. The chapter's short final section discusses the overall quality of the research done in both fields. Here we focus primarily on two methodological issues, namely the problem of a selection bias of participants and the issue of rigorous evaluation, and draw some conclusions on how research on socio-psychological approaches to peace-making can be advanced in the future.

ELITE LEVEL CATALYST FOR POSITIVE PEACE

In situations of intractable conflict in which destructive behavior becomes institutionalized over time (Gray, Coleman, & Putnam, 2007), political agreements are difficult to achieve because barriers of fear, mistrust, and suspicion make negotiations problematic even when joint-gains solutions are possible (Chigas, 1997). Thus, many socio-psychological approaches to conflict management focus on how the "cognitive-affective repertoire" (Bar-Tal, 2007, p. 1435) of politically influential members of the adversaries maybe transformed so that official agreements become possible. Following the aforementioned socio-psychological line of thought on the emergence and institutionalization of cultures of conflict in intractable disputes, these top-down approaches start from the basic assumption that while being a necessary condition the availability of joint-gains solutions to conflict is not sufficient for achieving political agreements at the negotiation table. Hence, pioneers of this kind of third-party intervention to conflict conclude that the value of the relationship between the conflicting parties needs to be enhanced by applying strategies "based on responsiveness to the adversary's needs and on reciprocity" (Kelman, 2006, p. 21) By assuming that the conflict-biased socio-psychological accouterment of politically influential members of the adversaries—a major obstacle for the parties to enter into a peace process—can be bridged, these top-down approaches aim to develop and apply methods and techniques that can facilitate this process. Their emphasis is on two components assumed crucial for this process, namely (a) on an unofficial, nonbinding setting and (b) on a rather passive role of a third party as a repository of trust. At the very general level researchers and practitioners presume that the individual is the critical unit of analysis. Secondly, these individuals are not treated as mere rational utility-maximizers following a logic of consequences but rather as social beings deeply enmeshed in the socio-psychological infrastructure of conflict, thus following a logic of appropriateness.

A prominent branch of literature addressing this realm of third-party interventions for a positive peace focuses on "track-two" diplomacy. These approaches are directed toward changing attitudes and perceptions, and allow parties to explore options and develop solutions outside formal negotiations (Fisher, 2007). They incorporate activities concerned with problem-solving and process-promoting, the former focusing on impacting policy, the latter concerned with impacting the participants (Funk, 2000). Contrary to "track-one" diplomacy, which refers to all official diplomacy, "track-two" encompasses all diplomatic activities that occur outside official governmental activities (Kaye, 2001).

Building on pioneering work of Burton (1969), Kelman and others (Fisher, 1972; Rouhana & Kelman, 1994) developed a socio-psychological approach toward the solution of international and intercommunal (Chigas, 1997) conflicts. Basically aiming at both problem-solving and process-promoting, interactive problem solving[°] is designed as an unofficial, academically based, third-party approach, suited to protracted conflict between identity groups (Kelman, 2005). Targeting the cognitive repertoire of politically influential members of societies in conflict, the central tool of the approach—problem-solving workshops—follows a dual purpose. By aiming for new conflict-resolution ideas among the particular individuals at the workshop table, the workshops are firstly designed to impact the participants themselves and are, thus, concerned with process-promotion. However, changes at the level of individual participants are not ends in themselves, but vehicles for promoting change at the policy level. Hence, workshops pursue secondly the aim of facilitating the negotiation process by maximizing the likelihood that insights developed by participants are transferred to the political debate and the policy-making process in their respective societies (Kelman, 2005).

Regarding the process-promotion purpose a situation of mutual distrust and suspicion is assumed as an a priori, so that workshops are required to provide participants with a context that allows them to interact at low levels of commitment so that the parties can develop a sufficient amount of working trust as a basis for promoting a cooperative process, a particular kind of trust not depending on sympathy or friendship (Pelzmann, 2005), but on the mutual conviction that the other party is moving in a conciliatory direction at its own interest (Kelman, 2005). Second, the process-promotion aspect of the approach is addressed by one of the core features of the workshops: Workshops take place in an "academic setting providing an unofficial, private, nonbinding context, with its own set of norms to support a type of interaction that departs from the norms that generally govern interactions between conflicting parties" (Kelman, 1999, p. 185).

Given the general situation of mistrusting enemies participating in the workshops, the third party plays a crucial role for workshop functioning in being required to provide a repository of trust (Kelman, 2005). Participating parties can place trust in the third party because academic practitioners implement a particular set of ground rules governing the workshop (Kelman, 1999). While the third party does not intervene directly with the interaction process of the

---

[°] For the evolution of the approach, its socio-psychological foundations and practical applications readers must be referenced to Herb Kelman's Web site: http://www.wcfia.harvard.edu/node/4262

participants by proposing solutions or by participating actively in substantial discussions it plays a facilitative role by guaranteeing privacy and confidentiality and by guiding the nature of the interaction toward a mode of Habermasian arguing, aimed at mutual understanding and an analytical mode of problem-solving rather than tactical communication. Ground rules ascertain that there is no expectation to reach an agreement and that the participating parties have the same right to serious consideration of their needs, fears, and concerns (Rouhana & Korper, 1997).

The selection of participants serves as a link between process-promotion and problem-solving. In order to maximize change in the individual, participants are required to be quite removed from the decision-making process and therefore less constrained by tactical considerations whereas to the end of maximizing transfer from the workshops to the decision-making level, participants should be as close as possible or even part of the decision-making apparatus, so that they can directly apply the new insights developed in the workshops (Kelman, 2005). In order to connect both aims participant selection tries to balance these contradictory requirements by focusing on individuals who are not officials but who are politi-cally influential.

In sum, track-two interventions following the problem-solving approach are assumed to fulfill three core functions: (a) increase the decision makers' sense of negotiation possibility by producing a feeling of shared identity among participants; (b) reduce threat perception through an exploratory function, in which participants can gauge the acceptability of specific proposals, and a verification function, in which each side can check the consistency of the other's position; and (c) strengthen negotiation-oriented leaders by providing them with track-two experiences (Lieberfeld, 2002).

Systematic interventions of effects of track-two evaluations are unfortunately rather rare, due to numerous conceptual and methodological challenges. Since there are often too many independent variables and possible interaction effects that may affect the development of a particular conflict most evaluative literature on track-two interventions builds primarily on utterances of workshop participants and concludes from rather unsystematic process tracing statements about their successfulness. Furthermore, the field is prone to a lack of conceptual clarity. Authors like Kaye (2001) come to the conclusion that regional security dialogues in the Middle East since 1991, involved some 750 regional elites have constituted an important mechanism in building regional understanding and knowledge by impacting the participants' preferences and subsequently policy incrementally. Others, like Kelman (1999), go further: For them approaches like interactive problem-solving are by definition unofficial and nonbinding interventions meant to provide an opportunity for exploratory interaction that can produce new ideas which subsequently can be fed into the decision-making process. They come to the conclusion that track-two activities "have made a modest, but not insignificant contribution to the Israeli–Palestinian peace process" (Kelman, 1999, p. 24), in that they have helped to develop *cadres* (individuals prepared to carry out pro-ductive negotiations), have provided important substantive inputs into the negotia-tions and have fostered a positive political atmosphere.

In another prominent case of protracted conflict Fisher derives an assessment of track-two interventions from his analysis of all varieties of mediation efforts in the Cyprus conflict. From his point of view Burton's initiative in 1966 (Burton, 1969) as well as Talbot's seminar in 1973 (Talbot, 1977) and the Kelman and Fisher workshops that took place over the years between 1979 and 1993 "have served a useful pre- or para-negotiation function" (Fisher, 2001, p. 323), but were in the end limited in scope and effect. In a more systematic way, Lieberfeld (2002) traces the processes of track-two diplomacy in South Africa, and comes to the conclusion that meetings between the ANC and dissident Afrikaners had a direct impact on white public opinion and introduced a more differentiated view of the ANC. In addition, the meetings helped to legitimize ANC as a negotiation partner and forced ANC officials to concretize their plans for the future and to specify their preconditions for negations which in turn facilitated subsequent track-one negotiations.

In sum it must be noted that although processes of changing individual participants are built on long-standing socio-psychological insights and should therefore be documented through empirical evaluation quite well, most literature relies heavily on anecdotic evidence and does not provide systematic assessment of particular interventions. The same is true for the channels through which the results are transferred to the policy level. They are neither clear nor certain. Building on "the hope and expectation that the results of unofficial dialog will trickle up to leadership" (Chigas, 1997, p. 412), the problem-solving aspect of the approach is still rather unexplored. As for difficulties to trace these processes of transfer over time it is quite problematic to evaluate to what extent the full meaning of the affect, trust and confidence building that comes from face-to-face interaction can be and is transferred to the decision-making apparatus.

Being aware of this central shortcoming of the classical interactive problem-solving approach Martinez and Susskind (2000) and Chigas (1997) utilize the basic premises of the approach by combining it with insights from other types of third-party interventions.

Martinez and Susskind (2000) make use of the experiences of the Consensus Building Institute (an NGO in Cambridge, MA) with the facilitation of international negotiations on climate change and biodiversity. They propose an effort dubbed parallel informal negotiations (PIN). Basically having the same aims as interactive problem-solving workshops, this approach tries to eliminate the issue of transfer by changing the criteria for participant selection: PIN tries to bring together official representatives of the adversary groups to engage in facilitated discussions aimed at both process-promotion and problem-solving. Hence, the critical gap of interactive problem-solving workshops is sought to be overcome by involving formal representatives of the adversaries and NGO experts in a non-public problem-solving process, under the supervision of neutral facilitators. The application of such talks presupposes that each side is to some extent motivated to explore possibilities for a political solution, so that certain circumstances must be present in order to render semi-official talks feasible.

Semi-official talks or track-one-and-a-half interventions were among others applied in the Palestine–Israel conflict and in South Africa. Here, Lieberfeld (2007) comes to the conclusion that the talks promoted tractability of both conflicts only in a minimal sense by providing for direct communication among the adversaries where there previously had not been any, and by moderating good-versus-evil images between participants. Although rarely tested in situations of intractable conflict it may be suggested that these track-one-and-a-half negotiations or semi-official talks might offer additional options for building "working trust" among the key actors in developing ideas that can form the basis of an official agreement.

Also aiming at eliminating the transfer gap in the interactive problem-solving approach, various methods of training* try to facilitate interactive conflict resolution by solely focusing on process-promotion. Such training brings together members of conflicting parties for a joint (Tyler-Wood, Smith, & Barker, 1990) or parallel (Chigas, 1997) learning experience which—in contrast to interactive problem-solving—excludes the substance of the conflict and focuses exclusively on the negotiation process. In these unofficial, confidential workshops members of official negotiation teams come together to learn either jointly or in separate settings about the conflict process, common negotiation and conflict dynamics, and how those are present in their conflict. Independent from the precise form, all approaches of training aim at replacing the common guiding metaphor of official negotiations— negotiation as a hard bargaining procedure (Mitchell, 1999)—by a new metaphor of negotiation seen as an endeavor of joint problem-solving. Hence, explicitly excluding the substance of the conflict, training approaches are designed to prepare the parties to be less adversarial and to cooperate in the official context of negotiations more creatively by teaching official representatives of the conflicting parties problem-solving-oriented techniques of negotiation.

Methods of training have been applied in conflict situations in Cyprus (Diamond, 1997), El Salvador and South Africa (Chigas, 1997), the Israel–Palestine conflict (Rothman, 1997), and also in the postwar reconstruction of Burundi (Wolpe & McDonald, 2006). Most of these interventions focus on facilitating the process of negotiation, and although scholars and practitioners agree that the evaluation of training at top levels is difficult, they come to the conclusion that experience with the applications of this method suggests that training may "contribute to a successful negotiation process" by dealing with obstacles to negotiation and improving the negotiation process (Chigas, 1997, p. 423). Furthermore, Wolpe and McDonald (2006) conclude from their analysis of initiatives for leadership training in Burundi that "peacebuilding and international post-conflict interventions can benefit significantly by focusing on the leadership dimension of institutional transformation and combining the skill-sets of both diplomats and organizational specialists" (p. 138).

Drawing together, socio-psychological approaches to the facilitation of negotiation processes provide a broad variety of techniques that may help to advance the process of official negotiation. Viewing them as an integral part of the larger negotiation process, explicates their theoretical relevance at all stages of that process. They are relevant at the pre-negotiation stage, where they can contribute to move the conflicting parties closer to the negotiation table. They can also be relevant

---

* For an overview on training as a socio-psychological approach to conflict resolution, see Fisher (1997).

alongside the negotiations, where they may help to overcome setbacks, stalemates, and loss of momentum by reanimating the process through new input and reviving a sense of possibility. They can be helpful at the post-negotiation stage where they can contribute to resolving the problems of implementing negotiated agreements, and, finally, in the post conflict process of peacebuilding and reconciliation, where they can help to transform the relationship between the former enemies by creating a sustainable culture of peace. However, further empirical research is needed in order to determine more systematically to what extent all these initiatives are truly contributive. What also has rarely attained sufficient systematic research attention is the status of the third party involved in these peace-building endeavors (Montiel & Boehnke, 2000).

GRASSROOTS LEVEL CATALYSTS FOR POSITIVE PEACE

Even if the process of peacemaking becomes successful and ends with a widely supported agreement between leaders of both parties, the political process is insufficient to guarantee the establishment of peaceful intergroup relations in the post-conflict era. While the official resolution of the conflict is a necessary step in achieving peace after a protracted conflict, it alone cannot transform the relations between groups at the grassroots level and create peaceful intersocietal relations. There is an increasing understanding among scholars in the field that without a socio-psychological change at the grassroots level, and without a fundamental transformation of the socio-psychological repertoire that maintains and perpetuates the conflict, the process of improving intergroup relations after a protracted conflict will not be successful (Rothstein, 1999). Society members themselves, and not only the political elite, must adapt to the peaceful relations to which they are subjected throughout the peacemaking process and after a peace agreement is reached.

The process through which the culture of peace is created and penetrates into the society is often referred to as reconciliation (Staub, 2006; see also Chapter 12). Bar-Tal et al. (2009, p. 23) propose that reconciliation must involve building positive relations that include "mutual recognition and acceptance, invested interests and goals in developing peaceful relations, mutual trust, positive attitudes as well as sensitivity and consideration of other party's needs and interests." On this route, long-lasting processes of de-humanization and de-legitimization must be overturned, and the opposing group must be recognized as trustworthy, legitimate partners, with valid goals and needs (Bar-Tal & Bennink, 2004).

However, the culture of conflict cannot be transformed overnight. Reconciliation must be perceived and implemented on the macro level and include a joint effort of educational institutions, media, and other social and cultural organizations through which positive messages about peace can be disseminated (Bar-Tal, 2009). A state of negative relations is usually accepted by society members as normative (Bar-Tal, 2004). Attempts to transform the negative relations often meet resistance and objection within each society. While endeavors for a change of negative intergroup relations often come from a few influential members or segments of societies in conflict, it becomes obvious that groups in conflict need assistance and interventions aiming at creating a more positive prism through which they can interpret and understand the conflict and intergroup relations, as opposed to the old prism that justified endless rivalry.

According to Bar-Tal (2009), reconciliation between members of former adversaries at the grassroots level can be promoted by various societal means such as mutual official apologies of each side in crimes and wrongs committed throughout the years of conflict, reconciliation and truth committees aiming at promoting justice and positive peace, compensations for victims of the protracted conflict on each side, writing of a shared history that will gradually be absorbed in each society's collective memory, recruitment of the mass media to the peacebuilding process, and joint cultural and economic projects.

Among measures aiming at society-level psychological change toward a culture of peace at the grassroots level, interventions in educational settings are crucial. While politicians struggle in attempts to resolve conflict at the political level and different groups and organizations engage in peace activism in civil society, educators, psychologists, and other scholars and practitioners, aware of the difficulties in promoting positive intergroup relations but motivated to work toward this goal, developed educational programs which are specifically designed to change attitudes and behavior on the individual or the small group level. These interventions usually take place in the education system, which is considered as one of the most important social institutes for the promotion of reconciliation (Gordon, 1994). The school system can promote the new culture of peace just as it served as an agent of socialization to conflict before. In addition, in the school system society has maximum control over transmitted messages and thus conducting large-scales intergroup interventions within its framework allows reaching a whole segment of a society (Bar-Tal et al., 2009).

Educational interventions aiming at cultivating an understanding between adversaries are referred to in the socio-psychological literature as peace education (Bjerstedt, 1995; Burns & Aspeslagh, 1996; Salomon & Nevo, 2002). The concept of peace education is rather elusive (Harris, 2002) and tends to overlap with "conflict resolution training," "democratic education," "civil education," and "multicultural education" (Salomon, 2002). Peace education obviously is an umbrella term for a variety of techniques and methods of interventions that differ in terms of ideology, objectives, emphasis, curricula, contents, and practices. However, they all aim at diminishing negative phenomena such as inequality, injustice, intolerance, and so on, by imparting values, attitudes, beliefs, skills, and behavioral tendencies that correspond with peace, and therefore try to intervene in socialization processes (Bjerstedt, 1995).

In peace education there is an attempt to develop a frame of mind and to change affective, attitudinal, and behavioral repertoires of young people, and not only to transit a body of knowledge. Interventions in this framework attempt to develop competencies, values, and attitudes, which will eventually manifest in peaceful cognition and behavior (Nelson & Christie, 1995; Staub, 2002). Peace education practitioners are motivated by the assumption that cognitive and affective changes among individual participants in educational intervention will create an overall bottom-up socio-psychological process, and will enable, in the long run, a transformation on the institutional and societal level. Therefore, despite the focus on the micro-level, many intervention projects wish to contribute to the creation of tolerance and mutual respect between opposing societies at the societal level and thereby to establish a culture of peace that will support the socio-political process of peacemaking.

Peace education does not mean the same in different socio-political contexts. In regions of relative tranquility, peace education emphasizes education to harmony and positive peace, and promotes basic ideals related to the concept of culture of peace such as democracy, tolerance of diversity, human rights, and peaceful global community. Peace education interventions in regions of tension and conflict will tend to educate for violence prevention, greater equality, and practical coexistence with real adversaries and minorities (Bar-Tal, 2002; Salomon, 2002; Stephan & Stephan, 2001). However, in cases of intractable conflict, peace education aims generally at facilitating the official process of conflict resolution and promoting reconciliation at the societal level by tackling the socio-psychological repertoire of societies involved (Bar-Tal et al., 2009; Salomon & Nevo, 2001). Peace education in such context attempts to directly change "[...] the individual's perception of the other's collective narrative, as seen from the latter's point of view" (Salomon, 2002, p. 9). Salomon enumerates four ideal outcomes of peace education: legitimizing the other's narrative, create willingness to critically examine one's own narrative and actions toward the other group, enabling empathy for the suffering of the other side, and promote readiness to engage in nonviolent activities.

Peace education can theoretically play a major role in transforming protracted negative intergroup relations before, during, and after the peacemaking process. Since peace education often encounters rejection among society members in its attempt to promote a new socio-psychological repertoire compatible with peace and to change beliefs and attitudes that are widely common among society members, Bar-Tal et al. (2009) spell out several conditions for successful peace education. These include conditions on the political–societal level, such as the existence of a parallel positive peacemaking process and enduring support for peacemaking and peacebuilding among at least some influential members of society, as well as conditions on the educational level, mostly high-level educational support, and a defined and decisive policy regarding the implementation of peace education (Johnson & Johnson, 2005).

Bar-Tal et al. (2009) suggest two models of peace education, based on the socio-political conditions of the relations between the groups mentioned above. When conditions are unfavorable, peace education should be indirect, that is, it must focus on general themes of peace such as tolerance, nonviolence, empathy, human rights, and conflict resolution, not on conflict specifics. However, when socio-political conditions are favorable, direct peace education that attempts to tackle the culture of conflict emerged throughout the years of the conflict and to facilitate an alternative culture of peace can be developed. Unfortunately, peace education rarely takes place within an all-encompassing school or societal approach aiming at promoting new educational objectives of peace and to create a climate conducive to peacebuilding and reconciliation (as suggested by Bar-Tal et al., 2009). Instead, it often carries the form of small-scale, short, and limited educational interventions in the framework of school based or off-campus workshops (Salomon & Nevo, 2002). These projects can be conventional, that is, performed in educational settings, or carry varied forms of secluded retreat, such as summer camps, trips, festivals, and more (Salomon, 2004).

Educational interventions of these forms are well practiced in societies involved in intractable conflict and are usually conducted by NGOs from both societies.[*] Peace education activities are also conducted in other societies involved in intractable conflict throughout the world (Northern Ireland: Niens & Cairns, 2005; Bosnia and Herzegovina: Clarke-Habibi, 2005; Rwanda: Staub, Pearlman, Gubin, & Hagengimana, 2005; Sierra Leone: Bretherton, Weston, & Zbar, 2003). Peace education work in a mono-national setting has been widely conducted in Northern Ireland (Church & Visser, 2001) and in the Middle East (Rosen, 2006). Despite major socio-political obstacles and the sectarian context of Northern Irish society, peace education interventions attempting to promote a culture of peace among Catholics and Protestants in that region have been widely implemented since the late 1960s. Particularly worth mentioning are the Quaker Peace Education Project (QPEP) that focused on reducing prejudice among schoolchildren, and the human rights educational program of the Community Relations Council, both conducted intensively during the 1980s and the 1990s (Duffy, 2000).

Peace education programs taking place during an intractable conflict, before a successful political peacemaking process has been completed, are challenged by unfavorable socio-psychological conditions such as competing collective narratives and historical memories of past events (Bar-Tal, 2004), as well as by undesirable socio-political factors such as ongoing violence and structural inequalities (Salomon, 2004). These obstacles are difficult to combat through mere participation in workshops that are limited in scope. And yet, systematic evaluations of peace education are necessary in order to establish the effects of those programs on their participants. Evaluation of peace education programs can also play an important role in their improvement by determining which models or particular aspects are more effective. The organizations and institutes involved should also have a vast interest in evaluation research, which can convince donors to supply funds for the programs and justify costs and efforts invested in their development and implementation.

In recent years there seems to be an increase in publications on the effectiveness of educational interventions in the field. Most studies on the effectiveness of educational interventions in intractable conflict were conducted in the Israeli–Palestinian context, especially pertaining to intergroup encounters between Jews and Palestinians. Evaluation studies were performed mostly through surveys in pre- and posttests, using a quasi-experimental design (Hertz-Lazarowitz, Kupermintz, & Lang, 1998; Maoz, 2000). A qualitative evaluation study was recently published by Halabi and Zach (2006), who conducted in-depth interviews with participants of Jewish–Arab encounters in Neve Shalom School for Peace. In addition, there is an increasing body of literature which focuses on the process of peace education programs rather then on their outcome, and evaluates their functioning, the dialogical transformative

---

[*] A thorough description of such activities in Palestine/Israel is available from Adwan and Bar-On (2000).

process occurring in bi-national programs (Sagy, Steinberg, & Faheraladin, 2002), and the discourse taking place in intergroup encounters (Bekerman, 2002). Most recent evaluation studies conclude that despite the unfavorable conditions under which peace education is conducted, even short and limited interventions can facilitate positive attitudes and perceptions among participants.

Salomon (2004, 2006) attempts to settle the inconsistency between the encouraging findings of peace education evaluations on the one hand, and the hurdles peace education encounters in regions of intractable conflict and the disappointment of scholars and practitioners in the field, stemming from their inability to have a major impact on the relations between the groups, on the other hand (Bar-On, 2006; Maoz, 2004b). First, Salomon (2004) concludes that peace education may have an "attitude reinforcing" or a "preventive function" in the sense that it reinforces existing views and blocks further deterioration of negative attitudes and beliefs (pp. 271–272). In a more recent publication, Salomon (2006) suggests that peace education in contexts of intractable conflict is likely to have a positive impact on peripheral attitudes and beliefs, which are more easily changed than core attitudes and collective societal beliefs that comprise most of the socio-psychological obstacles to peace (Abelson, 1988; Krosnick & Petty, 1995).

In addition, studies on the long-term effectiveness of peace education can shed more light on this inconsistency. It seems, however, that there is hardly any data available on the long-term impact of interventions (Hertz-Lazarowitz et al., 1998; Salomon, 2004). Recent studies with a delayed posttest have not yielded encouraging findings. Bar-Natan (2004), for instance, repeated her measurements examining whether interpersonal friendships that emerge in Israeli–Palestinian encounter groups lead to greater acceptance of members of the rival group after six month and found no positive correlations as were found immediately after the encounters. Rosen (2006) examined the possible influence of a peace education program conducted in a mono-national framework on attitudes and beliefs of participants. While the program was found to have a positive short-term influence on stereotypes, prejudice, and negative emotions, a repeated post-test two months afterwards revealed that these changes wore out substantially after the intervention and even returned to their initial level. Only a follow-up intervention a few months after the initial intervention improved again the positive attitudes and beliefs of former participants.

In addition to interventions at the educational level, attention must be paid to another prominent socio-psychological method of intervention, which strives to promote face-to-face contact between members of societies negatively impacted by conflict, known as *intergroup encounters* (Fisher, 1997; Maoz, 2000, 2004a). When encounters take place in an educational setting (Bar & Eady, 1998; Maoz, 1997) they can be seen as a particular method of peace education. However, intergroup encounters are widely practiced among group members of all ages, in a variety of social and professional settings (Baskin, Al-Qaq, & Yes, 2004; Sagy et al., 2002).

Encounters as a means of reducing negative beliefs and attitudes have largely been resting on the foundations of the *contact hypothesis*, a pioneer theory in social psychology, assuming that intergroup relations can be improved by facilitating positive contact between members of adversaries. To allow a positive impact on the cognitive level, intergroup contact must be close and durable, and must occur between members of equal status in an environment of institutional and societal support (Allport, 1954; Pettigrew, 1998). Based on this hypothesis, for instance, large-scale interventions in Northern Ireland sought to facilitate cross-community contact and thereby to promote values of tolerance and acceptance of cultural and political differences among local communities (Cairns, Dunn, & Giles, 1992).

The initial contact hypothesis proposes an interpersonal or decategorized contact, according to which people need to get to know each other as individuals rather than as members of groups, so that barriers between them can fall (Brewer & Miller, 1984). However, several socio-psychologists studying encounters between groups of societies involved in intractable conflict (Suleiman, 2004; Wilder, 1984) propose a revised contact theory, based on the notion of categorized contact in which group categories remain salient during the interaction (Hewstone & Brown, 1986), suggesting that encounters should focus on the intergroup level, that is, contact between group members who are encouraged to identify with their respective groups.* Studies have shown that while the interpersonal encounter is more likely to create a positive and pleasant experience for participants, and interaction on the intergroup dimension risks reinforcing beliefs and perceptions about intergroup differences, generalization to the out-group is more plausible in the intergroup encounter (Kenworthy, Turner, Hewstone, & Voci, 2005; Pettigrew, 1998).

The differentiation between categorized and decategorized interactions led to the developments of different models of planned and structured intergroup encounters. Katz and Kahanoff (1990) and Rothman (1998) mention two ideal-types of encounter structures. Encounters are traditionally performed in workshops in the spirit of the "human relations" tradition (the psychological model), which focus on psychological aspects of the encounter experience, emphasize common characteristics of members of both groups, and attempt to avoid political and intergroup discussions. These workshops usually aim at increasing intergroup empathy, decreasing stereotypical perceptions and negative attitudes, and nurturing more trust and friendly relations among the participants from both groups (Maoz, 2004a). More recent structured intergroup encounters are often based on a conflict-resolution or "collective identity" approach (the political model), utilizing experience from problem-solving workshops as described above. In this model of encounters, the interpersonal and the psychological dimensions are de-emphasized by a facilitator and an emphasis is put on a dialogical process between individuals who are asked to represent their groups. According to Maoz (2000, p. 722), dialogue encounters based on categorized interactions aim at facilitating a process by which "the sides deal with disagreement or conflict between them through expressing themselves, listening to the other and taking in or emphasizing with the emotions, experiences, views and values of the other."

While these are the two main "ideal types" of people-to-people educational interventions, many other models combining different approaches to positive contact and effective processes of intergroup relations' transformation were developed and

---

* The interpersonal versus the intergroup contact models are based on the *interpersonal–intergroup continuum* developed by of Tajfel and Turner (1986) to describe dimensions of interactions between people and groups.

applied in different regions of intractable conflicts. For instance, the common in-group identity model, suggested by Gaertner and Dovidio (2000), emphasizes that intergroup interactions in face-to-face workshops should not focus on distinctions between the two opposing groups but on superordinate categories that includes both groups, and thereby members of both groups will see themselves as one unit, which will maximize the likelihood of pleasant contact. Another interpersonal–intergroup bridging model is the cross-categorization model, offered by Brewer (2000), according to which crosscutting distinctions make social categorization more complex and reduce both the magnitude and implications of in-group–out-group distinctions.

DISCUSSION

While we recognize the contribution of recent studies to the understanding of the effectiveness of socio-psychological interventions in intractable conflict, there is a central crux of sound empirical research on the effects of propeace interventions on both the elite and the grassroots level, namely that of "preaching to the converted," and of engaged peace researchers, favoring their cherished hypotheses to a degree that prevents coming up with rigorous evaluation studies.

Let us briefly discuss both aspects. We do not know of a single study in the field of propeace interventions that was able to work with a random sample, in the sense this label is used in social science methodology. We do not mean random assignment in experimental studies. Studies of the latter kind do exist (Staub et al., 2005), although neither in abundance, we mean random, chance-driven selection of intervention participants, ideally without any element of volunteerism. To achieve this goal admittedly is not easy, because all social research today tends to rely on volunteer studies, due to informed consent regulations. Nevertheless, what is needed is the study of nonvolunteers. Taking the demand to an extreme, this could be done on the elite level if participation of elite members in propeace interventions are part of a sanction "package" of an international body, just like reckless drivers can be forced into reeducation workshops or otherwise they will not be able to reacquire their drivers license. Whether this will ever be feasible remains to be seen. On the grassroots level, it may be possible to gather random samples for propeace interventions using the usual incentive approach to participation in social research. The evaluation studies of the future, furthermore, need a true experimental design with real control groups. Thirdly, such studies need to employ not just the classical pretest–posttest design, but a time-series design or a longitudinal design with a grossly delayed follow-up.

How about the second part of the crux mentioned above? Many of "us" engaged psychological peace researchers would rather engage in a new propeace intervention than in a rigorous evaluation of it. We have not heard of many studies that report an intervention that did any harm, though anecdotal evidence and talk among colleagues does occasionally report about interventions that have done certain harm, mainly in cases where outsiders lacked the necessary cultural knowledge and sensitivity to do interventions in an alien setting. What is a truisms, though, is the fact that engaging in propeace interventions makes "us" feel good and thereby a priori has a positive effect, though, per se only for "us" and not for the participants of interventions. In order to minimize this obstacle to state-of-the-art evaluation studies on propeace interventions, it might be a good idea if these evaluation studies were in the future done by independent groups of researchers. Foundations that engage in funding propeace interventions are presumably well-advised, if, in the future, they offer funds for propeace interventions typically only when proposals for such interventions also contain an element of independent evaluation, not done as action research. Propeace activists will presumable forward the counterargument that sound evaluation studies do cost money that might better be spent on the interventions themselves. However, we are not speaking about short-range emergency interventions. These should rather than not simply take place. What we are arguing is that researchers from the propeace "camp" should in the future refrain from outlining and pursuing the umpteenth intervention, but should invest into rigorous evaluation studies that allow them to in the long-run argue much more convincingly for the necessity of a widespread establishment of propeace intervention programs.

REFERENCES

Abelson, R. (1988). Conviction. *American Psychologist, 43*, 267–275.

Adwan, S., & Bar-On, D. (2000). *The pole of non-governmental organizations in peace-building between Palestinians and Israelis.* Jerusalem: Peace Research Institute in the Middle East.

Allport, G. W. (1954). *The nature of prejudice.* Garden City: Doubleday.

Bar, H., & Eady, F. (1998). Education to cope with conflicts: Encounters between Jews and Palestinian citizens of Israel. In E. Weiner (Ed.), *The handbook of interethnic coexistence* (pp. 514–534). New York: Continuum Press.

Bar-Natan, I. (2004). *Does friendship between adversaries generalize?* Haifa: University of Haifa, unpublished doctoral dissertation (in Hebrew).

Bar-On, D. (2006). *Tell your life story: Creating dialogue among Jews and Germans, Israelis and Palestinians.* Beer Sheva: Ben-Gurion University of the Negev (in Hebrew).

Bar-Tal, D. (2002). The elusive nature of peace education. In G. Salomon & B. Nevo (Eds.), *Peace education: The concept, principles and practice in the world* (pp. 27–36). Mahwah, NJ: Lawrence Erlbaum.

Bar-Tal, D. (2004). Nature, rationale, and effectiveness of education for coexistence. *Journal of Social Issues, 60*, 253–271.

Bar-Tal, D. (2007). Sociopsychological foundations of intractable conflicts. *American Behavioral Scientist, 50*, 1430–1453.

Bar-Tal, D. (2009). Reconciliation as a foundation of culture of peace. In J. de Rivera (Ed.), *Handbook on building cultures for peace* (pp. 363–377). New York: Springer.

Bar-Tal, D. (in press). Challenges for constructing peace culture and peace education. In E. Matthews, D. Newman, & M. Dajani (Eds.), *The Israeli-Palestinian conflict: Parallel discourses.* London: Routledge.

Bar-Tal, D., & Bennink, G. H. (2004). The nature of reconciliation as an outcome and as a process. In Y. Bar-Siman-Tov (Ed.), *From conflict resolution to reconciliation* (pp. 11–38). Oxford: Oxford University Press.

Bar-Tal, D., Rosen, Y., & Nets-Zehngut, R. (2009). Peace education in societies involved in intractable conflicts: Goals, conditions, and directions. In G. Salomon & E. Cairns (Eds.), *Handbook of peace education* (pp. 21–43). New York: Psychology Press.

Baskin, G., Al-Qaq, Z., & Yes, P. M. (2004). Years of experience in strategies for peace-making: Israeli–Palestinian people-to-people activities 1993–2002. *International Journal of Politics, Culture and Society*, 17, 543–562.

Baumeister, R. F., & Hastings, S. (1997). Distortions of collective memory: How groups flatter and deceive themselves. In J. W. Pennebaker, D. Paez, & B. Rime (Eds.), *Collective memory of political events: Social psychological perspectives* (pp. 277–293). Mahwah, NJ: LEA.

Bekerman, Z. (2002). The discourse of nation and culture: Its impact on Palestinian–Jewish encounters in Israel. *International Journal of Intercultural Relations*, 26, 409–427.

Bjerstedt, A. (1995). *Peace education: A world perspective for the 1990s*. Malmö, Sweden: School of Education.

Brenes, A., & Weseels, M. (2001). Psychological contributions to building cultures of peace. *Peace and Conflict: Journal of Peace Psychology*, 7, 99–107.

Bretherton, D., Weston, J., & Zbar, V. (2003). Peace education in a post-conflict environment: The case of Sierra Leone. *Prospects*, 33, 219–230.

Brewer, M. B. (2000). Reducing prejudice through cross-categorization: Effects of multiple social identities. In S. Oskamp (Ed.), *Reducing prejudice and discrimination* (pp. 165–184). Mahwah, NJ: LEA.

Brewer, M. B., & Miller, N. (1984). Beyond the contact hypothesis: Theoretical perspectives on segregation. In N. Miller & M. B. Brewer (Eds.), *Groups in contact: The psychology of desegregation* (pp. 281–302). Orlando, FL: Academic Press.

Burns, R. J., & Aspeslagh, R. (Eds.). (1996). *Three decades of peace education around the world*. New York: Garland.

Burton, J. W. (1969). *Conflict and communication: The use of controlled communication in international relations*. London: Macmillan.

Burton, J. W. (1990). *Conflict: Human needs theory*. London: Macmillan.

Cairns, E., Dunn, S., & Giles, M. (1992). *Surveys of integrated education in Northern Ireland*. Coleraine, UK: Centre for the Study of Conflict.

Chigas, D. V. (1997). Unofficial interventions with official actors: Parallel negotiation training in violent intrastate conflicts. *International Negotiation*, 2, 409–436.

Church, C., & Visser, A. (2001). Single identity work. *Derry/Londonderry: Local International Learning Project, INCORE*. Retrieved October 16, 2008, http://www.incore.ulst.ac.uk/publications/occasional/single_i.pdf

Clarke-Habibi, S. (2005). Transforming worldviews: The case of education for peace in Bosnia and Herzegovina. *Journal of Transformative Education*, 3, 33–56.

Cohrs, C., & Boehnke, K. (2008). Social psychology and peace: An introductory overview. *Social Psychology*, 39, 4–11.

De Rivera, J. (2004). Assessing the basis for a culture of peace in contemporary societies. *Journal of Peace Research*, 41, 531–548.

Diamond, L. (1997). Training in conflict-habituated systems: Lessons from Cyprus. *International Negotiation*, 2, 353–380.

Duffy, T. (2000). Peace education in a divided society: Creating a culture of peace in Northern Ireland. *Prospects: Quarterly Review of Comparative Education*, 30, 15–29.

Fernández-Dols, J., Hurtado-de-Mendoza, A., & Jiménez-de-Lucas, I. (2004). Culture of peace: An alternative definition and its measurement. *Peace and Conflict: Journal of Peace Psychology*, 10, 117–124.

Fisher, R. J. (1972). Third-party consultation: A method for the study and resolution of conflict. *Journal of Conflict Resolution*, 16, 67–94.

Fisher, R. J. (1997). Training as interactive conflict resolution: Characteristics and challenges. *International Negotiation*, 2, 331–351.

Fisher, R. J. (2001). Cyprus: The failure of mediation and the escalation of an identity-based conflict to an adversarial impasse. *Journal of Peace Research*, 38, 307–326.

Fisher, R. J. (Ed.). (2005). Evidence for the essential contributions of interactive conflict resolution. *Paving the way: Contributions of interactive conflict resolution to peacemaking in protracted ethnopolitical conflicts* (pp. 203–230). Lanham, MD: Lexington Books.

Fisher, R. J. (2007). Assessing the contingency model of third-party intervention in successful cases of prenegotiation. *Journal of Peace Research, 44,* 311–329.

Funk, N. C. (2000). Theory and practice of track-II diplomacy: Impact and dynamics of the search for common ground in the Middle East initiative. Washington, DC: American University. Unpublished PhD dissertation.

Gaertner, S. L., & Dovidio, J. F. (2000). *Reducing intergroup bias: The common ingroup identity model.* Philadelphia, PA: Psychology Press.

Galtung, J. (1969). Violence, peace, and peace research. *Journal of Peace Research, 3,* 176–191.

Gandhi, M. (1950). *Satyagraha in South Africa.* Ahmedabad: Navajivan Publishing House.

Gordon, H. (1994). Working for peace in the Middle East: The educational task. In E. Boulding (Ed.), *Building peace in the Middle East: Challenges for states and civil society* (pp. 311–317). Boulder, CO: Lynne Rienner.

Gray, B., Coleman, P., & Putnam, L. L. (2007). Introduction: Intractable conflict—New perspectives on the causes and conditions for change. *American Behavioral Scientist, 50,* 1415–1429.

Halabi, R., & Zach, M. (2006). *Youth encounters at the School for Peace* (in Hebrew). Neve Shalom: School for Peace. Retrieved October 17, 2008 from http://sfpeace.org/index.php?_lang=heandpage=articleandid=164and_section=publication

Harris, I. (2002). Conceptual underpinnings of peace education. In G. Salomon & B. Nevo (Eds.), *Peace education: The concept, principles, and practices around the world* (pp. 15–25). New York: LEA.

Hertz-Lazarowitz, R., Kupermintz, H., & Lang, J. (1998). Arab-Jewish student encounter: Beit Hagefen coexistence programs. In E. Weiner (Ed.), *The handbook of interethnic coexistence* (pp. 565–584). New York: Continuum Press.

Hewstone, M., & Brown, R. J. (1986). Contact is not enough: An intergroup perspective on the contact hypothesis. In M. Hewstone & R. J. Brown (Eds.), *Contact and conflict in intergroup encounters* (pp. 1–44). Oxford: Blackwell.

Johnson, D. W., & Johnson, R. T. (2005). Essential components of peace education. *Theory into Practice, 44,* 280–292.

Katz, I., & Kahanoff, M. (1990). Some dilemmas in the analysis of Arab-Jewish encounters (in Hebrew). *Megamot: Behavioral Sciences Quarterly, 23,* 29–47.

Kaye, D. D. (2001). Track-two diplomacy and regional security in the Middle East. *International Negotiation, 6,* 49–77.

Kelman, H. C. (1999). Experiences from 30 years of action research on the Israeli-Palestinian conflict. *Züricher Beiträge zur Sicherheitspolitik und Konfliktforschung* (Nr. 54, pp. 173–197).

Kelman, H. C. (2005). Building trust among enemies: The central challenge for international conflict resolution. *International Journal of Intercultural Relations, 29,* 639–650.

Kelman, H. C. (2006). Interests, relationships, identities: Three central issues for individuals and groups in negotiating their social environment. *Annual Review of Psychology, 57,* 1–26.

Kenworthy, J. K., Turner, R. N., Hewstone, M., & Voci, A. (2005). Intergroup contact: When does it work and why? In J. Dovidio, P. Glick, & L. Rudman (Eds.), *Reflecting on the nature of prejudice* (pp. 278–292). Malden, MA: Blackwell.

King, M. L. (1963). *Why we can't wait?* New York: New American Library.

Krosnick, J., & Petty, R. (1995). Attitude strength: An overview. In R. Petty & J. A. Krosnick (Eds.), *Attitude strength: Antecedents and consequences* (pp. 1–24). Mahwah, NJ: LEA.

Lieberfeld, D. (2002). Evaluating the contributions of track-two diplomacy to conflict termination in South Africa. *Journal of Peace Research, 39*, 355–372.

Lieberfeld, D. (2007). Promoting tractability in South Africa and Israel/Palestine: The role of semiofficial meetings. *American Behavioral Scientist, 50*, 1542–1562.

Maoz, I. (1997). A decade of structured educational encounters between Jews and Arabs in Israel. In D. S. Halperin (Ed.), *To live together: Shaping new attitudes to peace through education* (pp. 47–56). Geneva: Geneva University and Paris, UNESCO International Bureau of Education.

Maoz, I. (2000). An experiment in peace: Reconciliation-aimed workshops of Jewish-Israeli and Palestinian youth. *Journal of Peace Research, 37*, 721–736.

Maoz, I. (2004a). Coexistence is in the eye of the beholder: Evaluation intergroup encounter interventions between Jews and Arabs in Israel. *Journal of Social Issues, 60*, 437–452.

Maoz, I. (2004b). Peacebuilding in violent conflict: Israeli-Palestinian post-Oslo people-to-people activities. *International Journal of Politics, Culture and Society, 17*(3), 563–574.

Martinez, J., & Susskind, L. (2000). Parallel informal negotiation: An alternative to second track diplomacy. *International Negotiation, 5*, 569–586.

Mitchell, C. R. (1999). Negotiation as problem solving: Challenging the dominant metaphor. *Peace and Conflict: Journal of Peace Psychology, 5*, 219–224.

Montiel, C. J., & Boehnke, K. (2000). Preferred attributes of effective conflict resolvers in seven societies: Culture, development-level and gender differences. *Journal of Applied Social Psychology, 30*, 1071–1094.

Montiel, C. J., & Wessells, M. (2001). Democratization, psychology, and the construction of cultures of peace. *Peace and Conflict: Journal of Peace Psychology, 7*, 119–129.

Nelson, L. L., & Christie, D. J. (1995). Peace in the psychology curriculum: Moving from assimilation to accommodation. *Peace and Conflict: Journal of Peace Psychology, 1*, 161–178.

Niens, U., & Cairns, E. (2005). Conflict, contact, and education in Northern Ireland. *Theory into Practice, 44*, 337–344.

O'Kane, M. (1992). Peace: The overwhelming task. *Veterans for Peace Inc. Journal, 19*, 3.

Pelzmann, L. (2005). Gegenseitige Rückversicherung—unverzichtbar für strategisches Vertrauen. In W. Krieg, K. Galler, & P. Stadelmann (Eds.), *Richtiges und gutes Management: Vom System zur Praxis* (pp. 329–343). Bern: Haupt.

Pettigrew, T. F. (1998). Intergroup contact theory. *Annual Review of Psychology, 19*, 185–209.

Reimann, C. (2004). Assessing the state-of-the-art in conflict transformation. *Berghof handbook for conflict transformation.* Retrieved October 17, 2008, http://www.berghof-handbook.net/std_page.php?LANG=e&id=1

Rothman, J. (1997). Action evaluation and conflict resolution training: Theory, method and case study. *International Negotiation, 2*, 451–470.

Rothman, J. (1998). Dialogue in conflict: Past and future. In E. Weiner (Ed.), *The handbook of interethnic coexistence* (pp. 217–235). New York: Continuum Press.

Rothstein, R. (Ed.). (1999). *After the peace: Resistance and reconciliation.* London: Lynne Rienner.

Rosen, Y. (2006). The impact of peace education programs on core and peripheral attitudes and beliefs regarding the Israeli-Palestinian conflict. Haifa: University of Haifa. Unpublished doctoral dissertation (in Hebrew).

Rouhana, N. N., & Kelman, H. C. (1994). Promoting joint thinking in international conflicts: An Israeli-Palestinian continuing workshop. *Journal of Social Issues, 50*, 157–178.

Rouhana, N. N., & Korper, S. H. (1997). Power asymmetry and goals of unofficial third party intervention in protracted intergroup conflict. *Peace and Conflict: Journal of Peace Psychology, 3*, 1–17.

Sagy, S., Steinberg, S., & Faheraladin, M. (2002). The personal self and the collective self in group encounters between Jews and Arabs in Israel: Two intervention strategies (in Hebrew). *Megamot: Behavioral Sciences Quarterly, 16*, 534–556.

Salomon, G. (2002). The nature of peace education: Not all programs are created equal. In G. Salomon & B. Nevo (Eds.), *Peace education: The concept, principles, and practices around the world* (pp. 3–13). New York: LEA.

Salomon, G. (2004). Does peace education make a difference in the context of an intractable conflict? *Peace and Conflict: Journal of Peace Psychology, 10*, 257–274.

Salomon, G. (2006). Does peace education really make a difference? *Peace and Conflict: Journal of Peace Psychology, 12*, 37–48.

Salomon, G., & Nevo, B. (2001). The dilemmas of peace education in intractable conflicts. *Palestine-Israel Journal, 7*, 64–68.

Salomon, G., & Nevo, B. (Eds.). (2002). *Peace education: The concept, principles, and practices around the world*. New York: LEA.

Staub, E. (2002). From healing past wounds to the development of inclusive caring: Contents and processes of peace education. In G. Salomon & B. Nevo (Eds.), *Peace education: The concept, principles, and practices around the world* (pp. 73–86). Mahwah, NJ: Erlbaum.

Staub, E. (2006). Reconciliation after genocide, mass killing and intractable conflict: Understanding the roots of violence, psychological recovery, and steps toward a general theory. *Political Psychology, 27*, 867–894.

Staub, E., Pearlman, L. A., Gubin, A., & Hagengimana, A. (2005). Healing, reconciliation, forgiveness and the prevention of violence after genocide of mass killing: An intervention and its experimental evaluation in Rwanda. *Journal of Social and Clinical Psychology, 24*, 297–334.

Stephan, W. G., & Stephan, C. W. (2001). *Improving intergroup relations*. Thousands Oaks, CA: Sage.

Suleiman, R. (2004). Jewish-Palestinian relations in Israel: The planned encounter as a microcosm. In R. Halabi (Ed.), *Israeli and Palestinian identities in dialogue: The School for Peace approach* (pp. 31–46). London: Rutgers University Press.

Tajfel, H., & Turner, J. C. (1986). The Social Identity Theory of intergroup conflict. In S. Worchel & G. Austin (Eds.), *Psychology of intergroup relations* (pp. 7–24). Chicago: Nelson-Hall.

Talbot, P. (1977). The Cyprus seminar. In M. R. Berman & J. E. Johnson (Eds.), *Unofficial diplomats* (pp. 159–167). New York: Columbia University Press.

Tyler-Wood, I., Smith, C. M., & Barker, C. (1990). Adversary into ally. *American School Board Journal, 177*, 26–28.

United Nations General Assembly. (1998). *Resolution adopted by the General Assembly 52/12*. Proclamation of the year 2000 as the International Year for the Culture of Peace. Annex. A/RES/52/15, January 15, 1998.

Wilder, D. A. (1984). Intergroup contact: The typical member and the exception to the rule. *Journal of Experimental Social Psychology, 20*, 177–194.

Wolpe, H., & McDonald, S. (2006). Burundi's transition: Training leaders for peace. *Journal of Democracy, 17*, 132–138.

Woolman, D. C. (1985). Education and peace in the thought of Johan Galtung, *Current Issues in Education and Human Development Education and Peace, 3*, 7–20.

Conclusion
To Open the Closet

DANIEL BAR-TAL*

*T*he present volume brought together complementing chapters that jointly illuminate the social psychological perspective of conflicts and their resolution in a systematic and coherent way. The chapters can be viewed as pieces of a puzzle that are assembled to provide a holistic and comprehensive picture of issues that stand at the heart of the discussion about conflicts. The chapters provide theoretical conceptions, review empirical evidence and few of them refer to specific conflicts, but none of the chapters analyzes a particular case of a conflict. This accumulated knowledge proposes that human beings whenever they are in harsh conflict situation perceive, think, experience, evaluate, infer, feel, make decisions and act on the basis of human principles that psychology in general, and specifically social psychology, elucidated.

Within this axiom, it is has to be recognized that there are wide individual, as well as collective, differences. Individuals differ in many diverse characteristics such as for example their skills, experiences, knowledge, attitudes, or values. Similarly, collectives vary in their repertoire and also come up to conflict situation with different history, political culture, structure, resources, level of economic development, cultural tradition, set of societal beliefs, and so on. There is no doubt that these factors play a role in the way societies approach the encountered conflicts, manage and resolve them. But with these differences, there is probably less degrees of freedom to behave when human beings face great existential threat to them and to their collectives.

The context of severe and violent conflict, wherever and whenever it is, has similar characteristics that imply threat, stress, danger, demands, pressure, insecurity, uncertainty, and unpredictability. It then has particular implications for human individual and collective behavior, leading to such reactions as fear, anger, sense of hardship and suffering, frustration, grief, pain, sense of victimhood, humiliation, resentment, will to revenge, hatred, hostility, closure and more; all mostly negative reactions. The stronger and self-evident are the negative characteristics of the conflict context (especially perceived threat), the more predictable are human reactions.[†] These reactions reflect human tendency to react in the context of severe, harsh and violent conflict which implies threat in line with more dispositional features that characterize human beings as a species. Reactions of self-control,

---

* I would like to thank Klaus Boehnke, Guy Elcheroth, Henning Schmidtke, Dario Spini, and Stephen Worchel for their helpful comments on the earlier draft of this chapter.

† I recognize that these negative characteristics of a conflict can be also be perceived as a result of persuasion by opinion leaders and/or mass media.

reflection, self-regulation, perspective taking or moral considerations take also place but are less frequent in such a context. They require use of higher level skills vis-à-vis the situation, the rival, or the consequences and not many individuals use them in the context of intractable conflict.

Conflicts do not erupt by themselves but every conflict needs agents that will formulate the epistemic basis for its eruption and later its maintenance; mobilize the society members for support and participation; and make decisions about its continuation. The epistemic basis includes rationales, explanations and justifications for carrying the conflict taken from the ethnic, historical, religious, political, economic, social, moral, and cultural arsenal. In some conflicts the agents of conflict selectively present, biased and distortive information, focus on threats, direct manipulatively identity, use arousing pieces of collective memory, utilize master symbols, wake up emotions; in many cases it works. These agents succeed with relative ease to recruit society members for the causes of violent confrontation.

I do not want to imply that societies involved in conflicts carry them homogenously. Although conflicts differ in their history, or context, in almost all of them it is possible to identify differing groups of participants with different quantity and power. For example, there are segments which vehemently support the conflict and are ready to sacrifice their lives for it, there are others who profit in the continuation of the conflict, there are passive bystanders who observe the events, there are those who are victimized in its course and suffer, or there are those who oppose the conflict. Certain categories are not mutually excusive, and there is also need to recognize that as the dynamics of the conflict change, so the composition of the groups and their power changes too.

With this understanding, one of the fundamental questions in the study of the socio-psychological dynamics of conflicts is whether it is possible to generate rules and principles, describe processes and outline concepts that apply to different conflicts. In other words, the question is whether each conflict is so unique that it necessitates specific analysis and creation of new knowledge that cannot be borrowed from the knowledge accumulated on other conflicts or different conflicts have similar socio-psychological foundations and dynamics that can be elucidated and then applied in the analysis of the specific conflicts.

KNOWLEDGE ABOUT CONFLICTS

My view is that although each conflict erupts and is maintained in a particular political–social–cultural–economic–geographical–historical context, it is possible to detect certain general knowledge that sheds light on the common socio-psychological features of different conflicts. It is true, as noted, that the context of every conflict is different and so are particular specific processes, factors and contents that characterize every group, but beyond the particular characteristics it is possible to identify a broad-spectrum of rules of human behavior in conflict situation.

Intractable conflicts, as the chapters of the book for example describe, erupt under certain general conditions and evolve with certain general processes, they necessarily lead to the development of socio-psychological repertoire of emotions, beliefs, and attitudes that accompany them, they go through cycles of violence and evolve socio-psychological barriers that prevent their peaceful resolution. Then certain general conditions signal the possibility of peace making which requires change of the conflict supporting socio-psychological repertoire. Also the process of peace building, including reconciliation, has particular general features and requires certain general conditions in order to succeed.

The possibility of generating general knowledge negates the well-entrenched view in many of the societies involved in conflicts that insist on the uniqueness of their conflicts. It is probably functional for these societies to perceive their conflict as very specific to which knowledge of other conflicts cannot be applied. This approach justifies usually lack of readiness and inability of society members to embark on the road of peace. The view of the conflict as unique phenomenon with particular dynamics and principles that is difficult to understand it, places it in spheres beyond the accumulated knowledge. According to this claim, it is very difficult to understand it on the basis of observations of other conflicts as they do not apply to the particular context. All this implies, for those who claim the contention, that the conflict cannot be resolved peacefully because of the specific extremely difficult conditions and special characteristics.

Moreover, often this claim is accompanied by another claim that external observers cannot understand the dynamics of the conflict and therefore their insights are useless. The enormous amount of well-thought out, creative and comprehensive contributions testifies otherwise. Social sciences including social psychology created considerable amount of understanding about dynamics of conflicts, their eruption, evolvement, maintenance as well as their peace building and peace making. This accumulated knowledge portrays a quite comprehensive picture, though there is no limit to this knowledge and it can be expanded and improved.

STUDY OF CONFLICTS AND SOCIAL PSYCHOLOGY

Study of conflicts should be one of the major areas of research in social psychology. First, conflicts are inseparable component of human intergroup relationship that should be studied as part of human social behavior in the same way that social psychologists study conformity, or aggression. It is their duty to extend knowledge about this social intergroup experience. Second, bloody and protracted intergroup conflicts constitute one of the most significant problems that preoccupy the entire international community and many individuals and collectives around the world, but especially societies' members that are involved in them. Study of societal conflicts contributes not only to the understanding of this real-life phenomenon, but may also have practical implications, for example, enlightening acts that can prevent conflicts and ways that can facilitate their peaceful resolution. Social psychology cannot allow itself to be bystanders to issues that concern humanity. It has to take part in the attempts to control conflicts in the same way as microbiologists contribute their share to exerting efforts to overcome various illnesses. Such direction will make social psychology more relevant and more tuned to the needs of human kind.

But it is not only the world that needs socio-psychological knowledge for better understanding of eruption, management, prevention, and resolution of conflicts. Social psychology should also be interested in studying individuals and collectives in the context of conflict as part of its mission. This context has special influences on the human behavior, as this book and other many contributions show. It leads to reactions that were noted above—such as perception of threat and insecurity, feelings of fear and hatred and thoughts about delegitimization of the rival, suffering, deep sense of self-collective victimhood, as well as to violent acts that may include also terrorism, mass killings, ethnic cleansing, and even genocide. It provides a unique opportunity to study human behavior at its limits of stress, abilities to endure and suffer, ways of mobilization, actions of leaders, feelings, thoughts and behaviors of victims and perpetrators, evilness as well as goodness of human beings, their conformity and obedience, strength of minorities who persistently struggle for changing the repertoire of society members in order to stop the bloodshed, and so on. The study of conflicts can be one of the fields of research that will move social psychology out of its dominant closet of individualistic orientation and experimentation to the study of collectives with different research methods. Such a movement can bring back to social psychology the spirit of the founding fathers of modern social psychology who saw the study of the behavior of groups and intergroup relations on macro level, and the investigation of real-life issues as an inherent part of social psychology.

The study of conflicts should represent one of the best of the directions social psychology can take. But this study, in order to make a meaningful contribution to basic and practical knowledge, must have a number of characteristics. First, it should use different research methods including survey polls, interviews, experimentation, content analysis, and case studies. There is no one preferable method for investigating conflicts. Research methods should be selected on the basis of the posed research question. This openness allows asking a variety of research questions and investigation of wide scope of problems. Second, the study of conflicts necessitates interdisciplinary approach. Social psychology cannot provide complete answers to the posed research questions without incorporation of knowledge accumulated in other social sciences and humanities such as political sciences, history, sociology, anthropology, communication, cultural studies, and so on. The study of conflict eruption, mobilization, or negotiation as examples should be viewed as multifaceted phenomena that require their illuminations from different perspectives with different accumulated knowledge.

Social psychology, as other social sciences, must learn to cooperate and open itself to knowledge coming from different disciplines. Such cooperation, first of all, allows learning different approaches that use different concepts, frameworks and data to illuminate the same phenomenon. And second it extends meaningfully the scope of study of the given phenomenon. This way can well advance the integrated knowledge that can be more explanatory and predictive. Finally, the study of conflicts in social psychology should go also to the real field, the natural laboratory. The researchers cannot stay in their laboratories only, they also ought to observe the real situations, interview participants in conflicts and experience the conditions of the context. Real-life situations can serve as a macro laboratory, in which, through collecting natural observations, a conceptual framework, may be constructed and/or data collected.

Many of the areas that were investigated still need considerable research to extend their knowledge. In addition there are areas that have been relatively neglected and need illumination. Examples of the latter areas are research questions about mobilization to conflicts, bystanders in conflict eruption, opposition to conflict eruption and later to its continuation, victims' reactions, perpetrators' behaviors, rise of minorities that oppose the violence, actions by agents of conflict, use of societal mechanism to maintain the conflict, development of peace movements, overcoming barriers to peace making, persuading the leaders and the public to support peaceful conflict resolution, effects of continuing violent conflict on the individuals and societies engaged in them, methods of reconciliation and its effects, or prevention of conflicts. In general it seems to me that we social psychologists know more about the eruption, foundations and dynamics of serious and harsh conflicts than about their resolution and prevention. But in general there is still much to study and reveal.

It is the responsibility and the duty for social psychologists to study conflicts with all their aspects and then make this knowledge public, at least in the academic channels. But the socio-psychological knowledge should not remain in academic journals and books which are almost never visited by individuals who are directly involved in conflicts and some of them even make decisions that have critical influence on their course. It is thus of minimal requirement to move one step further to publicize the formed knowledge widely to the public. Of special importance is to publicize the knowledge in societies involved in conflicts and especially these parts that specifically enlighten the specific processes, factors and contents of the particular conflict. This accumulated knowledge should also serve the practitioners who work in international agencies, national NGOs, and governmental offices. Such participation in a public discourse enriches it with critical information that is relevant to the needs of the societies involved in a conflict. For example, participation in public discourse can become part of the persuasive process that may lead to peaceful conflict resolution, even if majority of society members do not want to hear these tunes. It is a must to show the manipulations and lies that are part of the selective, biased and distortive process of information supply. There is also a need to listen to the victims and extend their plight for humanitarian assistance, relief, justice, and healing. I assume that there are different segments of societies involved in harsh and violent conflicts that have different goals, agendas, and needs. Social psychologists are supposed to identify them and refer to them.

I realize that it is not simple to find attentive ears among the decision makers. High barriers often separate between academic social psychologists and the decision makers who have the power to select the course of action for their societies. Decision makers are rarely tuned to the voices that can enlighten them with knowledge about the conflictive way of their society. They usually have other social circles of advisers, preferences and priorities. Social psychologists are usually outsiders to the political and military leadership who manage the conflict. In this situation, as noted, social psychologists have to participate at least in public discourse to turn their knowledge into public domain.

LIMITATIONS OF STUDIES OF CONFLICTS

Although it is desirable that social psychologists who specialize in studying conflicts should not close themselves in an ivory tower; they should also be aware of their limitations, especially when it comes to propose concrete and specific ways to peaceful resolution of a conflict. Their contributions illuminate processes of eruption of conflict, evolvement of conflict shed light on conflict supporting repertoire or describe barriers that prevent peaceful conflict resolution. They can also present steps that are needed for initiating peace making and later maintaining it. But they often face difficulty in proposing specific and concrete acts that can change the views of leaders and of many of the society members to abandon the direction of violent conflict and instead to begin progress toward peaceful settlement of the conflict and reconciliation. Our academic knowledge not necessarily assures its successful application to resolve specific practical challenges that practitioners and decision makers face. This challenge requires proposals of concrete steps, messages, conditions, or acts that can cause unfreezing of held beliefs and attitudes and adopting new alternative repertoire that is facilitating peace making. Formation of such knowledge is not easy, in view of the complex conditions.

Numerous factors described in the chapters of the book explain why it is so frustrating to launch successful interventions that will establish a peaceful world. Powerful psychological, political, societal, economic, military, and/or cultural factors play a detrimental simultaneous role in preventing peace making. From the socio-psychological perspective, overcoming hostility, suspicion, prejudice, mistrust, fear, hatred, and other negative parts of human repertoire that evolve in conflicts is one of the most important challenges for our discipline.

The described limitation is especially pronounced in intractable conflict. In intractable conflict that lasts through at least decades and the societal institutions as well as communication channels support its continuation, the attempts to change the views about the conflict, can be equated to attempts to move a person from his/her deep-seated religious beliefs into secular world views. The well-entrenched ideological beliefs supporting the conflict are rigid, well-seated coherently in the cognitive system, related to emotions, validated by experiences and therefore can easily stand against persuasive communications, inconsistent information or invalidating experiences.*

We, social psychologists, must be aware that we are unable to control the different operating complex conditions that have a determinative influence on people. Also a major change is a long process that requires favorable conditions to be implemented that cannot be controlled. This means that it is not easy to provide specific practical advice about changing the socio-psychological repertoire of individuals and collectives and impart one that cherishes peace, compromises, negotiations and so on is a very difficult mission. This does not imply that the general principles are useless or that we are unable to provide on their basis an advice that is unique

---

* Obviously I am speaking about these types of conflicts (the great majority of them) that are morally viewed by the international community as required peaceful conflict resolution.

and helpful, as well as practical. In such state of mind, social psychologists need to use all their wisdom, critical reflections, knowledge, creativity, and real-life experience and at the same time be aware that there is no one existing magic proposal. Change of the ideological repertoire that supports the conflict requires also involvement, activism, and participation with a long breath, but many of us prefer to be closed in the ivory tower, disconnected from the reality of real-life conflicts. It was Kurt Lewin who told us that there is nothing more practical than a good theory. He served as the ultimate example in integrating rigorous science with practical involvement in real-life issues.

In conclusion, I would not like to imply that all the conflicts are symmetrical in their moral evaluation. Conflicts differ in their causes and goals. Although the initiators of conflicts always find them justified, with years, have emerged moral criteria to judge them and evaluate them. I believe that there are justified conflicts in which society members try to abolish slavery and discrimination, to stop inequality, exploitation, occupation, colonialism, or even genocide. Without these conflicts, important values of equality, justice, or freedom would not be implemented as individuals and collectives do not yield usually voluntarily status, prestige, dominance, control, wealth, territories, or resources, even if they have it unjustly. In these conflicts, principles of justice have to be addressed in their peaceful resolution as it took place in the resolution of the Algerian or South African conflicts. Also conflicts are not symmetrical in many parameters, including military power and/or violation of humanitarian and moral codes. In addition there are conflicts in which one side initiates a conflict and tramples on every basic principles of moral and humane codes of behavior as, for example, the Nazis did. In these latter cases often the only solution that international community decides and supports is a total victory in order to stop the total evilness. I believe that all these types of conflict require from us, on one hand, well-performed research, but at the same time differentiation between victims and perpetrators and voicing our values that should differentiate between right and wrong.

I would like to say that life without conflicts cannot always bring moral values, progress and innovations, but it is the duty of human beings to learn to manage conflicts in a constructive way for the benefit of humanity. Destructive conflicts bring death, suffering and misery. Social psychologists have a crucial role in the attempt to unveil the dark side of human beings that lead them to carry violent and vicious conflicts with relative ease. Social psychologists, having the role to elucidate human social behavior, should take the responsibility not only to understand the reasons and factors that lead human beings to carry destructive conflicts but also as social activists devote much scientific efforts to know and instruct human beings to manage their intergroup conflicts constructively. More than that, it is not only our duty as members of the intellectual human community to unveil the forces that lead to eruption of destructive conflicts and later their maintenance, but also to elucidate ways that enable human beings engaged in conflicts to embark on the road of peace. But of special importance is to exert un-exhausting efforts to reveal ways how to prevent bloody and protracted conflicts from occurring, without compromising on the achievement of the cherished moral values and goals. This is our vital mission.

Author Index

Subject Index

Note: n = note.